Flexible Stones

Excavations at Franchthi Cave, Greece
Thomas W. Jacobsen, general editor
with Karen D. Vitelli

Fascicle 1
Jacobsen, T. W., and W. R. Farrand, with contributions by F. A. Cooper and C. J. Vitaliano. *Franchthi Cave and Paralia: Maps, Plans, and Sections*

Fascicle 2
van Andel, Tjeerd H., and Susan B. Sutton, with contributions by Julie M. Hansen and Charles J. Vitaliano. *Landscape and People of the Franchthi Region*

Fascicle 3
Perlès, Catherine. *Les Industries lithiques taillées de Franchthi (Argolide, Grèce), Tome I, Présentation générale et industries Paléolithiques*

Fascicle 4
Shackleton, Judith C. *Marine Molluscan Remains from Franchthi Cave.* With a report on the Oxygen Isotope Analyses of Marine Molluscs from Franchthi Cave by M. R. Deith and N. J. Shackleton

Fascicle 5
Perlès, Catherine, with the collaboration of Patrick C. Vaughan, Colin Renfrew, and Arnold Aspinall. *Les Industries lithiques taillées de Franchthi (Argolide, Grèce), Tome II, Les Industries du Mésolithique et du Néolithique Initial*

Fascicle 6
Wilkinson, T. J., and Susan T. Duhon, with contributions by John A. Gifford and Sytze Bottema. *Franchthi Paralia: The Sediments, Stratigraphy, and Offshore Investigations*

Fascicle 7
Hansen, Julie M. *The Palaeoethnobotany of Franchthi Cave*

Fascicle 8
Vitelli, Karen D. *Franchthi Neolithic Pottery, Volume 1, Classification and Ceramic Phases 1 and 2*

Fascicle 9
Talalay, Lauren E. *Deities, Dolls, and Devices: Neolithic Figurines from Franchthi Cave, Greece*

Fascicle 10
Vitelli, Karen D. *Franchthi Neolithic Pottery, Volume 2, The Later Neolithic Ceramic Phases 3 to 5.* With a contribution on the Post-Neolithic Remains by James A. Dengate

Fascicle 12
Farrand, William R. *Depositional History of Franchthi Cave: Stratigraphy, Sedimentology, and Chronology.* With a report on the Background of the Franchthi Project by Thomas W. Jacobsen

Fascicle 13
Perlès, Catherine. *Les Industries lithiques taillées de Franchthi (Argolide, Grèce), Tome III, Du Néolithique ancien au Néolithique final*

Fascicle 14
Stroulia, Anna. *Flexible Stones: Ground Stone Tools from Franchthi Cave*

Flexible Stones: Ground Stone Tools from Franchthi Cave

ANNA STROULIA

INDIANA UNIVERSITY PRESS
Bloomington & Indianapolis

This book is a publication of

Indiana University Press
601 North Morton Street
Bloomington, Indiana 47404-3797 USA

www.iupress.indiana.edu

Telephone orders 800-842-6796
Fax orders 812-855-7931
Orders by e-mail iuporder@indiana.edu

∞ The paper used in this publication meets the minimum requirements of the American National Standard for Information Sciences—Permanence of Paper for Printed Library Materials, ANSI Z39.48-1992.

Manufactured in the United States of America

Cataloging information is available from the Library of Congress.

ISBN 978-0-253-22178-0

1 2 3 4 5 15 14 13 12 11 10

to Mike

CONTENTS

PLATES: https://www.iupress.indiana.edu/media/flexiblestones/

TABLES

FIGURES

PLATES

Active

Acut
63. FS 36
64. FS 116
65. FS 117
66. FS 118
67. FS 1
68. FS 893
69. FS 600
70. FS 212
71. FS 23
72. FS 11
73. FS 21
74. FS 153
75. FS 159
76. FS 38
77. FS 226
78. FS 899
79. FS 221
80. FS 157
81. FS 428
82. FS 22
83. FS 577
84. FS 789
85. FS 229

Adisc
86. FS 113
87. FS 300
88. FAN:61/1
89. S 18
90. FS 14
91. FS 188
92. S 19
93. FS 608
94. FS 596
95. FS 258
96. FS 317

Arect
97. FS 256
98. FS 297
99. FS 132
100. FS 167
101. FS 123
102. FS 125
103. FS 84
104. FS 848
105. FS 53
106. FS 774
107. FS 95
108. FS 110
109. FS 133
110. FS 134
111. FS 786

Asquare-circ
112. FF1:6E
113. FS 223
114. FS 231
115. S 72
116. S 62
117. FS 115
118. FS 318
119. FF1:6B

Aend
120. FS 7
121. FS 50
122. FS 108
123. FS 109
124. FS 420
125. FS 602
126. FS 362
127. FS 25
128. H1:64
129. FS 120
130. FS 192
131. FS 225
132. FS 228
133. Q5S:90/18

Aglobe

Aglobe-stain
134. FS 371
135. FF1:40B1a
136. O5:116/13
137. FS 111
138. FS 298
139. FS 372
140. P5:178/13

Aglobe-nostain
141. FS 315
142. FS 841
143. FF1:35B
144. FS 85
145. FF1:6
146. FS 695
147. FS 889
148. FS 272
149. FS 273
150. P5:179
151. QR5:6/2
152. FS 876
153. FS 760

ACKNOWLEDGMENTS

My involvement with ground stone tools started long before I had anything to do with the Franchthi project. It was an August afternoon of 1987 in one of the storerooms of the Kozani Archaeological Museum. I was an undergraduate student at Aristotle University at Thessaloniki participating in the Kitrini Limni archaeological project. Mihalis Fotiadis, director of the project, passed me a few boxes with ground stone tools from the excavation and survey and asked if I would like to 'play' with them. I said 'yes'.

It was eight years later, a November afternoon of 1995—I was then a graduate student at Indiana University, Bloomington—when Tom Jacobsen invited me to undertake the publication of the ground stone tools from Franchthi. Once more I responded positively.

My Franchthi journey did not start until May 1997 after I completed my Ph.D. dissertation on an entirely different topic. Being now at the end of the journey, I would like to express my gratitude to both Mihalis and Tom for having started it all.

The journey was essentially solitary, as preparations of monographs usually are. Yet, it would not have been possible without the direct or indirect, practical, intellectual, or emotional support from a host of people. I am deeply grateful to Kaddee Vitelli for her continuous, most often gentle, occasionally tough, encouragement through the years. She did an extremely careful reading of an earlier draft of the volume and offered very thoughtful comments. These and the heavy editing that she, 'being a daughter of an English professor', could not resist doing, benefited this volume immensely. Kaddee's own work on Franchthi, moreover, has provided inspiration and the context for my own work.

Catherine Perlès read earlier drafts of both individual chapters and the whole volume. Her comments and suggestions were (of course!) provocative and pushed me to think deeper and better about my material and about Franchthi. I have repeatedly cited her work on the site and on Greek Neolithic and I can only hope that I reproduced her ideas accurately.

Curtis Runnels also read and commented upon an earlier draft of this volume. I thank him for this and, most importantly, for being a great source of inspiration with his own work on ground stone tools.

Laure Dubreuil served as the external reviewer. My thanks for her close reading of this study and for offering specific substantial comments that helped make my ideas clearer.

With five exceptions, all the drawings were done by Ayla Akin. Ayla did a meticulous job putting the complex use wear of the Franchthi tools on to paper. Unfortunately, she will not be here to see her work in print. The exceptions (see Figures 3, 14, 23, 26, and 29) are drawings that were produced before I started my study and were kept in the Franchthi archives. I have not been able to identify the artist who produced these drawings except that her or his initials are A.L.S. My thanks to her or him too. The photographs were taken by me with the help of Mike Strezewski. Anne Chippindale was my editor and she did a great job improving the language and putting it all together.

The study of the material took place in the Leonardo, the storage facility of the Nafplion Archaeological Museum where all ground stone tools and other material found at Franchthi are kept. I spent several months there in 1997 with subsequent visits in later years for further study, drawing, and photography. At the Leonardo, museum guards and conservators offered well-needed breaks from intensive and frustrating observations of tools that were or maybe were not *a posteriori*, of surfaces that were used abrasively and also percussively, actively but perhaps also passively, of use wear found on this face and on the other face, and on the sides, and on one of the ends too . . . They wanted to know what life in 'America' is like, why Americans invaded Iraq, and what the hell I think I can learn by looking, and looking again and again, at all these rocks. I am indebted to them all for reminding me that my work as an archaeologist does not take place in a vacuum and that my ground stone tool research makes little sense to people outside a small circle of experts. Extra thanks should go to the museum guards who, always with a great sense of humor ('will you rebuild Palamidi with these rocks?'), helped lift heavy boxes off of storeroom shelves.

Many friends and colleagues helped through the years by responding to my questions, reading different sections of the study, providing references and offprints, comparing their notes with mine, discussing Aegean prehistory, sharing their writing space, or simply offering a sympathetic ear to my whining. Olga Mantzari, Ada Kalogirou, Tasos Bekiaris, Rosalia Christidou, Alexandra Christopoulou, Nina Collins, Tracey Cullen, Jennie Ebeling, Hanadi Al'Samman, Bill Farrand, Julie Hansen, Ismini Ninou, Hara Procopiou, Roberto Risch, Thomas Strasser, Kosmas Touloumis, Christina Tsoraki, Tania Valamoti, Jennifer Webb, Seiji Kadowaki, Barbara Voytek, and probably others—thank you all!

Little did I know in 1997 that the gestation period of this volume would be for some time parallel to two other pregnancies: those that brought my two sons to the world. The oldest, John, often complained that mommy was spending too much time in the office or was not 100% there when playing Bob the Builder or Star Wars Lego with him. The little one, Andrew, is too young to talk but he would probably express similar complaints if he could. I apologize to both of you and I am so very lucky to be your mother. I am, moreover, greatly indebted to my parents Yannis and Amalia Stroulia for taking care of John for weeks at a time while I was off in Nafplion.

The biggest thanks and the hardest to reduce to words I owe to Mike Strezewski. As my husband and also an archaeologist, he took this journey with me and suffered accordingly. He was there to check my wildest ground stone hypotheses, had the enormous patience to read and comment upon the earliest drafts, lifted my spirits with his sharp sense of humor, and loved, encouraged, and pushed me in every step of the way. It is to him that I dedicate this book.

The study of the assemblage and the accompanying drawing and photography projects were funded by a Postdoctoral Fellowship and two Summer grants from the E.A. Schrader Endowment Fund of the Program in Classical Archaeology at Indiana University, an NEH grant (awarded to Thomas W. Jacobsen), as well as a Publication Subvention grant from the Institute for Aegean Prehistory. My thanks to the above institutions and foundations for their support.

Flexible Stones

CHAPTER ONE

Introduction

INTRODUCTION TO THE SITE AND ASSEMBLAGE

The site of Franchthi Cave is located on the tip of a limestone headland on the northern side of Kiladha Bay in the southern Argolid, northeastern Peloponnese (Fig. 1). Excavations carried out between 1967 and 1976 under the direction of Thomas W. Jacobsen revealed a rare, long, and complex sequence of human occupation spanning the Upper Palaeolithic through the end of the Neolithic period. Evidence of human activity came from two integral but distinct areas: the cave and the so-called Paralia.

The cave is a karstic formation about 150 m in length and 45 m in maximum width. At the very back is a small pool of water. About two-thirds of the interior of the cave is covered by huge boulders, the result of massive rock-falls at various points in the cave history. That is why excavation trenches were opened only in the front portion of the cave as well as on the terrace just outside the cave mouth. The trenches dug in this part of the site are: A, B, BE, C, D, E, F, F1, FF1, FA, FAN, FAS, G, G1, H, H Pedestal (or 'HPed'), HA, HB, H Terrace, H1, H1A, H1B, H2, H2A, H2A Pedestal (or 'H2APed'), and H2B (Jacobsen and Farrand 1987:2, 20–21) (Fig. 2).

Paralia (the Greek word for beach) refers to a zone about 15 m wide located below the cave mouth and along the modern shoreline. The trenches excavated on Paralia are: L5, L5NE, O5, O5N, O5NE, P5, PQ5, Q4, Q5S, Q5N, Q6N, Q6NE, and QR5 (Jacobsen and Farrand 1987:20–21) (Fig. 2). For the way the trenches of both cave and Paralia were defined, and combined or subdivided as excavation progressed, see Jacobsen and Farrand (2000:11–25). From now on I will use the term Franchthi to refer to the site as a whole (both cave and Paralia).

The investigations at Franchthi brought to light huge quantities of cultural and environmental remains. Among them are the 522 artifacts that make up the subject of this study: ground stone tools, raw material used for ground stone tool manufacture, as well as byproducts of such manufacture. This number includes a few uncertain cases. I should clarify here that I use the term 'tool' in this study to refer to a kind of artifact that is used to alter matter. For all other kinds of artifacts that do not qualify as tools in the above sense I use the term 'non-tool object.' This category includes, for example, vessels (they contain matter but do not alter it), figurines, and ornaments. The single ground stone figurine found at the site has already been published along with the figurines made of clay in a separate volume in the Franchthi series (Talalay 1993). The ground stone ornaments, along with those made of shell, clay, and bone, have been presented in the context of a dissertation thesis (Miller 1997). They will all be published in another volume in the Franchthi series (Perlès and Miller in preparation). The same volume will include a separate document on the few Franchthi ground stone non-tool objects that are not classified as figurines or ornaments (e.g., vessels).

My study comprises all the ground stone tools, related raw material, and byproducts of manufacture recovered on the surface of the site or during the excavations. However, not all specimens contained in the investigated area were necessarily recovered. Depending on their experience and background, some excavators may have been more able than others to identify this kind of material—especially tools modified through use rather than manufacture (*a posteriori* tools as I call them here), tools with minor evidence of use, or small fragments—in the rather rocky sediments of the site. Moreover, not all excavated sediments were water sieved, a factor that may have affected the degree of recovery for some of the smallest specimens (fragments of small cutting edge tools, for example).

Despite their ubiquitous presence among prehistoric remains in Greece (and elsewhere), ground stone tools have not attracted the kind of attention received by other categories of archaeological material (e.g., pottery or lithics). It is probably accurate to say that these constitute one of the most neglected prehistoric artifactual categories. Even today, it is not unheard of for some ground stone tools never to leave the excavated site, having been discarded by the very archaeologists who unearthed them. The most common treatment of such tools, however, consists of a few superficial pages in a preliminary report or final publication written (ironically) as part of a 'small finds' chapter by scholars with often no background in the study of this kind of material (e.g., Winn and Shimabuku 1989; Mould, Ridley, and Wardle 2000). Exceptions to this rule do exist, nevertheless: See, for example, the Ph.D. dissertations of Christopoulou (1979), Moundréa-Agrafioti (1981), Procopiou (1998), and Runnels (1981).

There are several reasons for this disciplinary neglect. 1. Ground stone tools consist of mostly mundane, unglamorous, sometimes simply unattractive, artifacts. It is not accidental that the formally manufactured, often polished tools usually referred to as axes or celts have received more attention in the literature than those known as handstones. 2. The large weight of many ground stone tools causes difficulties in transportation and storage, eventually affecting their study. 3. Perhaps most importantly, ground stone tools seem to be surrounded by a widespread assumption that they constitute straightforward pieces of evidence in no need of further scrutiny. The natural consequence of this neglect is that the potential of this material—as much as any other—to illuminate aspects of prehistoric life remains unexploited[1] (see also Ebeling and Rowan 2004:108; Galdikas 1988; Lidström Holmberg 2004:199; Rowan and Ebeling 2008:2–3; Zurro, Risch, and Clemente Conte 2005:57–58).

The neglected status of ground stone tools is perhaps nowhere better reflected than in this very term used to describe them. The term 'ground stone tools' is a misnomer: the category that goes by this name includes not only tools made or used by grinding, but also others produced or used by percussion (see also Adams 1997:2; Ebeling and Rowan 2004:108; Wright 1991:21, 1992:53, 1993:93). In the last analysis, 'ground stone tools' is but a catch-all category that includes any stone tool that does not qualify as a chipped stone implement (see Fratt 1992:16). If negative, this is the most accurate definition of the 'ground stone tool' category to date and it is in this sense that the term is used in this volume. In spite of its problems, I decided to keep this term to avoid the negative 'non-chipped stone tools'[2] and because I have been unable to come up with an alternative term that is accurate, concise, and positive at the same time. It is this definition of ground stone tools as a catch-all class, moreover, that underlines best the artificial nature of this category. It is likely that neither the category of ground stone tools as such nor the distinction between chipped and ground stone tools would have made much sense to the prehistoric makers and users of these artifacts. The same could probably be said about the distinction between stone and bone tools (see also Adams 2002:1; Perlès 2001:227–228). All may be no more than archaeological constructs that respond to the need for division of labor within the discipline rather than reflections of any prehistoric concepts, ideas, or distinctions.

If this marginalized subfield of Aegean (and other) archaeology is to be developed, it is important that we get to know what these artifacts referred to as ground stone tools actually are. For that, detailed analyses of specific assemblages are necessary. Such analyses will help us: 1. appreciate and understand the diversity and complexity of this artifactual category; 2. identify specific research problems; 3. begin to clarify the role of this material in the social, economic, and symbolic systems of which it was certainly part; 4. understand better other kinds of materials (e.g., lithics, bone tools, and ornaments), since ground stone tools were in one way or another involved in most, if not all, the prehistoric *chaînes opératoires*.

My goal in this study is to start filling some of the gaps in the Aegean prehistoric literature regarding this kind of material by providing the level of detail that is missing from the existing ground stone tool publications—a cause of frustration every time I tried to compare the Franchthi assemblage with other Aegean assemblages at other than the most superficial level. To this end I discuss the Franchthi material systematically in terms of raw material (and its procurement); manufacture; use; and morphological characteristics as these are determined by the form of the raw material used, by manufacture, and by use—I call these characteristics technomorphological. It is the emphasis on these aspects that make this a technological study. In its technological approach my work follows studies that are current in other subfields (e.g., lithics, pottery, bone tools) and, closer to home, the published studies of the Franchthi pottery and lithics by Vitelli (1993, 1999) and Perlès (1987, 1990, 2004) respectively. It is my belief that a close look at the choices made and not made in the technological domain is an important means to understanding something about the people responsible for these choices (see also Vitelli 1993:3–5).

Classification

Another symptom of the underdeveloped state of ground stone tool studies is the confusion characterizing nomenclature and classification. The situation is such that, as has been accurately pointed out, each study introduces a different system—this certainly applies to the existing publications of Aegean ground stone assemblages. The problem is exacerbated by the characteristics of the material itself. Ground stone tools constitute a notoriously difficult material to classify: many of them are *a posteriori*, having never been given a formal shape through manufacture, whereas the form of both *a posteriori* and fashioned tools often changed dramatically throughout their use life (see Agatzioti 2000:3–4; Dubreuil 2002:77–78).

I have not been able to find among the existing classification/nomenclature systems one that I consider suitable for the presentation of the Franchthi ground stone tool assemblage. The system I devised, however, is influenced to a large extent by the French tradition and in this respect leaves behind the confusion of classification and nomenclature that characterizes the Anglo-Saxon literature on ground stone tools (see Carter 1977:694–696; Kraybill 1977:487–488).

My system is rather simple and differs for the Neolithic and the pre-Neolithic components of the assemblage. I divided the Neolithic specimens—representing the vast majority of my material—into two large categories: passive and active. Introduced by Laming-Emperaire in 1979 (cited in de Beaune 1989b:28), this distinction is often used by French (speaking) tool specialists. The term 'passive' refers to tools that remain stable during use, 'active' describes tools that move during use. I should emphasize that in the Franchthi material (as in others), these two categories are not mutually exclusive, since many specimens played both active and passive roles at different stages of their use life. The specimens with both passive and active use wear were placed in one or the other category on the basis of what I considered the primary of the two kinds of use wear.

Both the active and passive categories were further subdivided into smaller groups. Most of these groups are more or less homogeneous; a single one in each category is heterogeneous. The relatively homogeneous groups are made up of tools that show similarities in use wear and its location on the tool body (again, since many specimens have multiple kinds of use wear, it was what I considered the primary among them that determined inclusion in one or the other group), in form (size and shape), and, to a larger or smaller degree, in raw material. Two such groups have been constructed for the passive category, six for the active one. An additional heterogeneous group in each category includes all the specimens that could not fit in any of the more or less homogeneous groups.

Thus, the passive category comprises a total of three groups:
1. Passive open tools (Popen);
2. Passive tools with cavity (Pcav);
3. Passive miscellanea (Pmisc).

The active category comprises a total of seven groups:
1. Active cutting edge tools (Acut);
2. Active discoidal tools (Adisc);
3. Active rectangular tools (Arect);
4. Active square or circular tools (Asquare-circ);
5. Active tools used with ends (Aend);
6. Active globular tools (Aglobe);
7. Active miscellanea (Amisc).

The terms I used for the relatively homogeneous groups emphasize either morphological or functional characteristics depending on what is the most distinctive feature for each group (for example, Passive tools with cavity, Active cutting edge tools, or Active globular tools).

The boundaries between the groups in each category are not always as clear-cut as I would have liked. Several tools could perhaps equally well have been assigned to a different group from that into which they were finally forced, or at least this is my conclusion after having transferred them back and forth between groups time and again during the multi-year process of my study. The classes of my classification scheme should thus be understood as fuzzier than they actually appear,[3] and in some cases as representing points in a continuum (see also Woodbury 1954:85). This classification is constructed for analytical purposes (for the purposes of organizing the material and presenting it to other scholars), and it is uncertain to what degree it would have been useful or meaningful to Neolithic Franchthiotes.

My classification of the Neolithic material is, as mentioned above, based on a combination of criteria: form, use wear, and raw material. I chose to avoid a classification based mostly on morphological criteria, such as that devised by Wright (1992) for Levantine prehistoric tools, since this would not do justice to the dynamic character of the Franchthi material. As already mentioned, form is not a stable feature of these artifacts; this changed through use, maintenance, reuse, recycling, and/or post-depositional processes. Equally important, the form of the (many) *a posteriori* tools is one determined by use, not manufacture. On the other hand, I consider a classification that capitalizes on use, such as those that include, for example, classes called 'axes' or 'milling stones' (see, e.g., Adams 2002), an equally inappropriate choice for this assemblage, since we still lack a firm grasp of the precise uses of these tools.

For the Pre-Neolithic component of the assemblage I used a different approach. Since this is a small sample consisting of stratified specimens that are most often unique, I decided to present them in detail by period. This also seemed appropriate given that the Aegean pre-Neolithic ground stone tools are *terra incognita:* this is the first publication of such material.

Describing the material

My description of the material provides information on four fields: raw material, aspects of manufacture, technomorphological characteristics, and aspects of use. I introduce each of these fields below.

Raw material

Detailed discussions of the raw material and procurement methods are presented in different sections of this volume dedicated to specific portions of the assemblage. This section is meant to serve as a background for more detailed discussions. Most of the kinds of rocks used for the Franchthi ground stone tools are found in the geological formations of the Franchthi-Ermioni region. These have been studied by geologist Charles Vitaliano (1987). The geological map of an area of 125 km^2 between Dhidhima in the north and Kranidi in the south surveyed by Vitaliano is published in Jacobsen and Farrand 1987 as plate 1.

Serpentinite, diabase, and basalt are found in the so-called Ophiolite Nappe underlying the Fournoi valley as well as in volcanic bodies in the Dhiskouria hills southwest of Ermioni and northwest of the Franchthi embayment at Vourlia. The formation called Flysch in the central part of the Franchthi-Ermioni region contains sandstones, whereas the so-called Later Cenozoic Deposits underlying most of the southern and southwestern part of the southern Argolid contain limestones, conglomerates, and sandstones. Limestone is the main ingredient of the formations called Pantokrator Limestone (from Megalovouni west to the sea near Vourlia bay), Breccia (found mostly along the south slope of the Dhidhima Range), and Limestone-Marl Sequence (in the chain of hills south of the Kranidi-Ermioni road) (van Andel and Vitaliano 1987; Vitaliano 1987). Peridotite deposits crop out north of Dhidhima (Vitaliano n.d.:11).

Most of the limestones, serpentinites, sandstones, etc. used for the Franchthi ground stone tools do not seem to have been extracted from primary sources, however. It is more likely that they originated in local stream and river beds or beaches. Andesite, a raw material used for several ground stone tools but with no compatible local sources, was probably imported from outside the region.

None of the 522 specimens that make up the Franchthi ground stone tool assemblage was subjected to thin section petrography. Three hundred and forty-five of them, however, were inventoried and their raw material identified through macroscopic examination by the several geologists involved in the Franchthi project. I should note here that in some cases the geologists came up with different identifications. In these cases I usually adopted those made by Vitaliano. As the only one of the Franchthi geologists who examined all the inventoried ground stone specimens, he was the most familiar with the ground stone material. Moreover, he was the most familiar with the geology of the Franchthi area. The identification of the raw material of the 177 non-inventoried specimens, on the other hand, was made by me on the basis of macroscopic similarities with the inventoried specimens.

Finally, a note on nomenclature: I use the term 'pebble' in this study to refer to a rock measuring no more than 6.0 cm in maximum dimension; 'cobble' for one measuring 6.0–30.0 cm in maximum dimension; and 'boulder' for one larger than 30.0 cm in maximum dimension (see Wilkinson and Duhon 1990:xvi).

Manufacture

I examined all the specimens macroscopically (with naked eye and/or 10× magnification) for the identification of traces of manufacture (as well as use). This examination showed that a large number of specimens are *a posteriori* tools, or, in other words, were never subjected to a process of manufacture. For the remaining specimens three techniques of manufacture have been recognized: chipping and/or flaking; pecking; and grinding. They were rarely used all together for the same specimen. I define 'chipping' and 'flaking' as the removal of smaller or larger flakes by percussion for the purpose of shaping a tool or a non-tool object (see Runnels 1981:255). I use the term 'pecking' to refer to the use of percussion to dislodge minute amounts of material from a mass of rock at each stroke for the purpose of shaping a tool or a non-tool object (see Dickson 1981:37; Runnels 1981:256). Pecking can be (and was) also used as a maintenance technique for the rejuvenation of a dull work surface. I refer to this kind of pecking as pecking of resharpening to distinguish it from the pecking of manufacture described above. 'Grinding' can be defined as rubbing a rock on an abrasive surface or with an abrasive material for the purpose of shaping a tool or a non-tool object. I do not make a distinction between grinding and polishing that other scholars may make, since I consider polishing as a stage—optional to be sure—in the grinding process. I do mention, however, the cases in which grinding produced a high sheen or luster.[4]

Technomorphological characteristics

The shape and size of the specimens for each pre-Neolithic period and for each of the relatively homogeneous Neolithic groups are discussed in detail. The length, width, and thickness of all specimens—always in centimeters—are provided in separate tables. Length refers to the largest measurement taken along the long axis of a specimen; width to the largest measurement taken at right angles to the long axis; thickness to the largest measurement taken at right angles to a plane defined by length and width. According to the above definitions, length is always larger than width. There is, however, an exception to this rule: the length given for several fragmentary specimens—they are noted with one asterisk in the relevant tables—is smaller than their width. In these cases, length was measured along what was obviously the long axis of the original complete tool, width was measured along what was obviously the wide axis of the original complete tool. For each of the relatively homogeneous Neolithic groups, I provide frequency distributions for length, width, and thickness, and, whenever this was meaningful, for the length/width ratio as well. Complete specimens only are represented in these distributions.

I often make reference to the longitudinal and transverse sections of the tools I discuss in the text and usually provide drawings of one or both of these sections in the illustrations. The longitudinal section bisects a specimen along the long axis, or at a plane that contains length and thickness. The transverse section bisects it along the wide axis, or at a plane that contains width and thickness.

Given the dynamic character of the assemblage, I tried to establish to what extent the tool form (i.e., size and shape) represents the original form of the raw material and to what extent it is the result of manufacture, use, maintenance, etc.

Finally, I should clarify a few terms that I use throughout this book and that pertain to the anatomy of the tools under study: The term 'face' refers to a broad flat, convex, or concave surface. A face that is utilized is called 'work face.' Most specimens have one or two work faces, a small number have more than two. The unutilized face opposite a work face is called 'dorsal face.' In the passive specimens the dorsal face serves as a base. 'Face' is also used to refer to the six surfaces of the single Franchthi specimen of a cubic shape. 'Sides' refers to the long narrow surfaces flanking the faces of tools of a roughly rectangular or ovate plan. The same term is also used for the four narrow surfaces flanking the two faces of tools of a roughly square plan. 'Ends' refers to the short narrow surfaces at the extremities of tools of roughly rectangular or ovate plan. 'Periphery' is the term I use for the curvilinear portion of tools of circular or elliptical plan. The term 'facet' refers to a portion of a larger surface (usually face) that has been more or less flattened as a result of use or, more rarely, manufacture. I call 'cavity' a hollow configuration more than 4.0 cm in maximum dimension. For hollow configurations that do not exceed 4.0 cm in maximum dimension I use the term 'depression.'

Aspects of use

As already mentioned, I studied the use wear of the Franchthi material macroscopically. I should also mention here that not all traces of use have been preserved on the surfaces of these tools: later uses as well as maintenance techniques (i.e., resharpening) and processes of redesigning (see below) must have covered or eliminated some traces of earlier uses. About half of the Franchthi specimens, moreover, are fragmentary, and it can thus be assumed that some traces of use have been forever lost along with the missing parts on which they were imprinted.

To describe the use wear of the Franchthi ground stone tools I adopted a framework from the French tradition of tool studies. I chose this particular framework because it allows me to describe the way/s these tools worked, that is, the way/s they moved over and contacted the worked material as well as the human gestures involved—even if their precise uses remain elusive; and without predetermining them. This framework was devised by Leroi-Gourhan (1971:47–57), complemented by Laming-Emperaire (1979, cited in de Beaune 1989b) and de Beaune (1989b), and finally adjusted here to the English language by me.

Leroi-Gourhan developed a hierarchical scheme to describe all possible mechanical ways in which tools work. He defined three major types of *percussion* or, as I would define them, three major ways in which the force of the tool is applied to the worked material:

1. *percussion posée*, which I translate as abrasion;
2. *percussion lancée*, which I translate as percussion;
3. *percussion avec percuteur*, which I translate as indirect percussion (this is percussion with an intermediate tool).

De Beaune added a fourth type: *percussion lancée et posée*, which I translate as combined abrasion and percussion.

At a second level, Leroi-Gourhan distinguished three directions in which the force of the tool is applied on the worked material. Only two of them are applicable to my material:

1. *perpendiculaire* (perpendicular); and
2. *oblique* (oblique).

Table 1.1. Modified version of Leroi-Gourhan's hierarchical scheme of all possible ways in which tools work (Leroi-Gourhan 1971:45–57; Laming-Emperaire 1979, cited in de Beaune 1989b:28; de Beaune 1989b:28–30, 1993:164).

<table>
<tr><td rowspan="20">ACTIVE
or
PASSIVE</td><td rowspan="6">PERCUSSION</td><td rowspan="3">perpendicular</td><td>linear</td><td></td></tr>
<tr><td>diffused</td><td></td></tr>
<tr><td>punctiform</td><td></td></tr>
<tr><td rowspan="3">oblique</td><td>linear</td><td></td></tr>
<tr><td>diffused</td><td></td></tr>
<tr><td>punctiform</td><td></td></tr>
<tr><td rowspan="6">ABRASION</td><td rowspan="3">perpendicular</td><td rowspan="2">linear</td><td>longitudinal</td></tr>
<tr><td>transversal</td></tr>
<tr><td>diffused</td><td></td></tr>
<tr><td rowspan="3">oblique</td><td rowspan="2">linear</td><td>longitudinal</td></tr>
<tr><td>transversal</td></tr>
<tr><td>diffused</td><td rowspan="3"></td></tr>
<tr><td rowspan="2">COMBINED ABRASION AND PERCUSSION</td><td>perpendicular</td><td>diffused</td></tr>
<tr><td>oblique</td><td>diffused</td></tr>
<tr><td rowspan="6">INDIRECT PERCUSSION</td><td rowspan="3">perpendicular</td><td>linear</td><td rowspan="6"></td></tr>
<tr><td>diffused</td></tr>
<tr><td>punctiform</td></tr>
<tr><td rowspan="3">oblique</td><td>linear</td></tr>
<tr><td>diffused</td></tr>
<tr><td>punctiform</td></tr>
</table>

At a third level, he distinguished three kinds of contact between the tool and the surface of the worked material:
1. *linéaire* (linear), which he subdivided into *longitudinale* (longitudinal) and *transversale* (transversal);
2. *punctiforme* (punctiform); and
3. *diffuse* (diffused).
Laming-Emperaire added to this scheme the distinction between tools *actifs* (active) and *passifs* (passive), which, as already mentioned, is a structural feature of my classification of the Neolithic component of the Franchthi assemblage. Table 1.1 presents the above scheme.

To understand how the Franchthi tools worked it was not enough to study their use wear. The results of this study were combined with data on the location of the use wear on the body of each particular tool, as well as information about the tool's shape and size.

I would, of course, have liked to use the above framework as my own classification system for the Franchthi assemblage, and I did in fact do so in an earlier draft of this study. However, the large number of specimens showing multiple use wear made this a very repetitive text, as such specimens were assigned to two, three, or more slots and therefore discussed in the context of two, three, or more classes. Thus for the sake of my audience I settled for a classification system that does not reflect the flexibility of the Franchthi ground stone tools and their users/makers as much as I would have liked. Nevertheless, I do ensure that I discuss the secondary use wear of these tools along with the primary one.

If useful in describing how the Franchthi ground stone tools worked, the framework presented above is not, however, sufficient to determine how these tools were actually used. In other words, it can be employed to specify that a certain tool worked, for example, in an active percussive perpendicular diffused mode, but not to determine whether it was used to pound grains, smash clay, or break bones, to mention but a few possibilities. For this second step, microwear and residue analyses are necessary. The Franchthi assemblage was not examined in either way. The microwear analysis of ground stone tools is still in its infancy (although in the process of rapid development), many problems are still untackled, and experimental work of the quantity and quality needed to support such an analysis still lacking.[5] The protocol for the treatment of specimens to be subjected to residue analysis (see, e.g., Formenti and Procopiou 1998:153–154), on the other hand, was not followed during the Franchthi excavations four decades ago: the material was washed after it was dug and handled repeatedly ever since. No soil samples from around the ground stone specimens were collected either.[6]

Nevertheless, hypotheses for possible uses of the Franchthi specimens have been attempted on the basis of: analysis of the ways in which they worked; ethnographic, ethnoarchaeological, and experimental literature; comparisons with other assemblages; and, whenever possible, the context of the tools themselves. I would, of course, have, liked to exploit context for this purpose much more than I actually did. This has not been possible, however, since half of the specimens under study come from the surface or from disturbed deposits (see below, this chapter), whereas a large number of the remaining specimens seem to come from secondary contexts (i.e., not the contexts of use).

Finally, a note on nomenclature: I use the term 'reuse' to refer to multiple uses of a tool that produced multiple occurrences of a single kind of use wear (e.g., passive abrasive wear) on the same or different parts of the tool. I use the term 'recycling,' on the other hand, to refer to multiple uses of a tool that produced different kinds of use wear (e.g., passive abrasive and active abrasive wear) on the same or different parts of the tool. A specimen is also recycled if it served a non-tool function after it was used as a tool. For example, a tool used originally in an active abrasive mode and later as a lid for a vessel is recycled.[7] The term 'redesigned' refers to a specific variety of recycled tools which, after having being used in a specific mode (e.g., passive abrasive), were intentionally modified—presumably following an accidental breakage—in order to be used in a different mode (e.g., active abrasive).

Why not a ground stone tool stratigraphy?

Against common archaeological practice, Jacobsen and his colleagues adopted an interpretive framework based on the concept of 'multiple stratigraphies'. According to this framework, each category of stratified material from Franchthi would be treated in relative isolation from other categories of remains and used to establish a separate phasing sequence based on the succession of excavated units. The logic behind this choice was that different kinds of material may vary through time independently of one another. The aim was to avoid the domination of an overall site phasing by a single kind of material (e.g., pottery) (Jacobsen and Farrand 1987:7).

With one exception, separate stratigraphies have been established for all Franchthi materials published so far: lithics (Perlès 1987, 1990, 2004), pottery (Vitelli 1993, 1999), marine mollusks (Shackleton 1988), botanical remains (Hansen 1991), and the cave sediments (Farrand 2000). The exception refers to the figurines, which, due to their very small number, were not used to draw a separate phasing sequence (Talalay 1993).

Although the ground stone tool assemblage is much larger than that of the figurines, despite my efforts I have not been able to establish a sequence for this material either. There are several reasons for that. A large portion of the assemblage (over 45%) comes from surface units or from deposits that were disturbed in prehistoric or recent times (see Vitelli 1999:8–9, 17). Moreover, the four cave trenches, FAN, FAS, H1A, and H1B, employed by other Franchthi scholars for sequencing their materials, did not yield a statistically satisfactory number of specimens to allow the establishment of an independent ground stone tool sequence.

But these are perhaps only the most superficial obstacles to the establishment of a sequence for the Franchthi ground stone tools. A more substantial problem has to do with the characteristics of the material itself. The Franchthi ground stone tools constitute dynamic and flexible entities in terms of both form and use. The *a posteriori* tools were never given a specific shape and size, since they never went through a process of manufacture; the shape and size of many tools, including *a posteriori* ones, changed dramatically through use; finally, many tools were used for a variety of purposes in a specific period or in different periods of the site occupation (in the latter case we are talking about tools that circulated through the stratigraphy of the site). On this basis, what exactly is one supposed to use as analytical units, as the basic blocks on which to build a ground stone tool stratigraphy? The original form of a tool as this was determined by the manufacturer or, in the case of *a posteriori* tools, by nature, or its (different) form at the end of its use life? The first function of a multifunctional tool, its last, or one in the middle? My point is that this assemblage simply lacks the pure and static units out of which stratigraphies are usually constructed. Each one of the Franchthi ground stone tools is instead a palimpsest of form and (most often) a palimpsest of function as well. In other words, it represents, itself, a stratigraphy. Thus, the same intrinsic characteristics of the material that resist the construction of a classification system with crisp clear classes, also resist the construction of a stratigraphy. Both stratigraphy and classification, the way we usually understand and employ them, are schemes too static to accommodate the dynamic outlook and flexible behavior of the Franchthi ground stone tools (and probably many others).

A last, but no less important, factor that may in some cases have prevented the construction of a ground stone tool stratigraphy is the possible conservative tendency of the material. The group I call Active cutting edge tools, for example, may show no significant diachronic variation, simply because—as argued for other Aegean Neolithic assemblages of similar tools (see Moundréa-Agrafioti 1992:174)—their forms or functions may not have changed significantly from the beginning through the end of the Neolithic.

In the absence of a ground stone tool stratigraphy, for dating purposes I used associations of my material with the Franchthi pottery and/or lithics. There is no guarantee, however, that the rhythms of continuities and discontinuities of the ground stone tools and of either of these materials coincided. On the basis of associations with lithics, twenty-six specimens (5%) excavated in the deeper aceramic deposits of trenches FAN, FAS, H1A, H1B, H2A, and G1 were identified as pre-Neolithic. Using Perlès' dating system (1987, 1990), I assigned the pre-Neolithic material to the following periods: Upper Palaeolithic, Final Palaeolithic, Lower Mesolithic, Upper Mesolithic, and Final Mesolithic. Three specimens were assigned to the Lower/Upper Mesolithic and Upper/Final Mesolithic interphases. The pre-Neolithic material comes exclusively from the cave.

On the basis of associations with pottery and, to a lesser extent, lithics, I assigned a large portion of the material (239 specimens or 46%) to the Neolithic period. Using Vitelli's dating system (1993, 1999) or, in a few cases, that of Perlès (2004),[8] I was able to assign each of these specimens to one of four main Neolithic phases: Early Neolithic (or EN), Middle Neolithic (or MN), Late Neolithic (or LN), and Final Neolithic (or FN);[9] one of two Neolithic interphases: Early/Middle Neolithic interphase (or EN/MN), and Middle/Late Neolithic interphase (or MN/LN); or a phase in the beginning of the Neolithic called Initial Neolithic.[10] Not all the

Neolithic dates given are equally secure, however: according to Vitelli, a number of deposits originating in a specific Neolithic phase appear to have been contaminated by later or mixed with earlier or later material (see, for example, Vitelli 1993:57–58). The less secure dates are given in parenthesis in both the text and tables, for example, (MN) or (FN). The EN, MN, and FN material comes from both the cave and Paralia. The LN material, on the other hand, comes exclusively from the cave. No trace of LN activity has been identified on Paralia (Vitelli 1999:7, 10, 18).

Still almost half the specimens in the Franchthi assemblage (n=257) have been assigned to neither a specific pre-Neolithic period or interphase nor a specific Neolithic phase or interphase. These specimens were found on the surface of the site or excavated in disturbed deposits that yielded Neolithic pottery, along with small quantities of pre-Neolithic lithics and fauna and/or post-Neolithic pottery (Perlès 2004:6–7; Vitelli 1993:31–34, 1999:7–9, 17). Nine of them have characteristics that make me suspect that they may come from the pre-Neolithic occupation of the site. They are thus discussed in chapter 2 as 'possible pre-Neolithic specimens'. One surface specimen (S 1), on the other hand, has characteristics that leave no doubt of its post-Neolithic origin. This is a fragment of one of two elements of a rotary quern made of conglomerate by flaking and pecking, and measuring 39.2×23.2×15.3 cm. It probably dates to the Roman period (see Runnels 1981:127–130). A photograph of this specimen is provided in Plate 209 (in the folder called 'Post-Neolithic' at https://www.iupress.indiana.edu/media/flexiblestones/). S1 is included in the master list of the material (Appendix C), but there is no other description of it in the text. Given the negligible quantity of post-Neolithic remains found at the site (Dengate 1999), I assume that the remaining 247 specimens originate in the Neolithic occupation of the site and they are treated as such in this study.

Tool names

As mentioned earlier, only 345 of the total number of ground stone tools and related specimens found at Franchthi are inventoried. The inventoried material includes excavated specimens as well as a few surface finds. The name given to each of the inventoried specimens is made of the prefix FS (standing for 'Franchthi Stone') and a number from 1 to 910 (e.g., FS 117). These numbers are not continuous, since the Franchthi Stone inventory comprises not only ground stone tools and related material but also ground stone vessels, ornaments, figurines, and other non-tool objects made of ground stone, as well as selected lithics.

Sixty-four specimens found on the surface or excavated in disturbed deposits of either the cave or Paralia were not inventoried, but each given a name made of the prefix S (standing for 'Surface') and a number from 1 to 73 (discontinuous) (e.g., S 57).

The remaining 113 specimens have neither an FS nor an S number. The name by which they appear in this study simply reproduces provenience information written on them with nail polish or on the tag that accompanies them. The name of each of these specimens consists of the name of the trench, in which it was excavated, followed by a colon and the number of the unit in which it was found (e.g., FF1:29). Different ground stone tools and/or non-tool objects made of ground stone (e.g., ornaments) excavated in the same trench and unit were distinguished from one another by a lowercase or uppercase letter suffix accompanying the unit number (e.g., FF1:14b or FF1:32A) or by a dash (/) following the unit number and followed by another number referring to the order in which a particular specimen was excavated in a particular trench (e.g., Q5S:91/19). Finally, there are four exceptions to the above rule: H:67B2 is the name of a specimen excavated in trench HB (or trench H, quadrant B), unit 67, pass 2. Suffix 'j' in the specimen called FF1:39Aj refers to the order in which it was excavated in trench FF1, quadrant A, unit 39. Suffixes 'a' and 'b' in the specimens called FF1:40B1a and FF1:40B1b respectively refer to the order in which these two specimens were excavated in trench FF1, quadrant B, unit 40, pass 1.[11]

Structure of the study

The material is presented in the three following chapters. Chapter 2 discusses the pre-Neolithic sample. It is divided into three sections. The first is devoted to the Palaeolithic period (Upper and

Final), the second to the Mesolithic period (Lower, Upper, and Final), and the third to a few possible pre-Neolithic specimens. Chapters 3 and 4 discuss the Neolithic sample: Chapter 3 is devoted to the passive tools, chapter 4 to the active tools. Chapter 5, finally, presents the summary and conclusions.

This study does not have a separate comparative component as do other studies in the Franchthi series (see, for example, Hansen 1991; Perlès 1987, 1990). Whenever possible, however, I do make specific references to and comparisons with other Aegean assemblages, thus indirectly placing the Franchthi assemblage in a more general context. It is not accidental that most of my references to other assemblages are found in the Neolithic group I call Active cutting edge tools. For reasons I explained at the beginning of this chapter, such tools have attracted most of the attention of Aegean prehistorians (and others). The fewest references to other Aegean assemblages are found in the sections on the remaining Neolithic active tool groups (these represent some of the most neglected ground stone tool varieties) as well as in the chapter presenting the pre-Neolithic material (no other Aegean pre-Neolithic assemblage has been published so far).

The text is accompanied by a large number of illustrations (tables, drawings, and photographs). All but three of the tables are interspersed within the text. The exceptions are three long tables presented as Appendices A through C. Appendix A is a list of all the studied specimens by trench and unit. Appendix B is a list of all the specimens dated to specific pre-Neolithic periods and interphases or specific Neolithic phases and interphases. Appendix C is a master list of all the material. All the drawings (presented as figures) are found at the end of this volume (after Appendix C). The photographs (sometimes in combination with drawings) are included as plates at https://www.iupress.indiana.edu/media/flexiblestones/

Abbreviations used in the text

EN	Early Neolithic	Acut	Active cutting edge tool/s
MN	Middle Neolithic	Adisc	Active discoidal tool/s
LN	Late Neolithic	Arect	Active rectangular tool/s
FN	Final Neolithic	Asquare-circ	Active square or circular tool/s
(EN)	probably(/e) Early Neolithic	Aend	Active tool/s used with ends
(MN)	probably(/e) Middle Neolithic	Aglobe	Active globular tool/s
(LN)	probably(/e) Late Neolithic	Aglobe-stain	Active globular tool/s with stains
(FN)	probably(/e) Final Neolithic	Aglobe-nostain	Active globular tool/s without stains
EN/MN	Early/Middle Neolithic interphase	Amisc	Active miscellanea
MN/LN	Middle/Late Neolithic interphase	Amisc1	Active miscellanea 1
PDA	passive diffused abrasive	Amisc2	Active miscellanea 2
Popen	Passive open tool/s	Fig.	figure
Pcav	Passive tool/s with cavity	Pl.	plate
Pmisc	Passive miscellanea		

NOTES

1. For a study that exploits some of this potential, see Risch 2002.
2. '*Pierre non taillée*' is indeed the term used by some French (speaking) scholars (see, for example, de Beaune 2000).
3. On the concept of fuzziness in the classification of ground stone tools, see Adams 2002:11–16.
4. I should also mention that the same effect can be achieved by means other than grinding, such as rubbing with a piece of leather.
5. For promising work in the field of microwear analysis of ground stone tools and related experiments, see, for example, Adams 1988, 1989a, 1989b; Dubreuil 2002.
6. Such a protocol has been in fact followed for the ground stone material from the recent excavations at Çatalhöyük (Baysal and Wright 2005a:308–309) and it will be interesting to see how fruitful the residue analysis of this material turns out. For promising research in the field of organic residues on ground stone tools, see, for example, Procopiou, Anderson, Formenti, and Tresseras Jordi 2002; Yohe, Newman, and Schneider 1991.
7. For different definitions of the term 'recycling,' see Adams 1997:4, 2002:23–24; Dubreuil 2002:239–240; and Shott 1989:18.

8. The reason I used mostly a ceramic dating system for the Neolithic material rather than a lithic one, as I did for the pre-Neolithic sample, is that Perlès' study of the Neolithic lithics was published several years after the beginning of my study. Yet I did use the probable dates given by Perlès for a few contaminated units that were not taken into account by Vitelli. I should note here, however, that overall the two dating systems are not too different from each other as far as the units they assign to each phase.

9. EN corresponds to Vitelli's Franchthi Ceramic Phase 1 or FCP1, MN to FCP2, LN to FCP3 and FCP4, and FN to FCP5. All but FCP1 and FCP3 have been subdivided into a number of subphases. In only a couple of cases throughout this study had I a reason to employ this finer dating system.

10. This is the term used by Perlès. Vitelli calls it Ceramic Interphase 0/1.

11. In trenches HA and HB, as well as trench FF1 quadrants A, B, C, and D, an excavation unit may have been dug in a single pass across the trench bottom, or in successive passes of 1.0 to 5.0 cm in thickness if no obvious changes in sediment type appeared. Successive passes in a given unit were labeled 1, 2, 3, etc. (Jacobsen and Farrand 2000:25, 27).

CHAPTER TWO

The Pre-Neolithic Material

INTRODUCTION

This is the first publication of a Pre-Neolithic ground stone tool assemblage from a Greek site and my hope is that its detailed nature will provoke an interest in this kind of material. The Franchthi sample consists of 26 specimens from the Palaeolithic and Mesolithic periods. None of them was excavated on Paralia. All come from stratified deposits inside the cave (trenches FAN, FAS, H1A, H1B, H2A, and G1). Nine additional specimens are presented at the end of this chapter as 'possible pre-Neolithic specimens.'

I follow here the phasing scheme designed for the Pre-Neolithic lithics by Perlès. She defined 10 lithic phases named 0 through IX (Perlès 1987, 1990).

THE PALAEOLITHIC PERIOD

Radiocarbon dates relevant to the Palaeolithic period, or lithic phases 0–VI, are listed in Table 2.1. Summarized information on all Palaeolithic specimens is listed in Table 2.2. The drawing of one specimen appears in Figure 3. Photographs of a few specimens are found in Plates 1–4 on the CD, folder: Pre-Neolithic/Palaeolithic.

The bedrock floor was never reached by the excavations inside the cave, but the lowest excavated deposits (in FAS and HIB) are dated before 33,000–40,000 Cal. B.P.—the date of a layer of tephra overlying them (Farrand 2000:37–38, 73–74, 86–88). These deposits are assigned to lithic phase 0 and belong roughly to the limit between the Middle and the Upper Palaeolithic period. A Middle Palaeolithic occupation at the site is indeed suggested by a handful of Mousterian points and lithics with Levallois preparation excavated at the bottom of FAS or found in surface or disturbed deposits of the cave; a few examples of fauna of Middle Palaeolithic affinity excavated at the bottom of FAS; and the substantial thickness of the unexcavated archaeological deposit that an electric resistivity survey showed to lie over the bedrock floor (Farrand 2000:37–38; Perlès 1987:18, 49–51, 85–88).

Above the layer of tephra are deposits assigned to lithic phases I–VI spanning the Upper/Final Palaeolithic. Perlès distinguished two broad periods in this long timespan. They are separated by a hiatus of several millennia and seem roughly to correspond to different functions and modalities of use of the site. The first period dates to ca. 30,000–17,000 Uncal. B.P., the second to ca. 12,700–10,150 Uncal. B.P. (Perlès 1987, 1999; see also Farrand 2000:Table 6.1).

During the first Palaeolithic period, the environment was cold, dry, and steppic and the shore about 5–6 km from the cave (Hansen 1991:105; Perlès 1999:312). The faunal, botanical, and lithic evidence suggests that 'The occupation of the site…must have been very limited, both in scope and intensity. The cave seems to have been used only briefly and sporadically as a hunting camp, and subsistence activities were restricted to small-scale big game hunting' (Perlès 1999:312). Apparently, the people who used the cave in this period also made a few ornaments, an activity that may not be incompatible with a hunting halt (Perlès, personal communication 2/2007).

The first Palaeolithic period comprises lithic phases I–III (Perlès 1987, 1999). The general impression of a very limited occupation of the cave during this period is reinforced by the fact that only two ground stone tools could be assigned to it (Table 2.2). No specimen derives from a deposit attributed to lithic phase I. The earliest specimen, FS 454 (Pl. 1), derives from H1A:215 attributed to lithic phase II. Two dates are available for this phase ranging from ca. 23,600 to 21,050 Uncal. B.P. (24,900–23,850 Cal. B.C.) (Table 2.1). FS 454 is broken both longitudinally and transversally and in its current state measures 11.0×6.1×3.2 cm. It is probably an *a posteriori* tool and its raw material is fine-grained sandstone. The preserved surface (shown in illustration) may represent part of the side of the original tool. It is convex and has at the center a small area with percussion marks, probably the result of brief use in a passive or active percussive mode. This use could have taken place before or after the breakage of the tool. A zone along one of the two long broken edges is smoothed from an abrasive use that was probably active. This may be the remainder of a larger smoothed surface that broke away rather than an area used after the tool was broken. In addition, parts of this tool show a bright red/orange stain. The fact that this is also found on broken surfaces suggests that the tool was stained after it had already broken. The stain may derive from the 'yellowish red' clayey sediment of the lithostratigraphic unit in which the tool was found (Farrand 2000:55–56) or represent a pigment. It is tempting to see the stain as deriving from the species *alkanna* and *anchusa*, the non-carbonized seeds of which were excavated in levels dated to the first Palaeolithic period. The roots of these plants are well known for their dying properties—they produce a red color [(Hansen 1991:104; http://www.answers.com/topic/anchusa-2 (checked 5/2006)]. According to Hansen (1991:104–107), however, these plants were probably brought to the cave by natural rather than human agents.

The second earliest ground stone tool is H1A:207/21. It comes from H1A:207 attributed to lithic phase III. This phase is not dated by radiocarbon but recognized between lithic phases II and IV

Table 2.1. Radiocarbon dates relevant to the Palaeolithic period (by lithic phase).

Lithic phase	Sample no.	Excavation unit	Uncal. B.P.	Cal. B.C.
0	n/a	n/a	n/a	n/a
I	n/a	n/a	n/a	n/a
II	P-2233	H1B:191-192	21,480±350	23,850
	I-6140	H1A:219	22,330±1270	24,900
III	n/a	n/a	n/a	n/a
IV	P-1827	H1A:199	12,540±180	12,760
V	P-1923	H1A:181	11,240±140	11,150
VI	I-6129	H1A:175	10,880±160	10,700
	I-6139	H1A:173	10,460±210	10,180
	P-2231	FAS:204	10,260±110	9330
	P-2232	FAS:207	10,840±510	10,650

KEY: Uncal.=uncalibrated, Cal.=calibrated, n/a=non available

Note: This list was compiled on the basis of information provided by Jacobsen and Farrand (1987:Plate 71), Farrand (2000:Table 6.1), and Perlès (1987:85–171). Samples considered problematic by Perlès (1987) are not included in this table.

Table 2.2. Palaeolithic specimens (by lithic phase).

Date	Name	Trench:Unit	Prov.	Pres.	Material	L	W	T	Illustr.
Lithic phase II	FS 454	H1A:215	C	f	sandstone	11.0	6.1	3.2	Pl. 1
Lithic phase III	H1A:207/21	H1A:207	C	f	limestone	6.6	5.4	4.0	
Lithic phase IV	H1A:198/20	H1A:198	C	f	limestone	9.5	3.8	1.3	
Lithic phase V	FS 386	H1A:181	C	f	limestone	8.9	3.4	2.6	
Lithic phase VI	FS 377	H1A:179	C	c	sandstone	4.2	4.0	2.4	Pl. 2
Lithic phase VI	FS 378	H1A:179	C	f	limestone	8.7	7.2	2.4	Pl. 3
Lithic phase VI	FS 750	FAS:204	C	c	sandstone	18.1	9.7	5.7	Fig. 3, Pl. 4

KEY: Prov.=Provenience, Pres.=Preservation, L=Length, W=Width, T=Thickness, C=Cave, Illustr.=illustration, c=complete, f=fragmentary, Pl.=Plate, Fig.=Figure

(Perlès 1987:108, 1999:312). H1A:207/21 is a fragmentary limestone pebble measuring 6.6×5.4×4.0 cm. A small area (ca. 2.3×2.5 cm) on its preserved end is smoothed and covered with dense parallel scoring, probably the result of active abrasive use. It is unclear whether this area was used before or after the breakage of the tool.

The second Palaeolithic period was characterized by a milder and more humid climate with a vegetation of Mediterranean garrigue, comprising *Pistachia*, *Prunus*, *Pirus*, wild cereals, and legumes (Perlès 1999:312). The cave was about 3–4 km from the coast (Hansen 1991:111). According to Perlès, this period

> witnesses the onset of a generalized, broad spectrum economy, based on the gathering of land and sea resources (plants, mollusks and fish) and the hunting of deer and boar… The nature of the cave occupation has now changed drastically: it is intensively occupied, and constitutes a stable basis for very diversified activities…Franchthi can be interpreted as a seasonal base camp, occupied not only by hunters, but by complete residential groups (Perlès 1999:315).

The second Palaeolithic period comprises lithic phases IV–VI (Perlès 1987, 1999). One date is available for Lithic phase IV: 12,540±180 Uncal. B.P. (12,750 Cal. B.C.); one for lithic phase V: 11,240±140 Uncal. B.P. (11,150 Cal. B.C.); four for lithic phase VI ranging from 11,350 to 10,150 Uncal. B.P. (10,700–9330 Cal. B.C.)[1] (Table 2.1). Three certain and two possible ground stone tools have been excavated in deposits assigned to these phases (Table 2.2). The transition from a hunting camp to a base camp—less pronounced in lithic phase IV, more pronounced in lithic phase V (Perlès 1999:314)—is not reflected in the ground stone material. These two phases are represented by one possible ground stone tool each: lithic phase IV by H1A:198/20, excavated in H1A:198 and measuring 9.5×3.8×1.3 cm; lithic phase V by FS 386, excavated in H1A:181 and measuring 8.9×3.4×2.6 cm. Both specimens are fragments of limestone cobbles (H1A:198/20 is indeed a flake) and carry no macroscopically visible use wear. H1A:198/20 was found near what has been identified as a hearth by the excavators, and close to a number of large bones—perhaps the remains of a meal. With their sharp edges these cobble fragments may have served in cutting meat or 'tearing flesh from a carcass' (comment in the inventory for FS 386).

Lithic phase VI represents the Final Palaeolithic at Franchthi, a period best known at this site for the first appearance of Melian obsidian (Perlès 1987:141–142). This is the first phase represented by more than one ground stone tool. The three specimens dated to this phase (FS 377, FS 378, and FS 750) support a picture of cave use that involved not only hunting-related activities but domestic activities as well. They are presented below.

FS 377 and FS 378 were found in the same unit: H1A:179. FS 377 (Pl. 2) is the earliest complete ground stone tool from the site. It is a small specimen of fine-grained sandstone, measuring 4.2×4.0×2.4 cm. It is probably *a posteriori*, and has an almost perfect circular plan and planoconvex sections. The face shown in the illustration is flat (probably flattened) and well smoothed; the other is convex with a lightly smoothed top. Additional smoothed areas are found on the tool's periphery. FS 377 was used exclusively in an active abrasive mode. The well smoothed texture of the flat face may be an indication that it was used for rubbing a hide or a wooden passive surface. I doubt that it was used in combination with a passive stone tool since no such implement was found in the Palaeolithic deposits of the site. However, the possibility of a use in conjunction with an unpreserved passive tool made of wood for grinding an intermediate substance cannot be ruled out. Given its small thickness, FS 377 may be at an exhausted state, something that may explain the abrasive wear in parts other than the flat face. Alternatively, it may have been used by a person with a small palm—perhaps a child.

FS 378 (Pl. 3) is a large flake from an *a posteriori* tool (a utilized limestone cobble), measuring 8.7×7.2×2.4 cm. It contains part of a face ('A' in illustration) that is flattened from active abrasive use. It is smoothed enough from use to reflect light and also carries groups of tiny stries (0.2–0.6 cm long). Part of a rounded end ('B' in illustration) and of a flatter side ('C' in illustration)—both of the same texture as A—are also preserved. The edges of all these surfaces are soft (rather than abrupt), an indication that they were not used on hard (i.e., stone) passive surfaces. The soft edges and the shiny appearance suggest that the surfaces of FS 378 were perhaps involved in rubbing hides (to make them soft, smooth, shiny, and flexible)[2] or wood. It is true that there is nothing abrasive enough on the hide surface to scratch the active tool used to rub it. The stries, however, may have been produced by intrusive abrasive particles or remains of sand used in an earlier treatment of the hide.[3] Whatever the use of FS 378 may have been, it must have been a prolonged one; or so much is suggested by the flattened configuration of the preserved face and side.

All specimens presented so far come from H1A. FS 750 (Fig. 3, Pl. 4) is the earliest ground stone tool excavated in a trench other than H1A. It comes from FAS:204 and is a large complete tool measuring 18.1×9.7×5.7 cm. With its subtriangular plan it looks like a pestle. I prefer, however, to call this and a few other Lower Mesolithic specimens (see below, this chapter) pestle-like tools, rather than simply pestles. The reason for this term choice is that, despite their shape, the tools in question have not been used exclusively or primarily with their ends in an active percussive mode, as are more stereotypical pestles. The shape of FS 750 as well as pecking marks seen on its rounded sides suggests that this tool is a product of manufacture. If so, it is the earliest manufactured ground stone tool found at Franchthi. One of the ends is small, circular, and rounded, of rough and regular texture, and perhaps unutilized. The other end is much larger and clearly distinct from the rest of the tool body. It is oblong and rounded, with a smoothed surface that shows some traces of red pigment—red ocher? These traces suggest that at least one of the uses of this end consisted of pigment processing or processing a material with the help of a coloring agent. Another may have been processing foods (e.g., nuts or acorns), although evidence for or against this hypothesis has not been identified. This end may have been utilized in an active abrasive mode reciprocally and/or a light active percussive mode, perhaps in combination with an unpreserved wooden passive tool with a cavity—no such tool made of stone was found in the Palaeolithic deposits of the site. The faces of FS 750 are flat or slightly convex, and lightly smoothed, probably the result of an active abrasive use. This tool is manufactured, large, and complete—all features that make it surprising that it was left behind by its users.

The following summarizes the information on the Palaeolithic sample. This sample consists of five certain and two possible ground stone tools. Only one of them is certainly fashioned, the rest are most likely *a posteriori* tools. Limestone and sandstone are the two raw materials represented. Pebbles and cobbles of these materials could have been, and probably were, picked up locally. However, given the nomadic lifestyle of the Palaeolithic inhabitants of the cave, it is also possible that a few of the tools came to the cave with their users from other areas. For FS 750 in particular, with its unique manufactured status and characteristic pestle-like shape, it is not inconceivable that it was obtained from another group through exchange. All Palaeolithic specimens were used in an active mode, although one of them (FS 454) may have been used passively as well. Both abrasion and percussion are represented in this small sample. Of the two, abrasion is the more common. In at least two cases (FS 377 and FS 378) different parts of the tool body were used in an abrasive mode, whereas in a couple of cases both abrasion and percussion are represented on the same tool (e.g., FS 454). The two tools with a single kind of use wear (FS 377 and FS 378) may have been used exclusively for a specific task and could thus be considered as more or less specialized. Pestle-like FS 750 shows different kinds of use wear on different parts of its body, a characteristic pointing to a non-specialized use. Yet, since it is manufactured into a distinctive shape, it is perhaps safer to assume that it had a main use but was also occasionally used for other purposes. It is also possible that the secondary uses took place after this tool was discarded by its original users. The tasks in which the Palaeolithic specimens were involved included some that were pigment-related and perhaps also rubbing of hide and wood. There is also the possibility that pestle-like FS 750 was involved in food processing.

The small size of the Palaeolithic sample indicates that the ground stone tool industry did not play a significant role in the life of the foragers who used the cave during this period. Yet this impression may be misleading. The production of chipped stone tools—for most Palaeolithic lithic phases there is no doubt that it took place at the site (Perlès 1987)—must have involved the use of active and perhaps passive percussive tools of some sort (flaking and retouching tools, anvils, etc.), as must their maintenance. How can the absence of such tools from the Palaeolithic sample be explained? Since many or most of the ground stone tools involved in lithic production and maintenance probably consisted of water-rolled pebbles (not occurring naturally at the site) and had characteristic use wear, I find it unlikely that none was recognized as such and therefore collected during the excavation. Given that lithic debris has been identified in the excavated areas, it is equally unlikely that these tools were discarded in portions of the site not hit by the excavation. I believe, instead, that these tools were so important in everyday life that they would not have been easily left behind. If so, they must have come and gone with their users (see also de Beaune 2000:82; Julien 1985:209).

Since no ground stone tools have been published from other Greek Upper/Final Palaeolithic sites, no comparisons can for the moment be made with such material.

THE MESOLITHIC PERIOD

The Final Palaeolithic occupation at Franchthi was followed by a hiatus that lasted perhaps 600–650 years (Farrand 2003:74, 78). The Mesolithic started ca. 9600 Uncal. B.P. and lasted until ca. 7950 Uncal. B.P. (8500–7000 Cal. B.C.) (Table 2.3). Perlès distinguished three broad phases in the Mesolithic occupation: Lower, Upper, and Final. They correspond to lithic phases VII, VIII, and IX (Perlès 1990, 1999, 2001:20).

Lower Mesolithic

Radiocarbon dates relevant to the Lower Mesolithic period, or lithic phase VII, are listed in Table 2.3. Summarized information on all Lower Mesolithic specimens [including one from the Lower/Upper Mesolithic interphase (lithic interphase VII/VIII)] is listed in Table 2.4. Photographs of some specimens are found in Plates 5–10 on the CD, folder: Pre-Neolithic/Mesolithic/Lower Mesolithic.

Table 2.3. Radiocarbon dates relevant to the Mesolithic period (by lithic phase).

Lithic phase	Sample no.	Excavation unit	Uncal. B.P.	Cal. B.C.
VII (Lower Mesolithic)	P-2097	FAN:197	9150±100	8095
	P-2102	H1B:126	9290±100	8265–8340
	P-2103	H1B:139	9300±100	8265–8345
	P-2104	H1B:139	9270±110	8260–8340
	P-2108	FAN:218	9250±120	8260–8335
	P-2227	FAS:195	9430±160	8425–8470
	P-2228	FAS:195	9060±110	8040–8070
VIII (Upper Mesolithic)	P-1664	H1A:101	8940±120	8005
	P-1666	H1A:117	8740±110	7710–7870
	P-2096	FAN:177	8710±100	7700–7830
	P-2106	FAN:177	8730±90	7700–7860
	P-2107	FAN:177	8530±90	7540
IX (Final Mesolithic)?	P-1526	FF1:43A1	8020±80	7010–7035
	P-1536	G1:22	8190±80	7095–7240

KEY: Uncal.=uncalibrated, Cal.=calibrated

Note: This list was compiled on the basis of information provided by Jacobsen and Farrand (1987:Plate 71), Farrand (2000:Table 6.1), and Perlès (1990:23-91, 2001:Table 2.1). Samples considered problematic by Perlès (1990) are not included in this table.

Table 2.4. Lower Mesolithic specimens (including one specimen from the Lower/Upper Mesolithic interphase).

Name	Trench:Unit	Prov.	Pres.	Material	Date	L	W	T	Illustr.
FS 183	G1:50	C	f	diabase	Lithic phase VII	9.3	7.5	6.0	Pl. 8
FS 184	G1:54	C	f	limestone	Lithic phase VII	9.2	6.3	4.5	Pl. 9
FS 274	H1A:124	C	f	metaquartzite	Lithic phase VII	8.1	4.8	3.6	
FS 275	H1A:127	C	f	sandstone	Lithic phase VII	7.0	5.1	3.9	
FS 530	H1B:121	C	f	steatite	Lithic phase VII	4.6	2.5	1.0	Pl. 5
FS 594	H1B:144	C	c	limestone	Lithic phase VII	5.9	4.6	2.2	Pl. 10
FS 706	FAS:184	C	f	sandstone	Lithic phase VII	9.1	6.9	5.1	Pl. 7
FS 725	FAS:191	C	c	limestone	Lithic phase VII	10.3	7.6	4.5	Pl. 6
FS 296	H1A:120	C	f	sandstone	Lithic interphase VII/VIII	8.5	8.5	4.9	

KEY: Prov.=Provenience, Pres.=Preservation, L=Length, W=Width, T=Thickness, C=Cave, Illustr.=illustration, c=complete, f=fragmentary, Pl.=plate

The Lower Mesolithic is dated to ca. 9600–8950 Uncal. B.P. (8450–8050 Cal. B.C.) (Table 2.3). Conditions during this period were warmer and moister than before; the landscape in the Franchthi area probably had the form of open woodland, and the shore was about 2 km from the cave. The lithic industry is characterized by an emphasis on tools related to activities of transformation (manufacture of tools, weapons, utensils, clothes, and vessels) with small quantities of hunting equipment. The latter may be due to a decrease in the importance of large game hunting or changes in hunting techniques. Both marine and terrestrial shells have been found in substantial quantities (Perlès 1990:26–27, 1999:315, 2003:80; Shackleton 1988:11–20, 39–41). The botanical remains are characterized by large quantity and diversity (pistachios, almonds, oats, pear, lentils, wild barley, etc.). These nuts, fruits, legumes, and grains were collected and consumed in spring, summer, and autumn. Some of them could have been stored and consumed through the winter, whereas plants that do not usually leave traces in the archaeological record (e.g., roots, mushrooms, and greens) may have been gathered in and consumed through the winter as well. Both hypotheses are likely since oxygen isotope analysis of marine shells indicated exploitation of marine resources in all four seasons (Deith and Shackleton 1988; Hansen 1991:123–127). Perlès, however, recently cautioned that the above evidence does not necessarily imply year-round occupation of the cave and may reflect no more than repeated short term visits to the cave and nearby coast throughout the year (2003). I can not see, nevertheless, how the latter scenario can accommodate the remains of more than fifteen inhumations and cremations and also the evidence for a substantial production of pebble and shell ornaments (Cullen 1995; Miller 1997:130–133; Cullen and Papathanasiou in preparation; Perlès and Miller in preparation). I consider it thus safe to assume that the cave was used for a longer rather than a shorter portion of the year in the Lower Mesolithic. This hypothesis is also supported by the very high sedimentation rate during this period—indeed the highest throughout the Franchthi sequence (Farrand 2000:93–99, 2003).

The Lower Mesolithic deposits yielded eight ground stone tools (Table 2.4), a number larger than that representing the whole of the Palaeolithic period. I discuss them below starting with FS 530 (Pl. 5). This specimen was excavated in H1B:121, is made of the soft material steatite, and measures 4.6×2.5×1.0 cm. It is broken transversally, but it is likely that its original plan was roughly ovate. It is the earliest tool of its kind at Franchthi, but one parallel (FS 156) is found in the Upper Mesolithic component, whereas another (FS 47) is considered here as a possible pre-Neolithic specimen (for both see below, this chapter). FS 530 has two faces. One (shown in illustration) is convex, smoothed and scratched. It carries part of what seems to be a U-shaped groove that is polished by use to a high sheen. The groove may have originally crossed the face transversally in the middle. The second face is flat and scratched all over, probably as a result of the manufacturing process. The above description matches well that provided by Rose and Ralph Solecki for a number of tools excavated in deposits of the 11th millennium B.P. at Zawi Chemi Shanidar and Shanidar Cave, Iraq. Physical and chemical analysis of a few of these specimens showed that they are made of the soft stone chlorite or a chlorite–related material, such as steatite, soapstone, or talc schist. The examples that mostly resemble the Franchthi specimens are called by the Soleckis 'plain transverse grooved.' These are

> roughly ovate in shape with one flat and one highly convex face. On the convex face a deep groove is cut across the short axis in the approximate center of the stone. The groove is polished. The surface of the stone is covered with striations from the shaping and has a greasy luster...All are fragmentary but the following dimensions can be determined. They range in length from 5.2 to 7.1 cm; the one width measurement is 3.65 cm; in thickness the range is 2.5 to 4.2 cm. The grooves cut across the width of the stones vary from 1.1 cm in length and 0.7 to 1.1 cm in depth (Solecki and Solecki 1970:831–832 and Figure 1:A–C).

The Soleckis consider these specimens as too soft and smooth to have been used as abraders or smoothers. On the basis of ethnographic evidence, they suggest instead that these may have been suitable for a use as shaft straighteners. As heat resistant stones, the chlorite, or similar soft materials of which these tools are made, is especially suited to undergo the heating that shaft straightening involves. The Soleckis, moreover, suggest that the shaft straightener may be linked to the spread of the bow and arrow (Solecki and Solecki 1970:836–839).

The similarities in shape, size, material, use wear, and date between the Iraqi examples on the one hand, and FS 530 and the Upper Mesolithic FS

156 on the other, make it likely that the Franchthi specimens had a similar function, that is, they served as (arrow)shaft straighteners.[4] If so, they may have been employed in an exclusive passive abrasive mode. According to the Soleckis, grooved specimens of steatite, soapstone, and schist were also found in Epipalaeolithic/Protoneolithic components of other Near Eastern sites, such as Karim Shahir (Iraq), Beidha (Jordan), and Suberde (Turkey). I am not aware of any grooved Mesolithic specimens of such soft non abrasive materials from elsewhere in Europe, and it is likely that no such tools were used in the rest of Europe during this period.[5]

Four of the Lower Mesolithic specimens represent pestle-like tools; that is, they are tools that have the general shape of a pestle, yet were not used exclusively or primarily with the ends in an active percussive mode as are more typical pestles. These tools are: FS 183, FS 184, FS 706, and FS 725. All but one are fragmentary. I describe them below starting with complete FS 725 (Pl. 6). This specimen was excavated in FAS:191 and measures 10.3×7.6×4.5 cm. It is an *a posteriori* limestone tool with a roughly trapezoidal plan and two roughly oval sections. Its two roughly parallel, slightly convex faces show some red traces close to the longer of the two ends (A) of the tool, where they are also battered. This wear is probably the result of an active percussive use in a pigment-related task. End A is rounded and varies in width from 1.3 to 1.7 cm. It has a rough and regular texture, having been used in an abrasive and/or light percussive manner against a passive surface that was probably concave. The rough and regular texture of this end is cut by battering in the area where it meets the faces—an indication that the faces were used after end A. The shorter end (B) is also rounded and was probably also used in a concave passive surface.

FS 706 (Pl. 7) comes from FAS:184 and in its fragmentary state measures 9.1×6.9×5.1 cm. It is of sandstone, probably manufactured, and preserves parts of one face, two sides, and one end. These surfaces show a variety of use wear. The partially preserved end is rounded and clearly distinct from the rest of the body. It seems to have been used in an active abrasive and/or light percussive mode, probably against a concave passive surface. This same end, however, has a facet that is smoother than its surroundings and shows scoring that is vertical to the end's long axis—probably the result of a localized oblique active abrasive use that took place after the use of the whole end surface. One of the sides of the tool was also used in an active abrasive manner, as indicated by an area that is flatter and smoother than its surroundings. A battered area more or less in the center of the preserved face, on the other hand, may have been produced from active percussive use. Some red stain appears on one side and also on some of the broken surfaces, but it is uncertain whether it resulted from a use of the tool in a pigment-related task (pigment processing, for example) or from accidental contact with a coloring agent.

The two remaining pestle-like specimens, fragmentary FS 183 and FS 184, seem indeed to have been used primarily with the faces rather than the ends. FS 183 (Pl. 8) was excavated in G1:50 and measures 9.3×7.5×6.0 cm. Its raw material is diabase, a kind of rock seen for the first time at Franchthi. This tool is *a posteriori* and has three faces and a subtriangular transverse section. Two of the faces are lightly convex, the third (shown in illustration) slightly concave. Their surfaces are all well smoothed by use to the point of reflecting light. The smoothed texture is interrupted by pitting, however. At least the slightly concave face carries traces of red pigment. All three faces were used in an active abrasive mode—the two slightly convex faces on passive surfaces that were lightly concave, the slightly concave one on a passive surface that was lightly convex. The sheen of these faces as well as their soft (not abrupt) edges may suggest use in hide processing. Red ocher may have been rubbed on the hide for decoration and/or for its anitiseptic properties.[6] The pitting seen on these same faces may be the result of a (secondary?) active percussive use. The preserved end is strongly convex. A few percussion marks located on its highest point suggest an occasional active percussive use, although an earlier use in an abrasive and/or light percussive mode in a (wooden?) tool with a cavity cannot be precluded.

FS 184 (Pl. 9) comes from G1:54 and in its current state measures 9.2×6.3×4.5 cm. This probably *a posteriori* sandstone specimen is missing one end, but seems to derive from an oblong tool with a roughly trapezoidal transverse section. One of the faces (A) is flat to lightly convex and seems to have been used in an active abrasive manner. The center of the preserved portion of this face shows percussion marks from a secondary passive or active percussive use, whereas the area between this use wear and the preserved end is dipping and carries parallel stries from an additional active oblique abrasive use. The second face (B) bears percussion marks too. These are combined with slight traces of red pigment, suggesting perhaps a use in processing a coloring agent. On the same face and close to the preserved end is a depression reminiscent of those produced close to ends of oblong tools from use as mallets in indirect percussion (de Beaune 1997, 2000:57–58). The two sides and the preserved end were also used. One side (C) exhibits percussion marks from an active or passive percussive use. The other side seems to have been used in an abrasive mode. Finally, the end seems to have been used in an active percussive mode in a task that brought it into contact with a substance of red color (ocher?); hence the traces of red pigment on its surface.

Another Lower Mesolithic specimen, FS 594 (Pl. 10), was excavated in H1B:144. It is a water-rolled limestone pebble of an ovate plan measuring 5.9×4.6×2.2 cm. It has two faces. One of them (A) is smooth probably from handling rather than an abrasive use. Three areas of its periphery have been chipped off. The second face (B) is chipped off in its largest portion, but its preserved part has a smooth texture similar to that of the first face. The small preserved water-rolled surface of one of the ends appears pitted, probably the result of use in active or indirect percussion. The edges produced by chipping on the other end and on parts of the sides may be reminiscent of those seen on some of the French Mesolithic utilized pebbles reported by Ricou and Esnard (1996). These were shown experimentally to have been employed in lithic manufacture, and more specifically, as *compresseurs* in producing stone drills (*perçoirs*) by abrupt retouch. FS 594 and a few later Mesolithic parallels (e.g., FS 701, below, this chapter) may have had similar uses. It is in fact tempting to see them as used in producing lithic drills for perforating the small *Cyclope neritea* that served as ornaments for the body or clothing during the Mesolithic (Perlès and Miller in preparation). According to Perlès, however, these fragile shells could not have been pierced with stone drills; instead, wooden or bone splinters were probably used for that purpose (personal communication 2/2007).

The last two of the eight Lower Mesolithic tools are FS 274 and FS 275. Both are fragmentary. FS 274 comes from H1A:124, is of metaquartzite, and measures 8.1×4.8×3.6 cm. It preserves parts of two parallel faces that have been flattened from active abrasive use, and part of a rounded side that seems pecked, probably as a result of manufacture. FS 275 comes from H1A:127 and its material is sandstone. It measures 7.0×5.1×3.9 cm and preserves only a small area of an abrasively used surface.

The following summarizes the information on the Lower Mesolithic sample. The Lower Mesolithic sees an increase in the number of ground stone tools, most likely a reflection of the more intensive use of the cave during this period. The quantitative increase is accompanied by an increase in the diversity of this assemblage at two levels: 1) In terms of raw material: diabase, steatite, and metaquartzite are added to the two kinds of rocks (limestone and sandstone) used during the Palaeolithic. These new raw materials could be found locally, although nothing precludes the possibility that some of them (or the tools themselves) came to the site with their users from outside the Franchthi region. 2) In terms of 'types' represented. See, for example, the grooved specimen FS 530, which may have been used as a shaft straightener, and FS 594, which may have been used in lithic manufacture and maintenance.

Grooved specimen FS 530 is certainly the product of manufacture and so probably are FS 274, FS 594, and FS 706. The remaining tools are probably *a posteriori*, or at least I see no evidence to the contrary. Grooved specimen FS 530 seems to be the only tool in this sample used in an exclusively passive mode. The limited traces of possible passive use in other tools seem always to accompany more extensive active wear. As in the Palaeolithic sample, abrasion is more often represented than percussion, and in the tools that show evidence of both, percussion again tends to be secondary to abrasion. Interestingly, this pattern characterizes the Franchthi ground stone tool assemblage as a whole. Half of the Lower Mesolithic specimens have the general shape of a pestle, but none of them has been used exclusively or primarily with the ends in an active percussive mode as are stereotypical pestles (although two have been substantially so used). All pestle-like tools show traces of red color, an indication that they were used in a pigment-related task. Ocher has been noted on pebble and shell ornaments excavated in Lower Mesolithic units. As suggested by Cullen (1995:282), it could also have been used for body paint, coloring for clothing (or shrouds?), in the preparation of hides, or in healing. There is no reason, however, to believe that pigment processing or processing other materials with the help of a pigment were the only contexts of use for the specimens in question. One of them seems to have been used as a mallet, whereas other uses, such as food processing (pounding meat or acorns, for example) are also possible. The multiple surfaces used, as well as the multiple kinds of use wear evident on most Lower Mesolithic specimens, imply that they served a variety of functions. Yet it is unclear whether these tools were used in multiple tasks by one group of people, if the multifunctional profile is the result of use by different groups at different times, or perhaps both. The activities that seem to be represented in the Lower Mesolithic assemblage—preparation of arrow shafts, lithic manufacture and maintenance, hide-, pigment-, and possibly food-processing—all fit well in the picture of the cave as a base camp.

It will be interesting to see if any tools similar to those described in this section have been found, for example, in the Mesolithic component of Theopetra Cave, Klisoura Cave 1, or the Cave of Cyclope at Youra. For that, however, we will have to wait until the ground stone tools from these sites are published.

One fragmentary specimen, FS 296, comes from the Lower/Upper Mesolithic interphase, or lithic interphase VII/VIII (Table 2.4). It was excavated in H1A:120 and measures 8.5×8.5×4.9 cm. It has two flat parallel faces that were smoothed from an abrasive use.

Upper Mesolithic

Radiocarbon dates relevant to the Upper Mesolithic, or lithic phase VIII, are listed in Table 2.3. Summarized information on all Upper Mesolithic specimens, including two that may come from the Upper/Final Mesolithic interphase (lithic interphase VIII/IX), is listed in Table 2.5. Photographs of some of them are found in Plates 11–15 on the CD, folder: Pre-Neolithic/Mesolithic/Upper Mesolithic.

The Upper Mesolithic is dated to ca. 9050–8450 Uncal. B.P. (8000–7550 Cal. B.C.) (Table 2.3). The vegetation in the southern Argolid at the time consisted of a largely open woodland and the shore was about 1 km from the cave. The Upper Mesolithic record at Franchthi is characterized by a paucity of botanical remains, a massive number of microliths, and large quantities of tuna bones. Perlès finds it likely that the microliths were used in tuna fishing and processing. It is tempting to see the cave as a seasonal fishing camp, an hypothesis that could explain the dramatic reduction in botanical remains (Hansen 1991:129–133; Perlès 1990:79). Yet, this may be too good a hypothesis to be true. As Perlès (2003:81) recently noted, terrestrial resources (mainly mammals) seem to have provided the bulk of the diet during the Upper Mesolithic.

Six ground stone specimens have been found in Upper Mesolithic deposits (Table 2.5). I discuss them below, starting with FS 551 (Pl. 11). This fragmentary specimen comes from FAN:177 and measures 10.7×8.9×5.8 cm. It probably belonged to a relatively large concave tool and was used in a passive abrasive mode. If so, it is unique in the pre-Neolithic Franchthi ground stone sample. FS 551 is, however, interesting for additional reasons. This specimen is made of a non-local raw material: a variety of vesicular porphyritic andesite that, according to Runnels, 'probably was obtained from Poros'—an island in the Saronic Gulf that in the Upper Mesolithic may have been accessible by land. It is not surprising that a material from the Saronic Gulf reached Franchthi during this time, since obsidian from the much more distant island of Melos had been brought to the site much earlier (Runnels 1981:100). It is surprising, nevertheless, that the raw material of FS 551—unlike that of

Table 2.5. Upper Mesolithic specimens (including two specimens that may belong to the Upper/Final Mesolithic interphase).

Name	Trench:Unit	Prov.	Pres.	Material	Date	L	W	T	Illustr.
FS 296	H1A:120	C	f	sandstone	Lithic interphase VII/VIII	8.5	8.5	4.9	
FS 156	G1:34	C	c	steatite	Lithic phase VIII	7.0	2.8	1.7	Pl. 12
FS 551	FAN:177	C	f	andesite	Lithic phase VIII	10.7	8.9	5.8	Pl. 11
FS 701	FAS:166	C	c	limestone	Lithic phase VIII	6.1	3.3	1.6	Pl. 13
FAS:159	FAS:159	C	f	limestone	Lithic phase VIII	3.8	3.5	0.5	
H1B:108	H1B:108	C	c	limestone	Lithic phase VIII	5.9	2.9	1.3	Pl. 14
H1B:114/25	H1B:114	C	f	limestone	Lithic phase VIII	6.7	3.1	2.0	
G1:32	G1:32	C	c	limestone	(Lithic interphase VIII/IX)	5.7	2.7	1.8	Pl. 15
H2A:163	H2A:163	C	f	limestone	(Lithic interphase VIII/IX)	5.4	2.4	1.8	

KEY: Prov.=Provenience, Pres.=Preservation, L=Length, W=Width, T=Thickness, C=Cave, Illustr.=illustration, c=complete, f=fragmentary, Pl.=plate, (Lithic interphase VIII/IX) = possibly Lithic interphase VIII/IX most of the Neolithic passive specimens discussed in chapter 3—is, because of its vesicular quality, excellent for grain grinding. FS 551 preserves a portion of a concave work face that may have originally had the shape of an elongated shallow basin—a shape not encountered among the Franchthi Neolithic passive specimens. As Runnels suggested, the original intact tool may have been similar to those reported by Rose Solecki from Zawi Chemi Shanidar and Shanidar Cave under the name of 'trough querns' (Runnels 1981:100–101; Solecki 1969:989). Solecki believes that these querns may have been used for processing wild grain and, to a smaller extent, acorns (1969:993). FS 551 was probably suitable for grinding the above foods, as well as others, such as lentils and dried fish. The paucity of Upper Mesolithic botanical remains, however, may be an indication that at least plant foods were not ground with this tool.

FS 156 (Pl. 12) comes from G1:34. It is a complete steatite tool measuring 7.0×2.8×1.7 cm. It is oblong and has one convex and one concave face. The convex face (shown in illustration) is crossed in the middle and slightly diagonally to its long axis by a U–shaped groove about 2.0 cm long. A shorter, also U–shaped groove (0.7 cm long) is found close to the end of one of the sides (shown in illustration). Both grooves have a high sheen; the surface around them is smoothed but also crossed by scratches following different directions. These scratches may have been produced during the manufacture of the tool. As I argued above (this chapter), FS 156 may have had a function similar to that hypothesized for Lower Mesolithic specimen FS 530, i.e., that of a shaft straightener. If the functions of FS 156 and FS 530 are similar, they may suggest a cultural continuity between the Lower and the Upper Mesolithic or at least a certain continuity in some of the activities of the groups occupying the cave in the two periods.

This impression is reinforced by FS 701 (Pl. 13), a small, complete, flattish, ovate limestone pebble that is reminiscent of Lower Mesolithic specimen FS 594 (above, this chapter). FS 701 was found in FAS:166 and measures 6.1×3.3×1.6 cm. A large portion of the tool's sides and ends is chipped/flaked. This chipping/flaking removed about half of one face. One of its ends carries pitting, as do some other non-chipped/flaked parts of the sides and ends. FS 701 may have been used in lithic production and maintenance, as I think was the case with FS 594.

H1B:108 (Pl. 14) was found in the homonymous unit and may represent a variation on the same theme. This is a complete, small, ovate, flattish, limestone pebble measuring 5.9×2.9×1.3 cm. One of its two ends has been shaped into a more or less straight edge in plan view by removal of one small discoidal flake from one face and by retouch on the other. The other end has been shaped into a curved edge in plan view in a similar manner. These edges may have been useful in the context of a retouching task. Fine striations are visible on the sides and close to the curved edge. They are more or less parallel to each other and to the sides' long axis. They may have resulted from an active (or passive) linear abrasive use, perhaps in the context of preparing striking platforms for the removal of flakes and blades (see de Beaune 2000:80–82).[7]

Yet another variation on the same theme is offered by fragmentary specimen H1B:114/25, excavated in H1B:114 and measuring 6.7×3.1×2.0 cm. This is an oblong limestone pebble with a roughly discoidal flake scar that covers two thirds of one face. An area at the edge of the flake scar seems scratched, probably from use. The preserved end of the tool is slightly battered and chipped, probably the result of a use in active or indirect percussion.

The last Upper Mesolithic specimen, FAS:159, is itself a small discoidal limestone flake. It measures 3.8×3.5×0.5 cm and has a scratched area next to the edge that is probably part of the use wear of the original pebble from which it derives. Perlès also found many limestone flakes, several of them discoidal, in the Upper Mesolithic lithic material that she studied (1990:48, and personal communication, 7/2000). All these discoidal flakes seem to be similar to those removed from H1B:114/25 and H1B:108 mentioned above as well as from possible pre-Neolithic specimens FF18a and S 68 discussed below (this chapter). Perlès suggested that the limestone flakes in her material may represent debitage from the manufacture of artifacts, such as '*meules*, *broyeurs*, *recipients*' (1990:48). I find this hypothesis unlikely, however: neither vessels nor active or passive abrasive tools manufactured in limestone by flaking have been identified in pre-Neolithic levels at Franchthi. In his *Handbook of Aboriginal American Antiquities*, Holmes mentions sharp-edged discoidal flakes 'made with a single blow of the hammer upon the convex surface of a bowlder [*sic*]' (1919:302). These flakes known as 'teshoas' were used 'as scrapers, knives, etc., and for the making of various small implements.' However, no wear compatible with such uses has been observed on the limestone flakes from Franchthi. Unless they carry macroscopically invisible use wear, it is more plausible that they were removed from limestone pebbles in order to produce edges useful in specific tasks in the context of lithic manufacture and maintenance (as retouchers, for example). If so, they provide evidence of on-site production of lithic manufacturing tools.

The following is a summary of the information on the Upper Mesolithic sample. The raw material for four of the six specimens making up this sample consists of limestone pebbles; steatite and andesite were used for one tool each. The andesite has a non-local origin (probably in the Saronic Gulf), a reflection of the wide range of movement of the Franchthi Upper Mesolithic groups and/or the extent of their networks.

All Upper Mesolithic specimens are manufactured, the techniques used being chipping/flaking, pecking, and grinding. These tools were predominantly used in an active mode. Abrasion is again more common than percussion. Moreover, they appear to be more or less specialized. Most of them seem to have been used in making other tools and implements (chipped stone tools or arrows, for example).

The fact that grooved tools of soft stone as well as utilized limestone pebbles are found in both Lower and Upper Mesolithic levels can be considered as an element of continuity between the groups that used the site during these two periods. The presence of pestle-like tools in the Lower Mesolithic sample and their absence from the Upper Mesolithic one, on the other hand, can be considered as a point of discontinuity. Elements of both continuity and discontinuity have been noted by Perlès in the lithic material from these two periods (1990, 2003). Like her, I have the impression that the Lower and Upper Mesolithic groups at Franchthi were in some sense culturally affiliated.

If tools similar to the characteristic grooved specimens from Franchthi turn up in the Mesolithic material of sites located far from it (e.g., Theopetra Cave and the Cave of Cyclope at Youra), they may suggest that there were indirect contacts between all these areas, and by extension that Mesolithic Greece was more populated than has been previously thought. The fact, furthermore, that the Mesolithic grooved soft stone specimens from Franchthi have parallels in the Near East may be an indication that the Greek Mesolithic was less isolated than has so far been considered (see Perlès 2001:36, 2003:83–84). The apparent absence, on the other hand, of such tools from the rest of Europe perhaps reinforces the impression of the idiosyncratic character of the Greek Mesolithic in relation to contemporaneous European cultures (ibid).

Two specimens may belong to the Upper/Final Mesolithic interphase, or lithic interphase VIII/IX: G1:32 and H2A:163 (Table 2.5). Both come from the respective homonymous units.[8] G1:32 (Pl. 15) is a small, complete, oblong, flattish, water-rolled limestone pebble measuring 5.7×2.7×1.8 cm. One end (shown in illustration) is crossed diagonally by an edge. This edge was produced by grinding the end bifacially at an angle, although the alternative scenario of an *a posteriori* formation can not be ruled out. The edge may have been used as a retouching device. Close to this edge on both faces are areas scratched as a result of a probably active, linear, abrasive use. The faces, moreover, carry occasional striations that are roughly parallel to the long axis of the tool—they may have developed from a use in regularizing the edges of striking platforms. The other end is battered either from an active percussive use or a use in indirect percussion.

H2A:163 is a limestone pebble that is broken longitudinally but was probably oblong when intact. In its current state it measures 5.4×2.4×1.8 cm. One of its ends is battered, probably as a result of a use in active or indirect percussion.

Final Mesolithic

Radiocarbon dates relevant to the Final Mesolithic, or lithic phase IX, are listed in Table 2.3. Summarized information on the Final Mesolithic specimens is listed in Table 2.6. Their photographs are found in Plates 16–17 on the CD, folder: Pre-Neolithic/Mesolithic/Final Mesolithic.

Table 2.6. Final Mesolithic specimens.

Name	Trench:Unit	Prov.	Pres.	Material	Date	L	W	T	Illustr.
FS 549	FAN:174	C	f	quartzite	Lithic phase IX	9.3	4.5	6.6	Pl. 16
FS 691	H2APed:203	C	c	limestone	(Lithic phase IX)	4.9	3.5	2.1	Pl. 17

KEY: Prov.=Provenience, Pres.=Preservation, L=Length, W=Width, T=Thickness, C=Cave, Illustr.=illustration, c=complete, f=fragmentary, (Lithic phase IX)=possibly Lithic phase IX, Pl.=plate

The Final Mesolithic is the period before the Neolithic. There are two radiocarbon dates that may derive from Final Mesolithic contexts (see Perlès 1990:85), placing this period between ca. 8270 and 7940 Uncal. B.P. (7240–7010 Cal. B.C.) (Table 2.3). During the Final Mesolithic, the sea level rose even more, creating an inlet that would eventually become Kiladha Bay. This period is characterized by an extreme paucity of botanical remains, and a dramatic decrease of lithic material (with almost complete disappearance of microliths), as well as faunal remains (including those of tuna). Sea-shells, however, remain in relative abundance (Hansen 1991:135–138; Perlès 1990:84–85, 91; Shackleton 1988:11–18). The general paucity of archaeological remains suggests a sparse occupation of the cave during the Final Mesolithic period. This picture is supported by the ground stone tool material, represented by one specimen (FS 549) securely dated to this period and another (FS 691) only tentatively dated to it (see Perlès 1990:22) (Table 2.6).

Fragmentary FS 549 (Pl. 16) comes from FAN:174 and measures 9.3×4.5×6.6 cm. It is circular in plan and was probably planoconvex in both sections when complete. It is made of quartzite, a raw material seen for the first time at Franchthi. If my understanding is correct, this tool must have been perfectly symmetrical when complete and perhaps as aesthetically pleasing to its maker and user(s) as it is to me. One face is flat and battered from active percussive use. The subtle traces of red pigment visible on this face could be the result of use (although perhaps not exclusive) in a pigment-related task. The other face is of hemispherical shape and smooth, probably the natural texture of the waterworn cobble used as raw material (no facets are visible).

FS 691 (Pl. 17) was found in H2A:203. It is a small, ovate, limestone pebble measuring 4.9×3.5×2.1 cm. This pebble has the appearance of a fragmentary specimen since it is missing some parts (especially a large piece that includes one of the ends). I consider FS 691 complete, however, because I see the missing parts as having been intentionally removed. More specifically, I believe that one of the tool's ends was flaked off to create a useful edge; another three small flakes have been removed from its periphery. The other end is rounded and also pitted from active percussive use or use in indirect percussion. The rest of the surface carries scratches running in different directions. It is likely that FS 691 was used—as, I believe, were other Mesolithic specimens with similar characteristics—in the context of lithic production and maintenance. I should note here that the utilized limestone pebbles I described in this and the previous sections are characteristic of the Mesolithic. No other period in the Franchthi sequence produced any such tools.

The near absence of ground stone tools in the Final Mesolithic reinforces the impression formed on other grounds that the beginning of the Neolithic at Franchthi is not an indigenous development (Farrand 2000:96–97; Hansen 1991:174–183; Perlès 2001:39–41; see also introduction to the Neolithic in chapter 3, this volume). It is worth noting that the period corresponding to the transition to farming and permanent settlement in the Levant (Late Natufian and PPNA) is characterized by increase in grinding equipment ('grinding slabs' and 'handstones') and the concurrent decline in tools used for pounding ('mortars') (Ebeling and Rowan 2004:110; Wright 1993:97–99, 1994:254–257). We see nothing of the sort at Franchthi.

POSSIBLE PRE-NEOLITHIC SPECIMENS

Summarized information on all possible pre-Neolithic specimens is listed in Table 2.7. Photographs of some of them—in one case combined with a drawing—are found in Plates 18–22 on the CD, folder: Pre-Neolithic/Possible pre-Neolithic.

The nine specimens I present in this section may also originate in the pre-Neolithic occupation of the site. The first two discussed below (FS 169 and H:67B2) were excavated in deposits of HA or HB that yielded no pottery but have not been studied or dated by Perlès (or any other Franchthi scholars). The rest derive from disturbed deposits or mixed surface layers of the cave. I include them here because, on the one hand, they do not look like secure Neolithic specimens, and on the other, they are reminiscent of some of the specimens found in pre-Neolithic deposits and presented in the previous sections of this chapter. If they actually represent pre-Neolithic specimens, they may have ended up outside stratified pre-Neolithic deposits as a result of prehistoric or more recent digging. Alternatively, they may have been picked up by Neolithic Franchthiotes on the cave surface or in pits dug through pre-Neolithic layers.

FS 169 comes from H:57A2. It measures 7.3×2.2×4.2 cm and is a fragment from a basalt tool that was perhaps circular in plan. It preserves parts of the periphery and two faces. The faces are flattened and smoothed from an active abrasive use. Some fine stries are noticeable on the flatter face. The periphery is generally rougher than the faces, but has, nevertheless, some smoothed areas, probably the result of an active abrasive use.

H:67B2 comes from the homonymous unit. Measuring 5.8×8.2×5.5 cm, this specimen is a fragment of a limestone pebble that has concretion over a large portion of its surface. One face is more flat, the other more convex. The flatter face is smoothed from an active abrasive use.

FS 47 (Pl. 18) comes from surface unit G:2, is made of steatite, and measures 4.3×4.4×1.8 cm. It is a fragment of a tool that probably originally had a roughly ovate plan. In what must have been the middle of one of its faces, FS 47 has a U-shaped groove. The groove is probably perpendicular to the original long axis of this face. It has a high sheen but also scratched longitudinally. Small dense scratches, moreover, fan out from its preserved end. This tool may have been used as, I believe, were the secure Mesolithic parallels, i.e., as a shaft straightener.

FS 252 (Pl. 19) was excavated in disturbed unit G:32. It is a small complete limestone artifact measuring 3.8×1.9×1.9 cm. It has a cylindrical shape with a rounded top and a flat, perfectly circular, base. With its characteristic shape, unique in the Franchthi ground stone tool assemblage, FS 252 is perhaps reminiscent of a few European Upper Palaeolithic tools (see de Beaune 2000:111–112, Figure 9, no 8). Despite its very regular shape, FS 252 may not be the product of manufacture, since no manufacturing evidence can be identified on it. All the surfaces of FS 252 are (probably) naturally smooth, with the exception of the base that is used and shows a pronounced luster. The central area of the base carries stries that follow two main directions. The lustrous surface may be the result of working a soft supple material such as leather (this is the use suggested for the European parallels), and the stries the byproduct of the use of this surface in an unknown, but certainly fine, task.

FA:42 is a disturbed unit which yielded Neolithic pottery as well as Palaeolithic lithics, bone, and shell, Mesolithic lithics, and post-Neolithic pottery (Perlès 2004:6–7; Vitelli 1999:17). From this unit come specimens FA:42a and FA:42b. Both are small oblong utilized limestone pebbles. FA:42a (Pl. 20) measures 8.8×3.1×3.0 cm. One of its two ends was chipped, probably intentionally, to form an edge that may have been used in lithic manufacture or maintenance. The other end is rounded and smoothed and carries scoring on its top from an active abrasive use. FA:42b measures 6.2×3.6×1.8 cm. It has a naturally smooth surface but one end and part of both sides appear scratched.

FF1:8a (Pl. 21) derives from disturbed unit FF1:8 and measures 6.1×2.6×2.4 cm. S 68 comes from an unspecified unit in FA and measures 11.2×8.4×3.5 cm. Both specimens are small limestone pebbles with one discoidal flake removed from their body. Once more, I would suggest that flakes similar to those found in Mesolithic deposits (e.g., FAS:159, above this chapter) were removed from these pebbles to produce edges that could be useful in lithic manufacture and maintenance.

The last possible pre-Neolithic specimen is S 54 (Pl. 22). It comes from surface unit F:3 and is a fragment of an original tool that seems to have been oblong and subtriangular in plan. In its current state S 54 measures 12.1×6.9×5.6 cm and has two faces flattened from an active abrasive use,

Table 2.7. Possible pre-Neolithic specimens.

Name	Trench:Unit	Prov.	Pres.	Material	Date	L	W	T	Illustr.
FS 47*	G:2	C	f	steatite	Pre-Neolithic?	4.3	4.4	1.8	Pl. 18
FS 169	H:57A2	C	f	basalt	Pre-Neolithic?	7.3	2.2	4.2	
FS 252	G:32	C	c	limestone	Pre-Neolithic?	3.8	1.9	1.9	Pl. 19
FA:42a	FA:42	C	c	limestone	Pre-Neolithic?	8.8	3.1	3.0	Pl. 20
FA:42b	FA:42	C	c	limestone	Pre-Neolithic?	6.2	3.6	1.8	
FF1:8a	FF1:8	C	c	limestone	Pre-Neolithic?	6.1	2.6	2.4	Pl. 21
H:67B2*	H:67B2	C	f	limestone	Pre-Neolithic?	5.8	8.2	5.5	
S 54	F:3	C	f	sandstone	Pre-Neolithic?	12.1	6.9	5.6	Pl. 22
S 68	FA	C	c	limestone	Pre-Neolithic?	11.2	8.4	3.5	

KEY: Prov.=Provenience, Pres.=Preservation, L=Length, W=Width, T=Thickness, C=Cave, Illustr.=illustration, c=complete, f=fragmentary, Pl.=plate

Note: The length of the fragmentary specimens whose names are accompanied by asterisks is smaller than their width. These measurements were taken along what were obviously the long and wide axes of the original tools respectively.

and two unutilized convex sides. The use of the faces involved a red pigment, hence their reddish appearance. The preserved end is circular in plan and rounded. It is unclear if it was used in any way. This specimen is reminiscent of Palaeolithic pestle-like FS 750.

Finally, I should mention here the three specimens that were excavated in Neolithic units but have characteristics that make me suspect that they may also originate in the pre-Neolithic occupation of the site. These are FS 230 (Pl. 198) (reminiscent of Upper Mesolithic H1B:108 (Pl. 14), FAN:142, and FAN:143 (both discoidal flakes similar to those found in Upper Mesolithic deposits). They are presented as part of the Neolithic group Active miscellanea 2 (set 2 and set 8). They may have ended up in Neolithic deposits when picked up by Neolithic inhabitants of the site.

NOTES

1. Note in Table 2.1 that the span of one of the four samples used for the dating of lithic phase VI (P-2232) overlaps the Uncal. B.P. dates for lithic phase V.
2. For experimental and ethnographic examples of the use of unmodified pebbles and cobbles in such a context, see de Beaune 1989a; González and Ibáñez 2002:74–76; Ibáñez Estévez and González Urquijo 1996:68–75; Roux 1985:51.
3. For example, scraping dry hide with a chipped stone tool can involve a fine abrasive substance, like sand or ocher. Such a hide treatment is documented at Franchthi by use wear analysis of Mesolithic lithics (Vaughan 1990:242).
4. For experiments in arrowshaft-straightening with a grooved stone of slaty shale as well as related ethnographic information, see Cosner 1951.
5. The Soleckis do mention the presence of grooved specimens made of abrasive materials (e.g., sandstone) in Epipalaeolothic/Protoneolithic contexts in a broad geographical horizon from southwest Asia to north Africa (Solecki and Solecki 1970:834–836). Residue analysis conducted on a Natufian grooved specimen made of an unspecified volcanic rock and found at the rock shelter of Erq el-Ahmar, Israel, pointed to a use in grinding bone or antler (Christensen and Valla 1999). Specimens with similar characteristics, and probably used for grinding/polishing, have also been reported from European Mesolithic sites (de Beaune 2000:103–109). See also Adams (2002:77–89) for a discussion of 'flat abraders' with grooves and 'grooved abraders' (including shaft straighteners) from the U.S. Southwest.
6. Ocher may not be a proper tanning agent, but, by facilitating drying, it slows down the decay of hide (Ibáñez Estévez and González Urquijo 1996:70; Philibert 1993:133). For ethnographic examples of the use of ocher for working hide and for some Upper Palaeolithic pebbles probably so used, see González and Ibáñez 2002:75–76.
7. The raw material of *préparateurs de nucleus* is usually sandstone, but limestone specimens have been also identified (de Beaune 2000:82).
8. For the uncertainty of the attribution of units G1:32 and H2A:163 to this interphase, see Perlès 1990:79, 83 and Table XV.

CHAPTER THREE

The Neolithic Material (1)

INTRODUCTION TO THE NEOLITHIC PERIOD

The vast majority of the Franchthi ground stone tools and related material, a total of 486 specimens (93%), derive (or probably derive) from the Neolithic period. All Neolithic phases and two of the interphases, and almost all trenches of both the cave and Paralia are represented in this material. The following brief introduction to the Franchthi Neolithic is intended as a background to the presentation of the Neolithic specimens, to which this and the following chapter are devoted.

The Neolithic period started at Franchthi around the beginning of the 7th millennium Cal. B.C., after a short hiatus that followed the Final Mesolithic (Table 3.1). By the start of the Neolithic, sea levels had risen even higher, bringing the shore to less than 1 km from the cave. The earliest Neolithic deposits belong to a distinct sedimentological stratum. They have been assigned to a phase Perlès called Initial Neolithic to distinguish it from the subsequent Early Neolithic. The Initial Neolithic

Table 3.1. Radiocarbon dates relevant to the Neolithic period (by phase).

Lithic phase	Sample no.	Excavation unit	Uncal. B.P.	Cal. B.C.
Initial Neolithic	P-2094	FAS:143	7930±100	7130–6500
	P-1527	FF1:44B5	7900±90	7060–6500
	P-1392	A:63	7790±140	7060–6400
EN	P-1525	FF1:42B1	7700±80	6680–6420
	P-1667	H:37Y	7280±90	6370–5980
	P-2093	FAS:129	6940±90	5980–5640
MN	I-6128	FAN:120	6855±190	6090–5420
	P-1537	G1:11	6650±80	5650–5420
	P-1824	FAN:137	6670±70	5650–5480
	P-1922	FAN:129	6790±90	5820–5500
	P-1922A	FAN:129	6730±70	5730–5490
LN	P-1662	FAN:114	6690±80	5720–5480
	P-1661	FAN:97	6160±70	5240–4905
	P-1630	FAN:89	6110±90	5240–4805
	P-1920	FAS:83	6170±60	5240–4940
FN	P-1660	FAS:72	5260±60	4310–3970
	P-1659	FA:39	5160±80	4230–3790

KEY: Uncal.=uncalibrated, Cal.=calibrated

Note: This list was compiled on the basis of information provided by Jacobsen and Farrand (1987:Plate 71), and Vitelli (1993:Table 13, 1999:Table 9). Samples considered problematic by Vitelli are not included in this table.

remains are scarce but show elements of both continuity and discontinuity with the Mesolithic period. On the one hand, occupation is still limited to the cave, shellfish of the same kind as in the Mesolithic, as well as some of the traditional wild plant species, continue to be collected, and lithics for the most part remain unchanged. There is, moreover, no indication that the site is now used on a more permanent basis than before. On the other hand, the faunal remains are dominated by domesticated sheep and goats, whereas the botanical assemblage is marked by the appearance of domesticated emmer wheat, hulled two-row barley, and probably also lentils, and the disappearance of wild oats and barley. According to Perlès, the Initial Neolithic represents a brief episode of acculturation, with local hunter-gatherers coming into contact with established farming groups, acquiring new resources, and modifying their subsistence base accordingly (Perlès 1990:94–105, 1999:317, 2001:46–48, 2003:84; see also Hansen 1991:139–144). It is still unclear whether the Initial Neolithic represents a pre-pottery Neolithic phase; it has not been possible to determine the intrusive or *in situ* character of the few sherds found in units dated to Ceramic Interphase 0/1, as Vitelli calls the Initial Neolithic in her phasing system (1993:37–40). Only one ground stone tool, FS 74 (Pl. 174), was excavated in a deposit dated to this phase and even this comes from a unit contaminated by later material.

The Initial Neolithic was followed, again after a hiatus, by the Early Neolithic (EN). This phase started at Franchthi ca. the middle of the 7th millennium Cal. B.C. (Table 3.1) and represents a full-fledged Neolithic occupation. More specifically, the EN deposits produced the complete range of plant and animal domesticates found in Greece and indeed in quantities that leave no doubt that the main subsistence activities at the site were farming and animal herding. Large quantities of sherds have also been excavated, confirming that clay vessels were made and used in this phase, although most likely for purposes other than cooking or storage. The quantities of bone tools and ornaments are much larger than those from earlier periods of occupation. For the first time the area outside the cave—the terrace in front of the cave mouth as well as Paralia—started to be used. During this and the following phase, Paralia seems indeed to have been part (probably the periphery) of a substantial open-air settlement that is now submerged in Kiladha Bay. It is also probable that during EN the focus of occupation shifted from the cave to Paralia and beyond, where walls and terraces were constructed, the result of a substantial investment of time and labor. These constructions, along with, the large spread and high density of remains, argue for a more or less year-round occupation during this phase (Perlès 1999:317, 2003:84, 2004:69, 135–136; Vitelli 1993:41–48, 213–219, 1999:96–97). Thus, as Perlès has concluded, the sharp sedimentological break between the Initial and the Early Neolithic reflects an equally sharp cultural break between the two phases. The group/s that settled Franchthi at the onset of EN had a way of life and repertoire of techniques radically different than the Initial Neolithic group/s. Indeed, their strong similarities to the newly established farming communities in central Greece suggest a spread of farming communities into the Argolid (Perlès 2003:84). The excavations produced 18 ground stone tools dated to EN (this number includes the specimens that are probably dated to this phase).

The following Middle Neolithic phase (MN) covers roughly the first half of the 6th millennium Cal. B.C. (Table 3.1). In terms of use of space and subsistence base it can be considered a continuation of the EN occupation (Perlès 2004:161). This same phase, however, witnesses dramatic changes in the quality of pottery produced at the site. The elaborate shapes and decoration of many MN pots—the products of very skillful potters—made Vitelli argue that they participated in ceremonies perhaps aimed at regulating the social conflicts that must have arisen as a result of sedentism (Vitelli 1993:215–218). The lithic domain shows a dramatic rise in exogenous materials, i.e., obsidian and honey flint (Perlès 2004:101–102). MN produced the largest number of ground stone tools—a total of 134 (specimens probably dated to this phase included).

After an abandonment of the site that was probably not lengthy (or at least not longer than those that appear to have occurred during the span of MN), the site started being used again ca. the middle of the 6th millennium Cal. B.C. (Table 3.1), marking the beginning of the Late Neolithic phase (LN). After a relatively short use the site remained empty for a few hundred years until it was occupied by a group of LN people with distinctively different pottery. All LN groups confined their activities to the interior of the cave. No remains of LN activities have been identified on Paralia, although there is no doubt that this was crossed frequently by those using the cave. The limited distribution and reduced frequency of ceramic remains, the predominance of finely finished and often decorated sherds, unusual items (e.g., four-legged rhyta), and an emphasis on herding (inferred from the strong dominance of sheep and goat in the faunal assemblage), as well as the limited botanical remains, suggested to Vitelli that during LN people lived in small scattered groups up in the hills for most of the year, but gathered periodically with their flocks, harvest produce etc. at Franchthi (perhaps among other places) to socialize, feast, and participate in ceremonies. It is in these ceremonies, she proposes, that fine pots made specially for the occasion were used (Vitelli 1999:10–11, 96–104). Perlès finds this hypothesis likely only for the earlier part of LN.[1] For the later part of this phase,[2] she argues, the evidence does not support the idea of infrequent social gatherings with a ceremonial element. Palynological data from coring in Kiladha Bay indicating cereal farming in the vicinity of the site, a density of ceramic, lithic, and botanical remains comparable to that seen in MN levels, and a relatively large range of domestic activities reflected in the material in general rather suggest, according to Perlès, that during later LN the cave was occupied, if not throughout the year, at least for a portion of the year long enough to allow work in the cereal fields nearby and also for the remains of a variety of activities to accumulate. Ceremonies, in this scenario, were but one of the activities that took place inside the cave (Perlès 2004:115–116). Eleven ground stone tools have been uncovered in LN levels (specimens probably dated to this phase included). The LN at Franchthi ended around the beginning of the 5th millennium Cal. B.C. (Table 3.1). The cave during this and the following phase was about 500 m from the coast (Vitelli 1999:1).

The Final Neolithic phase (FN) started at least half a millennium after the end of LN and lasted for several hundred years (Table 3.1). The FN occupation was more extensive than that of LN: FN activities took place over a larger portion of the cave—including the dark rear and pool area—and on Paralia as well. According to Vitelli, nevertheless, the FN activities—like the LN ones—probably took place in a series of relatively brief visits separated by periods of limited, if any, occupation. FN pots have characteristics (e.g., they were subjected to very brief firings) which suggest that the potters were concerned in all steps of the process with making vessels quickly while at the same time focusing on superficial visual effects. Much of the ceramic evidence points to ceremony and ritual provided for by potters of varied backgrounds (Vitelli 1999:89–93). Perlès recently offered a different scenario. She finds the density of the FN lithic and other material too high to be explained by brief visits of a ceremonial purpose. Neither does she think that such brief visits can explain the rather specialized character of the lithic remains or the presence of large storage vessels, cattle remains, glumed cereal grains or spikelet fragments, large numbers of spindle whorls, etc. On this basis, she sees FN as consisting of a series of occupations by people who stayed at the site, if not year round, at least for a large portion of the year, and got involved in some specialized activities. During these stays ceremonies must have taken place (Perlès 2004:129–130, 166–167). The FN ground stone tool sample is substantial, comprising 59 specimens (specimens probably dated to this phase included).

I divided the Neolithic specimens into two large categories: passive and active. I subdivided each category into several groups—some more homogeneous than others. The groups distinguished for the passive category are:
1. Passive open tools (Popen);
2. Passive tools with cavity (Pcav);
3. Passive miscellanea (Pmisc).

The groups distinguished for the active category are:
1. Active cutting edge tools (Acut);
2. Active discoidal tools (Adisc);
3. Active rectangular tools (Arect);
4. Active square or circular tools (Asquare-circ);
5. Active tools used with ends (Aend);
6. Active globular tools (Aglobe);
7. Active miscellanea (Amisc).

I should note here that, although all groups have been defined on the basis of a combination of functional and morphological criteria, the names I chose for some groups emphasize morphological characteristics, those for others emphasize functional characteristics. I allowed this discrepancy for the sake of clarity and convenience; each of these names makes it easy to distinguish the group it refers to from the other groups because it promotes this particular group's most distinctive trait. I present the passive groups in the rest of this chapter, the active groups in chapter 4.

PASSIVE TOOLS

Introduction

Passive tools comprise 112 specimens (23% of all Neolithic specimens). The term 'passive' describes tools that functioned primarily, although not exclusively, in a passive mode. A passive tool remains stationary (or stable) during use, while another active implement moves over it. A tool is stationary when it rests upon or is fixed in the ground during use. However, if its size and shape and the task to be performed permit, a tool may also be stationary by resting on the user's lap. Sometimes this arrangement is more user friendly than one that involves placing the passive tool on the ground. Finally, a tool can be stationary by being held in one's hand. In fact, some small tools could not have been used in a passive mode unless hand-held.[3]

I split the passive tools into three groups on the basis of the general morphology of their work faces and the presumed ways these were utilized. Two of the groups are relatively homogeneous, one is heterogeneous. The first group includes a large number of specimens with one or more flat or concave, open, unbounded work face/s. They functioned primarily—but not exclusively—in a passive diffused abrasive mode. I call these tools Passive open tools or Popen. The second group comprises a small number of tools, among which are some of the largest specimens in the Franchthi ground stone assemblage. All are characterized by a cavity of larger or smaller depth. They functioned only passively and in a percussive or abrasive mode, or in a combined abrasive and percussive mode, although it is possible that two of them functioned as containers and not as tools. I call the members of this group Passive tools with cavity or Pcav. The third group comprises two passive specimens that fit neither of the above groups, since, unlike Popen, they have not been used in a primarily diffused abrasive mode, and, unlike Pcav, they have no cavity. I call them Passive miscellanea or Pmisc. I present these three groups in the following three subchapters.

1. Passive open tools (Popen)

Introduction

Summarized information on all Passive open tools, or Popen, is listed in Table 3.2. Drawings of some specimens appear in Figures 4–13. Photographs are found in Plates 23–55 on the CD, folder: Neolithic/Passive/Popen.

The Popen group comprises 102 specimens that have one, or more rarely, two open unconstrained work face/s used primarily, albeit not exclusively, in a passive diffused abrasive mode. The purpose of the passive diffused abrasive function is to change the shape and/or texture of an active component that moves over the passive tool (as in shaping a bone tool) or to alter the physical form of a substance that is placed between the passive tool and an active implement moving over it (as in the pulverizing of grains) (see also Adams 1994:69, 1995:17). In the second case the passive abrasive tool is one part of a pair that also includes an active tool. Tools morphologically similar to Popen are known by various names in the literature: 'millstone,' 'quern,' 'grinding slab,' 'metate,' 'whetstone,' 'abrader,' etc. (see also Carter 1977:694–696). These names may be suitable for other assemblages. However, by implying an exclusive passive diffused abrasive function, they are inadequate or even misleading for the Franchthi specimens in question, which often bear additional evidence of other than passive diffused abrasive functions. If the ancient people were flexible in their uses of these tools, then our archaeological treatment of the same tools—starting from their naming!—must reflect this flexibility.

Eighty-six specimens in the Popen group (84%) were excavated inside the cave,[4] sixteen (16%) on Paralia (Table 3.2). The high concentration in the cave can be explained by the fact that this is the part of the site most excavated—the percentages of Neolithic deposits removed by the excavation from the cave and Paralia are about 76% and 24% respectively (Jacobsen and Farrand 2000:28–29; Farrand, e-mail communication 1/1998). If, however, the distribution of Popen between the two sectors of the site is broken down by (Neolithic) phase, the picture becomes more complex, as I discuss later in this subchapter. We should remember that Paralia probably represents the periphery of a settlement that is now under water. It is more than likely that a number of specimens were submerged along with other remains from this settlement.

Only 16 specimens (16%) are complete (Table 3.2). The term 'complete' in this context describes not only intact specimens but also almost intact specimens, or, in other words, specimens missing a part so small or from such a location that the values of their three basic dimensions remain essentially unaffected; and one specimen, FS 390 (Fig. 4, Pl. 23), found broken in two pieces and glued back together by conservators. Although fractured, FS 390 is grouped here with the complete specimens, since its whole body is preserved. I found it necessary to adopt a more inclusive definition of the term 'complete,' for, if only intact specimens had been taken into account, the number of complete specimens would have been even lower with all the implications for statistical analysis that this would entail.

Eighty-six specimens (84%) are fragmentary (Table 3.2). In this context, a piece of a tool is considered a fragment even if it was reused or recycled as if it were a complete specimen (for definitions of the terms 'reuse' and 'recycling,' see chapter 1). I am referring here to: 1. tools, which, after being accidentally broken, were reused or recycled as preserved; 2. tools, which, after being accidentally broken, were intentionally modified to serve new uses; 3. and possibly also tools, which, albeit intact, were subjected to intentional modification, because they were no longer useful in their original form. The two latter kinds of tools make up the specific variety of recycled specimens that I call 'redesigned' (for a definition of the term 'redesigning,' see chapter 1). For the sake of clarity, I decided to consider as fragments the pieces of tools that were reused or recycled as if they were complete specimens. Without this compromise, I would have ended up with a very confusing classification, in the context of which some specimens would have been defined as fragmentary regarding their pre-breakage use/s, and complete regarding their post-breakage one/s. Obviously the above distinction between complete and fragmentary specimens serves analytical purposes and does not always reflect the different stages of the use-lives of the tools in question. I will, nevertheless, attempt to describe these stages—to the degree that I comprehend them—below where I address the uses of these tools.

Even if some of the fragments were reused or recycled as if they were complete specimens, the fact remains that all of them are the result of breakage episodes. The question then is: why were so many tools broken? It is hard to see the large number of broken specimens as an unintended consequence of use. The mostly abrasive uses of these tools could not have exposed them to destructive forces, as would percussive uses. Neither is there evidence that they often broke during use, as they became exhausted (i.e., too thin to withstand the pressure exerted on their work face/s). The shape of many of these tools, nevertheless, with one open, elongated, flat or concave face, may have made them vulnerable when accidentally dropped, and certainly more vulnerable than tools of small convex forms (see, e.g., active cutting edge tools, chapter 4). Moreover, a substantial number of fragmentary specimens (over 30) come from deposits in FA, FF1, and H1 that were severely disturbed by post-Neolithic digging (Vitelli 1999:8–9, 17). It is possible that tools originally discarded in a complete state were broken when the disturbance occurred.[5] Finally, in some cases, perhaps other more intriguing fracturing processes may have been at work. One of them I explore towards the end of this subchapter. I should clarify here that the Popen group is not unique in the fragmentary status of most of its members. High percentages of fragmentary specimens have been noted in other Greek Neolithic assemblages of similar tools.[6]

Only 24 Popen come from undisturbed deposits. They are dated through their ceramic contexts to the four main Neolithic phases (i.e., EN, MN, LN, and FN) (Table 3.2). The remaining 78 specimens include: 1. Twenty-three items recovered in specific MN or LN strata that are or may be mixed with earlier or contaminated by later material. For these items only probable dates are available (Table 3.2). 2. Four items deriving from strata dated to EN/MN or MN/LN (Table 3.2). 3. Fifty-one items found on the surface or excavated in disturbed deposits that yielded Neolithic and some pre- and post- Neolithic material too (see Perlès 2004:6–7; Vitelli 1993:31–34, 1999:7–9, 17). Given the absence of passive tools with one or more unconstrained work face/s in undisturbed pre-Neolithic deposits,[7] the discovery of only one certain post-Neolithic ground stone tool, S 1 (Pl. 209), and the negligible amount of post-Neolithic remains in general (Dengate 1999), it is very likely that these 51 specimens are also remnants of the Neolithic occupation of the site. For these reasons, I consider and treat them here as Neolithic. This is the date assigned to them in Table 3.2.

If only the twenty-four securely dated tools are taken into account, their distribution among the four main Neolithic phases is as follows:

EN	4
MN	13
LN	3
FN	4

More than half of these specimens derive from MN, while the rest are more or less evenly

Table 3.2. Passive open tools (Popen).

Name	Trench:Unit	Prov.	Pres.	Material	Date	L	W	T	Illustr.
FS 73*	A:55	C	f	sandstone	Neol.	11.1	16.5	4.9	Pl. 37
FS 81	G:lot28	C	c	sandstone	(MN)	19.8	13.5	4.5	Pl. 33
FS 82	G:lot28	C	c	sandstone	(MN)	27.1	14.2	7.1	
FS 83	G:lot28	C	f	sandstone	(MN)	14.7	8.9	4.0	Fig. 12, Pl. 51
FS 114*	FF1:8	C	f	andesite	Neol.	11.5	12.6	5.4	Pl. 27
FS 124	FF1:10	C	f	andesite	Neol.	12.0	11.8	5.7	Pl. 28
FS 126	G1:11	C	c	sandstone	(MN)	27.0	13.6	6.0	Fig. 9
FS 165	H:23	C	c	sandstone	(MN)	19.1	10.7	5.0	Fig. 10, Pl. 49
FS 168	G1:20	C	f	sandstone	MN	9.8	2.6	4.5	
FS 170	FF1:39A	C	f	sandstone	(MN)	21.1	16.3	7.0	Pl. 36
FS 173	G1:19	C	c	sandstone	(MN)	18.9	16.4	6.5	Pl. 30
FS 174	G1:10	C	c	sandstone	(MN)	20.0	13.2	6.1	Fig. 11, Pl. 46
FS 175	G1:10	C	c	sandstone	(MN)	25.3	12.1	7.5	Pl. 35
FS 247	H1A:72	C	f	sandstone	Neol.	7.3	6.6	3.3	
FS 285	FAN:117	C	c	sandstone	LN	24.0	13.4	4.7	Pl. 48
FS 301	H1B:92	C	f	sandstone	Neol.	14.3	9.9	4.1	
FS 320	FAS:71	C	f	sandstone	FN	11.5	10.6	4.1	
FS 321	HPed:37Y	C	f	sandstone	EN	8.0	7.3	5.1	Fig. 13, Pl. 51
FS 324*	FAS:71	C	f	andesite	FN	10.1	13.9	6.2	Pl. 38
FS 368	FAS:93	C	f	sandstone	LN	12.9	10.9	5.3	
FS 380	FAS:102	C	f	andesite	LN	12.2	6.5	4.6	Pl. 26
FS 388	H2A:84	C	c	sandstone	MN	21.3	20.2	7.1	Pl. 32
FS 390	H2A:77	C	c	andesite	(MN)	26.1	14.5	5.6	Fig. 4, Pl. 23
FS 395	H2B:13	C	f	sandstone	(MN)	14.5	7.8	4.6	
FS 396	FAN:121	C	f	sandstone	MN/LN	8.1	7.7	3.7	
FS 418	FAN:132	C	f	sandstone	MN	14.1	10.9	5.6	
FS 419	FAN:132	C	f	siltstone	MN	10.8	6.5	1.9	
FS 423	FAN:134	C	f	sandstone	MN	11.5	11.4	11.1	Pl. 29
FS 424	FAN:134	C	f	andesite	MN	13.6	9.7	6.3	
FS 433	FAN:136	C	f	sandstone	MN	9.2	9.1	3.8	
FS 434	FAN:136	C	f	sandstone	MN	10.0	8.6	5.8	
FS 442	FAS:116	C	f	sandstone	MN/LN	12.7	9.1	5.1	
FS 464	FAS:121	C	f	sandstone	MN	10.3	4.0	3.5	Pl. 53
FS 465	FAS:123	C	f	sandstone	MN	18.2	15.1	4.7	
FS 466	FAS:123	C	f	sandstone	MN	12.2	8.2	4.8	
FS 467	FAS:124	C	f	sandstone	(MN)	8.1	8.0	4.3	
FS 468	FAS:125	C	f	sandstone	MN	11.6	7.9	5.6	
FS 509	Q5N:42	P	f	sandstone	Neol.	15.3	7.5	3.8	
FS 603*	L5NE:18	P	f	sandstone	FN	10.6	14.7	5.1	Pl. 39
FS 624	Q5S:92	P	c	sandstone	Neol.	20.5	11.7	5.4	
FS 645	H2APed:186	C	f	sandstone	Neol.	10.2	6.1	4.5	
FS 661	Q5S:131	P	f	sandstone	(MN)	9.6	5.7	5.3	
FS 668	Q5S:154	P	f	sandstone	Neol.	14.8	12.3	4.5	
FS 723	Q5S:177	P	f	sandstone	Neol.	15.7	12.5	6.1	Fig. 6, Pl. 31
FS 759	O5:81	P	f	sandstone	EN	24.9	14.9	5.0	Pl. 45
FS 765	P5:89	P	f	conglomerate?	(MN)	8.2	6.8	4.6	
FS 795	FA surf.	C	c	andesite	Neol.	23.3	15.6	4.1	Pl. 25
FS 830	H1:9	C	f	sandstone	Neol.	9.3	8.4	4.6	Pl. 54
FS 832	H1:8	C	f	andesite	Neol.	9.6	7.4	4.3	
FS 852	H1:13	C	c	sandstone	Neol.	18.3	13.1	5.7	
FS 873	L5:61	P	f	conglomerate	FN	17.1	15.4	5.5	

KEY: Prov.=Provenience, Pres.=Preservation, L=Length, W=Width, T=Thickness, C=Cave, P=Paralia, surf.=surface, Illustr.=illustration, c=complete, f=fragmentary, EN=Early Neolithic, MN=Middle Neolithic, LN=Late Neolithic, FN=Final Neolithic, (MN)=probable Middle Neolithic, (LN)=probable Late Neolithic, EN/MN=Early/Middle Neolithic interphase, MN/LN=Middle/Late Neolithic interphase, Neol.=Neolithic, Pl.=plate, Fig.=figure

*Table 3.2 (*continued*). Passive open tools (Popen).*

Name	Trench:Unit	Prov.	Pres.	Material	Date	L	W	T	Illustr.
FS 892*	QR5:29	P	f	sandstone	EN/MN	14.5	18.8	3.7	Fig. 7, Pl. 50
FAN:86	FAN:86	C	f	sandstone	(LN)	13.1	6.1	5.9	
FF1:6a	FF1:6	C	f	andesite?	Neol.	14.1	13.7	5.8	Pl. 40
FF1:6c	FF1:6	C	f	sandstone	Neol.	14.7	10.6	4.7	
FF1:14a*	FF1:14	C	f	sandstone	Neol.	13.2	14.2	4.1	Pl. 41
FF1:14b*	FF1:14	C	f	sandstone	Neol.	11.4	14.8	4.2	Pl. 34
FF1:20	FF1:20	C	f	sandstone	Neol.	11.3	8.5	4.7	
FF1:32b	FF1:32	C	f	sandstone	(MN)	15.3	6.6	4.4	
FF1:34f	FF1:34	C	f	sandstone	(MN)	12.3	8.5	6.6	
FF1:34g	FF1:34	C	f	sandstone	(MN)	12.5	10.9	4.7	
FF1:36	FF1:36	C	f	sandstone	(MN)	12.6	7.9	4.9	
G1:18/1	G1:18	C	c	sandstone	(MN)	21.5	13.6	3.5	Fig. 5, Pl. 24
G1:18/2*	G1:18	C	f	sandstone	(MN)	10.7	14.7	5.1	
H1:25*	H1:25	C	f	sandstone	Neol.	9.5	14.5	5.0	
H1:47*	H1:47	C	f	sandstone	Neol.	12.2	13.2	3.9	Pl. 47
H1:52	H1:52	C	c	sandstone	Neol.	18.5	12.5	4.8	
H1:58*	H1:58	C	f	sandstone	Neol.	10.9	13.1	5.2	Pl. 42
H1:68	H1:68	C	f	sandstone	Neol.	14.6	13.9	5.7	Fig. 8, Pl. 43
H2A:41/7	H2A:41	C	f	sandstone	Neol.	18.2	11.6	5.4	
H2B:16	H2B:16	C	f	sandstone	(MN)	15.9	12.5	8.1	
H2B:34	H2B:34	C	f	sandstone	(MN)	13.2	8.9	5.3	
L5:79/47	L5:79	P	f	sandstone	Neol.	11.1	7.9	3.4	
Q4:86/11	Q4:86	P	f	sandstone	EN	8.8	6.7	5.9	
Q4:87/14	Q4:87	P	f	sandstone	EN	12.5	9.5	6.7	
Q4:109/19	Q4:109	P	f	andesite	EN/MN	8.9	8.8	6.0	
Q5N:103/13	Q5N:103	P	f	sandstone	MN	22.4	16.5	5.9	
S 4	Paralia surf.	P	f	sandstone	Neol.	11.8	9.1	3.5	
S 9	Cave surf.	C	f	sandstone	Neol.	18.0	13.1	6.5	
S 11	FA:10	C	f	sandstone	Neol.	14.4	11.2	12.4	
S 21	FA:42	C	f	sandstone	Neol.	13.5	7.2	4.4	
S 24	FA:7	C	f	andesite	Neol.	14.1	9.0	5.2	
S 25*	FA:10	C	f	sandstone	Neol.	9.3	12.2	5.1	
S 26	FA:41	C	f	sandstone	Neol.	20.2	15.7	4.9	
S 29	FA:34	C	f	sandstone	Neol.	10.8	9.1	5.1	
S 30	FA:33B	C	c	sandstone	Neol.	15.7	12.5	4.1	
S 32	FA:29	C	f	sandstone	Neol.	9.4	9.3	7.1	Pl. 55
S 34*	FA:15	C	f	sandstone	Neol.	12.5	14.1	6.0	Pl. 44
S 37	FA:35	C	f	sandstone	Neol.	19.9	6.2	6.5	
S 38	FA:33B	C	f	sandstone	Neol.	11.7	11.1	4.3	
S 38a	FA:10	C	f	sandstone	Neol.	15.9	10.4	3.5	
S 39	FA:29	C	f	sandstone	Neol.	13.2	7.1	4.9	
S 41	FA:34	C	f	sandstone	Neol.	10.1	9.3	3.1	
S 43	FA:44	C	f	volcanic rock	Neol.	11.3	8.8	4.5	
S 44	FA:42	C	f	sandstone	Neol.	11.2	11.1	3.1	
S 52*	F:6	C	f	andesite	Neol.	11.2	14.2	4.4	
S 53	FA:41	C	f	conglomerate	Neol.	17.2	13.3	3.5	
S 55	F:15	C	f	andesite	Neol.	13.9	9.3	4.0	
S 59	FA:6	C	f	andesite	Neol.	7.0	6.7	4.4	
S 61	FA	C	f	andesite	Neol.	12.7	11.4	5.1	
S 66	FA:43	C	f	andesite	Neol.	11.6	11.1	3.6	
S 71	H1B surf.	C	f	andesite	Neol.	14.5	13.6	3.7	

Note 1: The length of the fragmentary specimens whose names are accompanied by an asterisk is smaller than their width. The length and width measurements were taken along what were obviously the long and wide axes of the original tools respectively.

Note 2: G:lot 28 refers to units G:19-24.

distributed among the other three Neolithic phases. If the 23 less securely dated specimens are also taken into account (specimens dated to interphases are not included), the number for MN rises to 35, that for LN becomes 4, and those for the two other phases remain unaltered. The heavy concentration of Popen in MN levels is an issue I take up at the end of this subchapter.

In this presentation, I treat all Popen as a single group, given the very high number of specimens recovered from disturbed deposits, and, more importantly, the lack of obvious internal distinctions that would call for a different approach.

Raw material

According to macroscopic analysis, sandstone, andesite, conglomerate, and siltstone are the types of rocks represented in the Popen group. Sandstone of several varieties (micaceous, ferruginous, arcosic, glauconitic, calcareous, feldspathic) was used for the vast majority of specimens (n=80 or 78%) (Table 3.2). These sandstones are hard, almost always of high cohesiveness, and fine-grained with a few medium-grained exceptions. As indicated by the naturally smooth, rounded surfaces preserved on the unworked areas of many specimens, for example, the dorsal face of G1:18/1 (Fig. 5, Pl. 24), sandstone was collected in the form of water-rolled cobbles and boulders (see also Runnels 1981:95). Since none of these tools was subjected to thin section petrography, the sandstone sources can not be securely determined. For several reasons, nevertheless, I consider it likely that the sandstone used was for the most part procured locally. The so-called Flysch formation in the central part of the Franchthi-Ermioni region contains 'suitable sandstones resembling those utilized' on the site (van Andel and Vitaliano 1987:20). Equally important, sandstone is the most common raw material not only for the Popen group but for the Franchthi ground stone tool assemblage as a whole; over 200 of the total number of specimens (close to 40%) are of this material. It is rather hard to assume that the material for all these tools, or the tools themselves, were imported to the site from outside the region. The idea of a local origin for the sandstone used is, finally, supported by the results of the Argolid Exploration Project (AEP). According to Runnels, a member of both the Franchthi project and AEP, and also familiar with Popen,[8] sandstone 'boulders' transported by streams occur in the Fournoi and Kiladha valleys less than an hour's walk from Franchthi. As he also observed, the rubbles of sandstone in the Kiladha valley are sorted by stream transport into uniform size groups and, interestingly enough, those closest to Franchthi have sizes and appearances similar to those used for ground stone tools at the site (Runnels 1981:79). It is, therefore, probable that for millennia Franchthi people collected local sandstone stream cobbles and boulders as raw material for such tools.[9] As noted, however, these boulders and cobbles 'are often highly fractured and weathered and ... suitable for manufacturing very small saddle querns and handstones' (Kardulias and Runnels 1995:112). If Franchthiotes preferred to collect the readily available sandstones despite their relatively small dimensions, it can be assumed that large tool size was not a significant enough consideration to make them commit to laborious and time-consuming quarrying activities.

The raw material of 16 and possibly 17 specimens (16 or 17%) has been identified as andesite; an additional specimen is made of an unspecified volcanic material (Table 3.2). Two varieties of andesite can be distinguished through macroscopic inspection: aphanitic and porphyritic. The aphanitic is non-vesicular and of brown/gray color. It was used for three specimens: FS 380 (Pl. 26), FS 390 (Fig. 4, Pl. 23), and FS 795 (Pl. 25). The porphyritic, used for 13 or 14 specimens, is mostly gray in color and flecked with white phenocrysts of feldspar and black phenocrysts of hornblende and biotite, e.g., FS 114 (Pl. 27), FS 124 (Pl. 28), S 59, S 61 (see also Runnels 1981:70). None of these tools has been thin-sectioned, but Runnels, who studied andesite sources in southern Greece, considers their andesite as visually distinct from that found in sources in the Argolid[10] (1981:66, 77–98). Macroscopic similarities between the porphyritic varieties used at Franchthi for Popen and other tools and those from sources in the Saronic Gulf point to the latter as a likely provenience for the porphyritic andesites found at Franchthi (see Runnels 1981:60–70, 104).[11] This hypothesis is supported by the thin section of a Franchthi LN sherd with porphyritic andesite inclusions in its fabric. The andesite found in this sherd has been identified as originating in Aigina, and at least macroscopically as being of the same kind as the (porphyritic) andesite used for some Popen (Vitelli 1993:208–209, 1999:38). Thin section analysis, moreover, has pointed to an Aiginetan source for the porphyritic andesite of two 'millstones' from Kitsos Cave in Attica (Cohen and Runnels 1981). This andesite 'appears to be identical' to that used for some Argolid Neolithic 'querns' (Kardulias and Runnels 1995:112–113). If the porphyritic andesite used at Franchthi for

Popen and other tools comes from the Saronic Gulf, the source of the rarer aphanitic andesite remains unknown. What can be said, nevertheless, is that it probably does not come from the southern Aegean where sources of aphanitic andesite are common, since these aphanitic varieties tend to be vesicular (Runnels 1981:60–70). Franchthi is not exceptional in the use of non-local materials for some of its passive abrasive tools. Such a practice has been documented by petrographic analysis for a number of 'stone processors,' including 'querns,' from Sitagroi (Dixon 2003a, 2003b; Elster 2003a:187), and by macroscopic study for specimens from Argissa and Achilleion (Winn and Shimabuku 1989:270–271; see also Perlès 2001:242).

The andesite used for Popen was apparently also collected in the form of stream boulders and cobbles, as suggested by the water-rolled surface of FS 795 (Pl. 25), and also by the curvilinear appearance of this and other specimens made of this material. Judging from the two complete andesite specimens, FS 390 (Fig. 4, Pl. 23) and FS 795 (Pl. 25), neither the size nor the shape of the tools made of the non-local material differ from those of tools made of local sandstone. This may be an indication that tools of both local and exogenous materials were manufactured by members of the same community, and by extension that the andesitic Popen did not enter the local system in a finished form (see also Runnels 1981:105). The possibility, though, that these tools were imported ready-made from a community that simply produced similar looking tools cannot be ruled out.[12] The similarities in size between the tools made of the two kinds of material, in particular, suggest that andesite was not used because it allowed the manufacture of larger specimens that perhaps would better meet the needs served by Popen. That contact (direct or indirect) with the andesitic sources was not taken advantage of to procure larger pieces of raw material reinforces the impression that large size was not a major concern for the producers and/or users of these tools. The small number of andesitic Popen, on the other hand, indicates perhaps that the import of the exogenous raw material (or the finished products made of it) to Franchthi was not crucial in the context of the Popen industry. Yet, whatever the reason for importing it to the site, it remained significant for a long time as andesitic Popen come from all but one (EN) of the four main Neolithic phases.

Finally, the material of two and possibly three specimens (2 or 3%) is conglomerate, whereas that of a single specimen is siltstone (Table 3.2). The conglomerate was probably also collected in the form of water-worn cobbles and boulders. Such cobbles and boulders could have been picked in the region (Vitaliano 1987:12–15).

Aspects of manufacture

Two techniques were used to modify the cobbles and boulders collected as raw material to the sizes and shapes desired for Popen: pecking and chipping/flaking. For both, active percussive tools must have been used. Some of them could have been provided by specimens in the group of Active globular tools discussed in chapter 4. No indication of the use of the technique of splitting (e.g., wedge holes or grooves) has been identified among Popen.[13] Neither is there any indication that large flakes struck off from cobbles or boulders served as Popen blanks (see also Runnels 1981:138).

Not all Popen show traces of manufacture: about 30 specimens carry no such evidence. I would consider, however, fewer than 10 of them as certain *a posteriori* tools—tools, that is, not modified prior to use: see FS 423 (Pl. 29), H1:52, and S 44. Given that most of the specimens showing no evidence of manufacture are fragmentary and also that it is quite common for manufacturing traces to appear on only parts of the complete specimens, I find it likely that in some cases the manufacturing evidence was lost with the missing parts. In other cases, the traces of manufacture were probably obliterated by use. But there is a more general reason to believe that there are not many *a posteriori* specimens in the Popen group: passive diffused abrasion tends to take place on flat or concave surfaces and such surfaces are rare in nature—especially in the water-rolled cobbles and boulders that seem to have made up the Popen raw material. If the natural surfaces of these stones were as convex as is suggested by the unworked parts of some specimens, then some modification process that would create a more or less flat (or concave), usable surface must have been necessary. The opposite is the case with active abrasive tools. An active abrasive use often involves convex surfaces; that is, surfaces natural in water-rolled stones.

But of what does the evidence of Popen manufacture consist? Regarding the work faces, most of the evidence of their preparation has been obliterated by use. The more or less clear pecking marks, however, preserved on the very edges of the work faces of many tools suggest that pecking was one of the techniques used to prepare them: see FS 173 (Pl. 30) and FS 723 (Fig. 6, Pl. 31). Distinguishing the pecking marks related to manufacture from those that resulted from resharpening—a process directed towards the rejuvenation of a dull work face—is not always an easy task. In the Franchthi context, I consider as traces of resharpening the dense systematic pecking that appears to have cut into an already used surface: see FS 82, FS 388 (Pl. 32), and FS 465. Resharpening of the work faces could have been conducted with active percussive tools similar to those used for the pecking of manufacture.

Flake/chip scars are visible on the edges of the work face of at least two specimens, FS 81 (Pl. 33) and FF1:14b (Pl. 34). That these scars are smoothed over by use is an indication that they preceded use, and are perhaps remainders of larger flaked surfaces. Flaking in these cases seems to have been used as a first stage of manufacture followed by a second stage of pecking.[14] The scarcity of traces of flaking on the Popen work faces can imply two things: this technique was rarely used for the shaping of the work faces; or it was more or less regularly used as a first stage in the manufacture of the work faces, but its traces were obliterated by the subsequent pecking as well as use of these faces. I would argue that flaking may have been a more popular technique for the shaping of the faces than its limited traces indicate: if the original surfaces of the water-rolled cobbles and boulders collected as raw material had been as convex as some remnants of them in Popen dorsal faces suggest, then pecking would have been too slow and time-consuming if exclusively used to create a flat or concave work face. As such, it was likely accompanied by a flaking stage.[15]

As for the dorsal faces, they sometimes received no treatment. In these cases the manufacturers modified only the area of the original cobble or boulder that was intended for use, leaving the rest of the raw material basically intact: see, e.g., G1:18/1 (Fig. 5, Pl. 24). Most specimens, however, have dorsal faces roughly or systematically pecked and, in some cases, also occasionally flaked: see FS 170 (Pl. 36), FS 175 (Pl. 35), FS 390 (Fig. 4, Pl. 23).

No debris from the manufacture of Popen has been identified at Franchthi. Debris from the stage of pecking is not expected: the dust that pecking produces, unless in massive quantities, is not recoverable by standard excavation procedures. Flaking, however, would have left behind many flakes, some of substantial size, as shown experimentally (see, e.g., Menasanch, Risch, and Soldevilla 2002:89–90; Risch 2002:89; Runnels 1981:249). The fact that no such flakes were recovered can hardly be attributed to the inadequacy of the excavation techniques or the inexperience of the excavators. Dry sieving, and to a lesser extent, water sieving were regularly used, whereas the excavation crew, being used to low quality microcrystalline materials and unconventional chipped stone tool forms, was certainly capable of identifying flakes of sandstone and other materials used for Popen and other ground stone tools. Neither can it be argued that such flakes may have been mixed with the lithics. Perlès found 'no andesite or sandstone flakes that might correspond to on-site roughing-out or shaping' among the lithic material that she studied (1992:130). If the absence of such flakes from the Franchthi remains is not an archaeological construct, it may be a result of prehistoric practices.

It is possible that the bulk of Popen flaking took place away from the site, perhaps at the sources of raw material. This archaeologically and ethnographically documented practice may have been considered attractive in the Franchthi context as in others, because it reduces both the transport weight and the risk of subsequent manufacture failure due to internal flaws in the raw material (see Hayden 1987a:26–41; Schneider 1996:304–307; VanPool and Leonard 2002:719–720; Wilke and Quintero 1996:245, 254). But if the first stages of the manufacturing process, and thus the production of roughouts, took place at the sources of raw material, one would expect such roughouts to have been recovered at the site during the excavation. Yet not a single Popen roughout was found. Moreover, the discovery in the talus north of trench L5 of 27, mostly sandstone, unworked cobbles (Wilkinson and Duhon 1990:11)—despite the lack of dates or evidence that they were intended for Popen manufacture—may also argue against this hypothesis.[16]

Is it possible that Popen were not manufactured by Franchthi people but rather imported to the site as finished products ready for use? If the raw material of most Popen is—as I argued—sandstone of probably local origin, to pursue this scenario, it is necessary to assume that there was another site in the area that produced such tools and 'exported' them to Franchthi. There are, however, no grounds for such an assumption: surface surveys in the region located only two other sites with evidence of use in MN[17]—the phase that yielded the majority of Popen—and even these do not appear to have been permanent settlements (Jameson, Runnels, and van Andel 1994:346; Runnels 1981:175).

Since the above scenario creates more problems than it solves, I prefer to see the production of most Popen as local in the sense that they were made of local raw materials by Franchthi people at the sources of raw material and/or on the site and its vicinity. The absence of both Popen flaking debris and roughouts may be due to a tendency on the part of the producers to complete some of the manufacturing stages that would leave recoverable traces at the sources and others in an area of the site or its vicinity not covered by excavation.[18] The aforementioned concentration of unworked sandstone cobbles in a particular spot may indeed point to a specific location, in which, perhaps for a certain period of time, some stages of the manufacturing process for Popen and/or other ground stone tools took place. It is true that, with one exception, specialized areas are absent at Franchthi.[19] The fact, however, that almost no debitage has been traced from the processes of Popen redesigning[20] (see redesigned specimens, below)—episodes that could not have taken place at the sources of raw material—makes the existence of a specific undiscovered area used for Popen manufacture/redesigning likely.

Yet I would not like to suggest that the production of Popen at Franchthi represents a case of craft specialization. The characteristics of the assemblage—simple shapes, small sizes, predominantly local raw material procured in ways that did not involve mining, a relatively simple manufacturing process,[21] a rather modest level of output—rather argue against the presence of full or part-time Popen specialists at Neolithic Franchthi.[22]

Finally, who (or which gender) was responsible for Popen manufacture (including procurement of raw material) at Franchthi? I can not address this question directly through the material and its contexts, but according to the ethnographic and historic record both women and men are equally good candidates for this job (see David 1998:25, 35; Davidson and McCarthy 1957:438; Ertug-Yaras 2002:217; Haaland 1987:80, 1995:165; Hayden 1987a; Schlanger 1991:461; Schneider 1996:302–303; Schön and Holter 1990:362).

Technomorphological characteristics

The 16 complete Popen range in length from 15.7 to 27.1 cm, with all but one falling into the 18.3–27.1 cm range (Table 3.3). With five possible exceptions, FS 170 (Pl. 36), FS 723 (Fig. 6, Pl. 31), FS 892 (Fig. 7, Pl. 50), FF1:6a (Pl. 40), and H1:68 (Fig. 8, Pl. 43), no fragmentary specimen seems to derive from a tool originally longer than 27.0 cm. And of these exceptions, only FS 170 and FS 723 could have been originally as long as 32.0–35.0 cm. If so, Popen can be considered rather small, at least for some activities (e.g., grain grinding).

The complete specimens range in width from 10.7 to 20.2 cm, with all but one falling into the 10.7–16.4 cm range (Table 3.4). The average is 13.8 cm. There is some basis for arguing that this may not be much different from the average width of the total Popen population: 17 of the fragmentary specimens seem to derive from original complete tools that broke transversally and more or less in half. As such they roughly preserve the complete tools' maximum width. The specimens in question are: FS 73 (Pl. 37), FS 124 (Pl. 28), FS 170 (Pl. 36), FS 324 (Pl. 38), FS 603 (Pl. 39), FS 723 (Fig. 6, Pl. 31), FS 892 (Fig. 7, Pl. 50), FF1:6a (Pl. 40), FF1:14a (Pl. 41), FF1:14b (Pl. 34), G1:18/2, H1:47 (Pl. 47), H1:58 (Pl. 42), H1:68 (Fig. 8, Pl. 43), S 25, S 34 (Pl. 44), and S 52. An additional specimen, FS 759 (Pl. 45), has one of the ends broken off and also preserves the maximum width of the original complete tool. The above 18 fragmentary tools are between 12.2 and 18.8 cm wide. If their width values are added to those of the 16 complete specimens, we end up with a total of 34 values or the widths of 33% of the total Popen population. The average width of these 34 tools is 14.2 cm, similar to that of the complete specimens (13.8 cm). If the average width of the complete tools can be considered as more or less representative of the whole Popen population, then one can argue that the Popen width is also small for at least some tasks (e.g., grain grinding). This hypothesis gains even more weight if considered against another feature of a large number of specimens: because of their particular shape, the maximum width is not maintained across their length (see below).

The complete Popen range in thickness from 3.5 to 7.5 cm (Table 3.5). The fragmentary tools are between 1.9 and 12.4 cm thick. The higher maximum thickness of the fragmentary tools compared to that of the complete specimens is due to two unusually thick fragments: FS 423 (Pl. 29) and S 11 (with a thickness of 11.1 cm and 12.4 cm respectively). In the absence of any indication that other fragments derive from tools with a comparable thickness, these two should be considered exceptional.

I should stress here that the Popen thickness (and, in some cases, the length and width as well) are not determined solely by manufacture or, in the case of *a posteriori* specimens, the form of the raw material, but also by use: the thickness of abrasively used passive tools (as well as the length

Table 3.3. Frequency distribution of complete Popen by length.

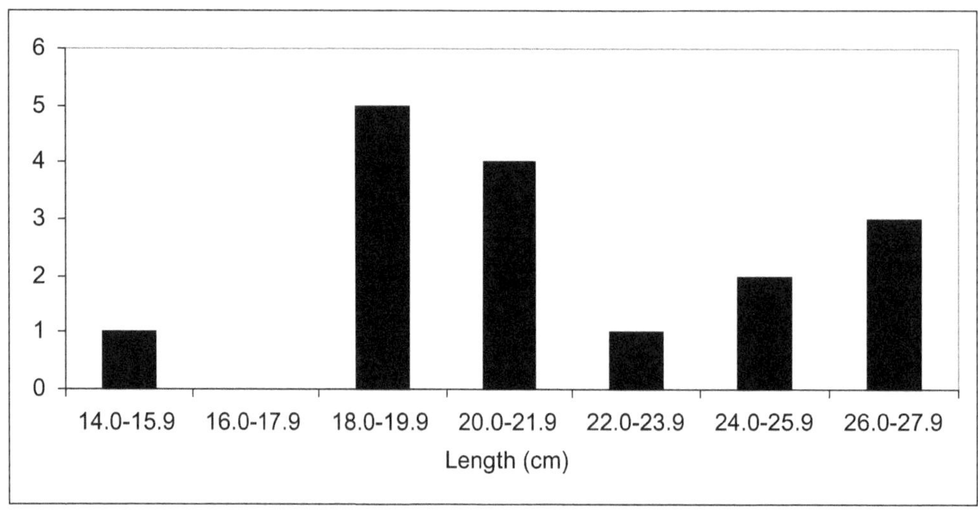

Table 3.4. Frequency distribution of complete Popen by width.

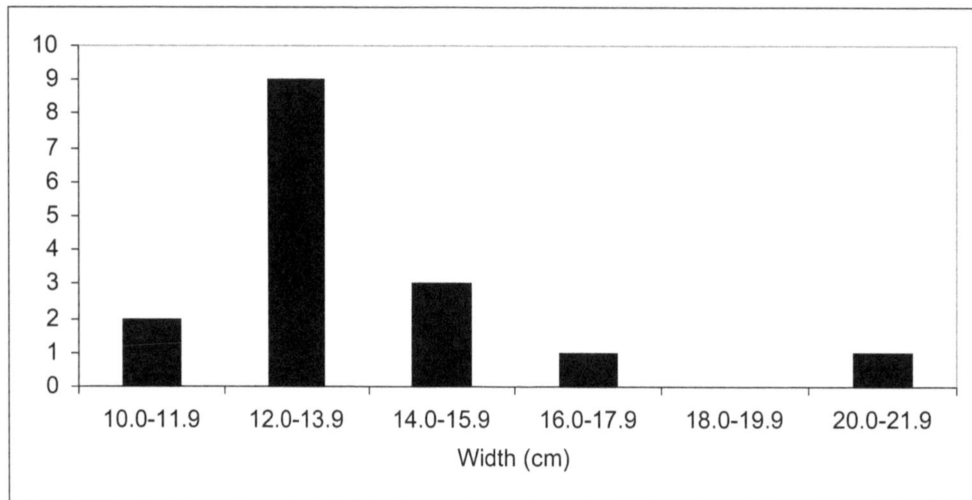

Table 3.5. Frequency distribution of complete Popen by thickness.

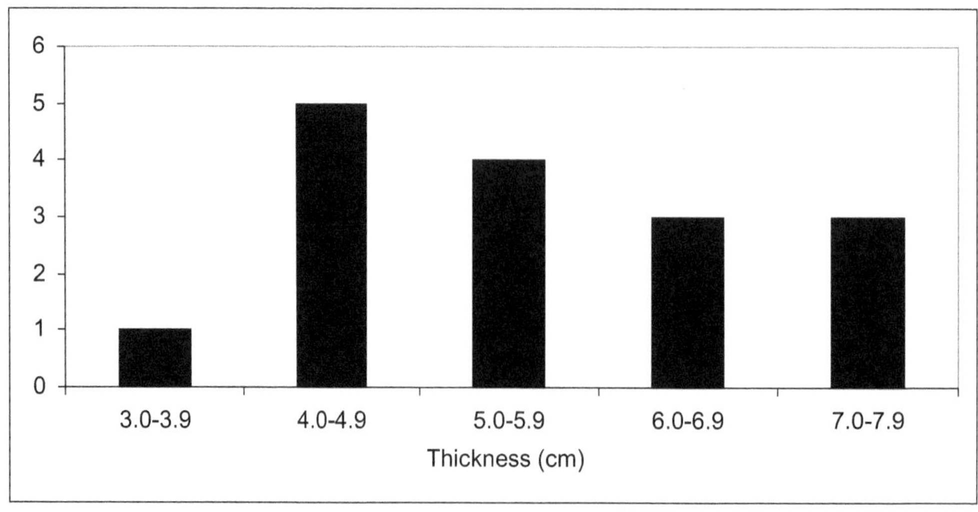

and width of tools with planoconvex or concave-convex sections) decreases through the use of the work face/s and through its/their resharpening, also related to use (see also Nierlé 1983:182). The amount of wear depends on the frequency and duration of the use episodes, the frequency of resharpening, the hardness and texture of both the raw material and the processed material, as well as the force exerted on the work face/s. On this basis, the thickness values reported for Popen (and the length and width values reported for specimens with planoconvex or concave-convex sections) should be assumed to be at least slightly lower than their original ones (i.e., those that the tools had before being put to use).

The above dimensions describe more or less small tools. In this respect, Popen are not different from tools recovered at Neolithic sites in the Argolid, Corinthia, and Attica (see Kardulias and Runnels 1995:112–118; Runnels 1981:102, 1985:33, 1996:41; Runnels and Murray 1983:62). Likewise, two northern Greek sites, Makri and Makriyalos, yielded no complete specimen longer than ca. 30.0 cm and no indication that the fragmentary specimens had a higher original length (Bekiaris 2007:45; Tsoraki 2007:293; Yeroussi 1999:33). Most Aegean Neolithic assemblages, nevertheless, include at least a few specimens longer than 30.0 cm and in most cases 40.0–56.0 cm long: see Sesklo and Dimini (Wijnen 1982:41 and personal observations at the Archaeological Museum of Volos 9/1998), Achilleion (Winn and Shimabuku 1989:268–271), Alepotrypa (personal observations at the Museum of Diros 7/1997), Dispilio (Ninou 2006:23; Touloumis 2002:108–109), Servia (Mould, Ridley, and Wardle 2000:146–151), Sitagroi (Elster 2003b), Gyali (Sampson 1988:171–186), Dikili Tash (Séfériadès 1992a:84–99), Stavroupoli (Alisøy 2002:587–608), and Apsalos (Ninou 2006:23).

Of the 16 complete Popen, 13 have an elongated (roughly ovate or rectangular/parallelogram) plan, e.g., FS 126 (Fig. 9), FS 165 (Fig. 10, Pl. 49), FS 174 (Fig. 11, Pl. 46), FS 175 (Pl. 35), FS 285 (Pl. 48), FS 390 (Fig. 4, Pl. 23), FS 795 (Pl. 25), G1:18/1 (Fig. 5, Pl. 24). The remaining three have a roughly polygonal or square plan: see FS 173 (Pl. 30) and FS 388 (Pl. 32). If this distribution is representative—and it seems that it is (see below)—it suggests that the elongated plan was the one preferred by the manufacturers and/or users of Popen. That the majority of the complete elongated specimens are ovate, rather than subrectangular/parallelogram, creates the impression that of the two elongated plans the ovate was the more popular. This impression is reinforced by a look at the fragmentary specimens: at least 18 of them are large enough to be identified as parts of ovate tools,[23] with many more candidates among the smaller pieces. If the ovate is the dominant Popen plan, some comments regarding the implications of this shape for the efficiency of the work face are in order. The main characteristic of ovate tools is that their maximum width is found at the middle section of their length, decreasing with distance from this central area. FS 390 (Fig. 4, Pl. 23) can illustrate my point: the maximum width of this tool (14.5 cm) applies basically to a central area of the work face 6.0–7.0 cm long and decreases towards its ends. If making the most out of the Popen work faces had been a serious concern among their users—something that certainly applies to uses such as grain processing—it would have been wise to choose a shape that maintains the same width across the tools' length. The rectangular is obviously such a shape. Since, however, the ovate, and not the rectangular, is the preferred Popen shape, it is reasonable to assume that this was not a serious concern for the users of these tools. This appears even more intriguing in light of the fact that—as already seen—the maximum Popen width is not large to begin with.[24]

A few of the elongated specimens (both complete and fragmentary) have a strongly concave (saddle-shaped) work face: see FS 390 (Fig. 4, Pl. 23), FS 174 (Fig. 11, Pl. 46), FS 723 (Fig. 6, Pl. 31), S 34 (Pl. 44). This, however, is the shape of the work face at the end of the tools' use life. The question, therefore, is: what was the original shape of the work face of these tools, and thus what kind of shape did the manufacturers choose to produce? Did they choose a concave shape or is this the result of use (and resharpening) of originally flat work faces? No rigid criterion exists for determining what the case is and it is conceivable that both are at work in this material. The fact, however, that the work faces of the complete elongated specimens can be placed in a sort of continuum according to their degree of flatness/concavity,[25] suggests perhaps that the concave shape is a byproduct of use (and resharpening) rather than the result of manufacture, and by extension that the work faces originally produced and intended for use were basically flat.

If the work face was originally flat, it may be possible to estimate roughly the thickness lost through use (and resharpening) by measuring the distance between the lowest point of the concave face and a hypothetical plane connecting its two ends. The thickness lost resulting from this calculation is never more than 1.2 cm. Not all originally flat work faces, nevertheless, seem to have acquired a concave shape after substantial use (and resharpening); or at least this is suggested by a couple of specimens with a flat work face but low thickness: G1:18/1 (Fig. 5, Pl. 24) and FS 795 (Pl. 25), with a thickness of 3.5 cm and 4.1 cm respectively.

Most Popen have convex dorsal faces and thus planoconvex or concave convex longitudinal sections, e.g., FS 126 (Fig. 9), FS 174 (Fig. 11, Pl. 46), FS 175 (Pl. 35), FS 390 (Fig. 4, Pl. 23). Convex dorsal faces do not sit well on flat surfaces. Franchthi people, however, may have preferred them, because they allowed an easier fixing of the tools into the rocky and irregular floors of the site.[26] A convex dorsal face may have been an equally convenient choice for the smaller tools that probably rested on the user's lap during use. A couple of complete specimens, FS 173 (Pl. 30) and FS 285 (Pl. 48), have a more or less flat dorsal face. These have a roughly bi-plano or concave flat longitudinal section. The bi-plano or biconcave longitudinal section in a few other (mostly fragmentary) specimens has to do with the presence of two opposite work faces, e.g., FS 165 (Fig. 10, Pl. 49), FS 723 (Fig. 6, Pl. 31).

Aspects of use

The use wear study I present in this section is macroscopic. Such a study allows the reconstruction—to a greater or lesser extent—of the gestures involved in the use of these tools. On the basis of this information, the tools' technomorphological characteristics, and, whenever possible, the contextual evidence, I do, however, sometimes attempt hypotheses on their possible uses.

Most Popen show only passive diffused abrasive (PDA) wear. A number of tools, however, exhibit combinations of PDA with non-PDA wear or with traces produced from a non-tool function. In these cases, instead of focusing exclusively on the PDA wear, I decided to discuss it along with the non-PDA wear or the evidence related to a non-tool function. Such a presentation best reflects the ways these tools were utilized and experienced by their producers/users.

Moreover, I decided to include in this discussion not only complete, but also fragmentary specimens. Fragments make up over 80% of the Popen population. Their number requires that they be taken into account in this context, the more so because they often exhibit use wear patterns that are absent among the complete specimens. My decision expresses my desire to do the most with what is available. I should finally note here that, unless otherwise noted, all specimens I describe below are of fine-grained sandstone.

An example of a complete tool with a single occurrence of PDA wear is provided by H1:52. This specimen comes from the homonymous (disturbed Neolithic) unit and measures 18.5×12.5×4.8 cm. It is probably an *a posteriori* tool with a single work face that is lightly concave and smoothed from PDA use, probably in shaping tools and/or non-tool objects of an unidentified material (stone, wood, bone, shell?). This face seems to be too small for a use with an active abrasive tool for grinding an intermediate substance.

An example of a fragmentary specimen with a single occurrence of PDA wear is provided by H1:68 (Fig. 8, Pl. 43). This tool comes from the homonymous (disturbed Neolithic) unit. It measures 14.6×13.9×5.7 cm and constitutes perhaps about one half of an original tool of ovate plan. H1:68 has a single work face that is pecked from what seems to be a process of manufacture. The work face is characterized by a wide, discontinuously smoothed, U-shaped groove, which is broken lengthwise, but seems to be perpendicular to the long axis of the original complete face. This groove starts at one of the sides of the work face and is about 11.0 cm long. It tapers towards its other end (see sections aa and bb in Figure 8), having a preserved maximum width and depth of about 6.0 and 0.5 cm respectively. Fine lines along the groove's long axis indicate that the active component/s moved reciprocally and parallel to this axis. The active component/s was/were probably longer than 11.0 cm (the groove's length) and at least 6.0 cm wide (the groove's extant maximum width). It/they must also have had a convex shape, as inferred from the groove's concave transverse section. The groove may have been formed *a posteriori* by shaping or smoothing tools or non-tool objects, or resharpening blunt tool edges. It is unlikely that the original complete tool broke accidentally in the middle during and because of use; H1:68 shows its maximum thickness (5.6 cm) at the breakage area. For a discussion of how or why this and other tools may have been split, see below.

Most of the complete specimens, as well as a large number of the fragmentary ones, exhibit combinations of PDA wear, combinations of PDA and non-PDA wear, or combinations of PDA wear and traces derived from a non-tool function. I present these combinations below.

1. Combinations of PDA wear

Three such combinations have been identified, named 1a–1c. I consider the tools showing these combinations as 'reused.' The term 'reuse' refers to multiple uses of a tool that produced multiple occurrences of a single kind of use wear (in this case passive diffused abrasive) on the same or different parts of the tool.

Combination 1a

This combination is represented by specimens that have more than one work face used in a PDA manner. All are fragmentary. Two of them I discuss here.

FS 723 (Fig. 6, Pl. 31) comes from disturbed Neolithic unit Q5S:177 and measures 15.7×12.5×6.1 cm. It seems to represent about one half of an original tool of ovate plan and of a width roughly similar to that preserved. This tool has two opposite, strongly concave work faces (A and B), a unique configuration in the Popen assemblage. Both are smoothed, although to a different degree, from a diffused abrasive use. The concave shape of the faces and the presumably relatively large size of the original tool (ca. 30.0–32.0 cm in length) point to a passive use, an impression reinforced by the fact that the abrasive wear of the work faces does not extend from edge to edge. If both faces were used in a PDA manner, they may have been involved in different tasks, as perhaps suggested by their different texture and color: face A is more smoothed than face B. It is also characterized by a slight orange color lacking in face B.

But in what order were the two work faces manufactured and used? They may have been fashioned at the same time to be used for different purposes—a practice documented ethnographically.[27] It is also possible that one face was made and put to use first, the other fashioned later to serve a different purpose. Or, according to a third scenario, one face may have been manufactured after the other was already used up. I tend to find more plausible the first two scenarios, that allow for some parallel use of the two faces: the manufacturer/s and/or user/s of this tool probably intended to have two different work surfaces available at the same time. That is, I believe, why they went to the trouble of producing a second work face opposite to the first—ending up in the process with a fragile tool—instead of continuing to use and resharpen a single one. If my hypothesis is correct, the two faces must have been used by one individual or by a number of individuals working in the same context and sharing tools, rather than by two different individuals or groups in two different time frames. Finally, it is likely that FS 723 split (more or less in half) during use, as a result of the pressure exerted on its vulnerable bi-concave middle section—the tool's lowest thickness (2.7 cm) is shown in this area.

The second specimen, FS 423 (Pl. 29), is a thick, *a posteriori* tool, measuring 11.5×11.4×11.1 cm. It is currently roughly square in plan, but may have been more or less rectangular when complete. FS 423 has five naturally flat surfaces, three of which served as work faces. All three were used in a diffused abrasive mode. The fact that the use wear does not extend to the edges of the work faces suggests that they were used passively. The most intensively used of the work faces (A) is now—although not necessarily originally—sloping. Its use wear consists of a well smoothed and slightly concave area measuring 8.8×5.6 cm. Subtle striations that are roughly parallel to the long axis of this area indicate a reciprocal movement of the active component/s along this axis. The other two work faces (B and C) are adjacent and roughly at right angles to face A. Both are broken and thus were originally larger. Their preserved used areas measure about 6.0×5.0 cm and are discontinuously smoothed. That of face B is basically flat, whereas that of face C (not shown in illustration) is slightly concave.

The three work faces could have been used in the context of shaping or smoothing tools or non-tool objects, or of resharpening blunt tool edges. In what order they were used is not clear. They could all have been used before the fracture of the tool; or face A may have been the one that continued or started to be used after the breakage, and because the other two had been rendered useless by it. The latter scenario is certainly plausible, since the flat, broken surface on which FS 423 now most comfortably rests, is opposite to work face A. As such, it could have served as an excellent base during the use of this face.

Equally puzzling is the question of how many people used this tool. FS 423 was excavated in MN unit FAN:134. It was, more specifically, found in an area referred to in the excavation notebooks as 'hearth strosis' (see also Vitelli 1993:71)—a possible indication that it was used close to a hearth. Was FS 423 used by a single person who took full advantage of the multiple faces of this block, as s/he shared the hearth space with other people involved in other activities? Is more than one individual from the same group or different groups responsible for the different work faces of this tool? I have no definite answer to this question. I am, however, more inclined to see all three work faces as used by one individual or by members of a single group.

Combination 1b

This combination is represented by specimens that show more than one occurrence of PDA wear on a single face. Two of these specimens I discuss here.

FS 390 (Fig. 4, Pl. 23) was found in two halves in MN unit H2A:77 and underneath a 'built fireplace' full of ash (see Vitelli 1993:65). The two halves were glued back together. That is why I consider it here as complete. Measuring 26.1×14.5×5.6 cm, FS 390 is one of the largest complete Popen. It is also one of the few specimens made of aphanitic andesite. This tool is ovate in plan, concave-convex in longitudinal section, and planoconvex in transverse section. Its single work face is one of the most concave in the Popen group and shows a smoothed central zone parallel to its long axis and 7.0–8.0 cm in maximum width. This zone is probably the result of PDA use with (an) active component/s (e.g., cutting edge tools) or with an active tool and an intermediate substance.

The central zone seems to have developed on a background carrying pecking marks, probably from resharpening. If so, the PDA use that produced the zone must represent the last use of a work face that had been already used in a PDA mode throughout its surface, causing the need for resharpening. Indeed, if I am right in my hypothesis that the work faces of Popen were in general made flat (see above), I would assume that, in the case of FS 390, the earlier PDA use of the entire work face was substantial enough to produce a strongly concave configuration.

In the second specimen I discuss as illustration of combination 1b, the secondary use of a limited area of a work face produced a groove. This specimen is FS 892 (Fig. 7, Pl. 50) which comes from unit QR5:29 dated to EN/MN. FS 892 measures 14.5×18.8×13.7 cm and likely represents about one half of an originally ovate tool. Both its longitudinal and transverse sections are concave–convex. Its single work face shows a well smoothed, lightly concave zone. This is cut by the fracture of the tool, but appears to be parallel to the long axis of the original complete face. Its preserved length is ca. 13.0 cm, whereas its width varies from ca. 3.0 cm at its preserved end to ca. 10.0 cm at the breakage line. This zone is the product of PDA use. During this use, (an) active component/s moved reciprocally along the long axis of the original complete work face. The well-smoothed texture of the zone may have been produced from use in shaping or smoothing tools or non-tool objects or from use in conjunction with an active tool for grinding an intermediate substance.

The work face of FS 892, however, carries one more kind of PDA wear: a small groove that is U-shaped in section and has a pointed end. This groove starts at one side of the work face and continues inwards for 5.3 cm. Its maximum width and depth are 1.2 cm and 0.2 cm respectively. It is somewhat smoothed and was perhaps used for grinding to shape pointed bone or wooden tools (e.g., awls and arrows). The groove is apparently an *a posteriori* formation as there is no evidence of manufacture (e.g., pecking traces). This is hardly surprising, given that—as I can tell from personal experience—it is relatively easy to produce a groove by, for example, grinding reciprocally and axially a sharp piece of bone on a sandstone surface (see also Adams 2002:82–84). The fact that the groove cut the smoothed zone leaves no doubt that it was formed after the zone and that it represents a secondary use of the work face. It may also indicate that the groove was formed after the tool's fracture.[28]

Combination 1c

This combination is represented by specimens which have both more than one face used in a PDA mode and more than one occurrence of PDA wear on a single face. I present below one example.

FS 126 (Fig. 9) is one of the largest complete Popen, measuring 27.0×13.6×6.0 cm. This tool is ovate in plan and planoconvex in both longitudinal and transverse sections. Its relatively large size suggests that it was used passively. Its work face is flat and discontinuously smoothed from PDA use. A portion of the face, nevertheless, is covered by subtle parallel striations that are roughly perpendicular to the face's long axis. This area is about 15.0 cm long, starts at one of the sides of the face, and continues inwards for about 5.0 cm. The use wear in question suggests a certain localized PDA usage that took place after the earlier, more comprehensive use of the work face. During this secondary use, (an) active component/s moved reciprocally and against the long axis of the face in a limited area. It is possible that in this context FS 126 was propped up, since that arrangement offers better control of the abrasive process in the area in question. This use may have consisted of grinding one or several tool/s or non-tool object/s. A yellowish stain, visible on the work face, and especially on the area affected by the secondary use, may represent the remains of an abrasive material (ocher?) employed to facilitate this use.

The dorsal face, sides and ends of FS 126 are generally rounded and in fact there are no boundaries between them; all continue each other smoothly.

One of the sides, however, contains a flat to slightly concave facet. This facet measures 13.6×5.6 cm and has a smoothed texture, pointing to PDA use. It could have been used for grinding to shape or smoothing tools or non-tool objects. Interestingly, some of the edges of the facet are cut by the work face, indicating that the facet was produced and used before the manufacture of the work face, and thus when the tool as a whole had a different shape. This could explain why the plane of the facet is now at a rather awkward angle in relation to the work face. FS 126 was excavated in G1:11, a unit of probable MN date. It was found close to a hearth. Since it is far from exhausted, this specimen may have been found more or less *in situ*.

2. Combinations of PDA and non-PDA wear, or of PDA wear and traces derived from a non-tool function

Four such combinations have been identified, named 2a–2d. The first three refer to the coexistence of PDA and non-PDA wear on the same tool. The last refers to the coexistence on the same tool of PDA wear and a color stain or a residue produced from a non-tool function. I consider all tools showing these combinations as 'recycled.' The term 'recycling' refers to multiple uses of a single tool that produced either different kinds of use wear or a combination of use wear and evidence of a non-tool function.

Combination 2a

This combination is represented by specimens in which both PDA and non-PDA wear have been imprinted on a single work face, and, moreover, on top of each other. I present two examples here.

G1:18/1 (Fig. 5, Pl. 24) comes from G1:18, a unit of probable MN date. This complete specimen measures 21.5×13.6×3.5 cm, is ovate in plan, and has an open, flat to slightly concave work face and a convex dorsal face. In the middle 13.0–14.0 cm of its length, the work face shows scratches that are roughly parallel to each other and perpendicular to the face's long axis. The ends of the work face, on the other hand, are smoothed and do not seem to have been affected by the use that produced the scratches. The smoothed texture of the ends of the work face is probably the byproduct of PDA use that involved the entire face and took place before the use that scratched its middle portion. The secondary, diffused abrasive use responsible for the scratches, on the other hand, was more likely active. Such a hypothesis can better explain the fact that the scratches extend to the edges of the work face. Moreover, a passive use against the long axis of the face seems rather inconvenient, as I realized when I tried to simulate it. In the context of the presumed secondary active use, G1:18/1 must itself have moved reciprocally over a passive surface that was flat, longer than 13.6 cm (the width of G1:18/1 itself), and no more than 13.0–14.0 cm wide (the length of the middle scratched portion of the face). The dorsal face of G1:18/1 retains the natural, open, convex, water-rolled surface of the original cobble used as raw material, and shows no anomalies or flake scars that could have served as finger grips. Such a dorsal face cannot be comfortably held for a reciprocal movement of the tool over a passive surface. Yet, since the scratched area does not extend to the ends of the work face, it is likely that G1:18/1 was held by its ends and moved, work face down, over the passive component. This is perfectly feasible given the tool's thinness. Thus, if the above reconstruction is correct, in the case of G1:18/1, a hitherto passively used face was turned over and used actively with the help of both hands.

FS 174 (Fig. 11, Pl. 46) represents, I believe, a variation on the same theme. This tool comes from G1:10, a unit of probable MN date. It measures 20.0×13.2×6.1 cm and is similar to the abovementioned G1:18/1 in plan, length, and width. Unlike G1:18/1, however, it has a strongly concave work face. This work face is smoothed across its surface, probably the result of PDA use. It is, however, more smoothed in the middle 14.0 cm of its length, where it is also crossed perpendicularly by subtle parallel striations. The latter characteristics probably resulted from a localized diffused abrasive use against the long axis of the work face. I believe that this use was active, since (a) the striations extend to the edges of the work face and (b) a passive use against the long axis of the work face must have been rather inconvenient. If my understanding is correct, the presumed active use of the middle portion of the face that produced the striations followed an earlier PDA usage of the entire face. During the secondary active use, FS 174 must have been held with both hands, work face down. Given the concave configuration of the work face, the passive component must have been at least lightly convex; and given that the parallel striations reach the edges of the face, this component was probably longer than the width of FS 174 (13.2 cm).

Combination 2b

This combination is represented by specimens that have one work face showing both PDA wear and non-PDA wear, and a second work face with either PDA or non-PDA wear. I discuss two examples here.

FS 165 (Fig. 10, Pl. 49) comes from H:23, a unit of probable MN date. This is a complete specimen measuring 19.1×10.7×5.0 cm. Its plan is that of a parallelogram, both its sections are roughly rectangular. This tool has two opposite work faces: A and B. Face A is generally flat and smoothed; it is, however, slightly concave in the central area, where it is also crossed by subtle parallel striations following the face's long axis. The central use wear was produced by a PDA use, perhaps related to shaping or smoothing tools or non-tool objects. The two ends of face A, on the other hand, carry subtle striations perpendicular to the face's long axis, whereas parts of the face around the central area show some red/orange coloring. The striations in this case are probably the result of a use that was active. In the context of such a use, the tool must have been held with both hands and face A moved over a passive surface. This use may have to do with grinding, for example, clay, or smoothing a large flat surface with the help of a substance, such as clay or ocher.

Face B is lightly concave and smoothed, carrying subtle striations along its long axis. All seem to have been the result of a PDA use. Interestingly, the smoothed texture is interrupted by dense pecking marks on the sides and ends of the face and by less dense pecking marks on roughly one third of the rest of the face. It is unclear what purpose this pecking served. If it has to do with resharpening, one wonders why only a portion, and not the entire face, was pecked. Are we witnessing here a resharpening process that for one reason or another was never completed? It is also uncertain whether faces A and B were fashioned at about the same time to be used for different purposes, or one was made or continued to be used after the use of the other had ceased. Once again, I find it more likely that, at least regarding their passive uses, the two faces were for some time used parallel.

FS 388 (Pl. 32) measures 21.3×20.2×7.1 cm and is roughly hexagonal in plan. It has two work faces (A and B), each one of which slopes when the tool rests flat. The large volume and weight of this tool (3.3 kg) suggest that they were used passively. Face A is slightly concave and smoothed, both probably results of PDA use. This same face, however, is dotted on a large portion of its surface by percussion marks. Attempting to reconstruct the use life of face A, I would suggest that a PDA usage took place first, giving the face a smoothed, slightly concave configuration. Later, another passive usage took place on this face. As suggested by the percussion marks, however, this secondary use was percussive rather than abrasive.

Work face B is flat to lightly convex and carries traces of systematic pecking all over its surface. The pecking cut a smoothed surface—produced probably from earlier PDA use—and must, thus, be the result of resharpening. Face B does not seem to have been used after being resharpened. Again, it is not known in which order the two faces were manufactured and used, and, again, I find it likely that, at least regarding their abrasive functions, these faces were for some time used in parallel.

FS 388 was excavated in MN unit H2A:84. It was found against a wall and thus perhaps *in situ*, since it is not uncommon for large passive tools to be placed against walls when not in use, so that they are kept clean and out of the way (see, for example, Roux 1985:37–39; Schlanger 1991:462; Baudais and Lundström-Baudais 2002:176). If my hypothesis is correct, this particular arrangement indicates that whoever left this tool behind had the intention of returning (see also Banks 1982:13). Such a scenario may also explain why work face B was not used after it had been resharpened. A large number of pistachio shells were found in the same unit as FS 388, as well as in neighboring units. It is possible that some of the uses of this tool consisted of processing pistachios—cracking pistachios to remove the shells and grinding the nutlets into flour (see Dubreuil 2002:136).

Combination 2c

The cases of reuse and recycling presented so far do not involve any intentional alteration of the tool form. The use-wear combination I discuss in this section does. This combination is represented by more than ten tools, which, after being used in a PDA mode, were intentionally modified to serve an active function. These modifications gave a tool a certain shape and size that would allow it to be held in one hand during use.[29] They may have taken place after the original tool was accidentally broken or (probably less often) while still intact, but no longer needed in that form.[30] I call this particular variety of recycled tools 'redesigned.'[31] The redesigned specimens are very characteristic in their mostly geometric shapes (triangular, rectangular, square, circular, half-circular). I have classified all redesigned tools as fragmentary. In reality, however, these specimens are fragmentary in respect to their pre-modification use(s), but complete in terms of their post-modification one(s). I present below four examples, divided in two groups.

The first group comprises specimens which, after being redesigned, were actively used with the same face that had been earlier used in a PDA manner. FS 83 (Fig. 12, Pl. 51) is one such specimen. It comes from G:lot 28[32] (of probable MN date) and measures 14.7×8.9×4.0 cm. Roughly rectangular in plan, it has a single work face that is flat to slightly convex along the long axis, and slightly concave along the wide axis. The dorsal face has an open convex shape. The most characteristic thing about this tool is that its two sides consist of more or less straight-cut parallel surfaces. I find it unlikely that such surfaces resulted from a breakage accident, and suggest that they are the product of an intentional modification process. If so, FS 83 comes from a larger (probably fragmentary) specimen that was redesigned to become a hand size tool. As I show below, it may be possible to reconstruct the shape and dimensions of the original tool.

The roughly planoconvex longitudinal section of FS 83 is strikingly similar in both shape and size to the transverse section of FS 390 (Fig. 4, Pl. 23), one of the complete ovate Popen described above. The concave-convex transverse section of FS 83, moreover, looks as if it is a part of that tool's longitudinal section. There are no tools in the Franchthi assemblage other than the ovate Popen that have one section that is planoconvex and about 15.0 cm long, and another that is concave-convex. I suggest thus that FS 83 derives from an original ovate Popen, that its current longitudinal section represents the transverse section of the original tool, and that its current transverse section is part of that tool's longitudinal section. If so, the current length of FS 83 (14.7 cm) must correspond to the width of the original tool. Since this figure is almost exactly the same as the width of FS 390 (14.5), it is possible that the original tool had a length similar to FS 390 and was therefore about 26.0–27.0 cm long.

If FS 83 comes from an ovate Popen, the slightly concave (in transverse section) configuration of its work face is likely related to PDA use of the original tool. With the exception of its middle section, the work face of FS 83 is covered by subtle striations that are roughly parallel both to each other and to the long axis of the face. As suggested by the fact that the straight-cut edges (sides) of the work face are worn smooth, the striations must have developed as a result of a diffused abrasive use that took place after the original tool was redesigned into the form of FS 83. The size and shape of FS 83 suggest that the use that produced the striations was active. During this use the tool must have been held in one hand, work face down. Moreover, the absence of striations from the middle section of the work face indicates that the two parts of the face carrying the striations were used one at a time. During each use episode, one of the two parts was moved reciprocally along the long axis of the face and over a passive surface that was probably flat. Finally, the work face shows slight traces of a red substance that could be remains of ocher used to facilitate its secondary function. I should note here that another tool, S 21, has a similar size to FS 83, and a roughly trapezoidal plan with two parallel sides that consist of straightly cut surfaces. I suggest that it also comes from a larger ovate Popen that was for one reason or another redesigned to serve as an active tool.

A second example is offered by FS 380 (Pl. 26). This specimen is made of an aphanitic andesite that looks very similar to that of FS 390 (Fig. 4, Pl. 23) described above. It measures 12.2×6.5×4.6 cm and is roughly triangular in plan. One of its sides is convex, the other two consist of straightly cut surfaces that meet in a right angle. From this particular shape and the way it was formed, it can be inferred that FS 380 comes from the circumference of a larger tool of a curvilinear (perhaps ovate) plan that was redesigned to a shape and size excellent for holding in one hand. FS 380 has a single work face that is slightly concave and discontinuously smoothed. The cut edges of this face are worn smooth, suggesting that the modified tool was actually used. The other face is convex and has a pecked surface that can be considered the result of manufacture. This surface probably represents part of the unutilized dorsal face of the original tool.

In reconstructing the biography of FS 380, guided by its use wear and morphology, I suggest that a larger tool formerly used in PDA mode (hence the slightly concave work face) was (perhaps after it accidentally fractured) redesigned into a hand-size tool and used in an active diffused abrasive mode with the same face (hence the latter's smoothed-over cut edges).

FS 380 comes from LN unit FAS:102. It was found near a hearth, and thus possibly *in situ*. Pointed bone tools and grain were also found in the area. I doubt that FS 380 is functionally associated with the bone tools, since I cannot see how it could have been used to grind them. FS 380 is perhaps suitable for a grain grinding task, although no passive tools were retrieved from this or neighboring units.

The second group comprises specimens, which, after being redesigned, were actively used on a face or area different from the one that had been earlier used in a PDA mode.

One example is FS 321 (Fig. 13, Pl. 52). It comes from EN unit HPed:37Y. Measuring

8.0×7.3×5.1 cm, its size is perfect for holding in one hand. It is triangular in plan with sides that consist of straight-cut surfaces of roughly equal length. At least two of the three corners of the triangle, on the other hand, are rounded and pecked. These corners represent remnants of larger surfaces that existed before the straight cutting that produced the sides of the triangle. This suggests that FS 321 comes from a larger tool with a pecked, rounded periphery.

FS 321 has two opposite work faces: A and B. Face A is flat to slightly concave and smoothed from probable PDA use. This use wear is cut on all sides, suggesting that face A was used before the original tool was redesigned into its current triangular shape. Face B is flat and discontinuously smoothed from a diffused abrasive use. Its three sides are smoothed over, suggesting that this face was used actively after the modification of the original tool. If so, the active diffused abrasive use of this tool followed its PDA use.

Thus, in the case of FS 321, a larger tool that seems to have been used in a PDA mode with one face (hence the flat to slightly concave configuration of face A) was redesigned into a hand-sized tool and used in an active diffused abrasive mode with the other face (hence the smoothed-over cut edges of face B).

FS 464 (Pl. 53) provides a variation on the same theme. This specimen comes from MN unit FAS:121. It measures 10.3×4.0×3.5 cm and has a very narrow rectangular plan. Its two ends and one of the sides consist of straight-cut surfaces that meet in two right angles. The second side is pecked and slightly convex in plan, most likely part of the circumference of a larger original tool. The rectangular shape of FS 464 is unlikely to be the result of accidental fracture and should thus be seen as part of a redesigning strategy. FS 464 has two opposite, slightly concave faces that are discontinuously smoothed. The concave configuration and the smoothed texture of both faces are cut on one of the sides and on the two ends, suggesting that they represent use wear of the original tool. The fact that this use wear does not reach the uncut second side of the two faces suggests that the latter originally served a PDA function.

There is no sign that FS 464 in its present form was used in an abrasive mode with the faces. What purpose, then, did the modification serve? The answer to this question lies, I believe, on one of the tool's ends that looks chipped, as if it had been involved in a percussive task. Both the elongated shape of the tool and its proportions make it perfect for holding in one hand and using with one end in an active percussive mode. I suggest, then, that FS 464 represents a Popen that, perhaps after being accidentally fractured, was intentionally modified into a much smaller active percussive tool.

Other redesigned tools include FS 468, FS 765, FS 830 (Pl. 54), FS 832, S 29, S 32 (Pl. 55), and S 41. Redesigned tools come from all but the FN phases, making them one of the characteristic features of the Franchthi Neolithic ground stone tool industry as a whole. Such a chronological distribution may be indicative of a certain cultural continuity among the groups that occupied Franchthi from EN through LN, something also hypothesized on the basis of pottery and lithics by Vitelli (1999:97–98) and Perlès (2004:164–165) respectively. The practice of redesigning points, I believe, to a flexible attitude towards tools and raw materials (see also below). If the people who used both the original and the redesigned versions coincide, this practice perhaps also suggests an attachment by the users that was strong enough to involve them in redesigning activities. On the other hand, the fact that two of these specimens (FS 832 and FS 468) were not used after they were intentionally modified suggests that, at least in some cases, redesigning took place in anticipation of future needs, the hallmark of a curation technology.

Combination 2d

The last combination is represented by two recycled specimens carrying on their work faces PDA wear as well as a stain or a residue produced from a non-tool function. These specimens were at some point converted into bases for tasks that involved liquid or semi-liquid substances. No modification of the original tool form took place in the process of recycling. I illustrate this combination with complete specimen FS 795.

FS 795 (Pl. 25) comes from the surface of trench FA and is made of aphanitic andesite. Measuring 23.3×15.6×4.1 cm, it is ovate in plan and planoconvex in both longitudinal and transverse sections. It has a single smoothed work face that seems to have been used in a PDA mode before serving as a base in a task that produced the patches of black stain visible on its surface. This stain has not been analyzed, but it may represent resin used as adhesive material. It may be similar to that found on some LN sherds (Vitelli 1999:28–29). In the case of FS 795, a slab used in a PDA mode was later employed as a surface over which a task perhaps involving melting or melted resin took place.[33] If so, it may have been used, for at least some portion of its use life, next to a hearth.

Discussion

About half of the 102 specimens that make up the Popen group show more than one occurrence of use wear. It can be assumed that tool fracture caused the loss of some evidence of use and thus that the number of tools with more than one occurrence of use wear was originally higher.

It is obvious that Popen were versatile tools used, reused, and recycled in ways that left behind different varieties of use wear. Equally clear is a tendency on the part of Popen users to combine PDA uses with active diffused abrasive ones rather than (passive or active) percussive uses. There is nothing extraordinary in Popen reuse and recycling. After all, these tools probably had long lives and their *raison d'être* was to serve the needs of their users as these emerged in everyday life. In fact, it is probably the tools with a single occurrence of PDA wear that should be considered anomalous. It is, however, still necessary to address the context in which reuse and recycling took place. Were tools used and reused or recycled by more or less the same people during a limited time frame? Or were they used by one group of people at one time, and then abandoned to be recovered and reused or recycled by another group at a later time?[34]

To address these questions, one needs first to examine whether there was a movement of Popen from one Neolithic phase to the next. If that were the case, one would expect the reused or recycled tools to come from the later Neolithic phases. Such tools, however, come from all four main Neolithic phases, not just the later ones. Characteristically, two of the four EN Popen show more than one occurrence of use wear. FS 759 (Pl. 45), with two work faces used in a PDA mode, is one of them. Although missing a part, this specimen is still large (24.9×14.9×5.0 cm) and usable, and as such, would have been a good candidate for reuse or recycling in MN or later phases. Yet it was never used after EN. Thus I would argue that, although a movement of tools from earlier to later Neolithic phases can not be ruled out, it cannot by itself account for the widespread presence of reused or recycled tools in the Popen group.

Given that most reused or recycled Popen come from MN, we should also explore the possibility of Popen movement within MN itself, and basically from earlier to later MN subphases—no fewer than five such subphases, named FCP2.1–FCP2.5, have been recognized on the basis of pottery analysis by Vitelli (1993:49–83). MN, after all, lasted for about 300–400 years. During this phase the site was abandoned and reoccupied several times. At the end of FCP2.2 and FCP2.4, in particular, there is the suspicion that the site was abandoned for substantial stretches of time (Vitelli 1993:210, 218, 1999:96). It is conceivable that when the users of these tools or their descendants returned after a period of abandonment, they took advantage of the tools available at the site. The fact, however, that the subphases with the largest numbers of reused or recycled specimens (FCP2.2 and FCP2.3) are also those with the highest numbers of Popen in general rather argues against this hypothesis. Thus, again, while the possibility of tool movement within MN cannot be ruled out, it is doubtful that such a movement took place to an extent sufficient to account for the large number of reused or recycled Popen found at the site.

On this basis, I would assume that in most cases use and reuse or recycling occurred in a single temporal context and involved a single group of people. This scenario may be supported by some internal evidence. I am referring here to specimens with two opposite work faces. As I argued earlier, an obvious reason for producing a second work face opposite to the first—ending up in the process with a fragile tool—instead of rejuvenating a single one, is so that two faces are simultaneously available for use. This implies that the individual/s who used one face was/were probably the same who used the other.

Whoever the people were who used and reused or recycled Popen, one thing is certain about them: they were flexible in the way they used these tools and, by extension, in the way they conceived and experienced them. They used the available complete or fragmentary tools regardless of their earlier uses, so long as they satisfied their needs at the time. Was this flexibility a response to constraints of the local environment? Can it be argued that this attitude was in a way forced upon them by a scarcity of suitable raw material? Most likely not, since regional surface surveys have shown that sandstone stream cobbles and boulders that could have been exploited must have been available in the Neolithic period, as they are today (see Runnels 1981:77–79; Kardulias and Runnels 1995:112). It is reasonable, therefore, to assume that the flexibility in use witnessed in this assemblage reflects a practical approach, according to which there is no reason to spend/waste time and energy collecting raw material and producing new tools if the available ones could, through reuse or recycling, equally well serve the existing needs. This was in fact a choice of increased productivity: the users of these tools got a higher return with the least possible effort/input.

Given the widespread assumption that broad-faced, abrasively used passive tools—often referred to in the literature as millstones or querns—most often served grain processing purposes, one interesting implication of my analysis of the morphology and use wear of the Franchthi tools is that even the largest of them are too small (and of inadequate shape) for efficient grain grinding. Runnels, who studied the same material for his Ph.D. dissertation, reached a similar conclusion (1981:152–154), a conclusion reinforced by experiments he and Stephen Diamant conducted grinding wheat and barley. They used two 'grinding slabs' measuring 30.0×21.0×10.0 cm and 37.0×18.0×7.0 cm and thus larger than the largest complete Franchthi specimens. As Runnels noted, they were 'too small ... for keeping the grain on them for efficient grinding. Only small amounts could be ground at one time' (1981:250–251).

Similar observations have been made by other scholars. Patrick O'Brien experimented with grinding wheat (among others) using 'metates' about 30.0×20.0×6.0 cm (again larger than the largest complete Franchthi specimens). He, too, found this tool size inadequate for efficient grinding (1994:31–32). According to Theresa Hersh, who studied food processing tools from Neolithic sites in Turkey, grinding stones under 25.0 cm are 'essentially too small to have functioned efficiently as lower slabs' (1981:464). Referring to prehistoric grinding equipment from eastern Sahara, Schön and Holter wrote that 'if 35 cm is the minimum length of a working surface for effective grinding, then it can be assumed that the smaller specimens were used for crushing spices and/or minerals' (1990:369). In the context of her ethnoarchaeological study in Tichitt, Mauritania, Valentine Roux observed the use of two kinds of passive grinding tools: those of the first kind are called *meules à grains* and have an average length and width of ca. 44.0 cm and 28.0 cm respectively. Those of the second kind have an average length and width of ca. 27.0 cm and 19.0 cm respectively, and thus are closer in size to the Popen. They are called *meules à végétaux* and are used for grinding plants other than cereals (Roux 1985:32–42). Another ethnoarchaeological study, this time at the village of Bata in Nepal, reported also the use of two categories of passive abrasive tools: the first (*meules*), measuring an average 58.0 cm in length and 34.0 cm in width, are used for grain grinding; the second (*meules à assaisonnement*) have an average length and width of 31.0 cm and 27.0 cm respectively, and are used for grinding spices, plant foods other than grains, and small quantities of salt (Baudais and Lundström-Baudais 2002:165–171).

The idea that Popen could not have been used, at least routinely, in cereal grinding[35] appears surprising in light of the palaeobotanical evidence. The botanical sequence at Franchthi is characterized by the continuous presence of domesticated cereal remains (wheat and barley) from the beginning through the end of the Neolithic, and suggests cereal consumption at the site throughout this period (Hansen 1991:141–153, 163–164). Indeed, cereals were not only consumed at the site but also cultivated in the vicinity (at least from MN through FN). This is confirmed by a pollen diagram from a core taken close to the site—in Kiladha Bay at a spot located between the village of Kiladha and the island of Koronis (Bottema 1990:117). The high percentages of cereal pollen shown in zone I of the diagram[36] suggest that the core was taken from or very close to an area where at one time cereals were grown or threshed (Bottema 1990:123; see also Hansen 1991:148). The fact that cereals were grown in the vicinity of the site and consumed at the site leaves little doubt that cereal processing took place at the site as well. But how did Franchthiotes process grains if they did not have adequate passive grain grinding implements?

In fact, the only reason the Franchthi situation may appear paradoxical is because of the common association of cereals with meal or flour. Contrary to what is usually assumed, however, grinding is not a necessary step in the preparation of cereal grains for consumption. Grinding produces meal or flour, but these, and by extension bread, are not the only forms in which cereals can be consumed. This assumption is rather an aspect of an ethnocentric approach that views as universal the dominant position of bread in modern Euro-American diets. It is true that grinding grains into flour offers a substantial advantage by maximizing the nutritional value of grains and in practice increasing the amount of food produced from the same amount of harvested grains (Wright 1993:97; see also Stahl 1989:172–174). As pointed out, nevertheless, grinding grains into flour is a very labor-intensive activity (Wright 1994:245). Given the sizes of even the largest Popen, it is probably not an exaggeration to argue that flour production at Franchthi would have been rather uneconomic by demanding more energy than the resulting flour would have produced. Grinding, thus, was probably not an attractive choice as the main cereal processing technique.

Equally ethnocentric may be the assumption that the only step in grain preparation for consumption that cannot be avoided is dehusking. According to this idea, nutrients in the seeds of glume wheats and hulled barley, such as those found at Franchthi and other Neolithic sites,[37] are tightly encased in indigestible fibrous husks that must be removed before consumption (see Moritz 1958:47; Wright 1994:242). Recent studies have shown, however, that cereal dehusking is not an indispensable stage in the preparation for consumption, that people in the past may have chosen not to dehusk their grains or to dehusk them only partially, and that they may not have had the same intolerance for fibrous foods or the same dietary preferences as modern people (see D'Andrea 2003; Procopiou 2003; Willcox 2002).

Yet, at Franchthi, it seems that dehusking did take place. This is suggested by rachis material (spikelet forks, glume bases, rachis fragments, and culm nodes) found in almost all Neolithic units studied for botanical remains (Hansen 1991:Appendixes A through D). Cereal dehusking can be accomplished by pounding (Wright 1994:243). As experimental work, archaeological evidence, ethnographic and ethnoarchaeological studies, as well as ancient written sources have shown, the preferred implements for this job are paired passive and active tools, known as mortars and pestles. Pounding cereal seeds in a mortar with a pestle makes husks 'rub off' each other, and leaves the grains relatively free. By contrast, the use of tools like Popen, in combination with active abrasive tools, is inefficient, as these tools tend to crush the seeds, making it virtually impossible to separate the grains from the chaff (see, among others, Dubreuil 2002:171; Ertug-Yaras 2002:214–215; Foxhall and Forbes 1982:75–77; Grégoire 1992:332; Hamon 2006:81; Harlan 1967:199–200; Hillman 1981a:154, 1983:5–8, 1984:129–131; Meurers-Balke and Lüning 1992:343–356; Nesbitt and Samuel 1996:47–54; Samuel 1993:278–281, 1999:131; Wright 1991:38–39, 1993:97, 1994:243; Yalouri 1994:62–65).

Nevertheless, no stone tools with a cavity and a raw material suitable to serve a grain pounding function have been excavated at Franchthi (see Passive tools with cavity, below this chapter). It is, moreover, unclear whether the very few excavated elongated active tools that could have been used with tools with cavity (see Active miscellanea 1 (set 4) and Active miscellanea 2 (set 4) (chapter 4)) were employed in a grain pounding context. Does this mean that Franchthi people had no dehusking tools? Not necessarily, since, like many ethnographic or historical groups (see Harlan 1967:199; Hillman 1984:130), they could for this purpose have used wooden mortars and pestles that simply left no trace in the archaeological record.

If cereal dehusking was accomplished at Franchthi with wooden tools, how could the dehusked grains have been prepared for consumption without the use of adequate passive abrasive tools? The ethnographic, historic, and archaeological record suggests that Franchthi people had several culinary choices. For example, they could boil the dehusked grain and eat it plain or mixed with honey, fresh or dried fruits, nuts, spices, etc. Boiling seems indeed to have been the most common cooking technique for grains (and other foods) at Çatalhöyük (Atalay and Hastorf 2006:306–309).[38] Modern examples of consumption of boiled grain also exist: Hillman reports that in Turkish villages small quantities of boiled grain are occasionally eaten as snacks (1984:135), and boiled wheat, mixed with ingredients such as raisins, sugar, almonds, and pomegranate seeds, makes up the traditional Greek dish '*κόλυβα*' (koliva) that is eaten in churches and cemeteries to commemorate the dead (Danforth 1982:21; Panourgia 1995:130–133).[39] Franchthi people could also have chosen to crack the dehusked grain by pounding in mortars, boil the cracked grain in water or milk, and consume it as gruel or porridge (see Runnels and Murray 1983:62). Or the dehusked grains could have been used to make bulgur by being boiled, sun-dried, and cracked.[40] Bulgur could have been consumed in the Neolithic in ways similar to today in the Near East and elsewhere: as porridge or like rice, added to stews or soups, or rolled into cakes mixed with meat or lentils (see Avitsur 1975:231; Hansen 2000:21; Hillman 1983:6, 1984:135–141).

The problem with all the recipes that involve boiling is that only a minimal amount of Franchthi pottery qualifies as cooking ware; as pottery, that is, that could have been and was used on or above a fire (Vitelli 1993:214–215, 1999:96–104). The paucity of cooking pots does not necessarily imply that boiling was not a common cooking technique at Franchthi, however. Ceramic vessels are not an indispensable element for boiling: food can be cooked very well in water that is heated with hot rocks inside baskets, wooden vessels, or leather containers (see Hansen 2000:21; Vitelli 1993:214–215).Yet it is likely that Neolithic Franchthiotes chose none of these alternative boiling techniques, since the Neolithic record at the site does not show large numbers of fire-cracked stones.[41] An additional argument against the use of flammable vessels for cooking comes from the—admittedly small—Neolithic human skeletal sample. The very low number of caries found in this material seems incompatible with the routine consumption of soft, cooked/boiled, sticky, starchy, and thus highly cariogenic foods, such as those noted above (see Cook 2000:101). For the same reason, it is unlikely that grains were soaked in water or milk and consumed as uncooked gruel[42] or, as Perlès suggested (personal communication, 2/2007), coarsely ground, soaked in water, and consumed in the form of roasted pancakes.[43]

The dehusked grains may in fact have been prepared for consumption in ways that involved neither grinding nor boiling. The Neolithic people of Franchthi could have chosen to eat dehusked grains parched or roasted on the fire. This is not totally unheard of for post-Mesolithic populations. Hillman reported possible evidence of consumption of roasted grains from a British Roman site (1981b:27). He also mentions the consumption of whole or cracked grains toasted on hot stones or metal or in clay pots in contemporary Turkish villages and in remote areas of Scotland (Hillman 1981b:27, 1983:6; see also Atalay and Hastorf 2006:299).[44]

Finally, Franchthi people could have used an even simpler technique to prepare cereal grains; one that does away with not only grinding and boiling, but also pounding. If exposed to heat, glumed cereals with an adequate moisture content explode or 'pop' and thus escape from their enveloping glumes. If, on the other hand, grains are not moist enough, heating at high temperature will char the glumes, allowing them to be rubbed off by hand. Indeed, it seems that the slight parching of the grains that this process involves makes them more palatable (Braidwood et al. 1953:520–521). According to Hansen (2000:20), seeds lightly heated to facilitate the removal of the glumes are eaten as an occasional snack food by Turkish farmers working in the fields during the harvest.

My analysis of Popen and the contextual evidence has suggested that at Franchthi grinding was not a technique commonly used in the preparation of cereal grains for consumption, that this preparation probably involved dry heat, and that grains were consumed in a rather hard state. If my hypothesis is correct, then we are witnessing at this site a certain continuity in diet—at least as far as the consumption of plants is concerned—between the pre-Neolithic and Neolithic populations, with the main change being the replacement of wild by domesticated plant species (see also Cook 2000:101; Hansen 2000:21; Vitelli 1993:214–215). A similar impression is given by human dental evidence. The wear is 'striking [*sic*] cupped' in both Mesolithic and Neolithic teeth, the result among others of the consumption of hard fibrous consistencies, such as grains (Cook 2000:101).

A closer look at tools similar to Popen and at their contexts from other sites may reveal that processing grains without grinding was more popular in the Neolithic Aegean than our narrow ethnocentric perspective has allowed us to see. The small sizes of such tools in Neolithic sites of the Argolid, Corinthia, and Attica (Runnels 1981:102, 1985:33, 1996:41; Runnels and Murray 1983:62) may indeed suggest common cooking techniques, dietary preferences, and eating habits for the communities that lived in these areas.

If grinding cereal grains into meal or flour was not the main Popen function, there is a variety of other functions that these tools could and must have served. Popen were probably used in the manufacture and maintenance of the roughly 90 cutting edge tools (or Active cutting edge tools, as I call them in this volume) found at the site. It is interesting in this respect that the chronological distribution of these tools parallels that of Popen, with the majority of them coming from MN deposits (see active cutting edge tools, chapter 4). There is, though, only one case of a spatial association between a Popen and an Acut: FS 892 (Fig. 7, Pl. 50) and FS 893 (Fig. 16, Pl. 68) respectively. It is unlikely, however, that the two tools are functionally associated: FS 892 is broken and there is no indication that it was used after the breakage to grind cutting edge tools, such as FS 893.

At Franchthi, grinding was an important stage in the ornament manufacturing process, through which the desired size, shape, and texture of these artifacts were obtained (Miller 1996:15–21, 1997:137–151, 2002). Popen must have been employed in the manufacture of the hundreds of ground/polished shell, stone, and bone ornaments found at the site.

Bone tools are another kind of Franchthi artifact, the smoothed or polished appearance of which indicates that they were ground on Popen (see also Adams 1989b:265; Campana 1987, 1989:31–34; Goodarzi-Tabrizi 1999:68–80). Moreover, the use wear on a few Popen, e.g., FS 892 (Fig. 7, Pl. 50), may, as I suggested above, have been produced by grinding or resharpening a bone tool. Bone tools were in some cases found in the same or neighboring units as Popen. Since, however, the bone tools from Franchthi are not yet published, I can not say in which cases a functional association between the two kinds of implements (i.e., use of Popen for bone tool manufacture and maintenance) is probable.

The above are some of the most obvious potential Popen uses. Others include grinding of dried meat or fish (Dubreuil 2002:126, 180–182; Haaland 1987:81; O'Brien 1994:21, 47), herbs and spices (Baudais and Lundström-Baudais 2002:170–171; Hayden 1987b:202), medicinal plants (Roux 1985:38), tubers and roots (Haaland 1987:81; Hayden 1987b:203–205; Roubet 1989:481), bark and wood (Adams 1989b:265; Adams and Greenwald 1979:41; Ebeling and Rowan 2004:109; Wright 1994:241), clay and pigments (Adams 1989a:266; Ebeling and Rowan 2004:109; Haaland 1987:81; Hayden 1987b:207–208; Schroth 1996:58), salt (Hayden 1987b:202), and insects, such as crickets and locusts (O'Brien 1994:20, 45–47; Schroth 1996:58).

I discuss below two more intriguing characteristics of Popen. The first refers to the high number of fragmentary specimens, the second to the unexpected spatial and chronological distribution of Popen in general.

Regarding the first topic, I try to shed light on the context in which the fracture of some specimens may have taken place. Most Popen probably broke as a result of accidents: the relatively small sizes of Popen indicate that they were portable and that they could have been taken wherever they were needed around the site.[45] Mobility, coupled with a vulnerable open shape, could explain most of the fragments in this group. For the breakage of some of the largest specimens, nevertheless, factors other than accidents may have been responsible. My suspicion is based on the two pieces into which FS 390 (Fig. 4, Pl. 23) is split as well as on the following 15 distinctive fragmentary specimens: FS 73 (Pl. 37), FS 124 (Pl. 28), FS 170 (Pl. 36), FS 324 (Pl. 38), FS 603 (Pl. 39), FF1:6a (Pl. 40), FF1:14a (Pl. 41), FF1:14b (Pl. 34), G1:18/2, H1:47 (Pl. 47), H1:58 (Pl. 42), H1:68 (Fig. 8, Pl. 43), S 25, S 34 (Pl. 44), and S 52. The two pieces of FS 390 and the above fragments have a broken edge that is regular, straight, and apparently perpendicular to the long axis of the original tool. Moreover, the break appears to be half way through the length of the original tool, an hypothesis reinforced by FS 390 (Fig. 4, Pl. 23), which is split exactly in the middle.

I find it unlikely that by some strange coincidence the original complete tools were all accidentally dropped and broken in the same way straight through the middle. Neither is there any evidence that these tools broke because of a particularly forceful pecking blow during the process of resharpening—not an uncommon accident.[46] It appears, moreover, that the original tools generally lacked features that would have favored an accidental fracture in the middle during and because of use: the fragmentary specimens mentioned above, or most of them, do not seem to come from worn-out tools. The area of the breakage (presumably the middle section of the original complete tools) is not thinner, and thus weaker, than the rest of the body. It is, in fact, usually thicker: see FS 73 (Pl. 37), FS 170 (Pl. 36), FS 324 (Pl. 38), FS 390 (Fig. 4, Pl. 23), FF1:14a (Pl. 41), H1:58 (Pl. 42) with a thickness at the breakage edge ranging from 4.1 cm to 7.0 cm. I should note here that an accidental fracture of a complete tool in the middle during and because of use is the best interpretation for FS 723 (Fig. 6, Pl. 31) described above. This specimen represents probably about one half of an original tool with two opposite strongly concave work faces. It is very plausible, as I have already suggested, that the original complete tool broke in its middle, thinnest section under the pressure exerted on it during use. A similar argument was put forward for a number of 'grindstones' from Arene Candide that are split in the middle. According to Starnini and Voytek (1997:450–457), 'the grindstones tended to break at the thinnest point,' a natural consequence of the prolonged use and rejuvenation of their work surface.[47]

If the Popen mentioned above were not accidentally fractured, could they have been broken deliberately? This hypothesis seems to find support in FS 390 (Fig. 4, Pl. 23). Percussion marks are found on the work face on both sides of the fracture line, suggesting that the intact tool was struck in this particular area. It is hard to assume that this tool fell accidentally on something hard or that something hard fell on it, causing a split exactly in the middle. It seems more plausible that FS 390 was intentionally hit on this spot.

But why would Franchthiotes have chosen to break some of their tools? The recovered fragments do not show evidence of post-breakage use. It cannot, thus, be argued that the original tools were deliberately broken to serve perhaps as smaller active tools, as is the case with the redesigned tools presented earlier. Could the missing parts have been the targets of modification and recycling? The fact that there are no traces of post-breakage use on either of the pieces of FS 390 (Fig. 4, Pl. 23) rather argues against this hypothesis. On this basis, the breakage does not seem to be linked to an intentional modification (redesigning) of an original tool. It may then have taken place in a non-utilitarian context.

Archaeological examples of deliberate breakage of ground stone tools in a non-utilitarian context do exist. The deliberate fracture of *meules* and *molettes* (active abrasive tools) in half or one third of their length has been attested in megalithic contexts in Britanny and in Neolithic sites of the Paris Basin and southern France (Bétirac 1956; Hamon 2006:143–144).[48] At Hallan Çemi Tepesi, many 'querns' and 'mortars' were rendered useless by intentionally perforating their bottoms (Rosenberg, Nesbitt, Redding, and Strasser 1995:7). 'Killed' 'metates' have been reported from Chaco Canyon (Schelberg 1997:1065–1066; see also Adams 2002:43), whereas in Arizona, destructive techniques observed on 'metates' include breaking them into fragments and manufacturing holes in their bottoms (Adams 2008:224–225). The suspicion of deliberate breakage has been raised for some tools similar to Popen at Megalo Nisi Galanis (Stroulia 2005a), Dispilio, and Apsalos (Ninou 2006:105), and for some 'grinding and pounding tools' at Çatalhöyük (Baysal and Wright 2005a:321). Chapman also envisions a process of deliberate fragmentation for 'querns' and 'rubbers' with a transverse, or more rarely, longitudinal fracture found in sites in the Balkans (2000:93–94).

The following are some of the possible non-utilitarian contexts in which the original complete Popen could have been deliberately split. Such a breakage may have aimed at preventing the reutilization of particular tools by people other than their original users/owners (see also Adams 2008:225). Or it may have taken place in a ritual context. In this scenario, some Popen were ritually 'killed' at some point in their use-life—and indeed before being worn out—to mark the death of the user/owner or important events (rites of passage?) in his/her life. A hypothesis of splitting of *meules* as part of a mortuary ritual has been put forward for the Languedocien Neolithic of southern France (Bétirac 1956). An ethnographic example of such a practice comes from the Walapai of Arizona and the Cahuilla of southern California, who are described as breaking the mortar of a dead woman (Euler and Dobyns 1983:260; Schroth 1996:62). Such breakage could also have been used to mark specific events in the life of the community. Ritual activity is not only expected to have taken place at Franchthi, as in any other (prehistoric or not) community, but has indeed been postulated by Vitelli from at least MN through FN on the basis of her analysis of the ceramic assemblage. During MN in particular, the phase which produced the majority of Popen, ritual activity, according to Vitelli, must have been crucial as a mechanism for negotiating the tensions constantly arising in the midst of the Franchthi community as a result of sedentism (Vitelli 1993:213–219, 1999:96–104).

An intentional breakage of some Popen may also have to do with processes of interpersonal and social interaction. In his *Fragmentation in Archaeology* (2000), Chapman made a case for deliberate fragmentation in southeastern European prehistory of a variety of artifacts (including 'querns,' as mentioned above) as well as dead human bodies, and manipulation of the resulting fragments. According to his model, in prehistoric societies objects were not as distinct from people as they appear to be today in the western industrialized world. In the prehistoric universe people were constructed through the objects they made, used, or owned as much as objects were constructed through their producers, users, and owners. Chapman sees fragmentation as linked to the process of enchainment. More specifically, two people who wish to establish some form of social relationship or conclude some kind of transaction, break an agreed-upon artifact, each keeping one or more parts as a token of the relationship. Each fragment of the object may itself be further broken and a part passed down to a third party. In Chapman's scheme the broken parts of a single object represent means to create and maintain lasting bonds between members of the same community or between different groups. I should note here that this interpretation is inadequate for at least FS 390, the two parts of which were, as mentioned above, found together under a 'built fireplace.'

Another possible scenario comes from the American Southwest. Referring to deliberately broken 'metates' found in sites in Arizona, Jenny Adams wrote:

> Large stones that were quarried for cooking slabs (pikistones) were considered by the Hopi to have been alive in the sense that the stones required feeding…It, therefore, seems possible that metates were destroyed so that their spiritual essence might return to the cosmos. (Adams 2008:225)

Similar beliefs may have been behind what I believe was the deliberate fracture of some Popen.

The actual systemic context of such a fracture for Popen is hard to pinpoint, but what we do know is the archaeological context of the two pieces of

FS 390 and four of the fragments that resulted from this process (FS 170, FS 324, FS 603, and G1:18/2). The remaining specimens can not be used in this discussion, because they come from disturbed deposits. The two parts of FS 390 (Fig. 4, Pl. 23) were found under a 'built fireplace' along with another ground stone tool fragment, whereas FS 170 (Pl. 36) was itself excavated with two other ground stone tools in a hearth context. G1:18/2 was found in the same unit as another Popen and two bone tools. FS 324 was excavated with two other ground stone tools and an unidentified fragmentary clay artifact. Finally, FS 603 (Pl. 39) was found, along with other ground stone tools and artifacts, in a FN pit formation excavated in Paralia trench L5 (Vitelli 1999:19, 90). This pit was probably used originally for the production of quick lime. The discovery in this formation, however, of intact, high-quality arrowheads as well as similarities with a pit feature at FN Lerna made Vitelli suspect a possible secondary ritual use (1999:90–91; see also Perlès 2004:118). There is no reason to assume, on the other hand, that there was at Franchthi (or other Neolithic sites) a strict division between ordinary utilitarian and extraordinary non-utilitarian contexts (see Perlès 2001:255–272; also Bradley 2005). There is in fact secure evidence from other parts of the world, such as the American Southwest, that artifacts deliberately broken upon somebody's death were discarded in domestic rubbish (Adams 2008).

Before I close this discussion, I should note that the intentional breakage of artifacts at Franchthi is not a new idea. Vitelli has suggested it for the exceptional MN Urfirnis pottery (1993:216), Talalay for the MN split-leg figurines (1987, 1993:45–46), and I for some active cutting edge tools (Stroulia 2003 and chapter 4, this volume). Perlès also hinted at an unusual destructive process (involving breaking and burning) for some FN foliate points (2004:148).

I turn now to the issue of the unexpected spatial and chronological distribution of Popen. A few general points can be made. As already mentioned, 86 (84%) of the total number of specimens were excavated inside the cave, 16 (16%) on Paralia. As also mentioned earlier, this differential distribution appears normal in that it roughly reflects the volumes of sediment removed during the excavations from the two sectors of the site: about 76% from the cave and 24% from Paralia (Jacobsen and Farrand 2000:28–29; Farrand, e-mail communication 1/1998). If, however, the 47 dated Popen from the two areas are broken down by specific Neolithic phase (tools of probable dates are included, tools assigned to interphases are not) a more complex picture emerges, as shown in this table:

	EN	MN	LN	FN
number of dated Popen	4	35	4	4
Cave	1	32	4	2
Paralia	3	3	0	2

This distribution reveals a very high percentage of MN specimens inside the cave (91%). This concentration cannot be considered entirely the result of excavation biases: other kinds of MN material (e.g., lithics and pottery) are distributed much more evenly between the cave and Paralia (see Perlès 2004:100; Vitelli 1993:50).[49] Assuming that the cave was not only the place of discard for the Popen recovered there, but also the place of their use—a more reasonable assumption than one that sees people working on Paralia and using the cave as a dump[50]—the high concentration of MN specimens inside the cave suggests that during this phase the activities involving Popen tended to take place in that part of the site. The preference for the cave as the locus of Popen-related activities in MN is intriguing: if the ethnoarchaeological record is a good guide, in areas with mild/warm climate, as is/was southern Greece, the activities involving such tools are at least as likely to have taken place in the open as in a sheltered area.[51] Why did Popen-related activities tend to take place inside the cave during MN? I do not have an answer to this question, but I find it interesting that some of the largest complete specimens, FS 81 (Pl. 33), FS 82, FS 126 (Fig. 9), FS 174 (Fig. 11, Pl. 46), 175 (Pl. 35), FS 285 (Pl. 48), as well as one large and presumably usable fragment, FS 170 (Pl. 36), were excavated in the vicinity of hearths.[52] Given the state of preservation of these tools, it is likely that the hearth areas represent the context not only of their discovery but also of their use. According to this scenario, the tools in question were used around hearths and were left there when their users—for one reason or another—abandoned the site, with or without the intent to return. Hearths were sources of heat and light. They were also the areas where cooking took place. As such, at Franchthi, as in other sites, they probably served as places of gathering. If so, the activities in which some of the largest Popen were involved took place in the presence of more than one individuals who worked along each other sharing the social space and practical benefits of hearths. It is possible that the cave was preferred as the locus of Popen-related activities because it provided the hearth contexts—contexts of work and social life—in which these activities tended to take place.[53]

And finally, why so many MN specimens? The dated Popen include 35 MN specimens compared to only 12 dated to all the other Neolithic phases (tools of probable dates are included, tools assigned to interphases are not). It can be assumed that the large number of MN specimens reflects a more intensive use and subsequent discard of such tools during this particular phase, and that the activities in which these were involved were more widespread during this phase than others. Yet, other factors may to some degree be responsible for the unbalanced chronological distribution of Popen. According to Vitelli (1993:44–47), later Neolithic as well as post-Neolithic activities may have destroyed some EN deposits inside the cave. If so, some EN Popen may exist among those found in disturbed or surface cave deposits and considered here as generally Neolithic specimens. It is, moreover, significant that some of the kinds of artifacts that were presumably made and/or maintained with the help of Popen appear in higher quantities in other than MN phases. Shell beads were produced in massive numbers in EN, as suggested by the very large quantities of lithic tools (flint points and drills) used for their manufacture as well as of shell bead manufacturing debris found on Paralia (Perlès 2001:223–226, 2004:151–154). Interestingly, not a single Popen was found in the EN units of L5 and Q5 identified as locations of two shell bead workshops by Perlès (2001:224, 226, 2004:152; cf. Miller 1996:22–24). This is even stranger given that shell blanks were ground both before and after being pierced with the drills found in these areas (Miller 1996:17–21). Moreover, a cursory study of the bone tool inventory suggests that these artifacts may occur in higher numbers in FN than in MN. Were shell beads and bone tools in the non-MN phases ground with the help of Popen in an area of the site or its vicinity not touched by the excavation? Were the Popen used in such contexts discarded in an unexcavated location? These questions for the moment remain unanswered.

2. Passive tools with cavity (Pcav)

Summarized information on all Passive tools with cavity, or Pcav, is listed in Table 3.6. The drawing of a single specimen appears in Figure 14. Photographs of some others are found in Plates 56–61 on the CD, folder: Neolithic/Passive/Pcav.

The Pcav group comprises eight specimens (Table 3.6). They are characterized by a cavity or, in other words, a hollow configuration more than 4.0 cm in maximum dimension. Four of them are large (they constitute indeed some of the largest items in the Franchthi ground stone tool assemblage), the remaining four are smaller. Tools morphologically similar to these specimens are often called 'mortars' in the literature. I chose not to use the term here because of its underlying association with an exclusive pounding (i.e., active percussive) function.

Five specimens were excavated inside the cave, three on Paralia. Four specimens are dated to specific Neolithic phases (EN, MN, and FN), one has a probable MN date, another is dated to EN/MN. The remaining two specimens (FS 214 and S 17) come from FA:35 and FA:41, excavated in disturbed deposits that yielded Neolithic as well as some pre- and post-Neolithic material (see

Table 3.6. Passive tools with cavity (Pcav).

Name	Trench:Unit	Prov.	Pres.	Material	Date	L	W	T	Illustr.
FS 13	A:25	C	c	sandstone	FN	26.5	22.5	11.7	Fig. 1
FS 59	A:40	C	c	sandstone	FN	19.5	18.5	7.5	Pl. 56
FS 214	FA:35	C	f	sandstone	Neol.	16.1	11.3	4.1	Pl. 57
FS 472	H2B:25	C	c	conglomerate	(MN)	38.3	29.3	20.4	Pl. 60
FS 634	Q5S:76	P	f	sandstone	MN	13.0	13.0	4.9	Pl. 58
FS 749	Q4:100	P	f	sandstone	EN	15.2	9.1	6.8	Pl. 59
FS 910	L5:91	P	c	sandstone	EN/MN	29.0	16.8	15.3	Pl. 61
S 17	FA:41	C	f	sandstone	Neol.	22.1	19.2	16.9	

KEY: Prov.=Provenience, Pres.=Preservation, L=Length, W=Width, T=Thickness, C=Cave, P=Paralia, Illustr.=illustration, c=complete, f=fragmentary, EN=Early Neolithic, MN=Middle Neolithic, FN=Final Neolithic, (MN)=probable Middle Neolithic, EN/MN=Early/Middle Neolithic interphase, Neol.=Neolithic, Pl.=plate, Fig.=figure

Vitelli 1999:17). Since no tools with a cavity were retrieved from stratified pre-Neolithic deposits, and given the negligible amount of post-Neolithic remains in general (Dengate 1999), I consider these two specimens as Neolithic and this is the date assigned to them in Table 3.6. The raw material of all but one Pcav is sandstone. The exception is made of conglomerate. I describe here the members of the Pcav group in detail, if for no other reason than because we know almost nothing about tools with cavities from the Neolithic Aegean.

The four smaller specimens are: FS 59, FS 214, FS 634, and FS 749. All have a work face that consists of a cavity.

FS 59 (Pl. 56) is missing a part, but this is from such a location that the reconstruction of the shape and dimensions of the original intact tool is not affected. That is why I consider this specimen complete. As such, FS 59 is the only complete among the smaller specimens. It comes from A:40 and measures 19.5×18.5×7.5 cm. It has a roughly square plan, a flat base, and a work face in the form of an open cavity. The exterior walls seem to have been roughly shaped by flaking. The cavity is about 2.0 cm deep and slopes when the tool sits flat. It has a generally smooth texture and was probably produced by first pecking, and then grinding. The central area of the cavity, however, appears somewhat scratched/scarred, the result of a passive percussive and/or abrasive use. Strangely enough, around this central area is a ring of light red color more than 5.0 cm wide. One possibility regarding the formation of this ring is that first the cavity was used in pigment processing or a pigment-related task, staining it red, and later another use removed the pigment traces from the cavity's center. The use that scratched/scarred the center of the cavity, however, does not seem to have been heavy enough to eliminate a red coloration similar to that seen around it. Alternatively, this ring may have served as decoration or had a symbolic connotation. If it does, it suggests a possible extra-utilitarian dimension for this specimen. It should be noted that this artifact is dated to FN, a phase in which the cave seems to have been used—although probably not exclusively—for ceremonial purposes (Vitelli 1999:96–104; cf. Perlès 2004:129–130). Uses in such contexts are not unheard of for tools described in the literature as mortars: for example, Bulmer and Bulmer (1962:192–195) reported the modern use of ancient 'mortars' in magicoreligious activities among the Kyaka of central New Guinea.

The two following specimens, FS 214 and FS 634, are fragmentary, but had probably comparable sizes when complete. FS 214 (Pl. 57) was excavated in disturbed unit FA:35 and measures 16.1×11.3×4.1 cm. FS 634 (Pl. 58) comes from MN unit Q5S:76 and measures 13.0×13.0×4.9 cm. I discuss here FS 214, since FS 634 is completely covered by a thin layer of concretion. FS 214 represents about half of, probably, a roughly circular original tool about 16.0 cm in diameter. The preserved part of the cavity has a half-circular plan and is about 1.2 cm deep. This cavity was probably shaped by pecking. It has a smoothed texture and a red/orange stain indicating a use in pigment processing or a pigment-related activity. According to the excavation notebooks, a certain 'reddish substance' was found next to this tool. It is tempting to see this as the source of the stain in FS 214, but one should keep in mind that the unit where both the tool and the red substance were excavated was disturbed. The presumed circular shape of the complete cavity, its low depth and smoothed texture point to a passive diffused abrasive use in a rotary mode, although some light passive diffused percussive use or a combined passive abrasive and percussive use can not be ruled out. The base of FS 214 is convex and irregular and has a depression at its highest point, and, indeed at what must have originally been its center. The depression is broken but its preserved length, width, and depth are 3.4 cm, 3.1 cm, and 0.5 cm respectively. It seems to have been used in a passive percussive mode, in the context, for example, of cracking nuts. Such a use may have been responsible for the tool's fracture.

The fourth of the smaller specimens, fragmentary FS 749 (Pl. 59), comes from EN unit Q4:100. This oblong artifact measures 15.2×9.1×6.8 cm. The preserved depth of the cavity is 1.2 cm. Its irregular texture and the absence of use wear suggest perhaps that in this case the process of manufacture was never completed.

The four large specimens in the Pcav group are: FS 13, FS 472, FS 910, and S 17. They have a cavity that covers part or all of one face. I discuss first two specimens that share a number of similarities: complete FS 13 (Fig. 14), measuring 26.5×22.5×11.7 cm, and fragmentary S 17, measuring 22.1×19.2×16.9 cm. Both tools are made of identical looking calcareous sandstone, are pecked to shape, and have flat bases. FS 13 has flaring exterior walls and one work face consisting of a large open cavity in the shape of a reversed cone. Judging from its preserved portion, this was probably the original shape of S 17 too. The cavity of FS 13 is about 5.0 cm deep and about 12.0 cm in maximum diameter; the very bottom of the cavity is more or less circular in plan and concave in section. This part of the cavity seems to have been most heavily used. The use was passive percussive as indicated by percussion marks located in this area. An additional passive abrasive use of rotary mode is possible. The active component probably had an oblong body and a rounded end. A few tools with such a shape, with active percussive and/or abrasive wear on their ends, and an appropriate size are found in Active miscellanea 1 (set 4) and Active miscellanea 2 (set 4) (chapter 4) and could have been used with these and other Pcav. Alternatively, the active components were made of wood. FS 13 and S 17 could not have been used for pounding grains in the context, for example, of dehusking (see discussion of Popen above): the calcareous sandstone of which they are made would have added a lot of grit in the pounded product. The flaring walls and low depth of the cavity, as well as the small diameter of its bottom, also argue against this hypothesis. These tools must then have been used for processing other substances. FS 13 was excavated in FN unit A:25 and indeed comes from one of two 'clay-lined pits' containing ashy carbonized earth, which was not searched for botanical remains (see excavation notebooks and Vitelli 1999:18). S 17 comes from disturbed unit FA:41. Given the similarities between FS 13 and S 17, it is not unlikely for S 17 also to date to FN, especially since FA:39 as well as FA:45–46 are dated to this phase (see Vitelli 1999:17).

FS 472 (Pl. 60) is the largest complete specimen in the whole Franchthi ground stone tool assemblage, measuring 38.3×29.3×20.4 cm. It was found inside the cave (close to its entrance), in H2B:25, a unit of probable MN date. Most of its work face is covered by a large cavity shaped by pecking. This cavity measures 21.0×18.0×6.0 cm and has more or less vertical walls. The shape and size of the cavity, as well as the vesicular conglomerate material of this specimen, are perhaps adequate for use in grain processing. The very irregular texture of the cavity, on the other hand, may be an indication that FS 472 was used not as a tool (in a percussive or abrasive mode), but rather as a container.

FS 910 (Pl. 61) was found in L5:91 dated to EN/MN. It is the second largest complete specimen in the whole ground stone tool assemblage, measuring 29.0×16.8×15.3 cm. It has an oblong plan produced by flaking an original sandstone boulder. The work face is flat and interrupted by a cavity measuring 8.7×9.8×2.2 cm. This cavity has a hemispherical shape produced probably by pecking and grinding. Its surface is rough and regular with no visible percussion marks, suggesting that it was either used in a passive abrasive rotary mode (for perhaps processing or mixing herbs, spices, medicinal plants, salt, or other substances),[54] or not used at all as a tool. According to the second scenario, FS 910 functioned as a container.

The small number of stone tools with a cavity at Franchthi fits the general picture of scarcity of such tools/artifacts in the Aegean Neolithic (examples are mentioned in, among others, Mylonas 1929; Tsountas 1908; Wace and Thompson 1912). The variety of sizes, shapes, and use wear seen in the Franchthi specimens, suggests that these tools served a variety of purposes. Grain processing (i.e., dehusking) was probably not one of them.

3. Passive miscellanea (Pmisc)

Summarized information on the Passive miscellanea, or Pmisc, is listed in Table 3.7. A photograph of one of these tools is found in Plate 62 on the CD, folder: Neolithic/Passive/Pmisc.

The Pmisc group comprises two tools that fit neither the Popen nor the Pcav. Unlike Popen, they have not been used in a primarily passive diffused abrasive mode; unlike Pcav, they have no cavity. These specimens are FS 51 and FAN:63 (Table 3.7). I present them below.

FS 51 (Pl. 62) comes from G:20, a unit of probable MN date. This fragmentary specimen measures 7.8×6.5×0.6 cm and consists of a very

Table 3.7. Passive miscellanea (Pmisc).

Name	Trench:Unit	Prov.	Pres.	Material	Date	L	W	T	Illustr.
FS 51	G:20	C	f	silstone	(MN)	7.8	6.5	0.6	Pl. 62
FAN:63	FAN:63	C	c	sandstone?	FN	15.5	12.6	3.5	

KEY: Prov.=Provenience, Pres.=Preservation, L=Length, W=Width, T=Thickness, C=Cave, Illustr.=illustration, c=complete, f=fragmentary, FN=Final Neolithic, (MN)=probable Middle Neolithic, Pl.=plate thin siltstone plaque with three preserved sides that consist of probably naturally beveled edges. One of the two faces carries several long scratches. The scratches form roughly two clusters with different directions and are the result of a linear abrasive use that was probably passive. They could have been produced, for example, from (re)sharpening bone points. Evidence of what might have been an active diffused abrasive use is visible on one of the edges of this face.

FAN:63 (from the homonymous unit) is a complete, *a posteriori*, tool of perhaps sandstone, measuring 15.5×12.6×3.5 cm. It is a generally flat piece of stone with an open work face that shows pitting in the center, probably from a passive percussive use as an anvil.

NOTES

1. FCP3 in Vitelli's phasing system (1999), FLP N III in that of Perlès (2004).
2. FCP4 in Vitelli's phasing system (1999), FLP N IV in that of Perlès (2004).
3. For an ethnographic example of hand-held passive abrasive tools, see Hampton 1999:93–97.
4. No Popen was excavated from the terrace just outside the cave mouth.
5. No refits, though, were found during the excavation of these areas.
6. See Dispilio (Ninou 2006:28; Touloumis 2002:108), Megalo Nisi Galanis (Stroulia 2005a), Stavroupoli (Alisøy 2002:562), Makri (Bekiaris 2007:42), and Makriyalos (Tsoraki 2007:293–294; Yeroussi 1999:33). Similar patterns have been noted in non-Greek assemblages. See, for example, Divostin (Galdikas 1988:338).
7. Upper Mesolithic specimen FS 551 (Pl. 11) probably had the shape of a shallow basin (see chapter 2).
8. Runnels studied them as part of his Ph.D. dissertation (1981). He calls them 'millstones.'
9. For Perlès, the many varieties of sandstone represented in the Popen group, and in the Franchthi ground stone tool assemblage in general, rather suggest importation from outside the Franchthi region (personal communication, 2/2007). Yet, Kardulias and Runnels have noted that 'many varieties of sandstone occur as outcrops in the Southern Argolid' (1995:112). See also Hamon (2006:13–14) and Schneider (2002:46–47), according to whom, it is common for sandstones of different types to appear in the same stratigraphic exposure.
10. Two of these sources are found in the general Franchthi region. One is located at Vourlia beach (about 10 km northwest of Franchthi), the other in the Dhiskouria hills southwest of Ermioni (van Andel and Vitaliano 1987:20).
11. According to Runnels (1981:60–70), the porphyritic biotite-, hornblende-, feldspar-rich andesites are characteristic of the Saronic Gulf sources and very distinct from the andesite sources of the southern Aegean.
12. Some of the 'millstones' from Neolithic Lerna presented by Runnels (1981)—see, for example, those shown in his Plate 4—would be at home among the Franchthi specimens.
13. Such a technique was, for example, used by Guatemalan full-time specialist Ramon Ramos as a first stage in the 'metate' manufacturing process (Hayden 1987a:24).
14. For flaking and pecking as the techniques used in the manufacture of the Franchthi specimens, see also Runnels 1981:75–76, 137–140, 249–252, 1985:33. For flaking and pecking as two of the techniques used in general in the manufacture of passive abrasive tools, see Dubreuil 2002:91–94; Hayden 1987a:9–44; Hersh 1981:306–386; Menasanch, Risch, and Soldevilla 2002:88–90; Moundréa-Agrafioti 2002:103; Risch 2002:89.
15. Given the convex water-rolled configuration of the surfaces of the cobbles and boulders used as Popen raw material, we have to assume that, during flaking, striking platforms were prepared by pecking (see Wilke and Quintero 1996:255).
16. I have not been able to locate any of these 'imports' and no information on their size has been reported. Since, however, Wilkinson and Duhon describe them as 'cobble-sized,' they must be between 6.0 and 30.0 cm in maximum dimension (1990:xvi, 11).
17. Dhidhima Cave and Mouzaki Cave.
18. I should note here that the absence of roughouts and other byproducts of manufacture of abrasive tools is not uncommon for prehistoric sites (see Dubreuil 2002:95).
19. The exception refers to two EN cockle-shell bead workshops identified on Paralia by Perlès (2001:223–226, 2004:151–154). See, however, the conflicting interpretation of the same areas as dumps by Miller (1996:22–24).
20. Such debitage has the form of flakes with ground surfaces indicating refashioning of an older tool rather than primary manufacture. Only one sandstone flake (FF1:37c) that may have originated in a redesigning process has been identified and included in the group I discuss in chapter 4 as Active miscellanea 1 (set 13). Such flakes have been identified at Çatalhöyük (Baysal and Wright 2005a:312, 2005b).
21. Runnels and Diamant produced experimentally two 'grinding slabs' larger than any of the complete Popen in two hours and three hours and twenty minutes

respectively. The raw material of both was andesite (Runnels 1981:249–252). For even lower experimental production times, see Menasanch, Risch, and Soldevilla 2002:88–90; Risch 2002:89.

22. I use the term 'specialist' here to refer to an individual who works on a full- or part-time basis to create a product for use by others in exchange for goods or money (see Nelson 1987:149). For comparative purposes, see the ethnographic account on 'metate' manufacture in a Guatemalan village by full-time specialist Ramon Ramos (Hayden 1987a).

23. These are the eighteen specimens mentioned above in the discussion of Popen width.

24. I should specify here that my observations may not be applicable to tools of more substantial sizes. This may explain why the ovate shape is common for larger passive tools used in grain grinding. For an ethnographic example, see Roux 1985:34–37.

25. See, for example, the sequence from the flattest to the most concave among the following complete tools: FS 126 (Fig. 9), FS 175 (Pl. 35), FS 795 (Pl. 25), FS 285 (Pl. 48), FS 82, FS 390 (Fig. 4, Pl. 23), FS 174 (Fig. 11, Pl. 46).

26. See also the Australian Aborigines who give their 'millstones' a convex dorsal face because 'a convex bottom rests securely on sand' (McCarthy 1941:332).

27. For example, the Southern Paiute of southern California used 'one side of the metate to grind seeds and the opposite to grind berries' or one side 'for hulling and the other for grinding' (Schroth 1996:58).

28. Similar hypotheses have been formulated for grooves found on fragmentary passive abrasive tools from Makri (Bekiaris 2007:45–46).

29. Similar processes of modification of larger passive tools into 'handstones' are attested at Çatalhöyük (Baysal and Wright 2005a:315, 2005b).

30. An example of the latter practice comes from Chaco Canyon. According to Schelberg (1997:1075), 'At some point, metates ceased to be used in their primary capacity of grinding. They were broken up and the pieces were often recycled into other tools and uses.' Interestingly, most of the original tools do not seem to have been worn out.

31. I borrowed the term 'redesigned' from Adams, but I did not fully adopt her definition. According to Adams (1997:4), 'redesigned tools were designed and used for one activity and then either remanufactured or altered through use in a second activity so that they could no longer be used for this activity.' Instead, I consider as redesigned only the tools that were remanufactured and not those that were simply altered through use.

32. G:lot 28 refers to units G:19–24. These were dug in the first excavation season (1967). The pottery recovered was lotted, although, as far as I know, not the ground stone tools (see Vitelli 1993:32, 34, 76).

33. For examples of abrasively used passive tools with traces of glue-like substances, and more specifically asphalt, see Hole, Flannery, and Neely 1969:171, 174.

34. The second practice is known ethnographically. See, for example, the reuse/recycling of Neolithic *meules* by the modern people of Tichitt in Mauritania (Roux 1985:34, 38).

35. For the same reasons I find it unlikely that these tools were used for grinding pulses. Pulse flour has been identified in Bronze Age Akrotiri (Sarpaki 2001:32).

36. This part of the diagram covers the period from MN to FN (Hansen 1991:147).

37. See Hansen 1991:163–164; Megaloudi 2006; Renfrew 1973.

38. Boiling, instead of grinding, of grains has also been suggested for the Middle and Late Neolithic of Northern China (Fujimoto1993:489–490).

39. A similar dish called *blilé* is eaten by some Christian communities in Israel at festive and mourning occasions (Avitsur 1975:231).

40. Remains of bulgur have been identified at Akrotiri (Sarpaki 2001:32).

41. The inhabitants of Çatalhöyük used heated fired clay balls instead of hot rocks (Atalay and Hastorf 2006:293, 308–309). No such heating devices have been identified at Franchthi.

42. For a related recipe, see Avitsur 1975:231.

43. I do not include here a discussion of grain preparation for consumption as beer because apparently this also involved grinding (Katz and Voigt 1986).

44. The consumption of roasted whole grains is also mentioned by Valamoti (1994:52, 2007:96).

45. This is not uncommon. The Mahria women of Darfur in Sudan 'do not hesitate to carry their grinding stone to the tent of another woman in order to do the grinding [of, mostly, millet] in the company of several women' (Schön and Holter 1990:363). For another example of 'metate' mobility, see the Rarámuri of Northwestern Mexico (Graham 1994:55–57).

46. According to Shelley (cited in Schlanger 1991:462), transverse fractures occur during resharpening when the user fails to provide sufficient support while pecking the grinding surface. See also Nierlè 1983:187.

47. Roberto Risch offered the same interpretation for similarly broken specimens from the early Bronze Age of the western Mediterranean (personal communication 6/07).

48. I should note that the two split molettes shown in Hamon's illustrations are about 22.0 and 27.0 cm long respectively (Hamon 2006:Plates XLV and XLIX).

49. According to Vitelli, however, particular MN wares are not evenly distributed between the two parts of the site (personal communication, 2/2007).

50. This hypothesis is refuted, among others, by the discovery of a number of hearths inside the cave.

51. The women of the nomadic group Mahria of northern Darfur are reported to normally grind millet in the open air, next to the tent (Schön and Holter 1990:363).

Those of Tichitt, Mauritania, on the other hand, rarely grind in the yard, preferring to stay in the interior of the house to avoid the wind that would disperse the flour (Roux 1985:37). In western Nepal, grain grinding using *meules* takes place inside or outside the house, depending on the season and the weather conditions (Baudais and Lundström-Baudais 2002:167, 176). If I am right in suggesting that Popen were not used routinely in grinding grain, the wind may not have been a significant factor for their users. In ethnoarchaeological contexts, the use of passive abrasive tools for the manufacture or maintenance of other tools or non-tool objects tends to take place in the open-air (see Hampton 1999:270–272; Pétrequin and Pétrequin 1988:68, 1993:373; Toth, Clark, and Ligabue 1992:91).

52. I should reproduce here Vitelli's observations regarding the meaning of the term 'hearth' in the Franchthi context: 'From repeated experience, the excavators came to identify 'hearths' by finding, first, a small collection of rocks next to, or sitting directly on 'hearth clay,' i.e., a thin layer of clay reddened by exposure to the heat of fire. As they uncovered the group of rocks, they generally found a more ordered arrangement, usually defining one or more rough circles (or 'burners,' as they describe them in the notebooks) and plentiful carbon and ash. The depth of these 'hearths' varied. Sometimes…it was as much as 0.40 m. Since the traces of 'hearth clay' were generally outside the area enclosed by the rock circles, and since fires burn poorly inside relatively deep and narrow pits because of poor oxygen flow, the 'hearths' may have been pits dug next to the fire itself. They may have been used for baking with hot coals, as discard pits, or for some other purpose' (1999:20–21, note 16).

53. Associations of tools similar to Popen and hearths have been reported from other Greek Neolithic sites. According to Winn and Shimabuku (1989:266–268), 'querns' in Achilleion 'were frequently found in food preparation areas near hearths and ovens along with other food processing tools.' Alisøy also reports an abundance of 'grindstones' (some of them lower) found associated with hearths in Stavroupoli (2002:573). These authors assume that the tools found in this context were involved in food processing, but a broader understanding of the function of both passive tools and hearths casts doubt on this interpretation.

54. These are the main uses of later Greek stone 'mortars' (Runnels 1988:270).

CHAPTER FOUR

The Neolithic Material (2)

ACTIVE TOOLS

Introduction

Active tools comprise the vast majority of Neolithic ground stone tools at Franchthi, a total of 374 (77%). These tools functioned primarily, although not exclusively, in an active mode, or, in other words, they moved over another passive component or surface during use. They were used in an abrasive or percussive manner.

In the context of this large category, similarities among a number of tools allowed the construction of six relatively homogeneous groups:

1. Active cutting edge tools (Acut);
2. Active discoidal tools (Adisc);
3. Active rectangular tools (Arect);
4. Active square or circular tools (Asquare-circ);
5. Active tools used with ends (Aend);
6. Active globular tools (Aglobe).

These groups account for 222 (59%) of the total number of active specimens. Unfortunately, the heterogeneity of the remaining 152 (41%) active tools did not allow the construction of similar groups. The seventh group, then, called Active miscellanea (Amisc), comprises all the active specimens that I was not able to fit into any of the above six groups. I present all seven active groups in the following seven subchapters.

Tools with a cutting edge are the most studied of all varieties of active tools. As far as the Aegean and the rest of Europe are concerned, it is fair to say that they are the most studied of ground stone tools in general. Despite their usually much higher numbers, other varieties of active ground stone tools have been largely neglected. The following is the first systematic and reasonably balanced presentation of active ground stone tools from a Greek Neolithic site.

1. Active cutting edge tools (Acut)[1]

Introduction

Summarized information on all Active cutting edge tools, or Acut, is listed in Table 4.1. Drawings of a number of specimens appear in Figures 15–19. Photographs (sometimes combined with drawings) are found in Plates 63–85 on the CD, folder: Neolithic/Active/Acut.

The group of Active cutting edge tools comprises the Franchthi ground stone tools that were used (although not exclusively) in an active linear mode. The diagnostic trait of Acut is an acute edge located on one of the ends. This edge is always the result of manufacture (by grinding), rather than an *a posteriori* formation. I should note that Acut (or most of them) represent only the stone portions of original composite tools that also included hafting devices made of (primarily) wooden shafts, and perhaps a binding and/or adhesive material (see below).

Tools with a cutting edge are known in the literature as celts, adzes, axes, chisels, knives, hatchets, choppers, gouges, hoes, etc.[2] I prefer, however, not to use any of these terms for the Franchthi assemblage, since they imply and reflect a classificatory system designed for modern metal tools, the capacity of which to describe prehistoric stone tools is dubious. As both use wear analysis

Table 4.1. Active cutting edge tools (Acut).

Name	Trench:Unit	Prov.	Pres.	Material	Date	L	W	T	L/W	Illustr.
FS 1	Cave surf.	C	c	diabase	Neol.	6.9	4.2	2.8	1.64	Pl. 67
FS 6	A:5	C	f	serpentinite	Neol.	3.3	4.3	2.3	n/ap	
FS 11	G:2	C	c	serpentinite	Neol.	2.2	1.1	0.7	2.00	Pl. 72
FS 12	A:30	C	c	serpentinite	Neol.	3.8	3.0	1.2	1.26	
FS 21	A:27	C	c	serpentinite	(FN)	5.8	4.0	2.2	1.45	Fig. 17, Pl. 73
FS 22	B:3	C	c	serpentinite	Neol.	2.8	2.5	1.0	1.12	Pl. 82
FS 23	G:3	C	c	serpentinite	Neol.	6.1	4.0	2.0	1.52	Pl. 71
FS 24	G:17	C	c	diabase	Neol.	3.1	2.4	1.3	1.29	
FS 32	A:45	C	c	diabase	Neol.	4.5	3.7	1.8	1.21	
FS 33	G:21	C	c	serpentinite	(MN)	6.5	4.1	3.0	1.58	Fig. 18
FS 34	A:40	C	c	serpentinite	FN	7.3	4.2	3.2	1.73	
FS 36	A:46	C	n/ap	andesite	Neol.	7.4	4.1	2.5	n/ap	Pl. 63
FS 37	A:37	C	c	argillite	Neol.	4.0	2.0	0.9	2.00	Fig. 16
FS 38*	G:20	C	f	serpentinite	(MN)	5.7	6.4	2.2	n/ap	Pl. 76
FS 44	G:12	C	c	serpentinite	Neol.	2.0	2.6	0.9	0.76	Fig. 15
FS 52	A:19	C	c	serpentinite	Neol.	4.6	3.4	1.9	1.35	Fig. 16
FS 90	G1:4	C	c	serpentinite	Neol.	2.9	2.9	2.0	1.00	
FS 93	FF1:7	C	c	serpentinite	Neol.	3.0	2.8	1.2	1.07	
FS 94	FF1:9	C	c	serpentinite	Neol.	3.5	1.3	0.7	2.69	
FS 98*	G1:8	C	f	serpentinite	(MN)	3.5	6.0	3.3	n/ap	
FS 112	FF1:24	C	f	serpentinite	Neol.	7.1	4.2	3.2	n/ap	Fig. 17
FS 116	G1:15	C	c	serpentinite	(MN)	9.6	4.5	2.7	2.13	Pl. 64
FS 117	FF1:26	C	c	serpentinite	Neol.	7.6	4.8	2.5	1.58	Fig. 19, Pl. 65
FS 118	FF1:26	C	c	serpentinite	Neol.	5.9	3.8	1.8	1.55	Pl. 66
FS 142	H:2	C	c	basalt	Neol.	2.8	1.7	0.8	1.64	
FS 149	FF1:39B2	C	c	serpentinite	MN	3.0	2.7	1.1	1.11	
FS 153	H:13	C	c	serpentinite	Neol.	4.5	3.7	2.4	1.21	Pl. 74
FS 157	H:35	C	c	serpentinite	(MN)	2.2	1.5	0.9	1.46	Pl. 80
FS 159	H:23	C	c	serpentinite	(MN)	7.1	4.5	3.1	1.57	Pl. 75
FS 160	H:34	C	f	serpentinite	(MN)	4.5	4.7	2.1	n/ap	
FS 178	G1:11	C	f	serpentinite	(MN)	2.2	1.8	1.7	n/ap	
FS 180	FF1:40B1	C	f	serpentinite	MN	4.3	0.8	0.6	n/ap	
FS 185	Cave surf.	C	c	diabase	Neol.	5.5	3.5	2.3	1.57	
FS 201	H1:12	C	c	serpentinite	Neol.	2.5	1.0	0.7	2.50	Fig. 15
FS 207	FA:24	C	c	serpentinite	Neol.	2.9	2.4	1.1	1.20	
FS 210	FA:33A	C	c	serpentinite	Neol.	5.3	4.0	1.8	1.30	
FS 212	FA:33A	C	c	serpentinite	Neol.	6.2	4.0	3.1	1.55	Pl. 70
FS 219	FA:37	C	c	serpentinite	Neol.	4.1	2.3	1.2	1.78	
FS 221	FA:39	C	c	felsite porphyry	FN	3.2	2.7	1.1	1.18	Pl. 79
FS 222	H1:41	C	c	serpentinite	Neol.	4.3	2.8	0.9	1.53	Fig. 16
FS 226	FA scarp	C	c	serpentinite	Neol.	7.4	4.7	3.0	1.57	Pl. 77
FS 227	FA:43	C	c	peridotite	Neol.	6.9	4.0	2.8	1.72	
FS 229	H1:56	C	c	serpentinite	Neol.	8.4	4.9	3.7	1.71	Pl. 85
FS 239	FA:54	C	c	serpentinite	Neol.	2.2	1.1	0.5	2.00	

KEY: Prov.=Provenience, Pres.=Preservation, L=Length, W=Width, T=Thickness, L/W=length/width ratio, Illustr.=illustration, surf.=surface, C=Cave, P=Paralia, c=complete, f=fragmentary, n/ap=non-applicable, EN=Early Neolithic, MN=Middle Neolithic, LN=Late Neolithic, FN=Final Neolithic, (EN)=probable Early Neolithic, (MN)=probable Middle Neolithic, (FN)=probable Final Neolithic, EN/MN=Early/Middle Neolithic interphase, Neol.=Neolithic, Pl.=plate, Fig.=figure

Table 4.1 (continued). *Active cutting edge tools (Acut).*

Name	**Trench:Unit**	**Prov.**	**Pres.**	**Material**	**Date**	**L**	**W**	**T**	**L/W**	**Illustr.**
FS 278	H1B:82	C	c	serpentinite	Neol.	3.4	2.3	1.4	1.47	
FS 289	H1B:94	C	c	serpentinite	Neol.	3.2	2.7	1.1	1.18	
FS 311	FAS:72	C	n/ap	peridotite	FN	7.0	4.5	3.2	n/ap	
FS 363	Q5N:3	P	c	serpentinite	Neol.	2.4	2.2	0.9	1.09	Fig. 15
FS 374	H2A:75	C	c	serpentinite	MN	7.1	4.3	3.0	1.65	
FS 385	FAS:107	C	f	serpentinite	LN	4.2	2.0	1.0	n/ap	
FS 398	H2B:17	C	c	serpentinite	(MN)	2.6	2.3	1.2	1.13	
FS 425	FAN:134	C	f	serpentinite	MN	4.0	3.5	0.8	n/ap	
FS 428	H2B:50	C	c	basalt	(MN)	4.2	3.2	1.3	1.31	Pl. 81
FS 430	Q5N:23	P	f	peridotite	EN	7.2	4.8	3.3	n/ap	Fig. 18
FS 436	Q5N:24	P	f	serpentinite	(EN)	3.6	1.3	0.5	n/ap	
FS 505	FAN:142	C	c	serpentinite	(MN)	3.9	3.0	1.5	1.30	
FS 577	Q5S:14	P	f	serpentinite	Neol.	1.6	1.4	0.8	n/ap	Pl. 83
FS 589	L5NE:7	P	c	steatite	FN	4.6	2.2	1.1	2.09	Fig. 16
FS 600	L5NE:19	P	c	serpentinite	FN	7.0	4.2	2.9	1.66	Pl. 69
FS 617	Q5S:50	P	f	peridotite	Neol.	1.3	0.7	0.3	n/ap	
FS 666	H2APed:195	C	f	limestone	Neol.	3.3	2.5	0.6	n/ap	
FS 680	O5N:14	P	c	serpentinite	Neol.	2.4	1.5	0.8	1.60	Fig. 15
FS 693	Q4:1	P	c	diorite	Neol.	6.6	3.7	2.3	1.78	
FS 714*	Q4:59	P	f	serpentinite	Neol.	3.1	3.8	0.8	n/ap	
FS 715	Q4:58	P	f	serpentinite	Neol.	6.2	5.2	1.5	n/ap	
FS 726	O5:34	P	c	serpentinite	(MN)	2.2	0.8	0.7	2.75	
FS 751	O5:59	P	f	basalt	EN/MN	5.1	3.7	2.5	n/ap	Fig. 17
FS 755	Q4:128	P	c	diabase	EN	4.4	3.6	2.3	1.22	
FS 767	P5:91	P	f	serpentinite	Neol.	1.8	2.5	1.3	n/ap	
FS 772	PQ5:9	P	f	serpentinite	Neol.	1.2	1.1	0.6	n/ap	
FS 779	PQ5:28	P	c	serpentinite	MN	4.0	2.9	1.4	1.37	Fig. 16
FS 789	P5:153	P	f	serpentinite	Neol.	2.0	1.4	0.9	n/ap	Pl. 84
FS 826	H1:5	C	c	serpentinite	Neol.	6.1	4.3	2.0	1.41	
FS 837	H1:16	C	c	serpentinite	Neol.	9.1	4.9	2.6	1.85	Fig. 19
FS 838	H1:16	C	f	serpentinite	Neol.	6.3	5.0	2.0	n/ap	
FS 883	P5:174	P	c	serpentinite	MN	2.7	1.0	0.6	2.70	Fig. 15
FS 884	QR5:12	P	c	basalt	EN/MN	3.3	1.1	0.4	3.00	Fig. 15
FS 885	L5:60	P	c	basalt	FN	4.1	1.1	0.8	3.70	
FS 893	QR5:29	P	c	serpentinite	EN/MN	4.0	3.7	1.8	1.08	Fig. 16, Pl. 68
FS 899	P5:190	P	c	serpentinite	MN	3.9	3.4	1.9	1.14	Pl. 78
FS 902	P5:191	P	c	steatite	MN	3.1	2.9	1.2	1.06	
FA:28	FA:28	C	f	serpentinite	Neol.	3.2	1.5	0.4	n/ap	
FAN:129	FAN:129	C	f	serpentinite	MN	1.2	0.4	0.2	n/ap	
FF1:29	FF1:29	C	f	serpentinite	Neol.	3.5	3.3	0.7	n/ap	
H:17	H:17	C	f	serpentinite	Neol.	6.3	3.9	2.2	n/ap	
O5:84	O5:84	P	f	serpentinite	(EN)	1.7	1.2	0.4	n/ap	
Q5S:91/19	Q5S:91	P	c	magnetite	Neol.	2.8	3.2	1.0	0.87	
S 57	F:20	C	f	serpentinite	Neol.	3.9	3.2	1.8	n/ap	

Note: The length of the fragmentary specimens whose names are accompanied by an asterisk is smaller than their width. The length and width measurements were taken along what were obviously the long and wide axes of the original tools respectively.

and ethnographic evidence suggest, prehistoric tools were in general less specialized than their modern counterparts (see for example, Blackwood 1950:17, 23; Sonnenfeld 1962; Steensberg 1980:40–44). Moreover, classifications of modern tools tend to emphasize formal characteristics. If such characteristics usually correspond to functional differences in these tools, this is often not the case with prehistoric specimens. This is best illustrated in the misleading distinction between 'axe' and 'adze,'[3] often encountered in the literature and borrowed precisely from a classificatory system of modern cutting edge tools (see below).

One reviewer of an earlier draft of this volume felt uncomfortable with my classifying 'celts' and 'grinding/pounding tools' in the same general category of active tools. This reviewer suggested that I treat instead the 'celts' separately from all other passive or active tools. However, to the degree that I use a classificatory framework based on function rather than manufacture (see chapter 1), I think my choice to present cutting edge tools as one among other active groups is justified. There is, moreover, a *political* message in my choice. If, as I suspect, cutting edge tools have been studied more intensively than other active tools because they look pretty, perhaps placing them in the same general category as other not so good looking active tools will make us pay more attention to the latter.

The Acut group consists of 88 specimens[4] (Table 4.1). This number includes 78 complete and fragmentary tools currently exhibiting an acute edge. It also includes 10 tools without such an edge. The latter specimens fall into two groups: those that were left in a roughout form, the shaping of their edge having never taken place; and those whose edge was obliterated at some point in their use life when they were recycled to serve a non-linear function. In addition to these 88 specimens, the excavations uncovered 15 fragments with their active part missing, but whose raw material and overall shape point to the likelihood that they were once parts of Acut. Finally, four serpentinite specimens may represent stages of the Acut manufacturing process: one complete unworked cobble which, as suggested by Perlès (personal communication 7/1997), may have been collected as Acut raw material; and three cobble fragments with evidence of pecking that perhaps constitute remains of accidents that occurred during Acut manufacture. Since other Franchthi ground stone tools besides Acut were made of serpentinite and with similar techniques as Acut—the group of Active tools used with ends or Aend (below, this chapter)—it is not possible to decide whether the above 19 specimens belong to

Table 4.2. Possible Acut fragments, possible remains of Acut manufacturing process (H2A:9/3a, FS 734, and FS 240), and a possible unworked Acut raw material (FS 119).

Name	Trench:Unit	Prov.	Pres.	Material	Date	L	W	T
FS 35	G:24	C	f	serpentinite	(MN)	7.7	4.2	3.4
FS 119	G1:17	C	c	serpentinite	(MN)	8.0	4.9	3.0
FS 181	FF1:30	C	f	serpentinite	(MN)	2.7	3.0	1.0
FS 204	FA:24	C	f	serpentinite	Neol.	4.3	2.1	1.8
FS 240	FA:54	C	f	serpentinite	Neol.	6.7	4.7	3.0
FS 288	FAN:117	C	f	serpentinite	LN	5.2	2.1	2.8
FS 344	H2A:40	C	f	slate	MN	4.2	2.9	0.9
FS 359	H2A:58	C	f	serpentinite	(MN)	2.2	2.0	0.7
FS 426	FAN:134	C	f	serpentinite	MN	4.5	2.7	0.5
FS 508	Q5N:43	P	f	serpentinite	EN/MN	4.5	3.1	0.8
FS 550	H2A:129	C	f	serpentinite	Neol.	5.6	4.5	1.7
FS 562	Q5S:4	P	f	serpentinite	(MN)	5.5	3.9	1.0
FS 644	O5NE:25	P	f	limestone	Neol.	7.5	4.3	2.2
FS 734	O5:43	P	f	serpentinite	Neol.	5.0	2.1	0.7
FS 790	P5:162	P	f	serpentinite	(MN)	6.1	4.7	2.3
FS 877	H1:14	C	f	serpentinite	Neol.	5.3	3.5	0.9
FA:28a	FA:28	C	f	serpentinite	Neol.	5.2	3.1	2.5
H:39	H:39	C	f	serpentinite	MN	3.1	1.7	1.2
H2A:9a	H2A:9	C	f	serpentinite	Neol.	7.4	7.1	2.8

KEY: Prov.=Provenience, Pres.=Preservation, L=Length, W=Width, T=Thickness, C=Cave, P=Paralia, c=complete, f=fragmentary, MN=Middle Neolithic, LN=Late Neolithic, (MN)=probable Middle Neolithic, EN/MN=Early/Middle Neolithic interphase, Neol.=Neolithic.

the Acut or the Aend group. The fact, however, that the Acut group is far more numerous than the Aend group makes me suspect that most of these 19 items originated in the Acut manufacturing process. For this reason, I include Table 4.2, summarizing their information, in this subchapter.

I consider 59 Acut (67%) to be complete, since they are either intact or missing a part too small to significantly affect the reconstruction of their original shape and dimensions. Twenty-seven specimens (31%) are fragmentary. The percentage of fragments among Acut is low compared to that among Popen.[5] This difference can, at least to some degree, be attributed to the small, closed, convex, and thus, less vulnerable, Acut forms. The remaining two specimens, FS 36 (Pl. 63) and FS 311, are roughouts. I consider them neither complete nor fragmentary (Table 4.1).

Acut were found in various trenches in both the cave and Paralia. Sixty-two (70%) were recovered in the cave,[6] twenty-six (30%) on Paralia (Table 4.1). These percentages are roughly proportionate to the volume of Neolithic sediment excavated from the cave and Paralia (about 76% and 24% respectively; Jacobsen and Farrand 2000:28-29; Farrand, e-mail communication 1/1998). The Paralia deposits, however, yielded a somewhat higher percentage of fragmentary specimens: 42% of the Acut recovered there are fragmentary compared to 25% of those found in the cave. If not accidental, the higher percentage of fragmentary specimens on Paralia may be indicative of a possible preference for this part of the site as the place for activities that resulted in a higher Acut breakage rate or as the area to discard broken Acut. However, given the nature of the occupation on Paralia during certain Neolithic phases, it is also possible that the fragmentary tools, or some of them, were deposited there as secondary discard (see e.g., EN; Vitelli 1993:45–47).

Only 18 Acut come from undisturbed units. On the basis of contextual associations with dated ceramics, they are securely dated to the four main Neolithic phases (EN, MN, LN, and FN). The remaining 70 specimens include: 1. Fifteen tools that come from specific EN, MN, and FN strata that are or may be mixed with earlier or contaminated by later material. For these items only probable dates are available. 2. Three specimens that have been assigned to EN/MN (Table 4.1). 3. Fifty-two specimens that were found on the surface or excavated in disturbed deposits that yielded Neolithic and some pre- and post- Neolithic material too (see Perlès 2004:6–7; Vitelli 1993:31–34, 1999:7–9, 17). Since no cutting edge tools were found in stratified pre-Neolithic deposits, and given the negligible amount of post-Neolithic remains in general (Dengate 1999), I consider these last 52 specimens as Neolithic and this is the date assigned to them in Table 4.1.

If only the 18 securely dated specimens are taken into consideration, the Acut distribution among the four main Neolithic phases is as follows:

EN	2
MN	9
LN	1
FN	6

None of the Neolithic phases produced more than 10 securely dated specimens, with EN and LN indeed having yielded no more than two specimens each. If the 15 less securely dated specimens are also included, the Acut distribution changes into the following:

EN	4
MN	21
LN	1
FN	7

This is an unbalanced distribution showing a very high concentration of tools in MN levels (64%). This concentration may reflect a more intensive use (and subsequent discard) of such tools during this phase. It may also to some degree, however, be the result of post-depositional processes (see below).

A look at the following distribution of the 33 securely and probably dated specimens between the cave and Paralia reveals some interesting patterns:

	EN	MN	LN	FN
number of dated Acut	4	21	1	7
Cave	0	16	1	4
Paralia	4	5	0	3

Paralia yielded 12 Acut distributed rather evenly among all but the LN phases—no traces whatsoever of LN activity were found in Paralia. The 21 dated tools recovered in the cave come from MN, LN, and FN levels, with the vast majority (16) coming from MN. The large number of MN specimens found inside the cave may suggest that during this phase the activities involving Acut tended to concentrate inside the cave, although it is also possible that the cave represents the locus where these tools were placed/stored when not in use, or brought for maintenance. On the other hand, the fact that no cave specimen is dated to EN may be taken as an indication that, prior to MN, Acut-related activities had the tendency to take place outside the cave: on

Paralia and probably also on the now submerged part of the settlement. It is also possible, however, that the absence of EN specimens from the cave has to do with post-depositional disturbances: undisturbed EN deposits inside the cave are limited. Vitelli finds it probable that the EN remains inside the cave were originally more extensive, but were disturbed by both later Neolithic and post-Neolithic activities (1993:44–47). If so, some of the Acut used and discarded during EN may occur among the specimens excavated in surface or disturbed cave deposits and considered here as generally Neolithic specimens.

I have been unable to distinguish any chronologically meaningful morphological or functional groups within the Acut group. This may be due to the limited number of available dates or to the conservative nature of the material itself. If the latter is true, the Franchthi assemblage is not unlike other Aegean Neolithic assemblages of cutting edge tools, which, as pointed out, have the tendency to show no significant variation through time (Moundréa-Agrafioti 1992:174; Perlès 1992:141, 2001:236).[7] A similar lack of chronologically significant variation has been noted for assemblages from Mediterranean France. The situation is apparently very different in other parts of France, where such tools show 'a distinct evolution in production techniques, shapes and sizes, both in the long term and short term' (Perlès 2001:236).

Given the lack of chronologically significant variation, all Acut are discussed together regardless of their date. I nevertheless distinguish two groups on the basis of a cluster analysis of the three basic dimensions (length, width, and thickness) of the 59 complete specimens. The first group includes 39 specimens with small dimensions (length ≤4.6 cm), while the second comprises twenty larger specimens (length >4.6 cm). I refer to the members of the first and second groups as 'small' and 'larger' Acut respectively. I should emphasize that it is unclear whether this simple distinction corresponds to any emic classifications.

Before I move to the presentation of Acut, I should clarify a few terms pertaining specifically to the anatomy of these tools. 'Distal part' refers to the portion of the tool containing the working edge. 'Proximal end' refers to the end opposite that consisting of the working edge, whereas 'proximal part' is the portion of the tool containing the proximal end. 'Median part' is the term I use for the portion of the tool between the proximal and distal parts (see also Moundréa-Agrafioti 1981:178; Ricq-de Bouard 1983:10).

Raw material

According to macroscopic analysis, the dominant raw material among Acut is serpentinite. This is a type of rock commonly used for such tools in the Neolithic Aegean.[8] Sixty-six specimens (74%) were made of this material, which at Franchthi appears in a variety of tones of green and gray. Peridotite, basalt, and diabase are represented by four or five specimens each, while steatite is represented by two specimens. A variety of other raw materials (andesite, felsite porphyry, argillite, diorite, magnetite, and limestone) are represented by one specimen each (Table 4.1).

Apart from the medium-grained peridotite of FS 311 and FS 227, all the stones used are fine-grained. They measure no more than 4 on the Mohs hardness scale, although three exceptions exist: the hardness of the diabase of FS 185 is 7, while that of the andesite of FS 36 (Pl. 63) and the peridotite of FS 227 is 5. The general softness of the raw material suggests that the Franchthi tools were relatively easy to shape, but rather vulnerable in the context of any use that involved high pressure or percussion.

According to Vitaliano's geological survey (see chapter 1), the main types of rocks used for the Franchthi tools (i.e., serpentinite, diabase, basalt, peridotite) are found in the ophiolite complex of the Franchthi-Ermioni region, as well as in volcanic bodies in the Discouria hills (southwest of Ermioni) and at Vourlia (northwest of the Franchthi embayment). These rocks, however, are everywhere deeply weathered and the acquisition of large pieces of fresh material from outcrops must have been very difficult. Stream pebbles or cobbles concentrated in the float by natural processes are, thus, a more likely source (van Andel and Vitaliano 1987:20; Vitaliano 1987:13-14). Such pebbles and cobbles could also have been obtained at the beach, which was not far from the site during the Neolithic (Vitaliano n.d.:11).

The hypothesis that water-worn pebbles and cobbles were used as raw material for such tools—a practice rather common in the Neolithic Aegean (see Perlès 2001:233)[9]—is reinforced by the mainly curvilinear appearance of Acut. Additional evidence comes from: 1. A couple of tools (e.g., FS 755) that retain rounded, water-worn cortex in their proximal part or even higher. The cortex was retained as this area was left untreated, since it did not interfere with the intended shape of the tool. 2. A small, unworked, water-rolled, serpentinite cobble (FS 119), which, as mentioned earlier, may have been collected and brought to the site to be converted into an Acut. 3.

Three fragments of water-rolled serpentinite pebbles or cobbles with traces of pecking (FS 240, FS 734, H2A:9a) that, as also mentioned earlier, perhaps represent remains of accidents that occurred during Acut manufacture.

The problem with the hypothesis of the use of water-worn pebbles and cobbles as Acut raw material is that sound cobbles are nowadays rare in the streambeds around Franchthi (van Andel and Vitaliano 1987:20). As for the ancient beach, it is today under water and thus difficult to explore. One can argue, however, that pebbles or cobbles suitable for the manufacture of Acut may have been more abundant in the past, having latterly been depleted by human exploitation (see Perlès, cited in van Andel and Vitaliano 1987:20). This idea seems to be supported by the findings of the Argolid Exploration Project (AEP). AEP covered a much larger area than that covered by Vitaliano's survey and, in the beds of seasonal streams, located cobbles that appear macroscopically to be of the same raw materials as those used for Acut (Kardulias and Runnels 1995:111). If such stream cobbles occur today in the wider region, then their scarcity in the Franchthi area might very well be the outcome of intensive exploitation by different groups over a few millennia. Moreover, the cobbles located by AEP were small, matching the generally small dimensions of Acut. If the Neolithic inhabitants of Franchthi collected the local raw materials despite their softness and small sizes, it is reasonable to assume that these were adequate for the purposes for which the tools were intended.

There are, however, two specimens, for which the use of non-local material is suspected. The first is FS 36 (Pl. 63), a tool made of aphanitic andesite. This material was also used to make three Popen: FS 380 (Pl. 26), FS 390 (Fig. 4, Pl. 23), and FS 795 (Pl. 25). The andesite of the first two of these specimens, in particular, has not only the same texture as FS 36 but also the same color—a possible indication of the exploitation of the same source? Aphanitic andesite is not found in the Franchthi area and must, thus, have been imported from sources outside the region (see discussion in chapter 3). Interestingly, FS 36 lacks a working edge, having been left in a roughout state. Given the exogenous origin of the raw material, it is possible that the early stages of shaping of this specimen (consisting of pecking and some grinding) took place at the source. The resulting roughout may have been brought to the site for the rest of the manufacturing process, which, for some unknown reason, was never completed. It is significant that, as mentioned earlier, the hardness of the andesite of FS 36 is 5, and, thus, is higher than that of the raw material of the majority of the Franchthi specimens—a possible incentive for import.

FS 589 (Fig. 16) may have been made of non local material too. Its raw material is steatite and macroscopically similar to that used for the large number of LN and FN 'opaque white' beads discovered at the site (Miller 1997:166, 1998). According to Miller (1998), the steatite used for these beads was fired, acquiring as a result a characteristic off-white color—very different from the natural grey-green color of steatite. I assume thus that the steatite of FS 589 was exposed to heat too. The fact that steatite must be heated at very high temperatures, perhaps as high as 1000 to 1200 degrees Celsius, to achieve this notable white coloring (Miller 1998), may be an indication that the steatite of FS 589 was heated intentionally rather than accidentally, or in other words, fired. Based on the similarities between the opaque white beads from Franchthi and other Greek Neolithic sites, as well as the absence of manufacturing debris from all these sites, Miller believes that the fired steatite beads were not manufactured at Franchthi but instead imported to it (1998). If so, it is possible that FS 589 was imported to the site too. This hypothesis is perhaps reinforced by this specimen's FN date as well as its unique, angular appearance.

Franchthi fits the general pattern in the Neolithic Aegean regarding the raw materials used for cutting edge tools. These materials appear generally to be local—an impression that for a couple of sites has been confirmed by petrographic analysis[10]—but cases of the use of non-local stones have also been reported.[11]

Finally, several concerns must have informed the selection of particular pebbles and cobbles as raw materials for Acut. The most crucial was to find rocks with physical properties adequate for the intended finished products. Probably another concern was to obtain rocks with shapes and dimensions as close as possible to those of the desired tools. This, as ethnography informs us,[12] would have been a rational choice that could save time and energy during manufacture. It also seems likely that some effort was put into finding rocks that during manufacture would acquire a glossy appearance. The lack of uniformity in the appearance of the Franchthi tools reflects, in my view, not only a wide range of functional variation, but also the uniqueness of each pebble or cobble used, coupled with a lack of specialization in the production of these tools and of strict norms as to what they should look like.

Aspects of manufacture

The pebbles or cobbles collected as raw material were transformed into Acut (at least their stone components) by pecking and grinding, two techniques commonly used in the manufacture of such tools in the Neolithic Aegean (see Moundréa-Agrafioti 1996:104; Perlès 2001:233). With one exception, no specimen shows evidence of flaking.[13] The exception is the longest tool in the group, FS 116 (Pl. 64), which shows a flake scar on one face next to the working edge. Light flaking is also responsible for the creation of a kind of waist on the proximal part of the tool, something also unique in this collection. These deviations from the 'norm' may be signs of an exogenous origin, although, it must be stressed, the raw material of FS 116 is serpentinite of the same appearance and hardness as that of other Acut. It is unlikely that flaking was used regularly in the manufacture of Acut, and that flake scars were obliterated by the subsequent treatment of the surface: the raw material does not lend itself to flaking. Moreover, its softness makes flaking rather unnecessary. I should also note here that no traces of sawing have been identified in this assemblage.[14]

The initial shaping of Acut thus involved pecking, for which active percussive tools must have been used. Such tools are found in the group of Active globular tools discussed later in this chapter. It appears, however, that pecking was not used universally. The lack of evidence of pecking in most small specimens, rather than being the result of obliteration by subsequent grinding, most likely reflects the omission of a pecking stage. Such a choice can be easily explained: grinding alone would have been sufficient to give the desired size and shape to the small, soft pebbles used as raw material for small tools. Moreover, pecking small pebbles must have been awkward, since the pebbles would have been hard to hold and strike with percussive tools that were larger than the pebbles.

Unlike the small specimens, most of the larger ones were pecked into shape. This is to be expected, too, given that grinding would have been quite time-consuming if used alone to shape a larger pebble or a cobble.[15] In this case a combination of pecking and grinding offered a labor-saving advantage. The extent of pecking evidence on the surface of the larger specimens varies. In a few of them the pecking marks are almost undetectable, having been largely obliterated by the subsequent treatment of the tools' surface, e.g., FS 117 (Fig. 19, Pl. 65). In one specimen, FS 116 (Pl. 64), pecking traces cover almost all of one face. The majority of the larger Acut, however, exhibit pecking marks mainly on their proximal part and/or the sides, e.g., FS 1 (Pl. 67), FS 33 (Fig. 18), FS 118 (Pl. 66). These were often left partially ground or unground, hence the pecking marks are visible. The differential treatment of the distal and proximal parts of the larger specimens saved time without jeopardizing the tools' efficacy, since it was only the distal part that had to be ground to create a working edge. Moreover, the makers of these tools may have been sufficiently practical to choose not to grind an area that would be inserted into a handle, and thus invisible—a choice that would not affect the aesthetic appeal of these implements.[16] Lastly, this treatment may have served a specific technical purpose: to leave a rough or semi-rough surface that would allow a more secure attachment of the stone head to its handle (see Dickson 1981:33, 99; O'Hare 1990:130; Roodenberg 1986:98).[17] One wonders, however, why the proximal part was left in a rough or semi-rough state in some tools but not in others. Did this differential treatment have to do with time pressure, personal preference,[18] the kind of hafting device used, or the contexts of use?

Grinding was the second manufacturing stage for the larger specimens, the sole one for the vast majority of the small items. This process served important practical purposes: to create an acute edge at one end of the roughout, increase the efficiency of the tool, and reduce the chances of breakage during use. No less important, however, must have been the aesthetic effect that grinding brought about as it highlighted the color of the stone and developed a smooth and often glossy body texture (see Edmonds 1995:51; Malinowski 1934:190; Toth, Clark, and Ligabue 1992:92; Woodbury 1954:42). Grinding is a time-consuming and tedious process[19] and the tools that are completely ground and, indeed, have a polished appearance, such as FS 117 (Fig. 19, Pl. 65), strike us as the product of a considerable amount of time and energy that cannot be justified in strictly utilitarian terms. Such a surface treatment and the investment of labor involved, may imply a certain symbolic and ideological value for these tools and/or a certain status for their manufacturers, users, and/or owners. Again, the Franchthi assemblage is not exceptional in the completely ground/polished appearance of many of its members. Examples of cutting edge tools subjected to a similar treatment come from other Neolithic (Aegean[20] and non-Aegean[21]) sites.

As experimental and ethnographic studies suggest, grinding must have taken place with the help of water on passive abrasive surfaces (see, for example, Blackwood 1950:15; Dickson 1972:208, 1981:42-44, 151-156; Hampton 1999:93-97; Nami 1984:104; Pétrequin and Pétrequin 1993a:181-194; Toth, Clark, and Ligabue 1992:91; Townsend 1969:200; Vial 1940-1941:159). The water is essential in this process: on the one hand, it washes away the detritus formed during grinding, and, on the other, it prevents overheating that can cause edge chipping and flaking (Dickson 1981:41; Nami 1984:104). No bedrock grooves or 'cup marks' that could have been used in, or formed by, grinding Acut have been identified at Franchthi.[22] Passive abrasive surfaces could, however, have been provided at the site by Popen. As I argued in chapter 3, the size of these tools seems rather inadequate for grain processing, but is suitable for grinding stone tools (among other things). Moreover, the use-wear on certain Popen is compatible with grinding Acut—see, for example, FS 423 (Pl. 29). There is, though, only one case of a spatial association between an Acut, FS 893 (Fig. 16, Pl. 68), and a Popen, FS 892 (Fig. 7, Pl. 50), and even in this case a functional association between the two is doubtful: FS 892 is fragmentary and there is no indication that it was used after the breakage to grind cutting edge tools, such as FS 893.

If we leave aside the angular-looking and perhaps exogenous FS 589 (Fig. 16), grinding in general created rounded faces that smoothly meet the sides of the tools, e.g., FS 1 (Pl. 67), FS 212 (Pl. 70), FS 600 (Pl. 69). In a few cases, nevertheless, it produced light facets, e.g., FS 117 (Fig. 19, Pl. 65), or stronger facets, e.g., FS 23 (Pl. 71). Strong faceting, in particular, is seen in some of the smallest specimens; see FS 11 (Pl. 72), FS 201 (Fig. 15). The faceting in these tools has probably to do with their small size, because of which only a small surface at a time could be subjected to grinding.

Given the polished appearance of most of the Franchthi specimens, it is likely that the last stage of grinding involved a fine abrasive, for example, fine-grained sandstone, clay, or ocher.[23] In fact, one of these tools, FS 289, has a subtle reddish stain on its body, which may represent traces of clay or ocher used in this last stage.[24] The makers of these tools may also have rubbed them with a piece of leather to achieve a similar effect—see experiments by M'Guire (1892:169) and Nami (1984:104).[25] As already mentioned, such a treatment did not improve the tools' efficiency. It did, however, greatly enhance their appearance; this must have been its purpose.

Apart from serving as an indispensable stage in the manufacturing process, grinding was also used, after Acut had been utilized, to rejuvenate their dull edge. Since grinding in this case tended to affect only the area of the edge, it resulted in unifacial or bifacial beveling next to the edge—the diagnostic trait of resharpening, e.g., FS 11 (Pl. 72), FS 201 (Fig. 15), FS 363 (Fig. 15), FS 589 (Fig. 16). It is also possible, if untraceable, for the whole tool to have been reground in the context of edge resharpening, especially if there was a need to redefine its shape and proportions.

Interestingly enough, pecking was also sometimes used after grinding (and utilization) of the tool had already taken place. It is possible to distinguish two cases of this secondary pecking. In the first case, pecking basically removed the smooth ground surface in the proximal and sometimes even the median part, e.g., FS 21 (Fig. 17, Pl. 73), FS 153 (Pl. 74), FS 159 (Pl. 75). In the second and rarer case, pecking roughened up the smooth ground surface of only the sides of the tool; see FS 23 (Pl. 71) and FS 837 (Fig. 19). In both cases, the secondary pecking may have been intended to facilitate the secure adjustment of the stone head to the handle, or to redefine the shape and/or proportions of a tool that for one reason or another had become dysfunctional (see also Moundréa-Agrafioti 1981:183).

In a single case, FS 893 (Fig. 16, Pl. 68), the grinding of the body and the creation of an acute edge were followed by an intentional unifacial retouch that produced a serrated edge.

The process of Acut making must have been completed with the manufacture of a haft and the adjustment of the stone head into it. The only direct evidence of hafting at Franchthi consists of four (unpublished) antler sleeves.[26] Unfortunately, the bad state of preservation of three of these sleeves renders them essentially useless for this discussion. The fourth, FB 607, was found in a MN Paralia deposit and measures 10.5×2.8×2.3cm. The diameter of its socket is 0.9 cm at the top, tapering towards the bottom; its depth is 1.2 cm. This socket is too small to fit even the smallest Acut and must have been used for other kinds of tools (e.g., chipped stone or bone tools). The scarcity of antler sleeves and the absence of other antler or bone hafting devices suggest that antler and bone were not commonly used at Franchthi for hafting purposes, and by extension that the hafts of Acut (and other tools) were most often made of wood.[27] The stone heads could have been adjusted to the hafts directly or, more likely, with the aid of a binding (e.g., leather or vine strips) and/or an adhesive substance (e.g., resin or beeswax), all perishable materials that—if used—left no traces.[28] It should be stressed here that both the preparation of a haft and hafting itself are time-consuming processes (see Dickson 1981:47). For the Franchthi tools in particular, with their rather soft raw materials, they may represent the lengthiest stages in the whole manufacturing sequence.

For reasons explained above, the following configurations found in larger specimens can be considered as indirect evidence for hafting: a proximal part left in an unground or semi-ground state; see FS 1 (Pl. 67), FS 33 (Fig. 18); a ground proximal part or ground sides roughened up by secondary pecking; see FS 21 (Fig. 17, Pl. 73), FS 23 (Pl. 71), FS 153 (Pl. 74), FS 159 (Pl. 75), FS 837 (Fig. 19).[29]

We do not know the mode of hafting of the different Franchthi specimens, but there are three possible ways of fixing the stone head in relation to the haft: the stone head can be placed in the same plane as the haft with the working edge parallel to the haft's long axis (as in a modern metal axe); it can be placed in the same plane as the haft with the working edge perpendicular to the haft's long axis (as in a modern metal chisel); or it can be placed in a plane that is perpendicular to the haft's long axis (as in a modern metal adze).

Where did pecking and grinding of Acut take place? Or, in other words, where were these tools produced? Neither of these processes leave behind traces recoverable by ordinary excavation techniques, such as those employed at Franchthi. No other direct evidence of on-site manufacture, such as that found in some other Aegean Neolithic sites,[30] has been identified at Franchthi. Yet there is enough indirect evidence to allow some reasonable hypotheses. If, as I suggested earlier, the raw material was for the most part local, I would argue that the manufacture of small specimens—consisting, with three or four exceptions, of grinding a small pebble—took place at the site. The large number of Popen discovered and the availability of water in the small pool at the rear of the cave or the now-submerged springs at the Franchthi shoreline (Hansen 1991:5, van Andel and Vitaliano 1987:18) make this a likely scenario. This hypothesis is further supported by evidence of a particular kind of Acut grinding—resharpening—which, as a tool maintenance technique, had to have taken place at the site (or at most in its vicinity). For the same reasons, I believe that grinding of larger specimens also occurred locally. This, moreover, is suggested by the discovery of two roughouts of larger tools—FS 36 (Pl. 63) (most likely an import) and FS 311—which were probably intended to go through the grinding stage at the site.

Regarding pecking of larger specimens, the following points can be made. The discovery of active percussive tools during the excavations (see Active globular tools, below this chapter) indicates that pecking of Acut could have taken place at the site. It must be noted, though, that the active percussive tools found are likely to have served a variety of pecking purposes. The single complete, unworked, serpentinite cobble found (see above)—if it was picked to serve as Acut raw material—may suggest that cobbles were taken to the site to be subjected to the stages of manufacture. If the three fragments of pecked serpentinite cobbles (see above) are indeed remains of accidents that occurred during the pecking stage in the Acut manufacturing sequence, they too may support the hypothesis that pecking of Acut was carried out at Franchthi. Lastly, the evidence of secondary pecking itself (which, like resharpening, must have taken place at the site or not too far from it) suggests that pecking was probably a manufacturing stage that took place locally.

The unworked serpentinite cobble (possibly Acut raw material), the three fragments of pecked serpentinite cobbles (possibly remains of Acut manufacturing accidents), and the two Acut roughouts, all mentioned above, come from a variety of trenches in the cave and on Paralia, an indication, perhaps, that no specialized area of production of Acut existed at Franchthi, as it did elsewhere.[31] Such an hypothesis fits well with the impression of a lack of craft specialization in Acut manufacture, as this emerges from the evidence for easy procurement of the raw material, the lack of evidence for specialized skills involved in the manufacture of these tools,[32] as well as the absence of morphologically homogeneous groups, and thus the lack of standardization, in the context of the Acut industry.

Yet a non-specialized process of manufacture for Acut does not necessarily imply a lack of specialization by gender in their making and/or use. A specialization of this sort, in which cutting edge tools are made and used exclusively or primarily by men, is encountered ethnographically in many modern New Guinea groups (see, for example, Godelier and Garanger 1973:197; Pétrequin and Pétrequin 1988:68, 1993a:361, 373, 387; Stout 2002; Strathern 1970:327; Toth, Clark, and Ligabue 1992:267).[33] Such an hypothesis for Franchthi is, however, for the moment untestable. Moreover it is possible that the Franchthi people who were involved in Acut-making were also involved in the production of other serpentinite tools (e.g., Active tools used with ends, below this chapter) as well as serpentinite ornaments, although, again, evidence for or against such an hypothesis has not been identified.

Regarding the two tools mentioned earlier as perhaps made of non local raw materials, FS 36 (Pl. 63), a roughout made of aphanitic andesite, suggests that a few tools reached the site in a roughout form. The initial shaping of FS 36 could have been completed at the source of the raw material by residents of Franchthi or (perhaps more likely) by people who were in direct or indirect contact with them. This tool could have come to the site through the same trajectories as the three Popen (mentioned above) made of the same material. This, however, can only remain a hypothesis, since it is unknown whether these Popen and FS 36 are contemporary. FS 589 (Fig. 16), of fired steatite, was probably imported to Franchthi in a finished state, perhaps through the same (exchange?) mechanisms that made possible the import of opaque white beads of the same material.

I should note here that both direct procurement of raw materials at the sources and exchange have been suggested as mechanisms that brought exogenous materials for cutting edge tools or the tools themselves to the few Aegean Neolithic sites in which these have been found.[34] There is plenty of archaeological evidence from elsewhere in Europe for the movement of such tools or their raw materials across large distances in the context of exchange networks (see, for example, Bradley and Edmonds 1993; Edmonds 1993, 1995; Hodder and Lane 1982; Leighton and Dixon 1992; O'Hare 1990; Patton 1991; Pétrequin and Jeunesse 1995:61–92). Ethnographic and ethnoarchaeological evidence for the participation of such tools in exchange networks also abounds (see, for example, Hampton 1999:275-290; Pétrequin and Pétrequin 1993a:388-392; Strathern 1965, 1970; Toth, Clark, and Ligabue 1992; Vial 1940-1941; White and Modjeska 1978).

Technomorphological characteristics

The 59 complete Acut range in length from 2.0 to 9.6 cm. Forty (66%) fall into the 2.0–4.6 cm range (these are the 'small' specimens); the remaining nineteen (34%) are between 5.3 and 9.6 cm long (these are the 'larger' specimens). The large number of small tools is reflected in the average Acut length of 4.5 cm (σ 1.9) (Tables 4.1 and 4.3). It is indeed interesting that in the context of some classification systems 85% of the complete Acut would be considered 'miniature' (see Wright 1992:73). There are, nevertheless, two fragments, FS 112 (Fig. 17) and FS 430 (Fig. 18), that are long enough to have been part of complete specimens measuring 10.0 cm or longer, leaving open the possibility that a few Acut longer than those represented among the complete tools were at some point used at Franchthi. The comparison between the average length of the complete specimens recovered in the cave and Paralia (5.0 and 3.5 cm respectively) shows a higher concentration of larger specimens in the cave. This discrepancy may reflect some differential use of the cave and Paralia in relation to Acut.

The complete specimens range in width from 0.8 to 4.9 cm. With the exception of 11 tools (19%), all fall into the 2.0–4.9 cm range. The average width of the complete tools is 3.0 cm (σ 1.1) (Tables 4.1 and 4.4). Four fragmentary specimens, FS 38 (Pl. 76), FS 98, FS 715, and FS 838 are, however, wider than any of the complete tools. The complete specimens range in thickness from 0.4 to 3.7 cm. The average thickness is 1.6 cm. (σ 0.8) (Tables 4.1 and 4.5).

With the above dimensions, the Franchthi tools are on the whole smaller than those of most other Greek Neolithic assemblages. For comparative purposes, see the tools from several Thessalian sites studied by Moundréa-Agrafioti (1981:199-200), Knossos (Evans 1964), Olynthos (Mylonas 1929:71-72), Dikili Tash (Séfériadès 1992a), Servia (Mould, Ridley, and Wardle 2000:129-136), Dispilio (Stratouli 2002:158), Stavroupoli (Alisøy 2002:562), and Sitagroi (Elster 2003a:179-180, 2003b:204-210). See, nevertheless, the specimens from Kitsos (Perlès 1981:198), Tharrounia (Sugaya 1993:446), and Saliagos (Evans and Renfrew 1968:65) that have sizes comparable to those of Acut.

How can the small size of a large number of Acut be explained? In fact, the large number of small specimens becomes even odder in light of their generally good state of preservation and sharp working edges, features that imply that these tools entered the archaeological record when they were still functional. It is tempting to see the small size as a result of repeated resharpening, something that seems to be suggested by the generally low length/width ratio of these tools (average ratio: 1.59, σ 0.55) (Tables 4.1 and 4.6). There are, however, problems with this hypothesis. First, there are highly significant correlations among length, width, and thickness of the complete specimens, whereas the correlation between length and length/width

Table 4.3. Frequency distribution of complete Acut by length.

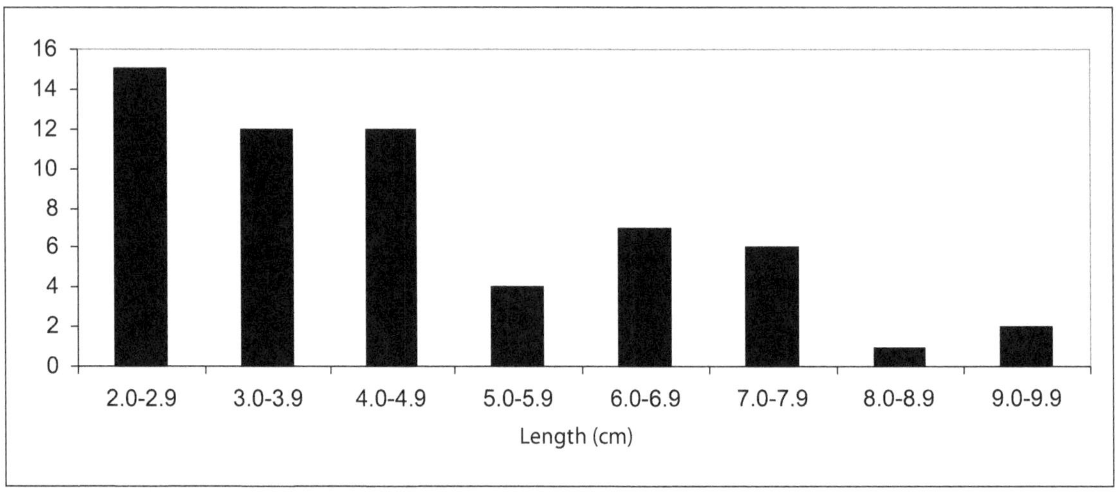

Table 4.4. Frequency distribution of complete Acut by width.

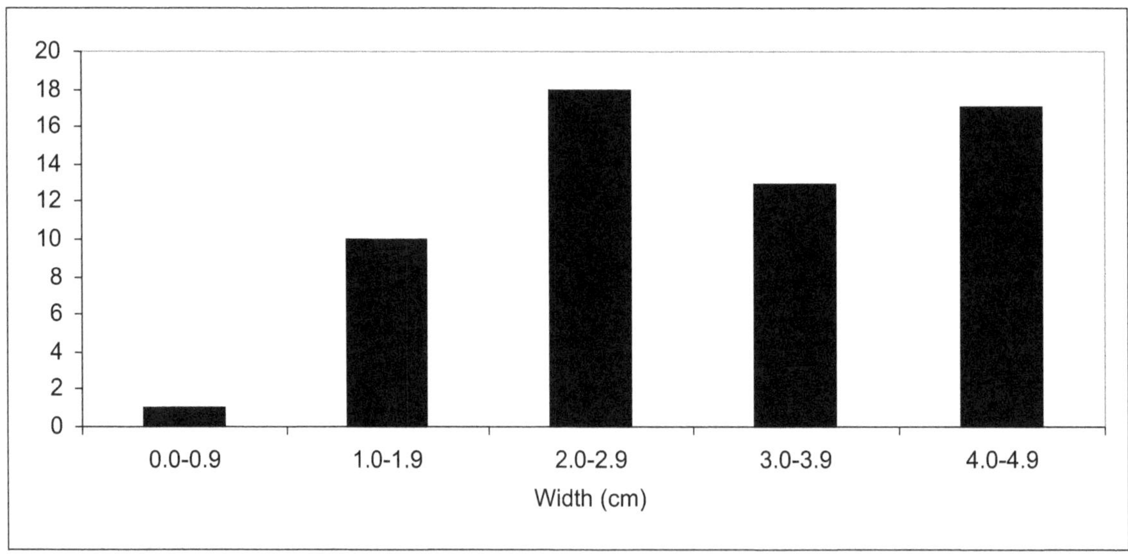

Table 4.5. Frequency distribution of complete Acut by thickness.

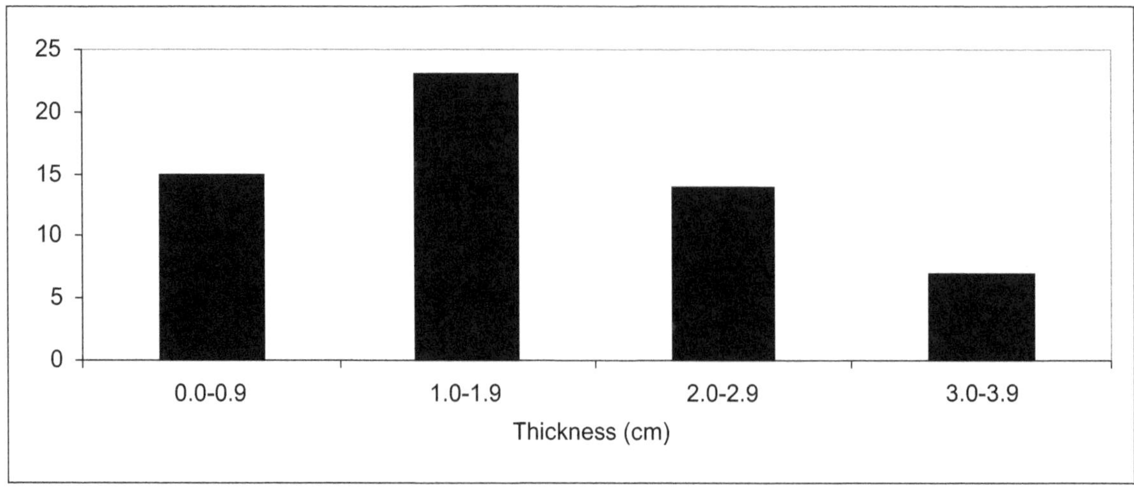

ratio is not significant. This suggests that resharpening was not practiced intensively enough to have a dramatic impact on the proportions of these tools (Table 4.7). Secondly, and most importantly, the resharpened tools account for only about half of the 39 complete small specimens and, moreover, there is no difference in the average length/width ratio between the small tools that were resharpened and those that were not. It is true, however, that, of the small specimens, those showing evidence of resharpening are as a rule the shortest (average length of resharpened small specimens: 2.9 cm; average length of those not resharpened: 3.7 cm). It could, thus, be argued that the very short length of the latter tools is the result of resharpening. Their small width and thickness, however, make it unlikely that these specimens were initially much longer. It is more reasonable to assume that the size of the small specimens, more than anything else, is a manufacturing choice—determined presumably by their functions—rather than the result of prolonged use and repeated resharpening.

Equally interesting is the scarcity of evidence of resharpening among the larger specimens. This suggests that these tools were not used intensively enough to require resharpening. It also suggests that the resharpened small tools do not represent the last stage in a long process of use of larger specimens or, in other words, that there is no continuity between larger and small specimens.

The preferred shape in plan view is (sub)triangular with 32 instances among the complete specimens (54%). In these tools the maximum width coincides more or less with the working edge. Tools of all sizes were made in this shape, e.g., FS 21 (Fig. 17, Pl. 73), FS 23 (Pl. 71), FS 44 (Fig. 15),

Table 4.6. Frequency distribution of complete Acut by length/width ratio.

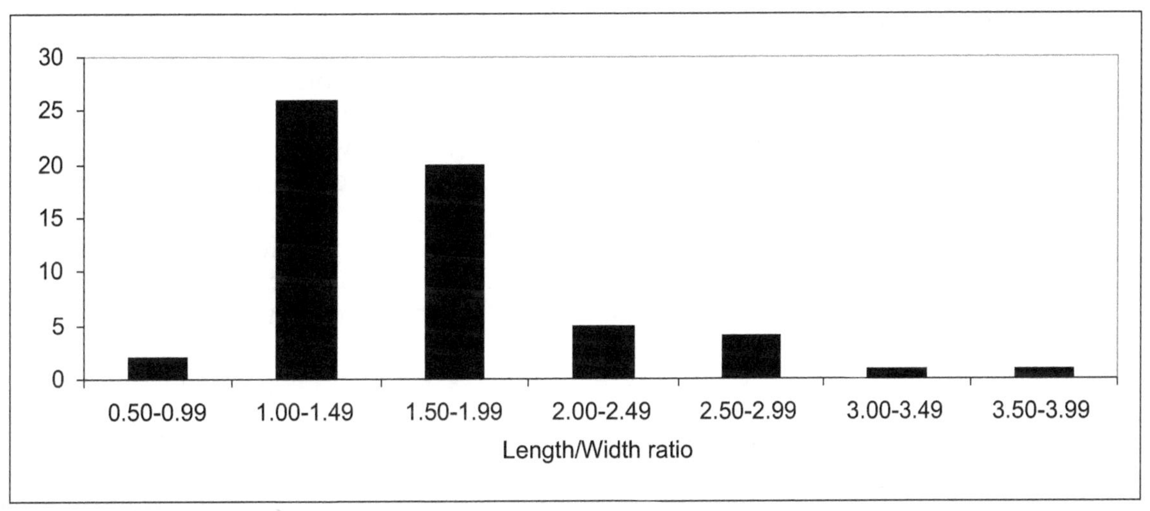

Table 4.7. Pearson correlations among the dimensions of complete small Acut.

		Length	Width	Thickness	L/W Ratio
Length	Pearson Correlation	1	0.579(**)	0.597(**)	–0.007(**)
	Sig. (2-tailed)		0.000	0.000	0.965
	N	39	39	39	39
Width	Pearson Correlation	0.579(**)	1	0.837(**)	–0.778(**)
	Sig. (2-tailed)	0		0.000	0.000
	N	39	39	39	39
Thickness	Pearson Correlation	0.597(**)	0.837(**)	1	–0.549(**)
	Sig. (2-tailed)	0.000	0.000		0.000
	N	39	39	39	39
L/W Ratio	Pearson Correlation	–0.007(**)	–0.778(**)	–0.549(**)	1
	Sig. (2-tailed)	0.965	0.000	0.000	
	N	39	39	39	39

** Correlation is significant at the .01 level (2-tailed).

KEY: L/W Ratio=length/width ratio.

FS 226 (Pl. 77), FS 837 (Fig. 19). The next most popular shape among the complete specimens is the (sub)rectangular with 16 instances (27%), e.g., FS 37 (Fig. 16), FS 589 (Fig. 16), FS 884 (Fig. 15). Six complete tools (10%) have a (sub)trapezoidal shape (e.g., FS 902, FS 93), whereas five (8%) have a roughly oval shape (e.g., FS 185).

Only three Acut have a perfectly symmetrical profile: FS 33 (Fig. 18), FS 600 (Pl. 69), and FS 899 (Pl. 78). Only seven specimens, on the other hand, have strongly asymmetrical profiles, e.g., FS 23 (Pl. 71), FS 52 (Fig. 16), FS 201 (Fig. 15), FS 589 (Fig. 16), and FS 751 (Fig. 17). With two exceptions, all the asymmetrical cases are, or come from, larger tools. Most specimens are indeed lightly asymmetrical in profile, e.g., FS 118 (Pl. 66). Thus, very few Franchthi specimens perfectly fit the classic definition of 'axe' and 'adze', according to which an axe has a symmetrical profile and a haft fixed parallel to its working edge, whereas an adze has an asymmetrical profile and a haft fixed perpendicular to the plane of the stone head. This suggests that the definition was not current among the Franchthi producers or users of these tools, who most of the time, showed no great concern with profile symmetry.[35] Such a definition, moreover, has proved problematic in light of ethnographic/ethnoarchaeological evidence: apparently modern groups in New Guinea haft their stone heads indiscriminately as 'adzes' or 'axes', depending on what is needed at the time, or in such a way that they can be rotated within their handle (Heider 1967:56; Malinowski 1934:191; Sillitoe 1988:43–44). The ways these tools are hafted (and used) can, moreover, change as they pass from group to group in the context of exchange (Pétrequin and Pétrequin 1993b:371). A similar flexibility in the use of prehistoric specimens is suggested by use-wear analysis (see Christopoulou 1992; Moundréa-Agrafioti 1981:167; Perlès 2001:235; Smoor 1976:186–188).

The majority of Franchthi specimens have a working edge that is lightly to strongly convex in plan view; see FS 23 (Pl. 71), FS 117 (Fig. 19, Pl. 65), FS 153 (Pl. 74), FS 837 (Fig. 19). The convex edge offered a significant technical advantage, since an angular connection of the working edge to the sides of the tool could have created fatal points of stress during use (see Dickson 1972:209, 1981:45, 102). A few tools have a straight edge in plan view. All are small, e.g., FS 11 (Pl. 72), FS 44 (Fig. 15), FS 157 (Pl. 80), FS 201 (Fig. 15), FS 221 (Pl. 79). Lastly, four specimens have an edge that is lopsided in plan view. In the literature, edge lopsidedness has been interpreted as the result of partial edge resharpening after localized damage (Spenneman 1987; see also Semenov 1964:129–130). This interpretation seems to apply to FS 680 (Fig. 15). In this small specimen a bevel that affected only one part of the edge clearly created a lopsided effect. The same interpretation, however, cannot account for the lopsided edge of FS 779 (Fig. 16), since this does not carry traces of resharpening. The lopsidedness in this case is probably a manufacturing choice, presumably related to the intended use of the tool. The two remaining specimens, FS 1 (Pl. 67) and FS 363 (Fig. 15), show evidence of unifacial resharpening, but it is not clear whether the lopsided edge has to do with manufacture or some subsequent intervention related to localized edge damage.

All but five tools have edges that are straight in front view. The edges of the five exceptions—all larger specimens—are curved in front view: FS 23 (Pl. 71), FS 117 (Fig. 19, Pl. 65), FS 118 (Pl. 66), FS 751 (Fig. 17), and FS 837 (Fig. 19). These edges are sharp and thus, beyond doubt, represent manufacturing choices, rather than the product of use with the faces (for perhaps polishing or scraping). The tools with a strongly curved edge also tend to have more asymmetrical profiles than other tools. Specimens with this edge configuration have been reported from a few other Aegean Neolithic sites.[36] Such tools are also known ethnographically/ethnoarchaeologically.[37]

Aspects of use

Small Acut

As we have already seen, the site produced a surprisingly large number of small Acut (39 out of 59 complete specimens). The size, coupled with a generally soft raw material and glossy appearance, makes one wonder whether these specimens were made not to be used as tools but rather to serve as miniatures, objects of status, articles of personal attire, or even toys.[38] Although a role as objects of status is likely for many of the Franchthi tools—such a role is after all very common among ethnographic specimens—the remaining hypotheses are hard to promote for these tools in general, given the abundant evidence of use wear or resharpening visible on their edges.[39] All were used and about half of them were also resharpened on one or both faces; see FS 201 (Fig. 15), FS 589 (Fig. 16). A few, indeed, show double resharpening on the same face; see FS 11 (Pl. 72), FS 363 (Fig. 15). The combined evidence of resharpening and use wear on some of the smallest specimens indicates that they were used after they were resharpened and thus when they had a very small length, e.g., FS 44 (Fig. 15), FS 157 (Pl. 80). If there is no doubt that the small specimens were used, how they were used is a much more complex matter, especially in the absence of microscopic use wear analysis[40] or experimental study. The following presents the results of the macroscopic study of the use wear of these tools, along with some suggestions about possible uses.

The working edge of a cutting edge tool enters the worked material through pressure exerted on the tool itself or its haft, or through percussion. Four use wear patterns are macroscopically visible on the edge of small specimens: chipping; a combination of chipping and scoring; a combination of chipping and rounding; and flattening, with or without chipping.

Some tools exhibit unifacial edge chipping, while others show bifacial edge chipping. The differential location of the chip scars may have to do with a specific use and/or hafting technique that exposed one or both faces of the edge to the resistance of the worked material. In the case of bifacial edge chipping, the two faces may have been exposed to the resistance of the worked material simultaneously or alternately. The bifacial edge chipping occurs on tools with different profiles and edge shapes, e.g., FS 157 (Pl. 80), FS 398, FS 505. No clear correlation thus exists between this particular use wear and a certain set of technomorphological characteristics.

Unifacial edge chipping occurs more rarely among small Acut; see FS 24, FS 726, FS 883 (Fig. 15). This use wear implies that primarily one face met the resistance of the worked material. I have been unable to detect any pattern linking the unifacial chipping to specific technomorphological features. In this context I should mention FS 222 (Fig. 16), which also has unifacial edge chipping. In this tool, however, the chip scars have clearly different directions, suggesting that different parts of the edge were at different times exposed to the resistance of the worked material. This kind of use wear is expected—if not exclusively—in the case of an indirect percussive function. This hypothesis is reinforced by percussion scars visible on the proximal end of the tool. Another specimen that should be mentioned here is FS 893 (Fig. 16, Pl. 68). This sturdy, stubby tool is unique in that it has a serrated edge produced by unifacial retouch. The chipping of the edge in this case represents a manufacturing choice rather than an unintended result of use, or such is suggested by the regularity of the notches.

In a second use wear pattern, represented by three tools, FS 12, FS 207, and FS 221 (Pl. 79), the chipping is accompanied by very fine, short (about 1 mm long) scoring. This scoring is perpendicular to the working edge and visible even without low magnification on one or both faces. The very short length and the direction of the scoring marks suggest that they are from use, rather than manufacture or resharpening, since it is very hard to grind the edge transversally for only one millimeter without flattening it out. Interestingly, on FS 207 and FS 221 the chipping appears on one face of the edge, the scoring on the other, raising the possibility that the two kinds of wear are the result of different uses. No correlation between the combination of chipping and scoring and specific technomorphological characteristics is detectable.

In a third use wear pattern, represented by FS 428 (Pl. 81) and FS 755, chipping appears on one face of a blunt or rounded edge. Are the dullness and chipping of the working edge the results of the same use, or do the two kinds of use-wear reflect two different uses? I tend to believe that they are the result of the same use. The dull edge on both tools may perhaps be the result of scraping and/or burnishing the interior of ceramic vessels. The chipping may have been caused from larger clay inclusions. Interestingly, the chip scars on the edge of FS 755 are consistently angled obliquely in relation to it. Moreover, they all have the same direction, pointing to an oblique and transverse movement of the edge over the worked material.

The last and most unexpected use wear pattern that I encountered on small specimens is a very narrow flat zone covering the entire edge or a part of it. Three specimens display this mysterious usewear pattern. On two of them, FS 22 (Pl. 82) and FS 363 (Fig. 15), chipping that followed the formation of the flat zone is also apparent on the edge.[41]

FS 11 (Pl. 72), one of the smallest specimens, deserves separate mention. The edge of this tool was unifacially resharpened twice but shows no evidence of use after the resharpening. At least three hypotheses can be put forward to explain this configuration: The tool was lost or discarded after it was resharpened and before being put back to use; it was curated to be ready for use when needed; or it was curated to serve a non-utilitarian function.

Finally, I discuss 14 fragments of small Acut, e.g., FS 577 (Pl. 83), FS 767, FS 789 (Pl. 84). These account for about half of all Acut fragments—a number curiously high for tools which, because of their small size and softness, were probably not systematically exposed to forces great enough to break them during use. If, in fact, that had been the case, one would expect their edges to be quite worn. Yet, although carrying some use wear, these edges are generally in very good condition, indicating perhaps that they were exposed to a destructive force only once: the time at which they were broken. Moreover, the breakage of these tools does not seem random. All 14 fragments retain part of the edge. Indeed 10 examples represent edge corners, consisting of part of the edge and part of one side. This pattern makes it hard to attribute the fracture to accidents that took place between episodes of use or after the discard of these tools—an impression reinforced by the complete absence of body parts missing the edge or part of it from the sample of small Acut. On this basis, I consider it possible that some of the small specimens at Franchthi were deliberately broken. This is further supported by a couple of fragments representing typical flakes; see FS 436, FS 789 (Pl. 84). An hypothesis of deliberate breakage could, in fact, explain the lack of fragments consisting of body parts. If some small Acut were deliberately broken, the body parts could have been equally deliberately removed and deposited in some undiscovered part of the site or even away from it.[42]

Deliberate breakage of whole entities and removal of certain parts of these are elements of ritual or symbolic treatment. As may have been the case for some Popen (see chapter 3), it is possible that small Acut were sometimes ritually 'killed' to mark the death of the producers/users/owners, or specific points in their lives or the life of the community; or alternatively to create and maintain a lasting bond between individuals or groups (see Chapman 2000). It is also possible that the deliberate destruction of Acut was only one part of a long and repeated ritual manipulation that also involved some kind of utilization that, if enigmatic, produced use wear on, and caused the need for maintenance (i.e., resharpening) of, the tool edges. The archaeological context is not of much help in testing this hypothesis, since, with one exception, all fragments in question came from disturbed deposits. The exception is FS 178, found close to a hearth in unit G1:11. A hearth, however, is a neutral place for this hypothesis, since it can be the locus of both everyday domestic and extraordinary ritual activities.

As noted in chapter 3, the deliberate breakage of artifacts is not a new idea for Franchthi or Balkan prehistory in general. It is not a new idea for prehistoric cutting edge tools either. There is evidence in Britain for deliberate smashing of 'axes' and their deposition in pits in causewayed enclosures, perhaps in a funerary context (Edmonds 1995:68–73). More generally, the use of such tools in ritual and funerary contexts and their association with megalithic monuments are well documented for western Europe (see, for example, Edmonds 1993, 1995; Patton 1991).

If I am correct in suspecting that some Acut had some (exclusive or not) ritual or symbolic function, they would not be the first Neolithic Aegean specimens to be so interpreted. Such an interpretation has already been proposed for the six largest such tools found in Greece. These vary between 18.0 and 27.8 cm in length, and, from the longest to the shortest, include: two specimens excavated at the so-called shrine of Nea Nikomeidia (Rodden and Rodden 1964:604); one found by a local shepherd together with three smaller specimens and other objects inside a clay vessel that was buried in the ground near the village of Anemodouri in the Peloponnese (Tsountas 1901); one excavated in the Athenian Agora; and two found by local people in the area of Ayia Anna, Euboea (Sampson and Sugaya 1988–1989:18; Sugaya 1992). The above specimens have been interpreted as votive offerings, cult objects for religious activities, or heads of acrolithic figurines. Interestingly enough, use wear seems to have been identified on most of them (Sampson and Sugaya 1988–1989:18; Sugaya 1992; Tsountas 1901:88), suggesting perhaps that at least some of these tools had both ordinary (i.e., utilitarian) and extraordinary (i.e., ritual) uses; this was probably the case with other Neolithic artifacts (e.g., figurines) and Neolithic spaces in general (see Perlès 2001:255–272; also Bradley 2005).

The ceremonial and symbolic dimension of cutting edge tools—well documented ethnographically (see, for example, Hampton 1999; Pétrequin and Pétrequin 1993b; Strathern 1965, 1970; Vial 1940–1941)—is perhaps expressed in the generally aesthetically pleasing appearance of the specimens from Franchthi as well as other sites. It may be also suggested for Neolithic Greece by a handful of very small stone artifacts that have the general shape of a cutting edge tool and carry a drilled hole, or evidence of an attempt at drilling, on the narrow end. They were found at the following sites: Franchthi,[43] Kitsos (Vialou 1981:409), Knossos (Sampson and Sugaya 1988-1989:20), Skotini Cave (Sampson and Sugaya 1988-1989:20, 34), and Findspot 39 from the Limnes-Berbati survey (Runnels 1996:42, 70). Such artifacts are often called 'axe pendants' as the hole (actual or incipient) is assumed to have served the purpose of suspension. They may have been worn as pendants, necklace elements, wrist or ear-pendants, or sewn onto clothing, as Skeates (1995:283) has argued for the much larger number of small and larger prehistoric perforated stone objects of an 'axe' shape found in the central Mediterranean region.[44] The Greek specimens have been interpreted as amulets or votive offerings (Sampson and Sugaya 1988–1989:20); their central Mediterranean counterparts, often found in ritual or funerary contexts, have been additionally seen as objects of cult, and more recently, as the last stages in the biographies of originally larger, functional tools, during which they acted as 'animate objects', serving a variety of social, ceremonial, spiritual, and personal roles (Skeates 1995). We do not know what purposes the Greek examples served, but, along with one ceramic object in the shape of a cutting edge tool from Franchthi,[45] a 'ceramic axe' from Achilleion (Winn and Shimabuku 1989:266), and two clay 'model axes' found at the 'shrine' at Nea Nikomedeia (Sugaya 1992:74), they perhaps constitute additional, if rare, evidence of the symbolic value of some Aegean Neolithic cutting edge tools and their shape.

Larger Acut

The excavations uncovered 20 complete larger Acut. Another 10 fragmentary specimens can be considered parts of larger Acut. With a few exceptions, the edges of larger Acut are in relatively or very good condition and, moreover, not resharpened. This implies that larger specimens were not used long or intensively enough to cause substantial damage and the need for frequent resharpening. In the absence of evidence for overuse or exhaustion of the larger tools, it may be assumed that, small though their number is, their users probably did not need more than those that were available.

Although most of the complete larger specimens could have been (and probably were) used in shrub clearing and woodworking, only three of them are massive enough to be considered as candidates for tree-felling tools: FS 116 (Pl. 64), FS 229 (Pl. 85), and FS 837 (Fig. 19). For two of them some qualification is necessary. FS 837 has a curved edge in front view. This, however, does not necessarily make the tool unsuitable for tree cutting, as is suggested by ethnographic examples of tree-felling tools with a similar edge configuration (see Hampton 1999:59–92; Pétrequin and Pétrequin 1993a:60–67). FS 229 was recycled at some point in its life to serve a non-Acut function that caused the obliteration of its working edge. Thus we can only hypothesize its use in a tree-felling task. On the other hand, the fact that it is recycled reinforces the suspicion formulated above that at Neolithic Franchthi there may have been no need for more larger Acut than those that were available.

In addition, four fragments come from tools that seem to have been large enough to carry out tree-felling: FS 98, FS 112 (Fig. 17), FS 160, and FS 430 (Fig. 18). With the exception of FS 430, all have chipped edges. The edge of FS 430 is missing, having been obliterated when the tool was recycled to serve a non-Acut function. The position of the break in these four tools—somewhere in the middle of the original body length or close to the edge—is perhaps an indication that they were broken during a usage that involved heavy percussion.

If the above seven specimens are/were large enough to carry out tree-felling, their raw material may be too soft for such a task. If they actually functioned in such a way, they must have been employed very cautiously, and certainly with numerous, light, short strokes, using mainly the elbow and wrist, nibbling or scraping (rather than cutting) the wood away. This is, according to ethnographic and experimental evidence, the way tree chopping tools made of stone are/were used in general—very differently than their modern counterparts made of steel (see Carneiro 1974:111–112; Iversen 1956; Malinowski 1934:192).

The scarcity of Acut that could have served for tree-felling might imply that this was not an important activity at Franchthi during the Neolithic. This idea is supported by palynological evidence, according to which the vegetation of the southern Argolid for most of the Neolithic was very open, with deciduous oak forming woodlands only at higher elevations (Bottema 1990:124; Hansen 1991:18). Land clearance for farming purposes, on the other hand, could have been carried out by burning. Experiments have, indeed, shown that the resulting ash acts as a fertilizer (see Iversen 1956:39). Additional tree-felling techniques not involving the use of cutting edge tools are described in the ethnographic literature: ring-barking (girdling), the driving tree fall or 'windrow felling', and the controlled use of fire (see, e.g., Brass 1941:561; Carneiro 1974:114–115; Steensberg 1980:58–61).

Theoretically, it is possible that the users of tree-felling tools took them along when they abandoned the site. In that case, however, one wonders why they left behind other specimens that were in a good and usable state. Given the small number of fragmentary larger Acut, it is also theoretically possible that some larger tools were discarded away from the site, where they were used and eventually damaged. I find it hard to believe, however, that the users of these heavy-duty, and thus probably precious, tools did not take the trouble to retrieve them and bring them back to the settlement for repair or recycling into other smaller tools or non-tool objects; nor is there any ethnographic support for such a scenario. There is, instead, ethnographic evidence from the Langda of New Guinea for a practice of returning the fragmentary and worn-out 'axes' to the village because their users '"feel sorry" for their handiwork' (Toth, Clark, and Ligabue 1992:92).

The majority of the larger specimens have straight edges in front view. These tools have symmetrical or asymmetrical profiles, e.g., FS 226 (Pl. 77), FS 600 (Pl. 69), and exhibit unifacial or bifacial edge chipping, e.g., FS 6, FS 21 (Fig. 17, Pl. 73), FS 160, FS 226 (Pl. 77). In two cases, FS 227 and FS 210, one edge corner is flaked off. Interestingly enough, on the remaining part of the edge of FS 210 one can see a narrow flat zone, similar to those identified on a few small Acut.[46]

As mentioned earlier, five larger specimens have a curved edge in front view: FS 23 (Pl. 71), FS 117 (Fig. 19, Pl. 65), FS 118 (Pl. 66), FS 751 (Fig. 17), and FS 837 (Fig. 19). These tools are characterized by a lighter or stronger asymmetrical profile, in which one face is more convex and the other more flat. This particular edge and body configuration may have been convenient for hollowing out logs—possibly with the help of charring—to create wooden bowls, ladles, and other artifacts similar, perhaps, to those known from the lacustrine sites of eastern France and Switzerland (Müller-Beck 1965:103–119; Pétrequin and Pétrequin 1988:121–123).

The above five specimens show some unifacial or bifacial edge chipping. In two cases, FS 23 (Pl. 71), FS 118 (Pl. 66), the chipping is accompanied by scoring, which resulted from use. Most of these tools were probably hafted with the plane of the stone head perpendicular to the long axis of the haft, although an attachment to a haft parallel to the tool's working edge can not be excluded (see discussion above). This does not seem to apply to FS 751 (Fig. 17), which has a strongly asymmetrical profile as well as oblique scars in different directions on both faces—a use-wear pattern that suggests that the edge was used in different directions at different times. This kind of chipping in combination with the scalar breakage of the proximal part indicates that FS 751 was used in indirect percussion (Perlès, personal communication 7/2000).

Three larger specimens, FS 38 (Pl. 76), FS 212 (Pl. 70), and FS 116 (Pl. 64), have a dull, rounded, chipped edge. One of them, FS 38, has a long edge (indeed, the longest in the whole Acut group), which is rounded for 3.3 cm and sharp for the remaining 1.5 cm. Both edge parts have some chipping, as well as some polish, although there is no doubt that they were used differently. With its long edge, FS 38 may have been suitable for hide dressing.[47]

FS 1 (Pl. 67), with a lopsided edge in plan view, must have been used with pressure, rather than percussion, and, moreover, obliquely, rather than perpendicularly, in relation to the worked material. Otherwise, only a few millimeters of the edge length would have been in contact with the worked material.

Finally, there are a few instances of recycling of larger specimens. In a couple of cases, the cutting edge was at some point used, not in a linear, but in a diffused percussive mode: FS 229 (Pl. 85), FS 430 (Fig. 18). These tools were, in other words, used as hammerstones, a use that caused the destruction of the acute working edge and the development of a rounded, battered surface. It is hard to understand why these Acut were turned into hammerstones. Perhaps their users no longer needed Acut or perhaps it was later users that changed their function. In two other cases, it is the proximal end that was apparently used in an active percussive mode: FS 212 (Pl. 70), FS 226 (Pl. 77). In some other tools, both the working edge and the proximal end were at some point used in that manner: FS 159 (Pl. 75), FS 374.

Unlike the small Acut, the size and use wear of the larger specimens leave no doubt of their practical functions. Yet the polished appearance of some of them, e.g., FS 117 (Fig. 19, Pl. 65), makes it likely that they had symbolic, ceremonial, or ritual dimensions as well.

Epilogue

The excavations at Franchthi yielded 88 Acut. They come from undisturbed or, more commonly, mixed Neolithic deposits or disturbed deposits that yielded Neolithic as well as some pre- and post-Neolithic material. None comes from a stratified Palaeolithic or Mesolithic deposit and there is no indication that such tools were made or used prior to the Neolithic period. The negligible quantity of post-Neolithic material at Franchthi (Dengate 1999) makes it equally unlikely that cutting edge tools were used at the site after the Neolithic. Serpentinite, the material of which most Acut are made, was not used for ground stone tools (above, chapter 2), and perhaps only rarely used for ornaments (Miller 1997:96–97, 129–133) in the pre-Neolithic times. The techniques of pecking and grinding were known to the pre-Neolithic inhabitants of Franchthi, but apparently not used in the *chaîne opératoire* later used for Acut. Thus, the Neolithic Acut assemblage at Franchthi represents a new industry that employed a new raw material and a new *chaîne opératoire*. These innovations can be used to support the argument—formulated on the basis of other Franchthi materials, and especially, geostratigraphy (see Farrand 2000: 96–97; Hansen 1991:174–183; Perlès 2001:39–41)—that the Neolithic culture at Franchthi is not a local evolution from a Mesolithic background but rather an exogenous development probably related to the arrival of a new group.

The introduction of a new tool, the employment of a new material, and a new technology, all point to an activity or activities first undertaken at the beginning of the Neolithic. It is not possible to say whether the scarcity of EN specimens in the Acut assemblage is representative (see above). If it is representative, however, it would suggest that the activity/ies in question were not central to the life of the Franchthi community during EN (i.e., at least the first 400 years of the Neolithic occupation).[48] It would, moreover, rule out the possibility that the activity for which Acut were first introduced to the site was tree-felling, a popular hypothesis based on the assumption that these tools were necessary to new farming communities for land clearing purposes. In this case Franchthi would be similar to other Greek Neolithic sites with small numbers of specimens dated to the beginning of the Neolithic (see Moundréa-Agrafioti 1981:244–245, 1992:175; Perlès 2001:231–232). Most tools from later phases at Franchthi were probably not used for tree-felling either given their dimensions, the properties of the raw materials, and the paleoenvironmental data. A number of Acut may have been used to clear shrubbery, work wood, butcher animals, process hides, or for tasks related to pottery production. Their use as weapons for killing animals or humans can not be ruled out, although no pertinent evidence has been identified at Franchthi (or other Greek Neolithic sites).[49] Nevertheless, there are quite a few specimens too small even for these tasks. Franchthiotes were certainly able to procure raw materials of better quality and larger dimensions through their own expeditions or through the exchange networks that brought, among others, obsidian and honey flint (used for chipped stone tools: Perlès 1989, 2004), andesite (this volume and Runnels 1981, 1985), and marble (used for figurines and vases: Herz 1992; Talalay 1993:12; van Andel and Vitaliano 1987:20) to the site. Yet they chose not to. This suggests that the qualities of the raw material were not inadequate for the uses intended for these tools or important enough to force them to do so. These points, along with features not justified on utilitarian grounds, may indicate that the symbolic/non-utilitarian functions of these artifacts were at least as, if not more, important than their practical ones. It is perhaps in this context that we should see a possible ritual killing of some small specimens.

2. Active discoidal tools (Adisc)

Introduction

Summarized information on all Active discoidal tools, or Adisc, is listed in Table 4.8. Drawings of three specimens appear in Figures 20–22. Photographs of several specimens are found in Plates 86–96 on the CD, folder: Neolithic/Active/Adisc.

The Franchthi ground stone tool assemblage includes many specimens with active diffused abrasive wear on their faces. Those that I call Active discoidal tools, however, stand out clearly as a group within the variety of specimens with this use wear, because they generally have a circular or elliptical plan and planoconvex or lenticular sections, a single, open work face, and similar raw material and size. These commonalities are accompanied by others that have to do with their chronological and spatial distribution. I should note here that there are specimens in the group of Active square-circular tools discussed below (this chapter) that also have a roughly circular or elliptical plan. These, however, are as a rule smaller than Adisc; have usually roughly rectangular sections, two work faces, and used peripheries; and their raw materials are different from those used for Adisc. That is why I decided to keep them separate from Adisc.

The Adisc group comprises 24 specimens. Nineteen are complete or almost complete, five are fragmentary. Sixteen were recovered inside the cave, eight on Paralia (Table 4.8). The horizontal distribution of Adisc in each of the two sectors of the site is very limited. The specimens with a cave provenience come mainly from the cluster of trenches in the rear portion of the excavated area (A, FA, FAN, FAS, FF1). Only one specimen, FS 113 (Pl. 86) comes from a trench close to the cave mouth (G1), but, since it was excavated in the first unit, it can be considered a surface find. As for the Paralia specimens, all were excavated in the northernmost trench L5, and mainly from its NE section (L5NE) (Table 4.8). It is tempting to see the limited horizontal distribution of Adisc as an indication that they were recovered in the general areas in which they had been used. As will become evident below, however, such an hypothesis may not be suitable for the specimens found on Paralia.

Contextual associations with dated ceramics or lithics yielded secure and probable dates for 15 specimens. Thirteen are securely assigned to FN, and two are assigned probable FN dates (Table 4.8). The remaining nine specimens were excavated in disturbed deposits that yielded Neolithic and some pre- and post- Neolithic material too (see Perlès 2004:6–7; Vitelli 1993:31–34, 1999:7–9, 17). Given their similarities with specimens dated to FN, I consider them also here as Neolithic and this is the date assigned to them in Table 4.8. I would indeed suggest that they were made, used, and discarded in the course of FN, given the homogeneity of the Adisc group in general; the fact that the rear of the excavated portion of the cave and the northernmost part of the Paralia, from which all but FS 113 (mentioned above) derive, are the two areas that yielded most of the evidence of FN occupation at Franchthi (Vitelli 1999:15–19); as well as the fact that, with the same exception, all these specimens were retrieved from units that yielded FN pottery. If the impression of a limited chronological distribution is accurate, it may argue for the involvement of these tools in specialized activities, an idea reinforced by their homogeneous use wear and standardized raw material, size, and shape.

Table 4.8. Active discoidal tools (Adisc).

Name	Trench:Unit	Prov.	Pres.	Material	Date	L	W	T	L/W	Illustr.
FS 14	A:24	C	c	calcar. sand.	FN	14.5	14.5	4.5	1.00	Fig. 21, Pl. 90
FS 113	G1:1	C	c	calcar. sand.	Neol.	14.6	12.6	4.4	1.15	Pl. 86
FS 121	FF1:6	C	c	calcar. sand.	Neol.	14.1	11.3	3.3	1.24	
FS 187	FA:8	C	c	calcar. sand.	Neol.	13.2	11.1	3.6	1.18	
FS 188	FA:6	C	c	calcar. sand.	Neol.	14.7	12.3	5.5	1.19	Pl. 91
FS 258	FAN:59	C	c	calcar. sand.	FN	11.9	9.5	3.6	1.25	Pl. 95
FS 260	FA:49	C	f	calcar. sand.	Neol.	12.1	6.3	3.3	n/ap	
FS 299	FAN:91	C	f	calcar. sand.	(FN)	12.8	7.9	3.6	n/ap	
FS 300	FAN:91	C	c	calcar. sand./congl.	(FN)	13.9	11.2	3.4	1.24	Pl. 87
FS 304	FAS:61	C	c	calcar. sand.	FN	16.5	15.1	4.0	1.09	
FS 317	FAS:69	C	c	calcar. sand.	FN	11.1	9.3	3.0	1.19	Fig. 22, Pl. 96
FS 575	L5:2	P	f	calcar. sand.	FN	11.1	7.4	4.3	n/ap	
FS 595	L5NE:7	P	f	calcar. sand.	FN	12.1	9.4	3.3	n/ap	
FS 596	L5NE:15	P	c	calcar. sand.	FN	14.0	11.1	4.3	1.26	Pl. 94
FS 598	L5NE:15	P	c	calcar. sand./congl.	FN	14.3	10.3	3.9	1.38	
FS 604	L5NE:18	P	f	calcar. sand.	FN	12.5	9.1	3.5	n/ap	
FS 608	L5NE:19	P	c	calcar. sand.	FN	14.2	14.2	3.6	1.00	Pl. 93
FS 621	L5NE:33	P	c	calcar. sand.	Neol.	13.9	11.9	3.0	1.16	
FAN:61	FAN:61	C	c	congl.	FN	16.5	16.0	5.1	1.03	
FAN:61/1	FAN:61	C	c	calcar. sand./congl.	FN	14.3	11.1	2.8	1.28	Fig. 20, Pl. 88
L5NE:19/25	L5NE:19	P	c	calcar. sand./congl.	FN	14.3	13.7	4.4	1.04	
S 18	FA:41	C	c	calcar. sand./congl.	Neol.	14.2	12.8	3.7	1.10	Pl. 89
S 19	FA:37	C	c	calcar. sand.	Neol.	14.0	12.5	5.5	1.12	Pl. 92
S 22	FA:33A	C	c	calcar. sand.	Neol.	11.7	10.7	3.7	1.09	

KEY: Prov.=Provenience, Pres.=Preservation, L=Length, W=Width, T=Thickness, L/W=length/width ratio, Illustr.=illustration, C=Cave, P=Paralia, c=complete, f=fragmentary, calcar. sand=calcareous sandstone, congl.=conglomerate, n/ap=non-applicable, calcar. sand./congl.=calcareous sandstone combined with conglomerate, FN=Final Neolithic, (FN)=probable Final Neolithic, Neol.=Neolithic, Pl.=plate, Fig.=figure

Raw material and manufacture

Macroscopic study of the raw material used for Adisc shows a preference for calcareous sandstone, a relatively soft and gritty material, of sometimes low cohesiveness and often of creamish color (Table 4.8). All but five tools are made in this material, suggesting that this may have been crucial for the particular function/s Adisc served. In four of the exceptions the selected material combined calcareous sandstone with conglomerate in such a way that the work face is in calcareous sandstone while the dorsal unutilized face is in conglomerate: FS 300 (Pl. 87), FS 598, FAN:61/1 (Fig. 20, Pl. 88), S 18 (Pl. 89). It is plausible that the material for these specimens was obtained at a single source either in a series of visits or in one raw material acquisition episode. The calcareous sandstone/conglomerate combination was perhaps chosen because the conglomerate gave the dorsal face an anomalous configuration that facilitated holding. Or it may have been an accidental choice simply related to the particular source exploited. The fifth and last exception, FAN:61, is made solely of conglomerate. For this reason, because it is the only specimen to have two work faces, and has additional evidence of passive percussive use, I consider it marginal in the Adisc group.

The raw material of FS 14 (Fig. 21, Pl. 90), FS 187, and FS 260, was obtained in cobble form, as suggested by the presence of natural water-rolled areas on the dorsal unutilized face. Suitable cobbles were probably available in the river or stream beds of the region or along the beach, which, during FN, was no farther than 500 m from the site (Vitelli 1999:1). The material I studied from Franchthi does not include unmodified cobbles of either plain calcareous sandstone or calcareous sandstone combined with conglomerate. However, some of the sandstone cobbles mentioned by Wilkinson and Duhon (1990:11) as found in the talus north of trench L5 (see Popen, chapter 3), may have been of a type, size, and shape appropriate for Adisc.

I detected no water-rolled surfaces on the remaining specimens. For some of them the lack of such surfaces may be the result of obliteration by the manufacturing process. For most tools, however, I believe it implies a different raw material acquisition strategy, in the context of which blanks were extracted from outcrops. This hypothesis is even more plausible given that the kind of sandstone used for Adisc is relatively soft and easy to work. The tools employed to extract these blanks need not have been anything more sophisticated than unmodified cobbles used in an active percussive mode. Such cobbles could have been picked up, used, and discarded at the source, never making it into the site. Outcrops that could have been exploited are found in the flysch formation that underlies the Franchthi-Ermioni region. Flysch outcrops are now rare in this region as a result of the extensive alluvium cover, but they were probably more common during the Neolithic (Vitaliano 1987:14–15).

The techniques used to shape the raw materials obtained through one or another acquisition strategy consist of flaking/chipping and pecking. Their traces are visible mainly on the periphery and the dorsal face of these tools. More specifically, the periphery of some specimens carries flaking/chipping marks. These were formed as the manufacturers trimmed the periphery of the blanks to give them the desired more or less circular or elliptical shape: FS 14 (Fig. 21, Pl. 90), FS 300 (Pl. 87), FAN:61/1 (Fig. 20, Pl. 88), S 18 (Pl. 89), S 22. In a few cases, flake scars show on the dorsal face; see FS 188 (Pl. 91), FS 300 (Pl. 87), S 19 (Pl. 92), but most often this face carries only traces of pecking; see FS 14 (Fig. 21, Pl. 90), FS 113 (Pl. 86). On the other hand, the pecking marks seen on the work face of four specimens, FS 14 (Fig. 21, Pl. 90), FS 113 (Pl. 86), FS 121, and S 18 (Pl. 89), are probably not from manufacture; if they were, they would imply that the work face was not much used, which does not seem to be the case. I consider these pecking marks, then, as evidence of resharpening. However, if the work faces of Adisc do not carry traces of manufacture, their flat (or at most lightly convex) configuration suggests that it was they, and not the more convex dorsal faces, that were subjected to the most extensive/intensive manufacturing process. The relevant evidence (consisting, presumably, of pecking marks and flake scars) must have been eliminated by the work faces' subsequent use.

No byproducts of the manufacturing process were recovered at the site. This may have to do with a tendency on the part of Adisc producers to carry out the manufacturing stages that leave an archaeological signature (i.e., flaking) at the sources and/or at an unexcavated area of the site or its vicinity (see also Popen, chapter 3). If their raw material is, as I suggested earlier, local, these tools could not have been imported to the site from other areas or come along with their users from outside the region.

Technomorphological characteristics

The impression of standardization emerging from the study of raw material is reinforced by the study of Adisc sizes. The 19 complete specimens show a small length range, from 11.1 to 16.5 cm (Tables 4.8–4.9). Their width range is also small, from 9.3 to 16.0 cm (Tables 4.8, 4.10). These lengths and widths could have allowed comfortable holding (with one or, in some cases, both hands) during use.

The picture, however, becomes more complicated when the dimension of thickness is added. The thickness of the complete specimens ranges from 2.8 to 5.5 cm (Tables 4.8, 4.11). Eleven of the nineteen complete specimens are less than 4.0 cm thick. As I can tell from my attempts to simulate an abrasive use, these specimens are too thin for a comfortable grip during use. The problem of holding is, indeed, exacerbated by the particular Adisc morphology: these tools tend to show their maximum thickness in the center, becoming gradually thinner towards the periphery; see FS 113 (Pl. 86), FS 608 (Pl. 93). The fact that many specimens appear dysfunctional suggests that they were originally thicker, that they were intensively/extensively used, and that they are now exhausted. The exhausted state of these specimens sheds light on the conditions of their discard: they were not discarded after an accidental breakage or because the users abandoned the site, but rather because they were worn out. I would assume that the exhausted tools had an original (pre-use) thickness of at least 5.0 cm.

Adisc show little variation in plan. These tools were fashioned in shapes that tend to have both axes more or less equal: the circular/elliptical, and in two cases, the subsquare and the polygonal: FS 14 (Fig. 21, Pl. 90), FS 113 (Pl. 86), FS 188 (Pl. 91), S 19 (Pl. 92). This rule does not apply to FS 598, which is subrectangular. I decided to include this tool in the Adisc group because of its

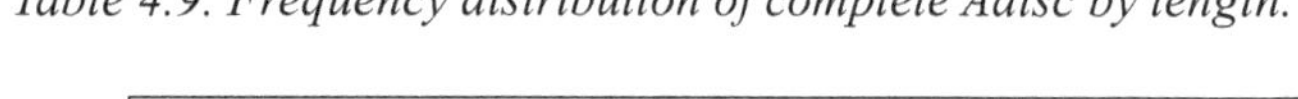
Table 4.9. Frequency distribution of complete Adisc by length.

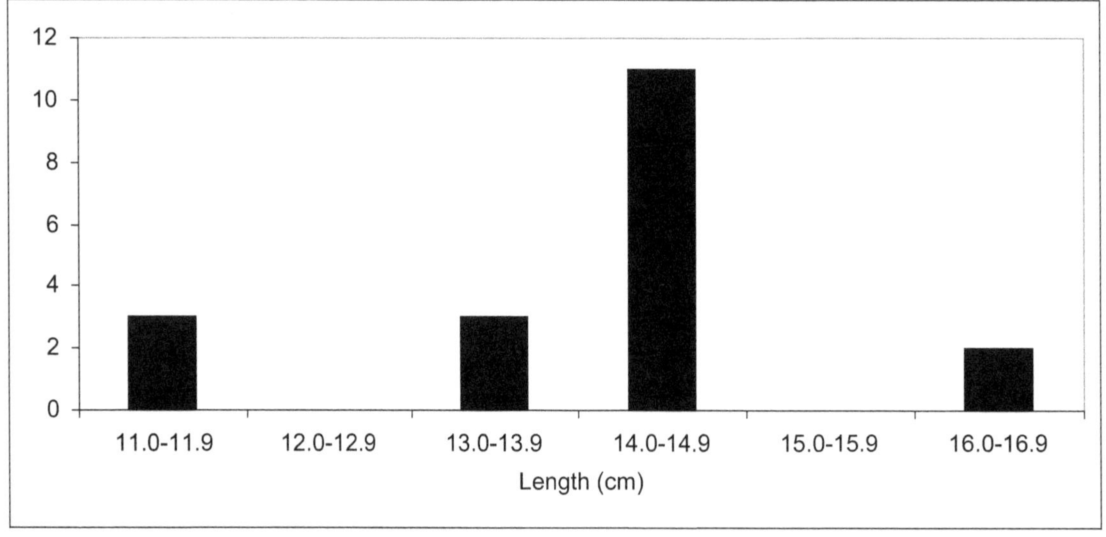

Table 4.10. Frequency distribution of complete Adisc by width.

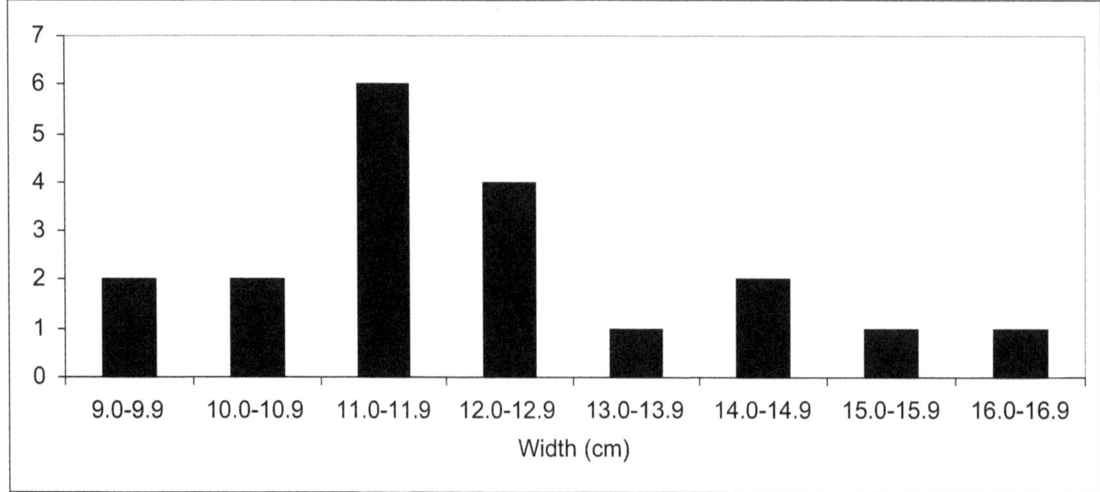

similarities in raw material (calcareous sandstone combined with conglomerate), size, use wear, and provenience/date (L5NE, FN) with more typical members of this group.

The preference for shapes that tend to have both axes more or less equal is reflected in the very low length/width ratios among the complete specimens. These range from 1.00 to 1.39 (average: 1.16) (Tables 4.8, 4.12). The limited shape variation suggests standardization and use of these tools for a short period of time, an impression reinforced by the relative absence of evidence for secondary uses.

The work faces are flat, e.g., FS 113 (Pl. 86), or lightly convex, e.g., FS 14 (Fig. 21, Pl. 90), FS 188 (Pl. 91), FAN:61/1 (Fig. 20, Pl. 88). The light convexity of some work faces seems to be the byproduct of use rather than the intended result of manufacture, implying that all Adisc work faces were made initially flat. The dorsal, unutilized face tends to be rounded or generally convex with an anomalous surface, giving the tools roughly planoconvex or lenticular sections: FS 14 (Fig. 21, Pl. 90), FS 113 (Pl. 86), FS 608 (Pl. 93), FAN:61/1 (Fig. 20, Pl. 88). In two cases, however, FS 188 (Pl. 91) and FS 596 (Pl. 94), the dorsal face has a ridge in the middle, making the longitudinal section planoconvex or lenticular, the transverse, triangular. The ridge of FS 596 seems to be part of the original cobble; that of FS 188 seems to be the product of manufacture. Whether natural or artificial, this ridge seems to facilitate holding the tool during use. If so, it is unclear why such a configuration was not provided for more specimens. I have in mind here tools such as FS 14 (Fig. 21, Pl. 90) and FS 113 (Pl. 86), which, despite the fact that they are about 4.5 cm thick, are not easy to hold

Table 4.11. Frequency distribution of complete Adisc by thickness.

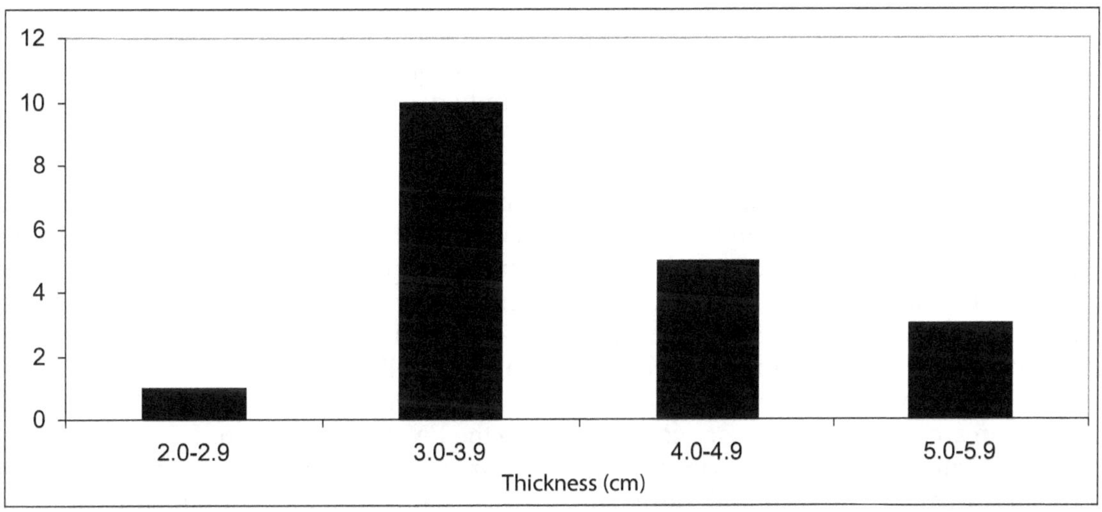

Table 4.12. Frequency distribution of complete Adisc by length/width ratio.

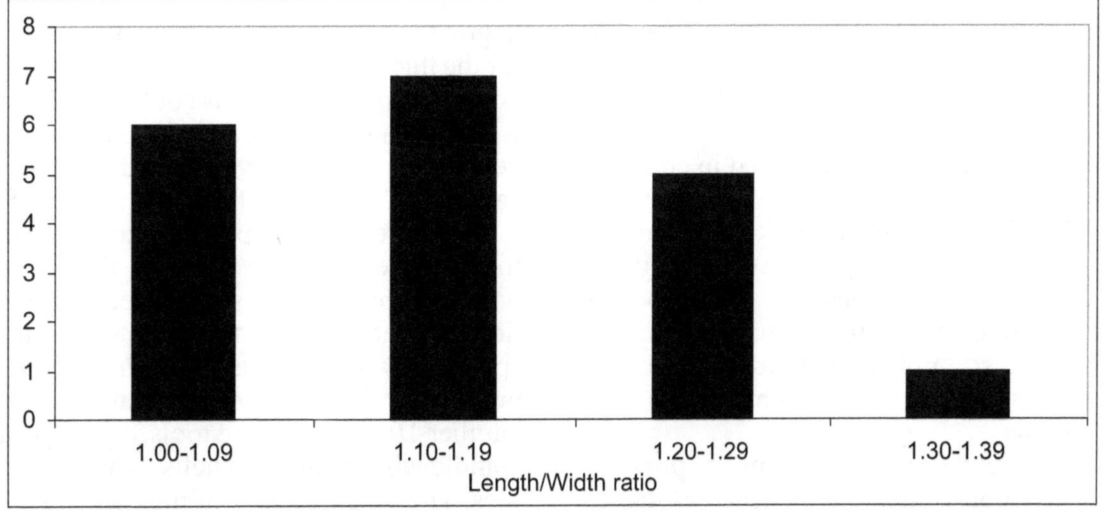

for use: their rounded dorsal face is too regular to grasp without finger grips.

Aspects of use

With two exceptions (FS 258 and FAN:61), Adisc were used with only one face and in an exclusively active, diffused, abrasive mode. The work faces of these tools are open, with a maximum dimension of 11.0–16.5 cm and, thus, in general larger than those of tools belonging to the two active groups I discuss below (this chapter) as Active rectangular tools and Active square or circular tools. I assume that the relatively large, open shape of the work faces of Adisc was crucial for the functions of these tools. Such faces are capable of handling a larger amount of worked material at once or affecting a larger surface than would smaller faces. This might explain why such a face morphology was selected by Adisc manufacturers/users.

The active diffused abrasive use wear of the work faces consists mainly of (discontinuous) smoothing that extends from edge to edge—the result of the movement of the work face over a passive surface. Given the generally circular or elliptical plan of most of these tools, one would perhaps expect the movement of the work faces during use to have been rotary or to have followed a variety of directions. Specific features, however, suggest that this was most often reciprocal. More specifically, the work face of FS 14 (Fig. 21, Pl. 90) shows a light convexity that follows a single axis; the work face of FS 300 (Pl. 87) shows scratches in a single direction; those of FS 595 and FS 608 (Pl. 93) have a certain area at the edges more continuously smoothed than the rest of the surface—this can only be interpreted as the result of consistent application of extra pressure on this particular spot; finally, the ridge crossing the dorsal face of FS 188 (Pl. 91) and FS 596 (Pl. 94) points to a reciprocal movement of the work face as well. In specimens with one axis slightly longer than the other, the reciprocal movement took place against the longest axis.

Could the passive surfaces used in conjunction with Adisc have been provided by Popen (chapter 3)? This is highly unlikely; if for no other reason than because there are extremely few Popen (four) dated to FN and thus contemporary with Adisc. Given the gritty texture of the raw material, it is also unlikely that Adisc were used in food processing, perhaps in combination with wooden boards.

Can context shed some light on possible Adisc uses? Good contextual evidence exists for seven specimens and comes from the FN deposits in the northernmost part of Paralia.[50] FN activities in this area left behind an interesting, if puzzling, formation, consisting of four shallow and two deeper pits excavated within L5 and L5NE. Most of these pits lack clearly recognizable boundaries and the relationship to each other is uncertain (Vitelli 1999:19, 90). The sediments of these deposits are distinguished from other sediments on Paralia and elsewhere at the site by their very high proportion of calcium carbonate, some of which appears in the form of very white clumps (Vitelli 1999:19; Wilkinson and Duhon 1990:44–46, 147–148).[51] It is not possible to say whether the high quantities of calcium carbonate derive from burning lime or crushing calcite, limestone, or shell (see Vitelli 1999:69). What is clearer, however, is, that white lime 'played an important role in FCP5 [FN] activities. In addition to use as a pigment, perhaps for the thick crusts on pots, and definitely for some painted decoration, it was sometimes mixed with clay to make the "smear" mixture used to glue broken pots. It was also used for whitewash, applied in multiple coats to pots of all sizes ...' (Vitelli 1999:90). The powdery white lime coatings and that used for painted decoration are too fine to have been ground mechanically and almost certainly represent burned lime. The thick white crusts on pots, on the other hand, have a granular crystalline texture that suggests finely ground rock rather than a plaster-like mixture made from burned lime (Vitelli 1999:69).

It is tempting to suggest that the Adisc found in the FN pit formation of L5 and L5NE were used to mix the lime with water and then the hydrated lime with the sand, ground limestone, or other material added to increase the lime's strength and volume (see Kingery, David, Vandiver, and Prickett 1988:221–222; see also Dubreuil 2002:124); and/or to grind a carbonate-rich rock to be used as material for the thick white crusts. It is, however, hard to see how these rather thin tools could have been used to work the caustic material that quicklime is. Moreover, neither of the above uses can explain the light convexity of the work face of a number of Adisc.

There is, perhaps, a reason that it is hard to associate the Adisc found in the pit formation with lime production: simply because this formation may not represent the context of use. More specifically, the excavation of the pits yielded not only Adisc but a variety of materials, including another 10 ground stone tools,[52] pottery, about 20 spindle whorls, lithics, shells, bones, and sea pebbles. The heterogeneity of the contents of the pits makes it likely that these were initially dug to burn lime, but later served as a place for depositing or discarding material that had been already used on various parts of Paralia (Vitelli 1999:90–91; see also Perlès 2004:118). This scenario may not illuminate the uses of the Paralia Adisc, but can at least explain how they ended up in the pit formation of L5 and L5NE.

I should mention here that one of the specimens found in the pit formation, L5NE:19/25, shows clear red traces on its work face. Interestingly, the pits are also rich in smectite, a clay mineral found in FN pottery (Vitelli 1999:65; Wilkinson and Duhon 1990:36, 44–46). On this basis, it has been suggested that they contained disintegrated FN pots/sherds (the short, low temperature firings used by FN potters produced pots fragile and prone to disintegration) or raw clay supplies intended for use in pottery making (Vitelli 1999:65). It is possible that L5NE:19/25 was used in grinding clay either exclusively or after having been used in another abrasive task.

No comparable contextual evidence exists for the specimens excavated inside the cave, but the similarities between the cave and Paralia specimens suggest that they had similar uses, whatever these may have been. I would indeed have argued that these tools participated in the very same activities, were it not for the fact that the study of both pottery and lithics suggests that the FN deposits of the two sectors of the site are not contemporary with each other, but rather belong to slightly different subphases (Perlès 2004:129; Vitelli 1999:89-90). In this light, I can only argue that the Adisc group points to a close affinity between the groups that occupied the site during these subphases, and to a continuity of the activities in which they were involved.

Whatever the uses of Adisc were, the characteristics of this assemblage suggest that they were probably intensive and rather specialized. The specialized outlook fits both the impression Perlès has for FN lithics and the large numbers of specialized artifacts, such as spindle whorls (Perlès 2004:129–130). For Vitelli (1999:99–104), in FN the site was used during brief visits for gatherings of a ceremonial character. Although the characteristics of the Adisc group may support Vitelli's hypothesis of brief visits, nothing in Adisc points to a use in ritual activities. The possibility, nevertheless, that these tools were used to prepare artifacts or substances that were involved in such contexts cannot be ruled out.

I close this subchapter with three specimens that seem to represent cases of recycling: FAN:61, FS 258, and FS 317. FAN:61 was used in an active abrasive mode on not only one, but two faces. After it was so used, it was apparently employed in a percussive mode, as suggested by a small depression in the center of both faces. The secondary percussive use was probably passive: the work faces of FAN:61 are about 16.0 cm in both length and width and an active percussive use would have been inconvenient. FS 258 (Pl. 95) was used in an active abrasive mode at least on one face. The ill-defined depression in its center (measuring 3.8×2.9×0.4 cm) and the more regular, almost circular one in the center of the other face (measuring 3.4×3.2×0.5 cm) represent evidence of secondary use, in a passive or active percussive mode (see also Active square or circular tools below, this chapter). In the case of FS 317 (Fig. 22, Pl. 96), recycling seems to have involved a process of redesigning. This tool has one work face used in an active abrasive mode. Its periphery was trimmed after the active abrasive use had taken place and in a way that made the tool too small for comfortable holding, at least by an average adult palm. I believe that FS 317 was originally used as other Adisc, but later redesigned and recycled to serve a non-tool function; it may, for example, have been used as a lid.

3. Active rectangular tools (Arect)

Introduction

Summarized information on all Active rectangular tools, or Arect, is listed in Table 4.13. Drawings of two specimens appear in Figures 23–24. Photographs of several specimens are found in Plates 97–111 on the CD, folder: Neolithic/Active/Arect.

The 19 specimens I discuss in this subchapter under the name Active rectangular tools have a generally subrectangular shape and a size good for use with one hand. These similarities are accompanied by others that have to do with raw material and use wear.

Sixteen Arect are complete or almost complete, three are fragmentary. Fifteen come from the cave, four from Paralia (Table 4.13). Four of the cave specimens were found close to hearths, a possible indication that they were used in a hearth context.

Contextual associations with dated ceramics or lithics yielded secure and probable dates for 12 Arect. Eight come from probable MN levels, one from a secure EN unit, one from a secure MN unit, and one from a probable LN unit (Table 4.13). The twelfth specimen, FS 256 (Fig. 23, Pl. 97), comes from an Upper Mesolithic unit (H1A:100) (see Perlès 1990:21), which is immediately below a pottery bearing unit (see Vitelli 1993:38) (Table 4.13). Since it is unlike any ground stone tool excavated in pre-Neolithic deposits, I consider it an intrusive Neolithic specimen. For the same reason, as well as because of the negligible quantity of post-Neolithic remains in general (Dengate 1999), I assume that the remaining seven specimens, found on the surface or excavated in disturbed deposits that yielded Neolithic and also some pre- and post- Neolithic material (see Perlès 2004:6–7; Vitelli 1993:31–34, 1999:7–9, 17), derive from the Neolithic component of the site too. They are all considered and treated here as Neolithic and this is the date assigned to them in Table 4.13.

Raw material and manufacture

With four exceptions, the raw material used for Arect consists of fine grained sandstone. The exceptions are less fine-grained sandstone of FS 297 (Pl. 98) and FS 771, metaquartzite of FS 132 (Pl. 99), and peridotite of FS 167 (Pl. 100) (Table 4.13). The heavy use of these tools has dramatically changed the form of the raw material, but the water-rolled texture of some unutilized surfaces, e.g., FS 84 (Pl. 103) and FS 848 (Pl. 104), as well as the curvilinear shape of most of the ends, e.g., FS 123 (Pl. 101), FS 125 (Pl. 102), FS 132 (Pl. 99), suggests that this consisted of river, stream, or beach cobbles. The cobbles may have been picked up at the same local river and stream beds or beaches where the similar looking sandstones used for most Popen were probably collected (see chapter 3).

Percussion marks that can be attributed to pecking are visible on unutilized parts of several Arect, an indication that some of the cobbles collected as raw material were subjected to a more or less extensive process of manufacture: see FS 84 (Pl. 103), FS 125 (Pl. 102), FS 256 (Fig. 23, Pl. 97), FS 774 (Pl. 106). Many more tools, however, do not carry such marks on areas not affected by use, suggesting perhaps that they are *a posteriori*. It is likely that the procurement of raw material aimed at the collection of cobbles not only of a particular type of rock, but also of a specific size and shape.

Table 4.13. Active rectangular tools (Arect).

Name	Trench:Unit	Prov.	Pres.	Material	Date	L	W	T	Illustr.
FS 53	G:19	C	c	sandstone	(MN)	13.2	7.3	3.6	Fig. 24, Pl. 105
FS 84	G:lot 28	C	c	sandstone	(MN)	11.0	6.5	5.0	Pl. 103
FS 95	FF1:6	C	c	sandstone	Neol.	9.5	4.9	3.1	Pl. 107
FS 110	G1:19	C	c	sandstone	(MN)	11.6	8.0	3.2	Pl. 108
FS 123	G1:9	C	c	sandstone	(MN)	11.1	6.7	3.9	Pl. 101
FS 125	G1:11	C	c	sandstone	(MN)	11.4	7.2	3.7	Pl. 102
FS 132	FF1:32	C	c	metaquartzite	(MN)	9.9	7.2	3.5	Pl. 99
FS 133	FF1:32	C	c	sandstone	(MN)	10.5	5.6	3.1	Pl. 109
FS 134	FF1:34	C	c	sandstone	(MN)	12.0	8.4	5.2	Pl. 110
FS 167	H:24	C	c	peridotite	Neol.	13.5	7.5	5.5	Pl. 100
FS 256	H1A:100	C	c	sandstone	Neol.	13.0	8.1	4.3	Fig. 23, Pl. 97
FS 297	FAN:119	C	c	sandstone	(LN)	12.1	8.4	4.3	Pl. 98
FS 771	PQ5:9	P	f	sandstone	Neol.	7.3	6.0	5.1	
FS 774	Q5S:216	P	c	sandstone	MN	11.1	7.7	5.8	Pl. 106
FS 786	Q5S:223	P	c	sandstone	EN	8.5	6.0	3.5	Pl. 111
FS 848	HTerrace:16	C	f	sandstone	Neol.	8.7	7.6	3.4	Pl. 104
FS 849	HTerrace:20	C	f	sandstone	Neol.	7.6	5.7	5.1	
S 6	Paralia surf.	P	c	sandstone	Neol.	10.6	7.5	3.3	
S 48	FA:34	C	c	sandstone	Neol.	11.5	7.0	3.9	

KEY: Prov.=Provenience, Pres.=Preservation, L=Length, W=Width, T=Thickness, Illustr.=illustration, C=Cave, P=Paralia, surf.=surface, c=complete, f=fragmentary, EN=Early Neolithic, MN=Middle Neolithic, (MN)=probable Middle Neolithic, (LN)=probable Late Neolithic, Neol.=Neolithic, Pl.=plate, Fig.=figure

Note: G:lot 28 refers to units G:19-24.

This goal may have been met more successfully in the case of the *a posteriori* specimens, less so in the case of the manufactured ones.

Technomorphological characteristics

The 16 complete specimens range from 8.5 to 13.5 cm in length, from 4.9 to 8.4 cm in width, and from 3.1 to 5.8 cm in thickness (Tables 4.13–4.16). The current thickness of the majority of Arect is less than 4.0 cm. As I can tell from trying to simulate an abrasive use of the faces of some of these specimens, such a thickness is too low for a comfortable grip during use. This is even more true, given the relatively small width of Arect in general: see FS 53 (Fig. 24, Pl. 105), FS 95 (Pl. 107), FS 110 (Pl. 108), FS 123 (Pl. 101), FS 125 (Pl. 102). Most Arect should, therefore, be considered exhausted for an abrasive use with the faces. However, these same tools are not worn out as regards other uses in which they were involved: an active abrasive use with the sides, and an active or passive percussive use with the faces, sides, or ends.

With two exceptions, FS 84 (Pl. 103) and FS 110 (Pl. 108), all complete specimens have a subrectangular plan. With four exceptions, FS 53 (Fig. 24, Pl. 105), FS 84 (Pl. 103), FS 167 (Pl. 100), and S 48, they are subrectangular in both longitudinal and transverse sections. However, this is a shape largely acquired through the intensive/extensive abrasive use of the faces and sides. Two of the exceptions, FS 110 and FS 84, illustrate my point: FS 110 is roughly trapezoidal in plan and subrectangular in both sections, having been used with both faces and one of the sides. If FS 110 had also been used with the second side, that, too, would have acquired the characteristic subrectangular plan of the other specimens in the Arect group. FS 84 is a water-rolled cobble with one flattened face. It is ovate in plan, and planoconvex in both sections, having been used primarily with one face and only slightly with the second face and one of the sides. If this tool had also been used intensively/extensively with the second face and both sides, like other specimens in this group, it, too, would have become subrectangular in plan and in both sections. FS 84, moreover, can serve as a guide for estimating the approximate original thickness of Arect. It is now 5.0 cm thick and can be comfortably held for abrasive use with the faces. Since one of the faces is already flattened, I assume that its original (pre-use) thickness was over 6.0 cm. Such a figure may be representative of the thickness of the cobbles used as Arect raw material.

Aspects of use

Arect are heavily used implements. They were used, reused, and recycled, as indicated by the multiple use wear visible throughout their surfaces. The use wear is both abrasive and percussive.

The abrasive wear is active and diffused. Given its extent—it has dramatically affected the shape of the cobbles used as raw materials—I consider it the result of the primary use of these tools. Consisting of more or less continuously smoothed surfaces, the abrasive wear is found in most cases on the two roughly parallel faces and the two roughly parallel sides, or, to be more accurate, it has produced them: e.g., FS 95 (Pl. 107), FS 123 (Pl. 101), FS 125 (Pl. 102), FS 133 (Pl. 109). The longitudinal sections of the Arect faces range from lightly convex to flat to slightly concave: for examples of the lightly convex configuration, see illustrated faces of FS 53 (Fig. 24, Pl. 105), FS 167 (Pl. 100), and FS 774 (Pl. 106); for examples of the flat configuration, see face B of FS 95 (Pl. 107) and FS 125 (Pl. 102); and for examples of the slightly concave configuration, see face A of FS 84 (Pl. 103), FS 95 (Pl. 107), and FS 125 (Pl. 102). All of the faces moved reciprocally during use, but not in the same direction. As suggested by subtle scratches seen on a number of them, most faces moved against their long axis, while a few seem to have moved along their long axis or diagonally: for scratches against the long axis, see illustrated face of FS 53 (Fig. 24, Pl. 105) and face A of FS 84 (Pl. 103); for scratches along the long axis, see both faces of FS 95 (Pl. 107); and for scratches diagonal to the long axis, see face A of FS 110 (Pl. 108) and illustrated face of FS 774 (Pl. 106). I doubt that the slightly concave configuration of some of the faces is the result of a passive use. The subtle scratches seen on the slightly concave face of FS 84 (Pl. 103) have a transverse direction. This means that if this face had served as a passive surface, it would have been crossed by active implements transversally. Holding this tool for such a use seems, however, very inconvenient as I realized when I tried to simulate it. I assume thus that the slightly concave faces of FS 84 and a few other Arect moved themselves reciprocally and against their long axis on convex passive surfaces.[53] The passive surfaces used in conjunction with those Arect faces that are flat or lightly convex, on the other hand, must have been flat or lightly concave respectively. The possibility, however, that the lightly convex configuration is the result of a rocking motion on flat passive surfaces can not be ruled out (see Adams 1997:8–9).

Table 4.14. Frequency distribution of complete Arect by length.

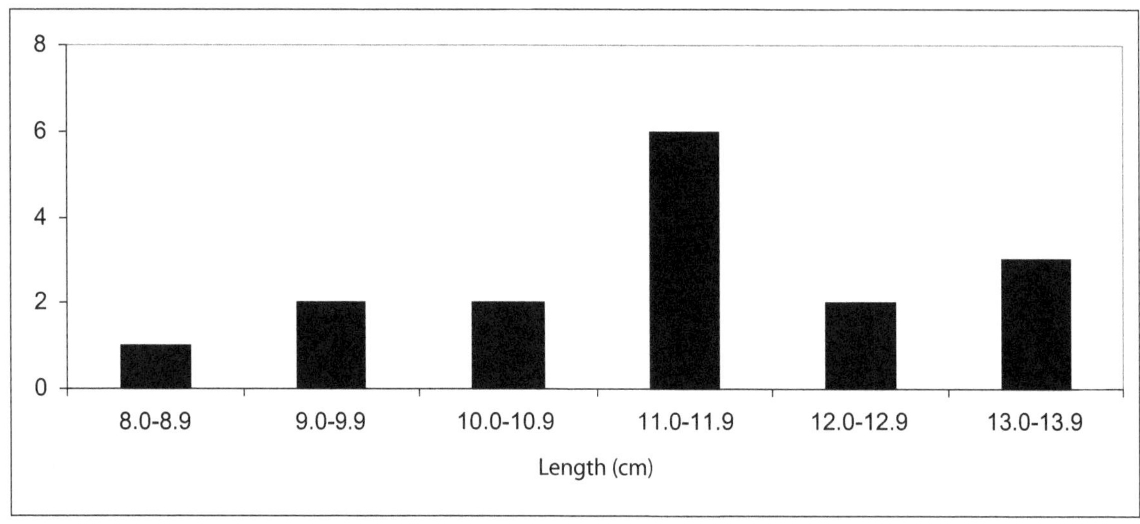

Table 4.15. Frequency distribution of complete Arect by width.

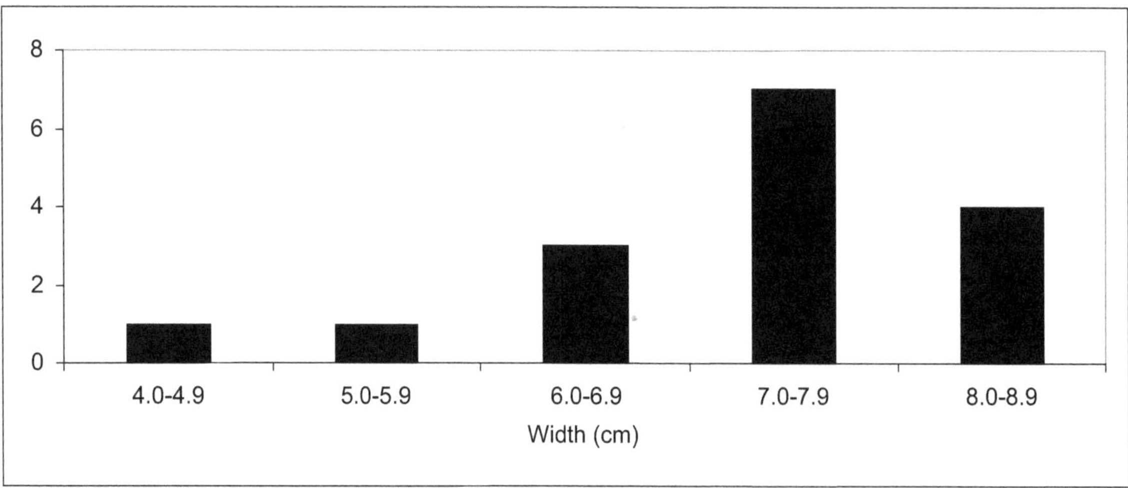

Table 4.16. Frequency distribution of complete Arect by thickness.

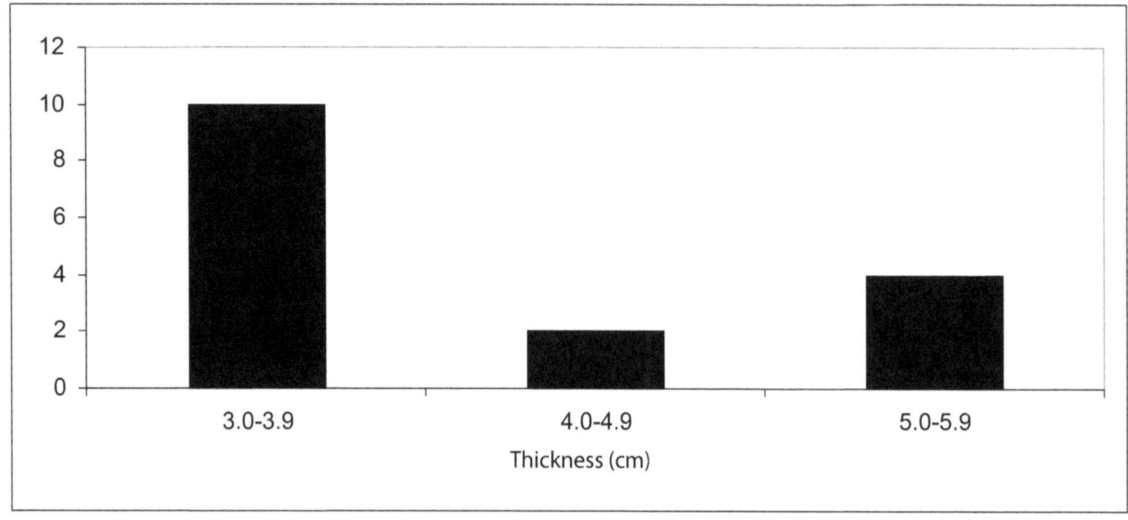

The sides of Arect were probably chosen for active abrasive use when the tools became too thin to be so used with the faces. These sides are narrow (about 3.0–3.5 cm wide), and flat or lightly convex: FS 95 (Pl. 107), FS 123 (Pl. 101), FS 125 (Pl. 102). Some are more, others less continuously smoothed. It is likely that the sides were used to process similar materials as the faces.

What was/were the active abrasive use/s in which both the faces and the sides of Arect were involved? Two specimens were found in the same units as two Popen: FS 110 (Pl. 108) and FS 173 (Pl. 30) in G1:19; FS 125 (Pl. 102) and FS 126 (Fig. 9) in G1:11. I doubt, however, that they were used together. Besides other reasons that have to do with the particular use wear of these specimens, the two Arect are shorter in length than the two Popen are wide (length of FS 125:11.4, width of FS 126:13.6; length of FS 110:11.6, width of FS 173:16.4). If they had been used together, the sides of the Popen work faces would not have been affected by use and would have had a different texture than the rest of the faces. This, however, is not the case. If my understanding is correct, Arect must have been used in conjunction with passive tools or surfaces of other materials (e.g., wood).

Arect have the right shape for grain-grinding, but their size is too small and the raw material perhaps too fine-grained for such a task. They may, however, have been adequate for grinding other materials, as suggested by the ethnoarchaeological literature. Tools of strikingly similar shapes, sizes, raw material, and with similarly smoothed surfaces are reported as being used in the village of Bata in Nepal in conjunction with passive abrasive stone tools (*meules à assaisonnement*) for grinding spices, plant foods other than grains, and small quantities of salt. The active tools (*molettes*) are *a posteriori*: the shape of the cobbles picked as raw material changes dramatically through the use of all surfaces. According to Baudais and Lundström-Baudais (2002:170–171), '*Celles qui sont encore neuves ont une section ovoide, mais plus elles vieillissent, plus la section évolue vers des formes subrectangulaires, carrées ou parfaitement circulaires selon la technique d'utilisation de chacun*'. As I suggested earlier, this is precisely what I believe is the case with Arect. The Nepalese tools are intensively used implements—their owners use them at least twice a day (Baudais and Lundström-Baudais 2002:170)—and such may very well have been the case with Arect. It is possible, then, that Arect, or some of them, were used in grinding some of the same substances as those ground with the Nepalese tools. I should note here that, according to the ethnographic and experimental record, ground stone tools of similar sizes and shapes to Arect are used in scraping off unwanted flesh, fat, and connective tissue from hides (Adams 1988; 1989a:269; Adams and Greenwald 1979:53–54; Hamon 2006:73; Dubreuil 2002:128, 189–191). Such tools, however, are made of medium to coarse grained sandstone, not fine-grained sandstone, which is the material of most Arect. Fine-grained sandstone, nevertheless, could have been adequate for an abrasive use in the last stage of hide cleaning—e.g., removing the epidermis—or in breaking the fibers aiming at increasing the softness and flexibility of the hide (see Hamon 2006:73, 99–102; Ibáñez Estévez and González Urquijo 1996:70).

Arect show substantial evidence of recycling. The same faces and sides that were used in an active diffused abrasive mode were often also used secondarily in a percussive mode. Percussive, moreover, is the primary mode of use of many of the ends of these tools. The percussive wear takes a variety of forms ranging from a few pits to a heavily battered surface. On a few faces, several pits formed a more or less linear pattern, probably the result of an active punctiform percussive use (as a mallet?): see, e.g., face B of FS 123 (Pl. 101). On some others, the pitting is limited to a central area, e.g., both faces of FS 132 (Pl. 99) and FS 256 (Fig. 23, Pl. 97). Yet others show in the center a more or less circular depression of U-shape section: FS 134 (Pl. 110), FS 786 (Pl. 111), FS 848 (Pl. 104). The central wear in both cases is probably the *a posteriori* result of (active or passive) percussive use (see Active square or circular tools, below, this chapter). Interestingly, some of the Nepalese *molettes* mentioned above were also used as nutcrackers (*casse-noix*) and as hammerstones (*marteaux*) for putting nails, causing the formation of a light depression in the center of the face (Baudais and Lundström-Baudais 2002:170). A use in nutcracking or hammering is possible for the Arect that carry central wear on their faces. Heavily battered surfaces, on the other hand, appear on some faces, sides, and ends, indicating an involvement in more heavy-duty percussion: see FS 53 (Fig. 24, Pl. 105), FS 133 (Pl. 109), FS 774 (Pl. 106), S 48.

I should finally mention in the context of recycling two specimens, FS 167 (Pl. 100) and FS 297 (Pl. 98), whose secondary wear on one of the ends gave them the appearance of a chopper. More specifically, these two tools have one of their ends chipped/flaked bifacially to form an acute edge, or, perhaps this edge was produced *a posteriori*, as a result of active percussive use (see Poissonnier 2002:146–147). The other end is battered from active percussive use and/or from involvement in indirect percussion. In the latter case, this end would have been struck by an active percussive tool so that the flaked/chipped edge attacked another passive component.

4. Active square or circular tools (Asquare-circ)

Introduction

Summarized information on Active square or circular tools, or Asquare-circ, is listed in Table 4.17. Drawings of a few specimens appear in Figures 25–30. Photographs are found in Plates 112–119 on the CD, folder: Neolithic/Active/Asquare-circ.

The group I discuss in this subchapter under the name Active square or circular tools comprises 14 specimens that have a roughly square or circular plan and a size good for use with one hand. The specimens with a circular plan are in general smaller than the Active discoidal tools described above (this chapter). Asquare-circ were primarily used in an active abrasive mode with both faces. I should note here that the term 'sides' in this context refers to the four narrow surfaces flanking the faces of specimens of a roughly square plan; 'periphery' to the curvilinear portion of the body between two faces of specimens of a roughly circular plan (see chapter 1).

Eleven tools are complete or almost complete, three are fragmentary. With the exception of one specimen found on Paralia, all were excavated inside the cave. Eleven of the thirteen cave specimens come from the rear of the excavated portion of the cave (FA, FAS, FF1). If not accidental, this limited distribution may reflect a spatial concentration for the uses of these tools.

Contextual associations with dated ceramics allowed the dating of only four specimens. Three are assigned a secure FN date, and one a probable FN date (Table 4.17). The remaining 10 specimens were found on the cave surface or excavated in disturbed deposits of the cave that yielded Neolithic as well as some pre- and post- Neolithic material (see Perlès 2004:6–7; Vitelli 1993:31–34, 1999:7–9, 17). No tools similar to Asquare-circ were found in stratified pre-Neolithic deposits, making it unlikely that these specimens originate in the pre-Neolithic component of the site. Since the post-Neolithic remains are, in general, negligible (Dengate 1999), I do not have any reason to view these 10 specimens as post-Neolithic either. I thus consider and treat them as Neolithic and this is the date assigned to them in Table 4.17. The fact that all the dated specimens come certainly or probably from FN, and that most of the specimens with no specific date were found in the rear of the excavated portion of the cave (the area that yielded most of the evidence of FN occupation inside the cave; Vitelli 1999:15–19), may be indications that all or most Asquare-circ were used and discarded during this particular phase.

Raw material and manufacture

The raw material used for Asquare-circ consists for the most part of relatively fine-grained sandstone. The individual grains of the sandstones used, however, are usually visible without magnification, making them less fine grained than those used as a rule for Arect. Other raw materials were used for three specimens: olivine gabbro for FF1:6E (Pl. 112), basalt for S 27, and perhaps metaandesite for FS 223 (Fig. 25, Pl. 113) (Table 4.17). The rounded appearance of the few unutilized surfaces (e.g., S 50) suggests that the raw material in most, if not all, cases, came in the form of water-worn cobbles. The sandstone cobbles were probably collected in local stream or river beds. They could also have been picked on the beach, which was not far from the site during the Neolithic.

Percussion pits that may be attributed to pecking of manufacture are visible on the periphery of FS 231 (Pl. 114). The chip/flake scars, on the other hand, that many Asquare-circ carry on their sides or periphery, seem to have cut used surfaces. They should thus be considered the byproduct of use rather than the result of manufacture; see FS 115 (Fig. 28, Pl. 117), FS 870 (Fig. 26), FF1:6B (Fig. 30, Pl. 119), and S 62 (Fig. 27, Pl. 116). Since most Asquare-circ surfaces have been heavily altered through use, it is not possible to determine how many of these tools were subjected to a process of manufacture and to what degree. It is therefore safe to say that some of the cobbles collected as raw material were converted to tools through manufacture. Others—perhaps, most—were not modified prior to use and thus represent *a posteriori* tools. In the latter case, extra effort must have been exerted during the procurement of raw material to locate cobbles of appropriate size and shape.

Technomorphological characteristics

The 11 complete Asquare-circ range from 7.9 to 11.0 cm in length, from 6.9 to 10.0 cm in width, and from 2.8 to 5.5 cm in thickness (Tables 4.17–4.20). The seven complete specimens that are less than 4.0 cm thick are too thin to be conveniently held for an abrasive use of the faces and thus should be considered exhausted, at least for such a use, e.g., FS 231 (Pl. 114), FS 870 (Fig. 26), S 62 (Fig. 27, Pl. 116). Their initial thickness must have been over 5.0 cm.

Given their roughly square or circular plans, Asquare-circ tend to have both axes more or less equal. This is reflected in the low length/width ratios, ranging from 1.01 to 1.27 among the complete specimens (Tables 4.17 and 4.21). Interestingly, the Adisc I discussed earlier (this chapter) and consider of FN origin also have a shape with two more or less equal axes. If my suspicion of a FN date for most or all Asquare-circ is accurate, this similarity suggests perhaps a certain cultural preference for this kind of shape in this particular phase. The two sections of Asquare-circ are usually (sub)rectangular, e.g., FS 115 (Fig. 28, Pl. 117), FS 870 (Fig. 26), more rarely (sub)trapezoidal, e.g., FS 318 (Fig. 29, Pl. 118), or planoconvex, e.g., FF1:6B (Fig. 30, Pl. 119).

Aspects of use

Asquare-circ are as heavily used as the Arect presented above (this chapter). Indeed the shape itself of Asquare-circ (as that of Arect) is largely the result of heavy use and reuse or recycling in an abrasive and/or percussive mode.

The two faces of most Asquare-circ were intensively/extensively used in an active diffused abrasive mode, as indicated by their more or less continuously smoothed texture and often flattened appearance. The faces range in shape from flat to convex, suggesting that they were abrasively used over flat or concave passive surfaces respectively. The possibility, however, that the convex configuration is the result of a rocking motion on flat passive surfaces can not be ruled out (see Adams 1997:8–9). At least some of the faces moved reciprocally over the passive surfaces, as inferred from subtle parallel scratches visible on them: FS 223 (Fig. 25, Pl. 113), face B of FS 115 (Fig. 28, Pl. 117) and S 72 (Pl. 115). With one exception, the faces moved perpendicularly over the passive surfaces. The exception is FF1:6B (Fig. 30, Pl. 119), which has two facets on the edges of face A—the result of a secondary active abrasive use that was oblique, not perpendicular as was the earlier abrasive use of the entire face. During the oblique use, the areas where the facets formed came into contact with the worked material at an angle. Interestingly, the two facets have a much rougher texture than the rest of the face, perhaps an indication that they were produced from processing a different material from that processed with the entire face. It is also possible, however, that the rougher texture resulted from a less intensive/extensive use. Face A of FF1:6B was used obliquely perhaps when a reciprocal movement over a passive surface, in a perpendicular mode, was no longer possible, because the tool had already become too thin.

Table 4.17. Active square or circular tools (Asquare-circ).

Name	Trench:Unit	Prov.	Pres.	Material	Date	L	W	T	L/W	Illustr.
FS 115	G1:5	C	c	sandstone	Neol.	9.1	8.1	3.8	1.12	Fig. 28, Pl. 117
FS 220	FA:35	C	c	sandstone	Neol.	11.0	8.6	2.8	1.27	
FS 223	FA:29	C	c	metaandesite?	Neol.	7.9	7.0	3.1	1.12	Fig. 25, Pl. 113
FS 231	FA:45	C	c	sandstone	FN	8.4	6.9	3.6	1.21	Pl. 114
FS 318	FAS:70	C	c	sandstone	FN	9.9	9.4	5.3	1.05	Fig. 29, Pl. 118
FS 360	FAS:83	C	f	sandstone	(FN)	8.4	7.3	3.9	n/ap	
FS 870	L5:61	P	c	sandstone	FN	8.6	7.8	3.4	1.10	Fig. 26
FF1:6B	FF1:6	C	c	sandstone	Neol.	10.8	10.0	3.8	1.08	Fig. 30, Pl. 119
FF1:6E	FF1:6	C	c	olivine gabbro	Neol.	9.1	9.0	4.9	1.01	Pl. 112
S 27	FA surf.	C	c	basalt	Neol.	9.5	8.4	5.5	1.13	
S 45	FA:30	C	f	sandstone	Neol.	10.3	7.4	3.3	n/ap	
S 50	FA:37	C	f	sandstone	Neol.	9.7	8.8	4.1	n/ap	
S 62	FA:33	C	c	sandstone	Neol.	9.8	9.2	3.5	1.06	Fig. 27, Pl. 116
S 72	H	C	c	sandstone	Neol.	10.2	8.7	4.9	1.17	Pl. 115

KEY: Prov.=Provenience, Pres.=Preservation, L=Length, W=Width, T=Thickness, L/W=length/width ratio, Illustr.=illustration, C=Cave, P=Paralia, surf.=surface, c=complete, f=fragmentary, FN=Final Neolithic, (FN)=probable Final Neolithic, Neol.=Neolithic, n/ap=non applicable, Pl.=plate, Fig.=figure

Some of the sides of the roughly square specimens and the periphery of a roughly circular one were also used in an active diffused abrasive mode: FS 115 (Fig. 28, Pl. 117), FS 231 (Pl. 114), FS 360, S 27, S 50, S 72 (Pl. 115). The sides, in particular—more or less flattened areas flanking the faces—were produced by such a use (see, e.g., FS 115, S 72). It is again plausible that the sides and periphery in question were employed when an abrasive use with the faces was no longer convenient.

It is unclear what the abrasive use/s of Asquare-circ was/were. I doubt, however, that Asquare-circ were so used systematically with Popen: as I argued for Arect, Asquare-circ are in general shorter in length than Popen are wide. If they had been used together, the sides of the Popen work faces would not have been affected by use and would thus have had a different texture from the rest of the faces. However, this is not the case. Moreover, if my suspicion of an FN origin for Asquare-circ is accurate, it offers additional support to the hypothesis that Asquare-circ were not used in conjunction with Popen: no more than four Popen were recovered from FN levels and only two of them were found in the cave, the main locus of discovery of Asquare-circ. Given their small sizes, I would also doubt that Asquare-circ were used in grinding grain. They could, nevertheless, have been used for grinding substances similar to those I suggested for Arect: spices, foods other than grains, and small quantities of salt. Other possibilities exist: two specimens, FS 223 (Fig. 25, Pl. 113) and S 27, show traces of red pigment on one or both faces, suggesting a use involving such a substance. The faces of FS 223, in particular, are also characterized by a greasy texture. They may have served for processing hides with the use of red ocher. Ocher could have been rubbed on the hide for decorative purposes or because of its antiseptic properties (see Hamon 2006:99–102; Ibáñez Estévez and González Urquijo 1996:70; González and Ibáñez 2002:75–76; Philibert 1993:133). Whatever the abrasive use/s may have been, the state of exhaustion of most specimens (at least for this kind of use and at least with the faces), may suggest that they were used rigorously in the context of intensive and specialized tasks. Such a profile reminds us of

Table 4.18. Frequency distribution of complete Asquare-circ by length.

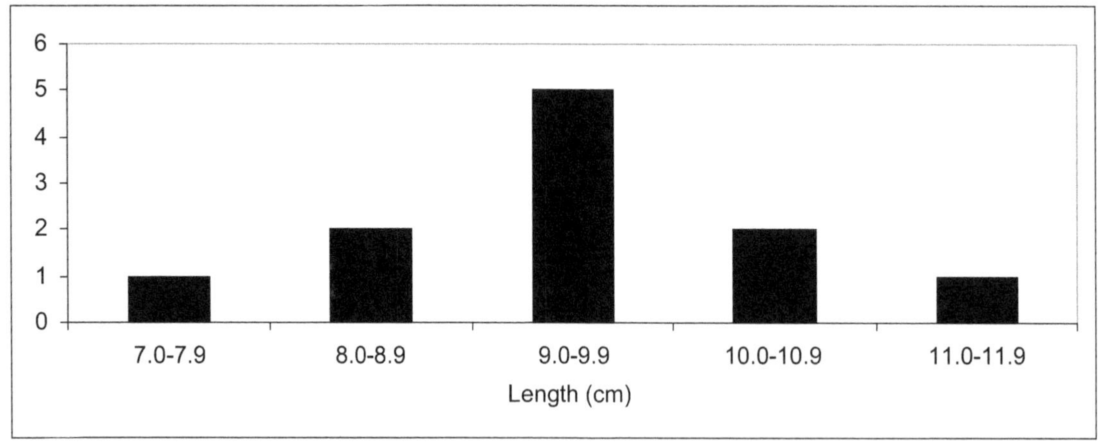

Table 4.19. Frequency distribution of complete Asquare-circ by width.

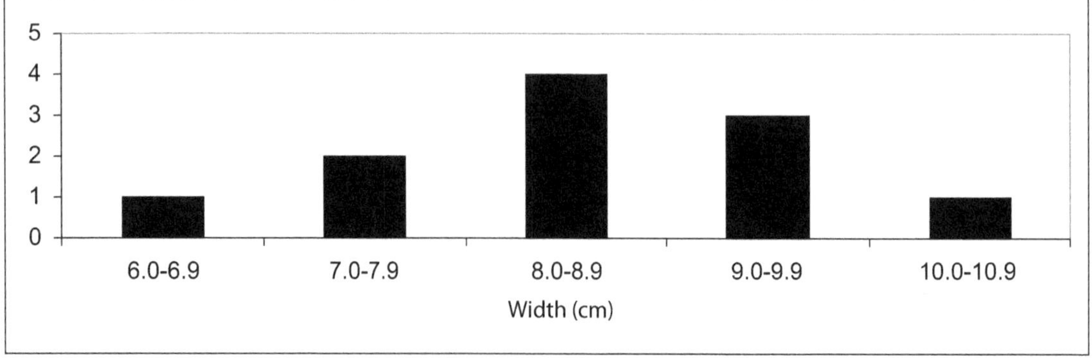

the impression given by Adisc and fits the general picture of FN Franchthi as the locus of specialized activities (see Perlès 2004:128–130).

In addition to the active abrasive wear, Asquare-circ show other traces on their faces and sides or peripheries. The traces seen in the center of the faces of a number of specimens vary from a few nicks, to a pitted area, to a rough and regular, more or less circular, U-shaped depression no more than 3.0–4.0 cm in diameter and up to 0.5 cm deep. Most often, the central traces are visible, albeit not equally strongly, on both faces; see FS 318 (Fig. 29, Pl. 118), S 62 (Fig. 27, Pl. 116), S 72 (Pl. 115). These traces cut through the abrasively-used surface and were thus produced after the active abrasive use of the faces. Since most Asquare-circ are currently exhausted for an active abrasive use with the faces, I assume that the central traces were formed on the faces when these could no longer be used in an active abrasive mode.

If it is evident that the nicks and the pitted areas represent use wear, what about the roughly circular depressions? Are these the intentional product of manufacture by pecking, the *a posteriori* result of use, or perhaps a combination of both? Comparable depressions found on North American tools of similar shapes and sizes as Asquare-circ have been interpreted as finger-grips, manufactured specifically to facilitate holding of the tool for active use with the sides/periphery (see e.g., Adams 2002:94–96; Holmes 1919:332; Woodbury 1954:90–93). In addition, tools with roughly circular depressions have been used as 'bead holders' by Pueblo Indians; the manufactured 'cups' hold the beads in place so that they can be drilled (Britt 1973). Yet the fact that, whenever depressions are found on both faces of Asquare-circ, one is deeper and more regular than the other, argues against the hypothesis that they are manufactured.

Tools with circular depressions are also known to have been used as spindle bases—the depressions serve as sockets while spinning yarn (Adams 2002:182–183; Britt 1973:26). Others are known to have been used as the top socket devices for bow drills used as fire-starters (Rowe 1995:14–15). In both cases initial manufactured depressions get larger and deeper through use. These depressions, however, have a smoothed ap-

Table 4.20. Frequency distribution of complete Asquare-circ by thickness.

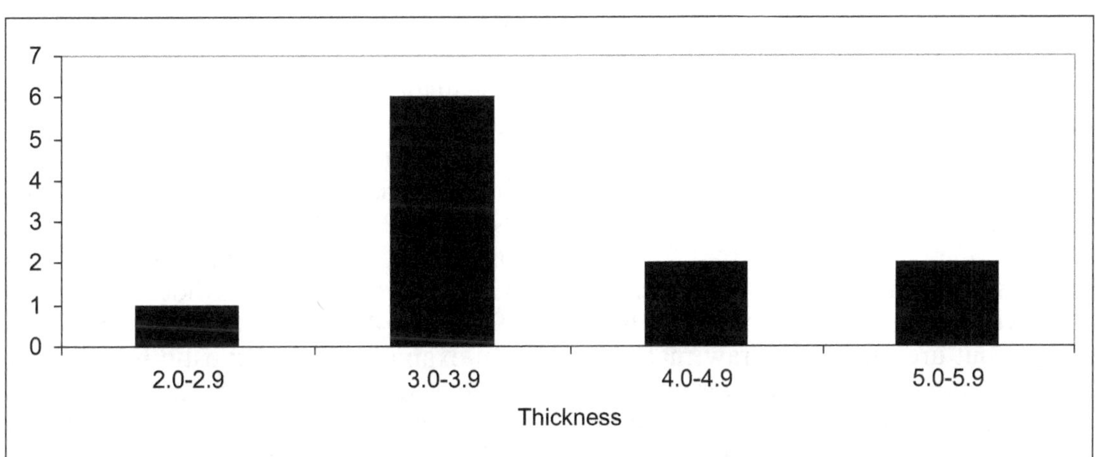

Table 4.21. Frequency distribution of complete Asquare-circ by length/width ratio.

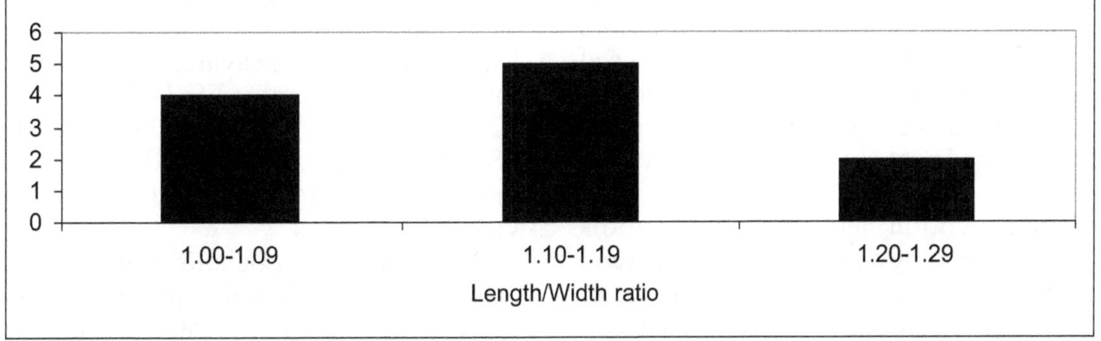

pearance as a result of use (Adams 2002:182–183; Rowe 1995:14–15), something that is not the case with the Franchthi examples.

It is thus more likely that the depressions seen in the center of the faces of several Asquare-circ represent use wear. If so, the nicks, the pitted areas, and the depressions may simply reflect different degrees of utilization. According to this scenario, the few nicks would represent perhaps nothing more than a single episode of percussive use; pitted areas would represent a relatively short use; the more regular, deeper depressions would be the result of a more sustained use. As regards the context in which the central use wear developed, there are two main possibilities: it could have been produced from an active or passive use of the tools in the bipolar knapping technique, or for cracking nuts (as hammerstones or anvils) (see Goren-Inbar, Sharon, Melamed, and Kislev 2002; de Beaune 1989b:35–38, 2000:65–70, Plate VI; Rowe 1995; Spears 1975). The first hypothesis should be rejected: the bipolar technique was not really used in the lithic industry at Neolithic Franchthi (see Perlès 2004). The second one may be more likely. The percentages of nut remains (i.e., pistachios and almonds) found in Neolithic levels are relatively low compared to those derived from Upper Palaeolithic and Mesolithic levels (Hansen 1991:164). Nut remains, however, appear in almost every Neolithic unit studied for botanical remains (Hansen 1991: Appendixes A through D). I would argue thus that the central wear in the faces of Asquare-circ was produced from the secondary active or passive use of these tools in nut cracking. Both the size and the shape of Asquare-circ (with two opposite flattened faces) may have been particularly convenient for such a use.

The percussive wear of many of the sides or peripheries is active and consists of flake/chip scars or percussion marks; see FS 870 (Fig. 26), FF1:6E (Pl. 112), S 62 (Fig. 27, Pl. 116), S 72 (Pl. 115). These seem to have cut the abrasive wear of the faces' edges, suggesting that the percussive use of the sides or peripheries followed the abrasive use of the faces. The percussive use may have had to do with breaking animal bones for creating raw materials for bone tools or for the extraction of marrow, crushing clay or materials that could serve as clay temper, flaking stone, pecking in the context of manufacture or resharpening, etc. (see Ritchie 1929:7).

5. Active tools used with ends (Aend)

Introduction

Summarized information on Active tools used with ends, or Aend, is listed in Table 4.22. Photographs of several specimens are found in Plates 120–133 on the CD, folder: Neolithic/Active/Aend.

The active tools I present in this subchapter under the name Active tools used with ends do not have an acute edge, but are made with raw materials and techniques similar to those used for Acut and in sizes and plans similar to the largest among them (see 'larger Acut', above, this chapter). These similarities and differences can create the impression that Aend are incipient or recycled Acut. As I show below, however, Aend share characteristics that suggest they make up a homogeneous, more or less functionally specialized group, neither used nor intended for use in an active linear mode as were the Acut. Aend were, instead, used primarily in an active diffused percussive mode, mainly with their ends.

I should mention here that several tools with similar morphology and use wear as Aend are found in the ground stone tool assemblage of Megalo Nisi Galanis, Kozani, which I have personally analysed (Stroulia in preparation). A group of morphologically similar tools has been reported from Dispilio by Stratouli. She considers most of them, however, to be recycled cutting edge tools (Stratouli 2002:160–161). The same interpretation has been offered for a number of tools of similar appearance from Arene Candide (Starnini and Voytek 1997:479–483). Prinz, on the other hand, suggested that examples from Divostin may have served as 'percussion flakers' (1988:262, Plate VII).

The Aend group is made up of 18 specimens. All but three are complete. With the exception of three tools found on Paralia, all Aend were recovered inside the cave (Table 4.22). No particular concentration in any part of the cave has been detected. Interestingly, however, at least seven of the fifteen specimens excavated inside the cave were found close to hearths: FS 7 (Pl. 120), FS 50 (Pl. 121), FS 108 (Pl. 122), FS 109 (Pl. 123), FS 277, FS 420 (Pl. 124), and FS 432. This is a possible indication that Aend in general were used in the vicinity of hearths.

Contextual associations with dated ceramics produced dates for eight specimens. All but one come from secure or probable MN deposits (three and four respectively). The exception is FS 602 (Pl. 125), which derives from a secure FN deposit. The remaining 10 specimens were excavated in disturbed deposits that yielded Neolithic and some pre- and post- Neolithic material as well (see Perlès 2004:6–7; Vitelli 1993:31–34, 1999:7–9, 17). Given the similarities between these specimens and those found in secure Neolithic deposits, I consider them also as Neolithic and this is the date assigned to them in Table 4.22. Since most of the dated Aend have a secure or probable MN date, it is possible that Aend, in general, were made, used, and discarded during MN—the same Neolithic phase in which most Acut originate.

Raw material and manufacture

As mentioned above, Aend were made of materials similar to those employed for Acut. Serpentinite was used for 16 specimens, diabase and basalt were used for one tool each (Table 4.22). As for Acut, the raw material for Aend was obtained in the form of pebbles or small cobbles. This is suggested by the curvilinear appearance of Aend, in general, and by the pebble or cobble appearance of specific specimens, e.g., FS 108 (Pl. 122), FS 362 (Pl. 126). It is possible that the pebbles and cobbles used for Aend were collected at the same, basically local, sources, and even by the same people and during the same expeditions, as were those used to fashion Acut. The discussion that addressed the Acut raw materials (at least the local ones) and their acquisition applies in this context too (above, this chapter).

With one possible exception (FS 136, see below), all Aend have been manufactured. This is indicated by traces of pecking and/or grinding visible on their bodies. Most tools carry evidence of both pecking and grinding, e.g., FS 7 (Pl. 120), FS 25 (Pl. 127), FS 109 (Pl. 123), FS 362 (Pl. 126), H1:64 (Pl. 128). A small number, on the other hand, seem to have gone through the grinding stage only, since they retain no pecking marks on their surfaces: see FS 120 (Pl. 129), FS 420 (Pl. 124), FS 602 (Pl. 125). The possibility, however, that such marks were eliminated by subsequent grinding cannot be ruled out. A single manufacturing stage of grinding may also be represented in FS 136. It is, however, also possible that the smooth body surface of this specimen is the result of an active abrasive use. If so, FS 136 should be considered an *a posteriori* tool. Two other specimens, FS 225 (Pl. 131) and FS 228 (Pl. 132), have been pecked to shape, but they show a smoothness that is probably not the result of grinding. This texture may represent hand polish in the case of FS 225, the product of an active diffused abrasive use in the case of FS 228. I should finally note that the Aend group includes a specimen with evidence of secondary pecking, or in other words, pecking that removed a ground surface: FS 192 (Pl. 130).

Table 4.22. Active tools used with ends (Aend).

Name	Trench:Unit	Prov.	Pres.	Material	Date	L	W	T	Illustr.
FS 7	A:18	C	c	serpentinite	Neol.	6.5	4.7	3.1	Pl. 120
FS 25	G:17	C	c	serpentinite	Neol.	8.2	4.2	3.5	Pl. 127
FS 50	G:20	C	c	serpentinite	(MN)	7.1	5.6	3.8	Pl. 121
FS 108	G1:11	C	c	serpentinite	(MN)	6.6	4.8	3.4	Pl. 122
FS 109	G1:17	C	c	serpentinite	(MN)	6.7	5.5	3.2	Pl. 123
FS 120	FF1:26	C	c	serpentinite	Neol.	6.6	6.2	3.5	Pl. 129
FS 136	FF1:37	C	c	serpentinite	Neol.	6.2	5.2	4.1	
FS 192	FA:10	C	c	serpentinite	Neol.	7.1	5.2	3.6	Pl. 130
FS 225	FA:42	C	c	serpentinite	Neol.	7.0	4.5	3.7	Pl. 131
FS 228	H1:59	C	c	serpentinite	Neol.	7.4	5.3	4.2	Pl. 132
FS 277	H1B:83	C	f	serpentinite	Neol.	7.6	4.4	2.0	
FS 362	H2A:66	C	c	serpentinite	(MN)	6.8	5.5	4.3	Pl. 126
FS 420	FAN:132	C	c	serpentinite	MN	5.8	4.5	3.0	Pl. 124
FS 432	FAN:136	C	f	serpentinite	MN	5.8	3.2	2.8	
FS 602	L5NE:18	P	c	diabase	FN	7.8	3.8	3.0	Pl. 125
FS 766	P5:92	P	f	basalt	MN	4.8	4.2	3.4	
H1:64	H1:64	C	c	serpentinite	Neol.	4.9	4.1	2.3	Pl. 128
Q5S:90/18	Q5S:90	P	c	serpentinite	Neol.	8.5	4.6	2.8	Pl. 133

KEY: Prov.=Provenience, Pres.=Preservation, L=Length, W=Width, T=Thickness, Illustr.=illustration, C=Cave, P=Paralia, c=complete, f=fragmentary, MN=Middle Neolithic, (MN)=probable Middle Neolithic, FN=Final Neolithic, Neol.=Neolithic, Pl.=plate

Similar cases have been noted among Acut (above, this chapter).

No remains of the Aend manufacturing process have been identified. Nevertheless, the complete, unworked serpentinite cobble mentioned earlier in this chapter as possible Acut raw material (FS 119) and the three serpentinite pebble/cobble fragments with evidence of pecking, also mentioned earlier as possible Acut manufacturing remains (FS 240, FS 734, and H2A:9/3a), could derive from the Aend manufacturing process. Moreover, some of the items I referred to earlier as possible Acut fragments (see Acut, this chapter) might be Aend fragments. Most of this material comes from MN deposits (Table 4.2).

The manufacturing process affected the faces and sides of these tools. It does not seem, however, to have altered the texture and the rounded pebble/cobble shape of the ends, the primary active parts of Aend. If so, one wonders why these tools were subjected to a process of manufacture in the first place. Why, in other words, were unmodified pebbles or cobbles not used? I believe that manufacture aimed to produce a particular body shape: most often roughly conical, e.g., FS 228 (Pl. 132), FS 362 (Pl. 126), or rectangular, e.g., FS 120 (Pl. 129), FS 192 (Pl. 130), less often cylindrical: FS 25 (Pl. 127). These shapes were probably chosen because they make tools convenient to hold in one hand and use with the ends. Moreover, while manufacture may have left unaltered the original convex configuration and rough regular texture of the ends, it did affect their contour. More specifically, the faces and sides of these tools were shaped in such a way that the ends acquired a roughly circular, oval, or elongated contour. The regularity in which the ends appear in the above shapes suggests that this was a conscious choice, presumably related to the intended use/s. This hypothesis is reinforced by a kind of incomplete beveling seen on one end (A) of at least two specimens: FS 7 (Pl. 120) and FS 25 (Pl. 127). This beveling, bifacial in FS 7 and unifacial in FS 25, did not produce an acute edge (in which case these items would have been classified as Acut), but precisely a convex surface of an oval or elongated contour. There is no possibility that these two specimens (or any other member of the Aend group for that matter) represent incipient Acut, since they carry use-wear on these particular ends. Neither can the two semi-beveled specimens or Aend in general be considered as recycled Acut: these tools tend to exhibit their maximum thickness at one of their ends, a configuration rarely found among Acut.

Technomorphological characteristics

The 15 complete specimens range in length from 4.9 to 8.5 cm (average: 6.9 cm) (Tables 4.22–4.23). A couple of tools, FS 420 (Pl. 124) and H1:64 (Pl. 128), are very short and should therefore be considered exhausted, at least for a use with the ends. The complete specimens range in width from 3.8 to 6.2 cm (average: 4.8 cm) (Tables 4.22 and 4.24). They are between 2.3 and 4.3 cm thick (average: 3.6 cm) (Tables 4.22 and 4.25).

If the average Aend length is comparable to the average length of the 20 complete 'larger' Acut (7.0 cm), their average width and, especially, thickness are higher than those of the complete larger Acut (4.3 cm and 2.6 cm respectively). These figures suggest that Aend are, in general, more massive than larger Acut, and support the hypothesis that these are not incipient or recycled Acut, but rather represent a distinct functional group. The comparison between the dimensions of Aend and larger Acut reveals, moreover, that Neolithic Franchthiotes could have produced slightly sturdier and more massive Acut than those recovered by selecting cobbles similar to those used for most Aend. That they did not reinforces the impression that this was a choice—not a passive submission to an ecological constraint.

Aspects of use

With one exception, all complete Aend have been used with both ends. The exception is Q5S:90/18 (Pl. 133), which was used with only one of the ends (A). The two fragmentary specimens are currently missing one end; it is probable that in their intact state they also had been used with both. All used ends are clearly distinct from the rest of the body. They were employed primarily in an active diffused percussive mode and in some cases also secondarily in an active diffused abrasive mode. I identified the following two main kinds of active diffused percussive wear on the ends of these tools.

The first is the least common and identified only on a handful of specimens. It consists of a battered, flat or concave surface; see end A of FS 120 (Pl. 129), end B of FS 192 (Pl. 130) and FS 228 (Pl. 132). This can be considered the result of a perpendicular diffused percussive use (the end attacked the worked material in a perpendicular mode). In one case (FS 120), this use followed an earlier one in a diffused abrasive mode, as suggested by pertinent wear seen around the battered surface.

The ends carrying the second kind of percussive wear are lightly or strongly convex and have a rough, and more or less regular texture with sporadic chipping that is most evident at the edges

Table 4.23. Frequency distribution of complete Aend by length.

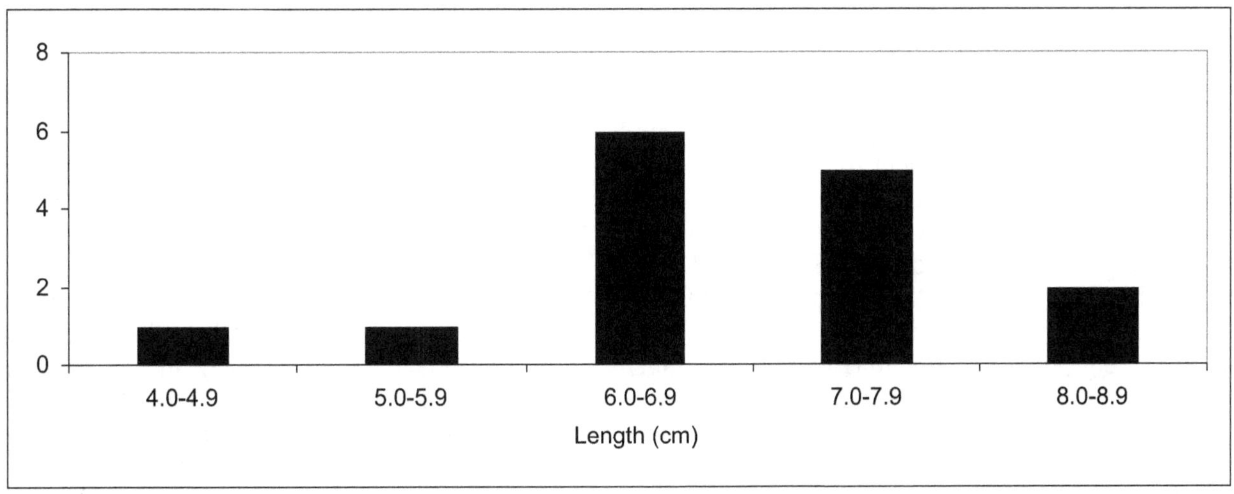

Table 4.24. Frequency distribution of complete Aend by width.

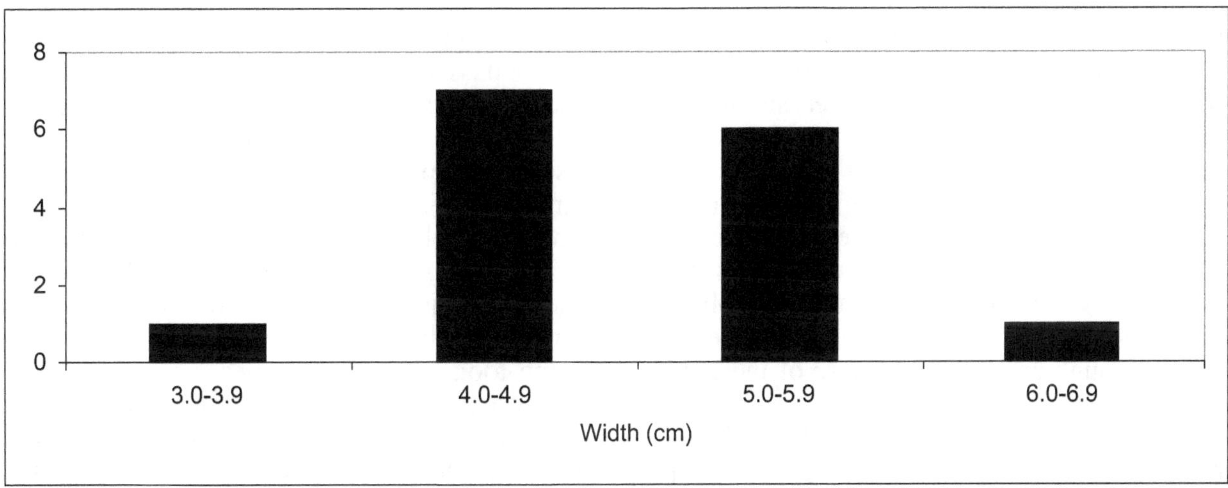

Table 4.25. Frequency distribution of complete Aend by thickness.

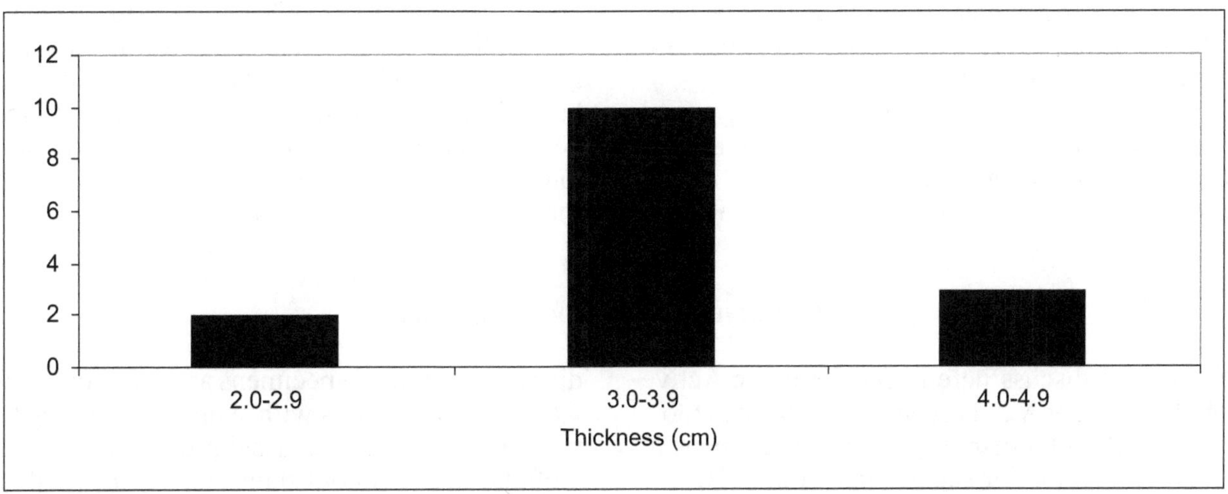

where the ends meet the body. They also show more or less subtle facets; see both ends of FS 108 (Pl. 122), end A of FS 228 (Pl. 132). Most of the elongated but also a few of the roughly circular/oval ends show a more or less subtle ridge in the middle as well. This ridge represents the edge of a facet, or the line where two facets meet. It can be straight: see end A of FS 109 (Pl. 123), end B of FS 420 (Pl. 124); curved: see end A of FS 362 (Pl. 126); or diagonal/sigmoidal: see end A of FS 192 (Pl. 130), FS 228 (Pl. 132), FS 420 (Pl. 124), and Q5S:90/18 (Pl. 133). It can be short, appearing on the highest end point, e.g., end A of FS 50 (Pl. 121), or long, crossing the end more or less longitudinally, e.g., end A of FS 109 (Pl. 123). Both the facets and the ridges suggest that the ends contacted the worked material obliquely, i.e., at an angle.

Similar oblique use wear is found on the ends of the morphologically similar—albeit *a posteriori*—tools that Poissonnier and his colleagues used experimentally to create the motif of a cross in faux relief on a block of granite. The ends of these tools—water-worn sandstone and quartzite cobbles—were used in an active oblique diffused percussive mode to peck the granite surface around the area reserved for the motif. The percussion was gentle, the percussive tools slightly touching—almost gliding over—the surface of the worked material in every strike. This use formed a ridge on the tools' ends (Poissonier calls the ends *biseautées*). A final, brief, oblique abrasive use, to regularize the granite surface, produced the rough and regular texture of these ends (Poissonnier 2002). A primary use of the ends of the Franchthi specimens in a gentle, oblique diffused percussive mode, and a secondary in an oblique diffused abrasive mode, could explain the use wear of the ends, consisting of facets and ridges, as well as a rough and regular texture. I suggest therefore that, in spite of the difference in the raw materials between the experimental tools and Aend, the ends of the Franchthi specimens that carry oblique use wear may have served pecking purposes.

It is tempting to see the obliquely used ends of the Franchthi specimens as having been employed for the last stage of pecking in the manufacture of stone vessels. The gentle oblique percussion I described above seems to have been right for the delicate task of finishing the shaping of the relatively thin walls of the Franchthi vessels. Moreover, most of these vessels are dated to MN, as are almost all of the dated Aend. The fact, however, that most of the materials used for the stone vessels are not local (see Herz 1992; van Andel and Vitaliano 1987:20), and that no byproducts of stone vessel manufacture have been identified at Franchthi, make it likely that these artifacts were imported to, rather than produced at, the site.

Some specimens show the oblique percussive (and secondary abrasive) wear on both ends, e.g., FS 108 (Pl. 122), FS 362 (Pl. 126). Others show it on only one, the other end showing perpendicular percussive wear: FS 192 (Pl. 130), FS 228 (Pl. 132); a primary diffused abrasive wear interrupted by a secondary perpendicular percussive wear: FS 120 (Pl. 129); or no use wear at all: Q5S:90/18 (Pl. 133).

Finally, a small number of specimens show use wear on the body as well. This use wear is active or passive, percussive or abrasive. For example, the oblique percussive wear of both ends of FS 420 (Pl. 124) extends also to one of the sides (C). This use wear is probably explained by this specimen's small size: FS 420, with a length of only 5.8 cm, is one of the shortest specimens in the Aend group. When this tool became too short for/from use with the ends, it is likely that one of its sides was used, since this allowed a more comfortable grip. The same tool, moreover, carries what appears to be active perpendicular diffused percussive wear on one face. Another tool, FS 602 (Pl. 125), carries active diffused abrasive wear on one side (B). It also shows a couple of scarred/scratched areas on one (illustrated) face, perhaps from an active percussive use as a mallet (see de Beaune 1997). Evidence of passive abrasive use is, on the other hand, found on one (illustrated) face of FS 192 (Pl. 130). It consists of a well polished U-shaped groove, formed probably *a posteriori*. Its current length is about 2.0 cm, but the fact that it is cut on one end by what seems to be secondary pecking, indicates that it was originally longer. It may have been used passively, for example, for polishing a pointed bone tool.

6. Active globular tools (Aglobe)

The group I discuss here under the name Active globular tools, or Aglobe, comprises 40 small tools of a generally globular shape. Some specimens in this group carry color stains, most do not. Here, I discuss the stained specimens as a subgroup called Active globular tools with stains, or Aglobe-stain; the unstained ones as a subgroup called Active globular tools without stains, or Aglobe-nostain.

6.1 Active globular tools with stains (Aglobe-stain)

Introduction

Summarized information on Aglobe-stain is listed in Table 4.26. Photographs of several specimens are found in Plates 134–140 in the CD, folder: Neolithic/Active/Aglobe/Aglobe-stain.

Aglobe-stain includes eight small tools with use wear that is for the most part related to processing a coloring agent. However, the possibility that this use wear derives from processing a certain material with the help of such an agent can not be ruled out. All specimens are complete or almost complete. Five specimens were excavated inside the cave, three on Paralia. The ceramic context has been useful in dating five specimens. Four are assigned a secure MN date, one a probable MN date (Table 4.26). The remaining three specimens were found on the surface or in disturbed deposits that yielded Neolithic and some post-Neolithic material as well (see Vitelli 1993:31–34). Given the homogeneity of the Aglobe-stain subgroup, I consider these specimens as part of the Neolithic assemblage and this is the date assigned to them in Table 4.26. For this reason they may even come from the MN occupation of the site too.

Raw material and manufacture

A single kind of raw material was used for all the tools in this subgroup: peridotite (Table 4.26). This is a material of high toughness, which is probably the quality that made it the rock of choice for Aglobe-stain. The globular shape of these tools suggests that the raw material came in the form of water-worn pebbles and small cobbles. Peridotite outcrops are found north of Dhidhima (Vitaliano n.d.:11); it is likely that pebbles and cobbles of this material were collected by Franchthiotes in local river and stream beds or on the beach which was not far from the site during the Neolithic.

I have not been able to identify any clear traces of manufacture (i.e., flaked or pecked surfaces). I assume that Aglobe-stain represent *a posteriori* tools. If so, the general homogeneity of this group in size, shape, and raw material must be the result of a particular effort to locate pebbles and cobbles with specific characteristics.

Technomorphological characteristics

Aglobe-stain range from 5.1 to 7.4 cm in length, from 4.1 to 7.3 cm in width, and from 3.4 to 7.3 cm in thickness (Tables 4.26–4.29). Four or five specimens are now too small to be comfortably held for use and may thus be considered exhausted: FS 371 (Pl. 134), FF1:40B1a (Pl. 135), 05:116/13 (Pl. 136), S 8, and perhaps also FS 372 (Pl. 139).

The generally globular shape of Aglobe-stain is interrupted by more or less substantial facets: see FS 111 (Pl. 137), FS 298 (Pl. 138), FS 371 (Pl. 134), FS 372 (Pl. 139), FF1:40B1a (Pl. 135), 05:116/13 (Pl. 136). The latter were produced as the original pebbles and cobbles were flattened in different areas in the course of use.

Aspects of use

Aglobe-stain were used in an exclusively active mode. With the exception of a couple of instances of diffused abrasive wear, these tools carry percussive wear as well as what seems to be combined diffused percussive and abrasive wear. Most of the use wear appears in the form of facets. Most, but not all, of the facets are stained with color, probably from processing a coloring agent. Some specimens, in addition, have occasional pitting on

Table 4.26. Active globular tools with stains (Aglobe-stain).

Name	Trench:Unit	Prov.	Pres.	Material	Date	L	W	T	Illustr.
FS 111	G1:16	C	c	peridotite	(MN)	6.5	6.0	5.2	Pl. 137
FS 298	H1B:95	C	c	peridotite	Neol.	7.4	7.3	7.3	Pl. 138
FS 371	H2A:75	C	c	peridotite	MN	5.5	4.4	3.5	Pl. 134
FS 372	H2A:75	C	c	peridotite	MN	6.4	4.1	4.0	Pl. 139
05:116/13	05:116	P	c	peridotite	Neol.	5.1	4.7	4.4	Pl. 136
FF1:40B1a	FF1:40B1	C	c	peridotite	MN	5.2	5.1	4.4	Pl. 135
P5:178/13	P5:178	P	c	peridotite	MN	5.8	5.5	4.8	Pl. 140
S 8	Paralia surf.	P	c	peridotite	Neol.	5.9	5.1	3.4	

KEY: Prov.=Provenience, Pres.=Preservation, L=Length, W=Width, T=Thickness, Illustr.=illustration, surf.=surface, C=Cave, P=Paralia, c=complete, MN=Middle Neolithic, (MN)=probable Middle Neolithic, Neol.=Neolithic, Pl.=plate

Table 4.27. Frequency distribution of complete Aglobe-stain by length.

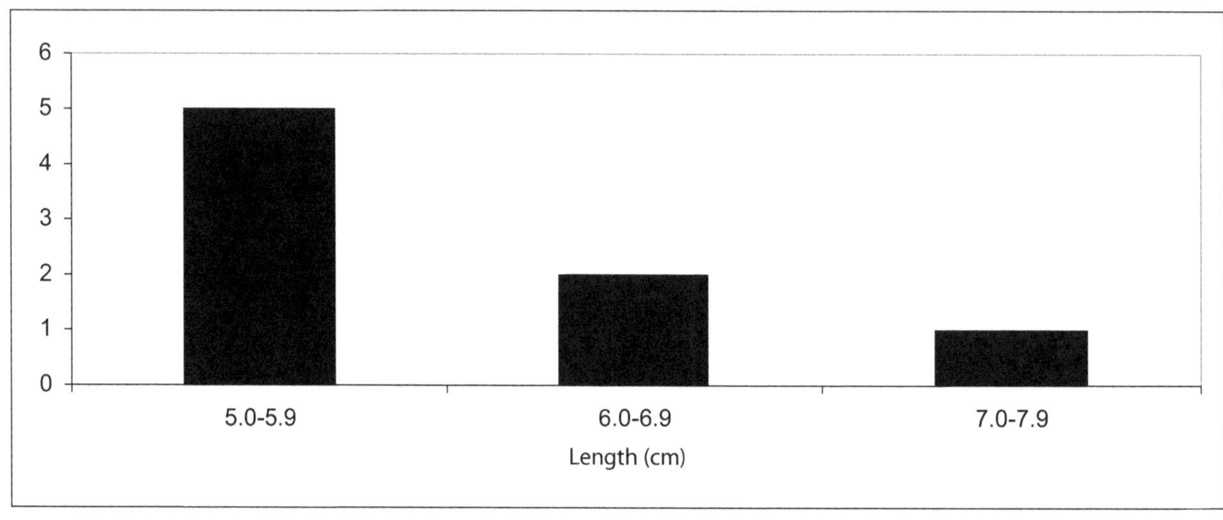

Table 4.28. Frequency distribution of complete Aglobe-stain by width.

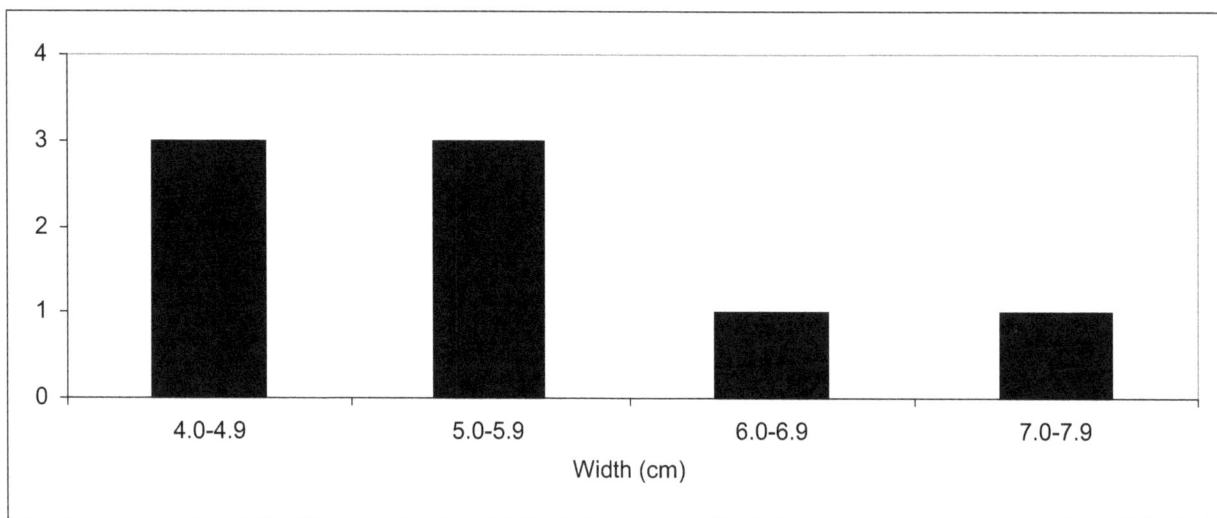

Table 4.29. Frequency distribution of complete Aglobe-stain by thickness.

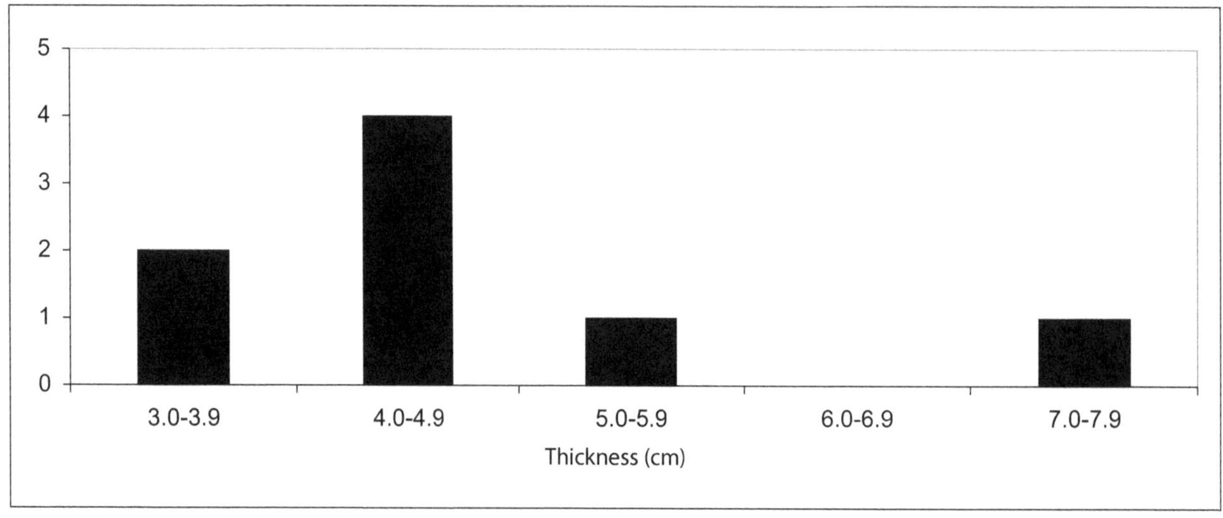

their surface from an episode or two of a percussive use not related to pigment processing.

There is no tool with only one facet. Most specimens have four facets, but some have fewer or more—S 8 has two, whereas FS 298 (Pl. 138) and O5:116/13 (Pl. 136) have five each. At least 33 facets are represented in the eight tools making up the Aglobe-stain subgroup. The facets are usually between 3.0 and 4.0 cm in maximum dimension. There are, however, both smaller and larger examples; see FS 298 (Pl. 138) and FS 371 (Pl. 134). Most of the facets are essentially flat, a small number of facets, on the other hand, are slightly convex.

It is unclear what the passive surfaces used with Aglobe-stain were; there are no specimens among the passive tools discussed in chapter 3 with both color stains and passive percussive wear or combined passive abrasive and percussive wear. There is, however, one medium size tool among the Active miscellanea 2 (set 7) (below, this chapter) that has use wear compatible with that found on Aglobe-stain. This tool is FS 829 (Fig. 32, Pl. 208). One of the faces was first used abrasively in an active mode (hence the classification of FS 829 as an active tool). Its central area, however, was used secondarily in a passive percussive or combined passive percussive and abrasive mode that stained it yellow. No other specimens with similar use wear were found. Passive surfaces convenient for use with Aglobe-stain could have been provided by the boulders dotting the cave. Nevertheless, I am not aware of any reports of stained boulders at the site. I would, thus, assume that the tools used in conjunction with Aglobe-stain were either discarded in non excavated areas or made of wood.

The small size of Aglobe-stain in general, and of their facets in particular, suggests that these tools were able to process only small amounts of pigment at a time. If so, one wonders why their users did not choose instead to grind the pigment itself against a passive surface—an ethnographically and experimentally documented technique (Vitelli 1993:101–103) that seems more convenient. An example of this technique may be represented by H1A:84 (Pl. 200), a piece of what seems to be ocher that is discussed below (this chapter) as one of the Active miscellanea 2 (set 2). The answer may lie in the fact that some ochres are found in pieces that are too small to be held for grinding. As such, they have to be crushed before being ground (Vitelli, personal communication 2/2007).

No chemical analysis of the color stains has been conducted, but the fact that they appear in different tones of red, orange, yellow, and brown suggests perhaps that they represent varieties of iron oxide. Iron oxide was used in the decoration of pottery during all Neolithic phases (Vitelli 1993, 1999). It was probably also used for the decoration of figurines (Talalay 1993:35), wooden tools or non-tool objects, hides and clothes, and the human body itself. The pigment in some cases, e.g., FS 372 (Pl. 139), may have been processed with the help of a binder. This could have been water but also urine, animal blood, fat, marrow, etc. (Schmandt-Besserat 1980:137).

Interestingly, two specimens, FS 371 (Pl. 134) and P5:178/13 (Pl. 140), are cracked. Of the two, FS 371 was found among the remains of a hearth (unit H2A:75), a possible indication that cracking was caused by exposure to high heat. This specimen seems, moreover, to be exhausted. The same unit yielded another specimen in the Aglobe-stain subgroup: FS 372 (Pl. 139). This is not cracked, but may be exhausted. Thermal treatment of ocher is a technique used to increase the available range of colors (Schmandt-Besserat 1980:129; see also Dubreuil 2002:124). This may explain why these two pigment processing tools were found in a hearth context: they may have been thrown in a hearth, when no longer useful and after they had been employed in pigment processing tasks that took place by, and involved this feature.

6.2 Active globular tools without stains (Aglobe-nostain)

Introduction

Summarized information on Aglobe-nostain is listed in Table 4.30. Photographs of several specimens are found in Plates 141–158 on the CD, folder: Neolithic/Active/Aglobe/Aglobe-nostain.

The Aglobe-nostain subgroup consists of 32 specimens that have a generally globular shape but carry no color stains. They were used in an exclusively active mode. Twenty-six of them are complete, six are fragmentary. Nineteen were excavated in the cave (including one from the terrace outside the cave mouth), thirteen on Paralia. Contextual associations with dated ceramics provided dates for half (n=16) of these tools. Six specimens come from secure MN levels, five from probable MN levels, three from secure FN levels, another two from EN/MN levels (Table 4.30). The remaining 16 specimens come from disturbed deposits that yielded Neolithic and some post-Neolithic material as well (see Vitelli 1993:31–34, 1999:7–9). Given the meager quantities of post-Neolithic remains at the site in general (Dengate 1999) and the similarities of these items to the Neolithic specimens, I consider them also as Neolithic and this is the date assigned to them in Table 4.30.

Raw material and manufacture

Several raw materials were used for Aglobe-nostain. Diabase is the most common, represented by 12 specimens; chert, diorite, peridotite, and limestone are represented by three to five specimens each. Serpentinite, sandstone, conglomerate, goethite, and, perhaps also, magnetite were used for one tool each (Table 4.30). These materials could have been found locally. Judging from the shape of these tools, and the unutilized, water-worn surfaces preserved on particular specimens, the different kinds of rock were probably collected as pebbles or small cobbles in stream or river beds or on the beach in the general Franchthi region (see van Andel and Vitaliano 1987:20).

A couple of specimens seem to have been subjected to a manufacturing process, consist-

Table 4.30. Active globular tools without stains (Aglobe-nostain).

Name	Trench:Unit	Prov.	Pres.	Material	Date	L	W	T	Illustr.
FS 85	G:lot 28	C	c	sandstone	(MN)	7.1	7.0	6.9	Pl. 144
FS 106	G1:15	C	c	limestone	(MN)	6.4	6.4	5.2	
FS 122	G1:13	C	c	diorite	(MN)	5.9	5.9	5.1	
FS 128	G1:19	C	c	conglomerate	(MN)	6.4	3.9	3.7	
FS 272	C:4	C	c	diabase	Neol.	5.9	5.8	5.6	Pl. 148
FS 273	A:5	C	c	diabase	Neol.	5.1	5.0	4.8	Pl. 149
FS 315	FAS:71	C	c	diabase	FN	5.8	4.4	3.3	Pl. 141
FS 375	H2A:75	C	c	limestone	MN	6.5	5.8	4.9	
FS 695	O5:4	P	c	diabase	Neol.	5.8	5.8	5.7	Pl. 146
FS 760	L5:34	P	c	diorite	EN/MN	5.8	5.8	5.0	Pl. 153
FS 827	Q4 backfill	P	c	chert	Neol.	5.5	5.3	5.3	Pl. 155
FS 840	HTerrace:21	C	c	diabase	Neol.	5.5	5.5	4.1	Pl. 154
FS 841	HTerrace:16	C	c	diabase	Neol.	5.2	4.8	3.2	Pl. 142
FS 871	L5:60	P	c	diorite	FN	5.2	4.6	4.5	Pl. 158
FS 876	P5:183	P	c	chert	MN	7.5	7.4	6.7	Pl. 152
FS 889	P5:186	P	c	limestone	MN	5.5	5.3	5.2	Pl. 147
FF1:6	FF1:6	C	c	diabase	Neol.	5.6	5.0	3.5	Pl. 145
FF1:9	FF1:9	C	f	peridotite	Neol.	5.7	5.4	2.6	
FF1:11	FF1:11	C	c	diabase	Neol.	5.1	4.7	4.4	Pl. 157
FF1:13	FF1:13	C	c	diabase	Neol.	5.8	5.5	4.0	
FF1:29C	FF1:29	C	c	diabase	Neol.	6.7	6.1	4.4	Pl. 156
FF1:35B	FF1:35	C	c	diabase	(MN)	5.9	5.6	4.6	Pl. 143
H1A:91	H1A:91	C	c	diabase	EN/MN	7.4	6.9	4.2	
H2A:75/21	H2A:75	C	f	peridotite	MN	5.2	4.7	2.2	
L5:99/51	L5:99	P	c	peridotite	MN	4.9	4.7	4.6	
L5NE:7	L5NE:7	P	f	chert	FN	7.0	6.2	4.9	
P5:179	P5:179	P	c	chert	MN	4.7	4.2	3.8	Pl. 150
Q4:3/2	Q4:3	P	c	goethite	Neol.	5.5	4.7	4.0	
Q5N:2/1	Q5N:2	P	f	magnetite?	Neol.	5.6	5.5	2.8	
Q5S:2/1	Q5S:2	P	f	serpentinite	Neol.	5.3	4.7	2.8	
QR5:6/2	QR5:6	P	c	chert	Neol.	5.2	4.2	4.0	Pl. 151
S 56	F:16	C	f	diorite?	Neol.	6.0	4.9	3.3	

KEY: Prov.=Provenience, Pres.=Preservation, L=Length, W=Width, T=Thickness, Illustr.=illustration, C=Cave, P=Paralia, c=complete, f=fragmentary, MN=Middle Neolithic, (MN)=probable Middle Neolithic, FN=Final Neolithic, EN/MN=Early/Middle Neolithic Interphase, Neol.=Neolithic, Pl.=plate

Note 1: G:lot 28 refers to units G:19–24.

ing of pecking and/or grinding: FS 85 (Pl. 144), which is an almost perfect sphere, shows evidence of pecking. FS 889 (Pl. 147), of the same shape, has a very regular, well smoothed surface that must be the result of manufacture by grinding. No pecking traces from an earlier manufacturing stage are visible on this specimen, but such traces may have been eliminated during the grinding stage. The unutilized, water-worn surfaces and the lack of manufacturing evidence in at least 10 specimens, on the other hand, leave no doubt that these constitute *a posteriori* tools; see, e.g., FS 315 (Pl. 141), FS 841 (Pl. 142), FF1:29C (Pl. 156), FF1:35B (Pl. 143), H1A:91, Q4:3/2, Q5N:2/1. Less straightforward cases exist. The four complete chert specimens (all more or less spherical) have most or all of their surface battered from a percussive use. I doubt that they were subjected to a process of manufacture. I believe, instead, that their spherical shape is a byproduct of use (see below) and I consider them to be *a posteriori* tools too; see, e.g., P5:179 (Pl. 150), QR5:6/2 (Pl. 151). Another 10 or so specimens with a more or less spherical shape may for several reasons not have been subjected to a process of manufacture either: see FS 695 (Pl. 146), FS 871 (Pl. 158), FS 122. First, there are no clear manufacturing traces on their surfaces—these do not show the characteristic dense and systematic pitting that results from pecking, nor are they ground all around. Secondly, all the specimens in question carry use wear, they are, in other words, tools. If so, it is hard to see them as stone balls manufactured to serve, for example, as gaming pieces, tokens, weights, etc.—a hypothesis offered for spherical objects recovered elsewhere (see Abu Hureyra; Moore 2000:172–173, Figure 7.8b, and sites in the Deh Luran plain in Iran; Hole, Flannery, and Neely 1969:200, Figure 84e). Thirdly, and related to the above point, the spherical shape does not seem to be crucial for the uses of these tools—there was no reason, in other words, to invest a substantial amount of time and energy in producing these spheres (yet, I have to admit that this seems to be the case for FS 889, Pl. 147— see above and below). I would suggest therefore, as I did for the aforementioned chert specimens, that the specimens in question attained a spherical shape as a result of use, and that they, too, are *a posteriori* tools. If my understanding is acurate, this shape was produced by the percussive use of original water-rolled pebbles or cobbles, a point to which I return below.

Technomorphological characteristics

The 26 complete specimens range from 4.7 to 7.5 cm in length, from 3.9 to 7.4 cm in width, and from 3.2 to 6.9 cm in thickness (Tables 4.30–4.33). Several specimens with surfaces substantially flattened by use cannot at this point be comfortably held, at least to use in an abrasive or combined abrasive and percussive mode, and should be considered exhausted for such uses: FS 272 (Pl. 148), FS 273 (Pl. 149), FS 315 (Pl. 141), FS 841 (Pl. 142), FF1:6 (Pl. 145), H1A:91. A couple of the relatively spherical specimens (and thus with no such flattened surfaces) are probably also exhausted, given their small size: P5:179 (Pl. 150), QR5:6/2 (Pl. 151). It can be assumed that the exhausted specimens represent heavily used implements that were originally larger. It is plausible that they were discarded when they became too small to serve the uses for which they were intended.

Aspects of use

As I said above, I consider the more or less spherical shape of a large number of specimens as the result of the percussive use of original water-rolled pebbles or cobbles. More specifically, I see these tools as having themselves been shaped by their use in shaping or resharpening other tools through pecking. The spherical shape is one commonly acquired by chert tools during their use as hammerstones for a variety of percussive tasks, including pecking.[54] Chert or quartz tools, comparable in size to the Franchthi specimens, and with a spherical shape produced by 'heavy pounding' have been reported from sites in the Deh Luran plain (Hole, Flannery, and Neely 1969:185–186. See also specimens from Çayönü: Davis 1982:116 and Plate 3.III:9). Closer to home, 'chert balls' similar in size and, from what I understand, use wear, to the Franchthi specimens, were recovered at Achilleion (Winn and Shimabuku 1989:272–273). Tools of a spherical shape acquired through percussive use, but of other materials, are mentioned in the ethnographic literature. Speaking of stones used to resharpen 'querns' in Africa, B.W. Walker wrote: 'These stones can become absolutely spherical from constant use, being turned about in the hand and dropped upon the rock (grindstone). They are just the size of a cricket ball and some consist apparently of granite, others of stone resembling limestone…' (Walker, cited in Boshier 1965:136).

If the above hypothesis is correct, the most intensive use of the relatively spherical specimens must have been the percussive one which produced this particular shape. This seems to have been the only use for at least two (of the four) complete chert

Table 4.31. Frequency distribution of complete Aglobe-nostain by length.

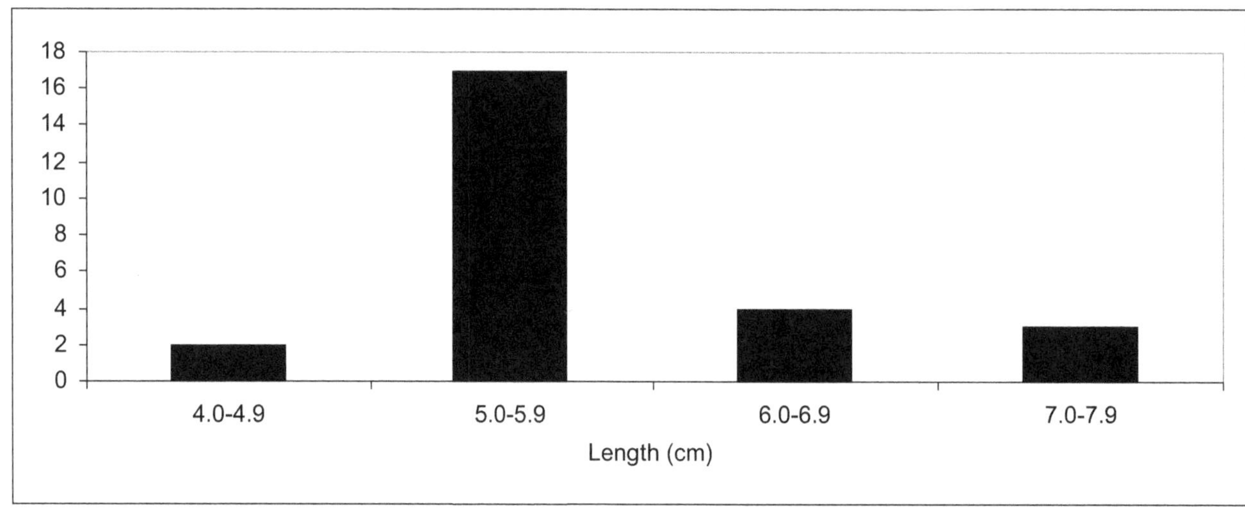

Table 4.32. Frequency distribution of complete Aglobe-nostain by width.

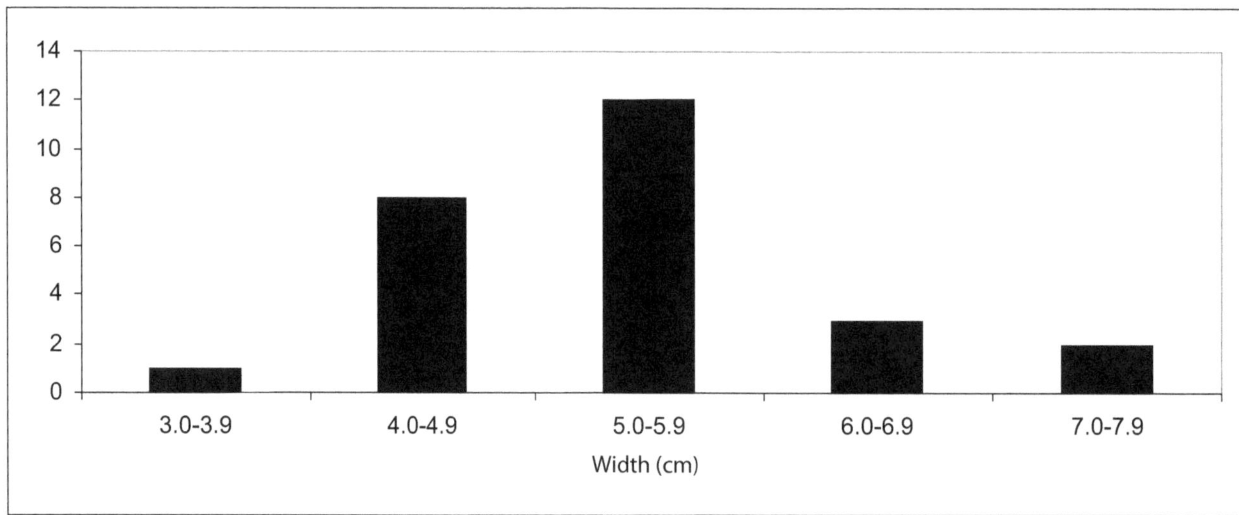

Table 4.33. Frequency distribution of complete Aglobe-nostain by thickness.

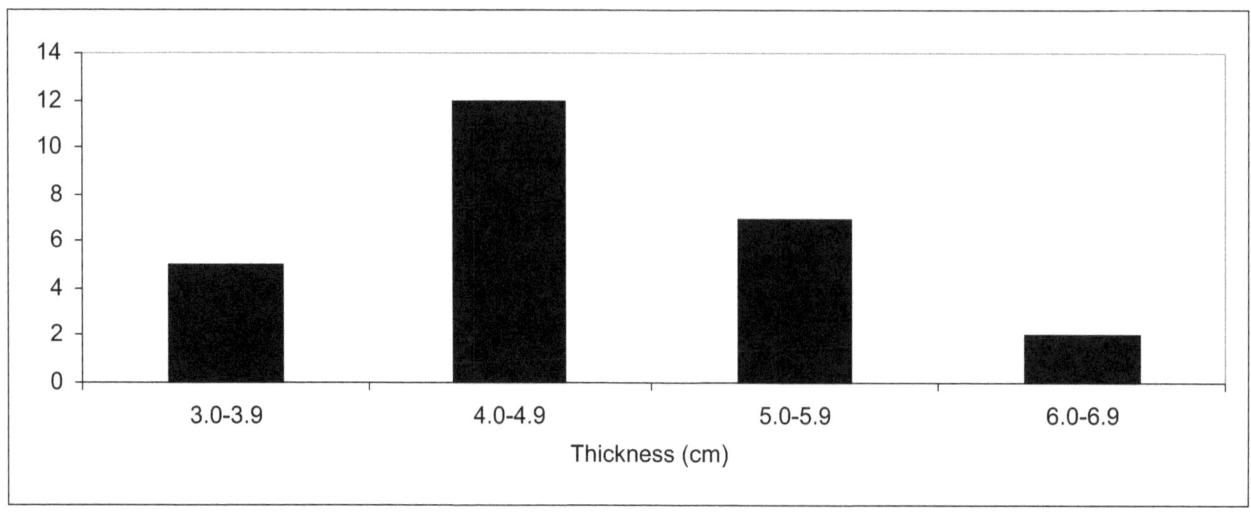

tools, which appear battered over the entire surface: FS 876 (Pl. 152) and QR5:6/2 (Pl. 151). Other spherical specimens, however, carry in addition localized use wear, suggesting that they were used secondarily as well. More specifically, at least six such specimens have on their surface one to three small (usually no more than 3.0 cm in maximum dimension) smoothed facets representing diffused abrasive wear, e.g., FS 122, FS 760 (Pl. 153), FS 840 (Pl. 154), FF1:11 (Pl. 157). These facets are flat or slightly convex. They have not really altered the spherical shape of the specimens in question, which is why I think that they are not the result of their primary use. Some of the same tools also carry small battered areas from an additional occasional percussive use that must have been different from the one that produced their spherical shape: FS 122, FS 760 (Pl. 153). An almost reverse process is, I think, illustrated in the near-perfectly spherical specimen FS 85 (Pl. 144), which, as mentioned above, was apparently manufactured by pecking. This specimen shows large smoothed convex facets around its surface that are probably the result of a substantial abrasive use. These facets are interrupted by four smaller ones, byproducts of more occasional abrasive and percussive uses: a flat, smoothed facet, measuring 4.5×3.7 cm, a more discontinuously smoothed, lightly convex area, measuring about 3.8×3.6 cm, and two battered facets measuring about 3.0×3.0 cm. The almost perfectly spherical FS 889 (Pl. 147), which was, I believe, ground to shape also has a small facet, measuring about 3.2×3.0, and a couple of tiny battered surfaces, the result of abrasive and percussive uses respectively.

The specimens that do not have a spherical shape are those that have two or three areas substantially flattened from intensive use. In most cases these areas have the form of flat or slightly convex faces or facets, e.g., FS 272 (Pl. 148), FS 273 (Pl. 149), FS 315 (Pl. 141), FS 827 (Pl. 155), FS 841 (Pl. 142), FF1:6 (Pl. 145), FF1:29C (Pl. 156), FF1:35B (Pl. 143), H1A:91. Some of the faces or facets seem to have been produced by an abrasive use (FS 272, FS 273, FF1:6), others by a percussive use (H1A:91), and still others by a combined percussive and abrasive use in a crushing mode (FS 315, FS 841). Almost all of these specimens have additional battered spots on their surface from an occasional percussive use. Similar-looking tools, with flattened areas, have been reported from Sitagroi (Elster 2003a:187, Plates 5.38 and 5.39).

7. Active miscellanea (Amisc)

Introduction

Active miscellanea, or Amisc, is a large heterogeneous group that comprises all the specimens—a total of 152—that I have not been able to include in one of the six relatively homogeneous active tool groups discussed above, or use to construct additional groups of comparable homogeneity and/or size.

The Amisc group includes various kinds of specimens: specimens that, although carefully manufactured and probably functionally specialized, are simply atypical in the Franchthi assemblage (or at least its Neolithic component)—similar specimens may, however, be more common in other assemblages that have not been systematically studied; specimens that do share a number of characteristics, but their number is not large enough to merit the construction of a separate group; *a posteriori* specimens, used expediently enough for no dramatic changes to occur on the shape (or texture) of the original pebbles or cobbles used as raw material; *a posteriori* specimens that may have been discarded before they were used sufficiently to develop shape and use wear characteristics that would allow placement into one of the six relatively homogeneous active tool groups, or construction of additional groups; fragmentary specimens that may, in their intact state, have had characteristics that would have made them suitable for inclusion in one of the six established active tool groups; specimens covered with a layer of concretion that precludes a study of use wear or, in some cases, even an assessment of the existence of such wear; finally, fragmentary specimens that have no visible use wear on the preserved parts, and could either have been used with the missing portions or represent parts of unutilized raw material.

Amisc is a large group whose detailed discussion aims at enhancing our understanding of the variability of the Franchthi ground stone tool assemblage. For the sake of presentation, I divided this group into two subgroups on the basis of raw material:

Active miscellanea 1, or Amisc1, comprises tools mostly of sandstone and, more rarely, andesite and conglomerate. Slate, as well as sandstone combined with conglomerate, is also represented in this subgroup with one and two specimens respectively.

Active miscellanea 2, or Amisc2, comprises tools mostly of limestone and serpentinite. Quartz, soapstone, steatite, peridotite, basalt, diabase, jasper, chert, chlorite schist, and, perhaps, also metaquartzite are also represented in this subgroup.

Again for the sake of presentation, I divided each subgroup into smaller sets. I constructed three kinds of sets for each subgroup: relatively homogeneous; totally heterogeneous/artificial; and generally/relatively heterogeneous. The relatively homogeneous sets comprise from two to seven specimens. If they had more specimens, I would have promoted them into actual groups of active tools, similar to the six discussed earlier in this chapter. Amisc1 has three relatively homogeneous sets, Amisc2 only one. The totally heterogeneous/artificial sets are made up of tools with unique characteristics in the Franchthi assemblage as a whole or its Neolithic component in particular. Amisc1 and Amisc2 have one such set each. The generally/relatively heterogeneous sets comprise specimens that have one or more characteristics in common (e.g., raw material, size, shape, or type of use wear). I can not claim that these specimens were similar in any functional sense, although some of them may have been. Most sets in each subgroup are of this kind: Amisc1 has eleven such sets, Amisc2 eight.

The discussion of each set is accompanied by a table summarizing basic information on the members of the set. The following KEY applies to these tables:

Prov.=Provenience, Pres.=Preservation, L=Length, W=Width, T=Thickness, Illust.=Illustration, C=Cave, P=Paralia, c=complete, f=fragmentary, EN=Early Neolithic, MN=Middle Neolithic, LN=Late Neolithic, FN=Final Neolithic, (Initial Neol.)=probable Initial Neolithic, (EN)=probable Early Neolithic, (MN)=probable Middle Neolithic, (LN) probable Late Neolithic, (FN)=probable Final Neolithic, EN/MN=Early/Middle Neolithic Interphase, Neol.=Neolithic, conglom.=conglomerate, sandstone/conglom.=sandstone combined with conglomerate, n/a=non available, Pl. =plate, Fig.=figure.

The name of some of the fragmentary specimens listed in these tables is accompanied by an asterisk. The length of these particular specimens is smaller than their width. The length and width measurements for these specimens were taken along what were obviously the long and wide axes of the original tools.

On the basis of contextual associations with dated ceramics or lithics, 74 specimens in the Amisc group were securely or probably assigned to a specific Neolithic phase or interphase. The remaining 78 specimens were found on the surface or excavated in disturbed deposits that yielded Neolithic and some pre- and post-Neolithic material too (see Perlès 2004:6–7; Vitelli 1993:31–34, 1999:7-9, 17). Given the Neolithic date of the majority of the pottery and lithics excavated in these deposits, as well as the small number of stratified pre-Neolithic ground stone tools (see chapter 2) and the negligible quantities of post-Neolithic material found at the site in general (Dengate 1999), I find it unlikely that these specimens (or most of them) have a pre- or post-Neolithic origin. I consider them thus as Neolithic and this is the date assigned to them in the tables that accompany the various sets.

Specimens such as those included in the Amisc group—especially those that I placed in totally heterogeneous/artificial or generally/relatively heterogeneous sets—are frustrating because they resist being squeezed into the neat pigeonholes of our classification systems. Yet they play an important role, reminding us that prehistoric people, including Neolithic Franchthiotes, did not live their lives trying to make our modern archaeologists' lives easier. They were flexible as they produced a material culture that served their needs as these emerged in everyday life. They used, reused, recycled, broke, and discarded tools and non-tool objects as they saw fit.

7.1 Active miscellanea 1 (Amisc1)

Amisc1 comprises 86 specimens. They are divided into 15 sets. Sets 1 through 3 are relatively homogeneous, set 4 is totally heterogeneous/artificial, sets 5 through 15 are generally/relatively heterogeneous. They are all presented below.

The drawing of one specimen appears in Figure 31. Photographs of several specimens by set are found in Plates 159–189 on the CD, folder: Neolithic/Active/Amisc/Amisc1.

Relatively homogeneous sets

Active miscellanea 1 – set 1 (Amisc1-set1)

Table 4.34. Active miscellanea 1 – set 1 (Amisc1-set1).

Name	Trench:Unit	Prov.	Pres.	Material	Date	L	W	T	Illustr.
FS 64	A:55	C	f	sandstone	Neol.	5.9	1.7	1.0	Pl. 161
FS 287	FAN:117	C	c	sandstone?	LN	6.2	1.8	1.0	Pl. 159
FS 531	H2A:122	C	c	sandstone	MN	5.7	2.4	1.2	Pl. 160
FS 752	Q6N:38	P	f	sandstone	EN/MN	5.6	2.2	1.1	Pl. 162
FAS:117	FAS:117	C	f	?	(MN)	2.5	0.7	0.5	Pl. 163

Amisc1-set1 comprises five small, oblong, thin, probably specialized, tools. They are mostly of fine-grained sandstone and were probably used in an active punctiform mode with their tip. The first four specimens listed above have the plan of a roughly isosceles triangle, with two long sides and a short straight or curved base. This shape is the result of a grinding process that seems to have aimed to create a tip at the apex of the triangle. The tip of the two complete specimens FS 287 (Pl. 159) and FS 531 (Pl. 160) is more or less rounded. That of FS 64 (Pl. 161) and FS 752 (Pl. 162) is broken off, but may have been originally similar. The use of these tools is uncertain. What is certain is that they could not have been suitable for punching holes on leather: their tip is not sharp enough for such a use.

Unlike the other four specimens in this set, fragmentary FAS:117 (Pl. 163) has a rod-like appearance with a very narrow shaft that is curved, not straight. The diameter of the shaft decreases towards the preserved end. This shape was given intentionally by grinding, as suggested by long, narrow, parallel zones formed around the shaft. The preserved end consists of a tiny flat facet. It is uncertain if FAS:117 served as a tool. If it did, it may have broken during use.

Active miscellanea 1 – set 2 (Amisc1-set2)

Table 4.35. Active miscellanea 1 – set 2 (Amisc1-set2).

Name	Trench:Unit	Prov.	Pres.	Material	Date	L	W	T	Illustr.
FS 605	L5NE:18	P	c	sandstone/conglom.	FN	24.0	17.1	8.6	Pl. 164
FS 612	L5NE:18	P	c	sandstone/conglom.	FN	17.5	14.0	6.8	Pl. 165

Amisc1-set2 consists of two complete large tools of elliptical or ovate plan. Their raw material is sandstone combined with conglomerate. Each has one work face that is generally flat and covered with concretion. The work face of FS 605 (Pl. 164) is smoothed from an abrasive use, as I discovered after removing some of the concretion. I have not been able to see any part of the work face of FS 612 (Pl. 165), but this may have been smoothed too. The work face of FS 605 slopes towards one end, an indication that—despite its large size—this specimen was used in an active mode. I assume that the work face of smaller FS 612 was used actively as well. An active use may also be suggested by the trimming of the periphery of both tools by chipping/flaking. Such trimming could have served to facilitate holding during an active use; the possibility, however, that it aimed to give the work face a particular shape cannot be ruled out.

Both tools were excavated in L5NE:18. This unit belongs to the FN pit formation of the northernmost portion of Paralia, described earlier in this chapter, and believed to have been used, at least originally, for the production of quicklime (Vitelli 1999:18-19, 90-91). Given their large size, these tools may have been suitable for crushing chunks of calcium carbonate that could then be burnt to produce quicklime. Or, since it is likely that the pit formation is a secondary context for these as well as other tools and non-tool objects found there (Vitelli 1999:90–91; see also Perlès 2004:118), FS 605 and FS 612 may not be at all related to lime production.

Active miscellanea 1 – set 3 (Amisc1-set3)

Table 4.36. Active miscellanea 1 – set 3 (Amisc1-set3).

Name	Trench:Unit	Prov.	Pres.	Material	Date	L	W	T	Illustr.
FS 597	L5NE:15	P	f	sandstone	FN	14.1	10.8	5.6	Pl. 169
FS 667	Q5S:154	P	f	andesite	Neol.	12.2	11.1	5.0	Pl. 168
FS 757	P5:77	P	f	sandstone	MN	12.7	10.2	5.6	
H1:41	H1:41	C	c	sandstone	Neol.	16.5	11.0	4.4	Pl. 166
H1A:72*	H1A:72	C	f	sandstone	Neol.	10.4	11.2	3.9	
S 73	n/a	n/a	f	sandstone	Neol.	14.3	11.4	6.3	Pl. 167

Amisc1-set3 comprises six mostly fragmentary, mostly sandstone tools. The single complete specimen, H1:41 (Pl. 166), has an elongated loaf shape with two generally planoconvex sections. This seems to have been the original shape of the fragmentary specimens. The limited evidence of manufacture consists of traces of pecking on the dorsal face of S 73 (Pl. 167) and the trimming of the sides/ends of this tool and H1:41 (Pl. 166). However, the flat or slightly concave configuration of the single work face of the specimens in this set suggests that, despite appearances, they underwent a more or less extensive process of manufacture.

All work faces have been used in an active abrasive manner, as suggested by a smoothed texture that extends from edge to edge, and in some cases, by the slopping of the face towards one end or side. Three of the work faces, FS 667 (Pl. 168), H1:41 (Pl. 166), and S 73 (Pl. 167), carry scratches with a general diagonal direction, suggesting that they moved diagonally during use (or at least that was the direction of the movement during the last use episode/s). The diagonal scratches further indicate that these three faces moved over relatively large passive surfaces—most likely larger than those offered by Popen (chapter 3). That these three tools and the tools in this set in general were not used in conjunction with Popen is also suggested by the length of complete H1:41 as well as the assumed original length of the fragmentary specimens. H1:41 is 16.5 cm long, and ca. 16.0 and more is a probable original length for the fragmentary specimens. These tools were, in other words, longer than Popen in general were wide (average width of complete Popen: 13.8 cm—see chapter 3). If Amisc1-set3 had been used with Popen, the ends of their work face would have remained unutilized and thus have had a different texture than the rest of the face—something that is not the case.

During use, Amisc1-set3 may have been held with one or both hands; the trimming of the sides/ends of two specimens may have served to facilitate holding during use. The ridge in the middle of the dorsal face of FS 597 (Pl. 169) may have served a similar purpose. The loaf shape and substantial size of these tools make them suitable for grinding grain. Their form is, indeed, reminiscent of the American tools known as 'manos' and used for such purposes. If the tools in this set, as well as a couple more I present below (Amisc1-set4) were actually used for grinding grain, their small number suggests that this was not an important activity at Neolithic Franchthi (see also Popen, chapter 3).

Totally heterogeneous/artificial set

Active miscellanea 1 – set 4 (Amisc1-set4)

Table 4.37. Active miscellanea 1 – set 4 (Amisc1-set4).

Name	Trench:Unit	Prov.	Pres.	Material	Date	L	W	T	Illustr.
FS 74	A:65	C	c	sandstone	(Initial Neol.)	8.0	6.0	6.0	Pl. 170
FS 154	H:13	C	c	andesite	Neol.	9.9	6.8	4.3	Pl. 171
FS 155	H:21	C	c	sandstone	Neol.	10.4	6.3	6.3	Pl. 172
FS 740	L5:26	P	c	sandstone	(MN)	6.0	5.6	4.9	Pl. 173

Amisc1-set4 comprises four complete specimens, each one of which is unique in the whole Franchthi ground stone tool assemblage. Each is described separately.

FS 74 (Pl. 170) is a tool of fine-grained sandstone and of a unique shape—nearly a cube. It is of a good size for holding with one hand. All six faces are flat or lightly convex, and smoothed from active abrasive use. The smoothed abrasive wear in four of the faces, however, is interrupted by battered areas, the result of a secondary active percussive use. This is the only tool that comes from a deposit dated to the Initial Neolithic. It was, however, found in a unit contaminated by later material. If it actually belongs to that phase, its uniqueness in the Franchthi assemblage may be considered as an additional argument for a cultural break between the Initial and the Early Neolithic (see introduction to the Neolithic period, chapter 3).

FS 154 (Pl. 171), of porphyritic andesite, has a wedge shape with a trapezoidal plan and a triangular longitudinal section. Its two trapezoidal faces (A and B) meet at a roughly 45° angle. Only A served as a work face. It is convex and has a well smoothed surface that reflects light, the result of an active diffused abrasive use, perhaps on a relatively soft or pliable material, such as wood or hide. The central area, nevertheless, is scarred, probably from a secondary localized active percussive use. Face B and both sides are generally flat, but have a somewhat irregular surface whose smooth texture probably represents handpolish. Given its unique shape and exogenous raw material, it is not unlikely that FS 154 came from outside the Franchthi region in a ready-made form.

FS 155 (Pl. 172) is made of fine-grained sandstone and has a unique, regular, cylindrical shape. It is missing a part, but this is from such a location that the reconstruction of the shape and dimensions of the original intact tool is not affected. That is why it is considered here as complete. This tool is about 6.0 cm in diameter and has two more or less convex used ends: one (A) has a smoothed surface interrupted in the center by a battered area. The other (B) has a rough, regular surface. The general texture of these ends suggests that they were used primarily in an active abrasive mode, and/or an active percussive mode on a relatively soft material. The small battered area of end A points to a secondary active percussive use against a harder material. The two ends could have been used in conjunction with a passive tool with cavity (see Pcav, chapter 3). The rest of the body has large smoothed areas, probably from active abrasive use, rather than grinding of manufacture.

FS 740 (Pl. 173), of fine-grained sandstone, has the shape of a cone with a rounded top. The base of the cone is almost circular, flat, and well smoothed from an active diffused abrasive use. Given the shape of FS 740, however, this base could also have been used (secondarily?) in an active percussive mode on a soft material, such as meat or hide (to break their fibers).[55] The rounded top is slightly smoothed and has pitting on the highest points, probably from occasional episodes of active abrasive and active percussive use. The body is battered at points, and thus probably was used occasionally in an active percussive mode as well. The more regular pitting on the body, on the other hand, probably resulted from a pecking process of manufacture.

Relatively/generally heterogeneous sets
Active miscellanea 1 – set 5 (Amisc1-set5)

Table 4.38. Active miscellanea 1 – set 5 (Amisc1-set4).

Name	Trench:Unit	Prov.	Pres.	Material	Date	L	W	T	Illustr.
FS 350	FAS:73	C	f	andesite	FN	14.1	9.5	6.0	Pl. 174
S 36	FA:35	C	f	andesite	Neol.	14.9	8.4	5.8	Pl. 175

Amisc1-set5 is made up of two fragmentary tools of an original elliptical or ovate shape. They were originally of substantial size (ca. 15.0 cm or more in maximum dimension), and probably used actively with both hands. Both are made, broadly speaking, of the same kind of porphyritic andesite. This may have come from the same exogenous sources as the porphyritic andesite used for some Popen (chapter 3). Both moreover are well shaped.

S 36 (Pl. 175) belongs to a tool of planoconvex sections. Its flat work face is smoothed, and also shows diagonal scratches, suggesting that it was used in an active abrasive mode diagonally (or at least that was the direction of its latest use episode/s) against a hard, relatively large passive surface. The unutilized, strongly convex, dorsal face seems to carry handpolish.

FS 350 (Pl. 174) represents perhaps one half of the original tool. Its strongly convex work face has a relatively smoothed texture (probably the result of a primary active abrasive use) interrupted by percussion marks in what must have been the central area of the original work face (probably the result of a secondary active percussive use). The work face, moreover, carries red traces, suggesting that this tool was involved in pigment-processing or a pigment-related task. I should note here that FAS:73, from which FS 350 was retrieved, is a 'hearth' unit (see Vitelli 1999:16) and that adjacent unit FAS:72 yielded a certain unidentified red substance. The unutilized dorsal face is, like that of S 36, strongly convex and seems also to carry handpolish.

The porphyritic raw material and the size, shape, and use wear of these two tools make them candidates for use in grinding grain. If they were so used, it was not exclusively, as suggested by the pigment traces on FS 350. Regardless of whether they were used in grain processing, however, these andesite specimens represent two atypical tools. This is perhaps an indication that they were imported to the site ready-made through a process of exchange, or that they came along with their users from outside the region. The latter scenario may be supported by the FN date of FS 350. The FN phase of the site is, after all, believed to have consisted of a series of occupations by groups who stayed for shorter or longer periods of time (Perlès 2004:129–130; Vitelli 1999:89–93).

Active miscellanea 1 – set 6 (Amisc1-set6)

Table 4.39. Active miscellanea 1 – set 6 (Amisc1-set6).

Name	Trench:Unit	Prov.	Pres.	Material	Date	L	W	T	Illustr.
FS 48	G:6	C	c	andesite	Neol.	9.5	8.5	6.0	Pl. 176
S 2	FA	C	c	conglom.?	Neol.	10.5	9.2	6.2	Pl. 177

Amisc1-set6 comprises two complete specimens of similar shape and size. They have an elliptical plan, roughly planoconvex sections, and are ca. 9.0–10.0 cm in maximum dimension and ca. 6.0 cm thick. The morphology and dimensions of these tools make them excellent for holding with one hand during active use.

FS 48 (Pl. 176), of porphyritic andesite, has a generally smoothed lightly convex work face that is scarred in its more central area. The use wear points to a primary active abrasive use and a secondary active percussive use. Given its lightly convex configuration, the work face must have been used (at least abrasively) in conjunction with a lightly concave passive surface. The possibility, however, that the morphology of the work face is the result of a rocking motion during use on a flat passive surface cannot be ruled out (see Adams 1997:8–9). It is interesting that the light convexity of the work face follows a single axis, an indication that it moved reciprocally along this axis. The work face also carries slight red traces, an indication that the tool was used (among others?) in relation to a material of red color (perhaps ocher or clay). The other face consists of a very rounded surface that continues without interruption into the periphery of the tool. The center of this face is very smoothed, suggesting that it was used in an active abrasive mode too. The periphery of the tool consists of lightly smoothed facets. Given their small dimensions and that FS 48 is not in an exhausted state, I am more inclined to see them as the result of manufacture rather than the byproduct of an active abrasive use.

S 2 (Pl. 177) is perhaps of conglomerate. It has two work faces. One (the illustrated) is lightly convex (again in a single axis) and smoothed from an active abrasive use. This, face, however, lacks both the percussive wear and the red traces seen on the work face of FS 48. The second work face of S 2 is strongly convex. It has a smoothed texture from an active abrasive use. This texture, however, is interrupted in the center by a rougher area measuring 5.2×3.1 cm—probably the result of a (passive or active) percussive use. The tool's periphery is in general rough and convex, probably the remainder of the original water-rolled surface of the cobble that served as raw material. It does, however, include a battered area, probably from active percussive use, as well as a flat to slightly convex facet, probably the result of a short active abrasive use.

It is possible that these two tools represent early stages in the process of use that ended in the formation of Arect or Asquare-circ (above, this chapter). It is equally possible, however, that they have nothing to do with these two groups and are simply atypical tools of, perhaps, exogenous origin.

Active miscellanea 1 – set 7 (Amisc1-set7)

Table 4.40. Active miscellanea 1 – set 7 (Amisc1-set7).

Name	Trench:Unit	Prov.	Pres.	Material	Date	L	W	T	Illustr.
FS 295	H1B:95	C	f	sandstone	Neol.	5.4	3.7	1.0	
FS 414	H2B:33	C	f	sandstone	(MN)	10.1	5.7	1.8	Pl. 178
FS 445	FAS:117	C	f	sandstone?	(MN)	6.8	6.6	1.4	
FS 737	L5:1	P	f	sandstone	FN	6.3	5.2	0.6	Pl. 179
FF1:5a	FF1:5	C	f	sandstone	Neol.	7.5	4.6	1.5	Pl. 181
H:40	H:40	C	f	slate	Neol.	4.3	2.6	0.6	
Q4:87/12	Q4:87	P	c	sandstone	EN	7.5	4.3	0.7	
Q5S:186/44	Q5S:186	P	c	sandstone	EN/MN	7.1	3.8	1.2	Pl. 180

Amisc1-set7 comprises eight mostly fragmentary, *a posteriori* specimens. Fine-grained sandstone is the raw material for most of them. I put all these specimens together because they are generally flat and thin—their thickness ranges from 0.6 to 1.8 cm. Neither of the two complete specimens is longer than 7.5 cm and the maximum dimension of the largest fragmentary specimen, FS 414 (Pl. 178), is ca. 10.0 cm. I doubt that any of the other fragments originally had a maximum dimension much greater than this.

Five specimens were used in an active abrasive mode with edges of their faces: FS 295, FS 445, FS 737 (Pl. 179), H:40, and Q4:87/12. FS 737 and Q4:87/12, in particular, have one side that is beveled as a result of active abrasive use with the edges of both faces. Q4:87/12 was also abrasively used with other parts of one of its faces.

Two other specimens, Q5S:186/44 (Pl. 180) and FF1:5a (Pl. 181), are flattish elongated pebbles. Complete Q5S:186/44 has one end that is curved in plan and this is also the shape of the preserved end of fragmentary FF1:5a. The curved end of Q5S:186/44 is smoothed from probably an active abrasive use and also slightly battered perhaps from an occasional active percussive use. That of FF1:5a is battered but not smoothed. One (illustrated) of the faces of Q5S:186/44 has a slightly concave central area that is smoothed from a (passive or active) abrasive use. FF1:5a has a small smoothed area close to the preserved end in its slightly concave (illustrated) face and another close to one of the sides on its slightly convex face.

A last specimen, FS 414 (Pl. 178), has a tabular shape. Its preserved narrow flat side is well smoothed from an abrasive use that was probably active. One of its two flat faces (shown in illustration) is also smoothed, especially in an area close to the used side.

Active miscellanea 1 – set 8 (Amisc1-set8)

Table 4.41. Active miscellanea 1 – set 8 (Amisc1-set8).

Name	Trench:Unit	Prov.	Pres.	Material	Date	L	W	T	Illustr.
FS 284	H1B:78	C	c	sandstone	Neol.	6.2	5.7	2.7	
FS 323	HPed:37N	C	c	sandstone	(MN)	7.0	7.0	3.7	
FS 471	H2A:95	C	c	sandstone	(MN)	5.9	5.3	2.5	
FS 828	HTerrace:9	C	c	sandstone	Neol.	4.3	4.0	3.0	Pl. 182
H1A:93	H1A:93	C	c	sandstone	(EN)	6.7	5.8	3.4	

Amisc1-set8 comprises five complete tools of fine-grained sandstone. They are all small, measuring no more than 7.0 cm in maximum dimension. FS 323, FS 828 (Pl. 182), and H1A:93 are circular or elliptical in plan, FS 471 is nearly square, while FS 284 is polygonal. They were all used exclusively in an active abrasive mode with one, or, most often, two work faces. FS 471 has, in addition, one of its sides flattened from similar use. FS 284, on the other hand, has a periphery that consists of a series of flat or slightly convex facets. The periphery was probably employed when the abrasive use of the faces made the tool too thin for a comfortable grip. All but one (FS 323) of the specimens in this set are too small for further abrasive use of the faces, and thus may be considered exhausted for such a use. Alternatively, these specimens may represent children's tools or educational toys.

Active miscellanea 1 – set 9 (Amisc1-set9)

Table 4.42. Active miscellanea 1 – set 9 (Amisc1-set9).

Name	Trench:Unit	Prov.	Pres.	Material	Date	L	W	T	Illustr.
FS 186	FA:4	C	c	sandstone	Neol.	9.0	7.4	2.0	
FS 276	H1B scarp	C	c	sandstone	Neol.	9.2	6.2	1.9	
FS 373	H2A:75	C	c	sandstone	MN	8.2	7.1	3.4	
FS 455*	FAS:120	C	f	sandstone	MN	4.8	5.6	1.6	
FF1:8b	FF1:8	C	c	sandstone	Neol.	9.4	3.8	0.9	
FF1:11a	FF1:11	C	c	sandstone	Neol.	5.1	4.7	4.4	
FF1:11b	FF1:11	C	c	sandstone	Neol.	6.8	5.0	1.7	
H:2	H:2	C	f	sandstone	Neol.	7.8	4.0	1.9	
H2A:9b	H2A:9	C	f	sandstone	Neol.	7.4	7.1	2.8	
H2A:23/4	H2A:23	C	c	sandstone	Neol.	7.9	6.7	3.4	

Amisc1-set9 consists of 11 complete and fragmentary *a posteriori* tools—basically used water-rolled pebbles and small cobbles. None of the complete specimens exceeds 10.0 cm in maximum dimension and probably none of the fragmentary ones did in its original intact state. Amisc1-set9 carry one, two, or three small, more or less smoothed, facets from use in an active abrasive manner. This use was minor enough not to have really changed the original form of the raw material. FS 186, FS 373, FF1:11a, and H2A:9b carry perhaps additional evidence of an active percussive use. The fragmentary specimens may have had additional used areas in their missing parts. I doubt, nevertheless, that these parts were more heavily used than those preserved.

Active miscellanea 1 – set 10 (Amisc1-set10)

Table 4.43. Active miscellanea 1 – set 10 (Amisc1-set10).

Name	Trench:Unit	Prov.	Pres.	Material	Date	L	W	T	Illustr.
FS 107	G1:11	C	c	sandstone?	(MN)	13.6	5.4	2.5	Pl. 185
FS 270	A:27	C	c	sandstone	(FN)	12.0	4.8	2.8	Pl. 184
FS 379	FAS:102	C	f	sandstone	(LN)	10.7	4.3	3.3	Pl. 183

Amisc1-set10 comprises two complete and one fragmentary *a posteriori* tools of an elongated, curvilinear plan and no thicker than 3.3 cm. FS 379 (Pl. 183) has both faces and sides flattened from an active abrasive use. The faces and sides of FS 270 (Pl. 184) have been used in the same mode, but only face A has been flattened by this use. FS 107 (Pl. 185) was so used only with the faces, but not intensively enough for the shape of the original water rolled cobble to change in any substantial manner. The reason I put these three specimens together in one set is that one or both of their faces carry percussion marks close to one of the ends. The percussion marks may have been the result of a secondary use of these tools in an active percussive punctiform mode as mallets. This is a function, for which their small thickness and elongated shape may have been particularly suited. FS 107 was apparently used in an active percussive mode with one of its ends as well resulting in flake scars in this area. FS 379 may have also been so used with one end of one of its sides (C).

Active miscellanea 1 – set 11 (Amisc1-set11)

Table 4.44. Active miscellanea 1 – set 11 (Amisc1-set11).

Name	Trench:Unit	Prov.	Pres.	Material	Date	L	W	T	Illustr.
FS 196	FA:11	C	c	sandstone	Neol.	9.8	6.6	2.9	
FS 257	H1A:94	C	f	sandstone	(EN)	11.7	11.7	5.4	Pl. 186
FS 261	FAN:59	C	c	sandstone	FN	15.9	11.9	6.3	Fig. 31, Pl. 187
FS 302	H1B:88	C	f	conglom.	Neol.	15.1	11.8	4.4	
FS 303	BE:4	C	c	sandstone	Neol.	10.6	9.2	3.5	
FS 322	FAS:72	C	c	conglom.	FN	18.0	9.4	5.0	Pl. 189
FS 435	FAN:137	C	f	sandstone	MN	11.2	10.5	7.5	
FS 607	L5NE:19	P	c	sandstone	FN	11.3	5.8	5.2	Pl. 188
FS 758	L5:37	P	f	sandstone	EN	9.4	7.9	7.1	
FS 788	P5:152	P	c	sandstone	Neol.	10.7	9.9	5.8	
FS 833	HTerrace:9	C	c	sandstone	Neol.	13.5	11.4	6.7	
FS 850	HTerrace:16	C	c	sandstone	Neol.	12.9	9.1	3.5	
FF1:32A	FF1:32	C	f	sandstone	(MN)	11.8	5.1	4.0	
FAN:89	FAN:89	C	c	sandstone	LN	14.2	10.6	3.7	
S 16	FA:21	C	f	conglom.?	Neol.	8.7	8.4	5.1	
S 33	F:4	C	f	sandstone?	Neol.	11.2	7.7	4.6	
S 40	FA:33A	C	f	sandstone	Neol.	10.5	7.8	3.0	
S 46	FA:19	C	f	sandstone	Neol.	13.0	8.8	4.2	
S 51	FA:34	C	f	conglom.?	Neol.	8.1	5.7	4.3	
S 58	FA surf.	C	c	sandstone	Neol.	13.0	12.1	6.5	

Amisc1-set11 comprises 20 complete and fragmentary, mostly *a posteriori* tools. The material of most specimens is sandstone; conglomerate is represented with a few cases. They have various shapes in plan view: perfectly circular, see FS 257 (Pl. 186); ovate, see FS 261 (Fig. 31, Pl. 187), FS 607 (Pl. 188); subsquare, see S 58; subrectangular, see FS 758; and lenticular, see FS 322 (Pl. 189). They come in a variety of sizes as well: the maximum dimension of the complete specimens ranges from ca. 10.0 to 18.0 cm. The largest among them may have been held with both hands when used. The specimens in this set have one work face that is flat or lightly convex and carries evidence of active abrasive use. The abrasive wear in the center of the work face of FS 303 is interrupted by a small depression similar to those seen on several Asquare-circ and a few Arect (see above, this chapter)—probably the result of a secondary (active or passive) percussive use. S 46 carries more extensive percussive wear in the central area—likely the result of a secondary passive use.

Three complete specimens deserve separate mention: S 257, FS 261, and FS 322. FS 257 (Pl. 186) has a circular plan and planoconvex sections. It has a size and shape excellent for active use with one hand. Evidence of systematic pecking on its unutilized dorsal face as well as some chip/flake scars point to a careful process of manufacture. With its shape and size, FS 257 may have been suitable for inclusion in the Adisc group (above, this chapter). Its raw material, however, is fine-grained sandstone and not calcareous sandstone (sometimes combined with conglomerate), as is the case with Adisc. Moreover, unlike all the dated specimens in the Adisc group, FS 257 comes from a unit of probable EN date. I decided, thus, to keep it separate from Adisc.

FS 261 (Fig. 31, Pl. 187) is manufactured, as suggested by pecking marks on its strongly convex, unutilized dorsal face and evidence of trimming by chipping/flaking on the sides and ends. The trimming may have been intended to facilitate holding. The work face also carries pecking marks that should, however, be attributed to a process of resharpening: the pecking cut through an earlier smoothed surface, small remnants of which can be seen on three spots on the edges of the face (named a–c on work face in Fig. 31). For some reason, the edges of the work face have also been trimmed.

FS 322 (Pl. 189) is made on a gritty kind of conglomerate. It has a lenticular plan and two planoconvex sections. According to the excavation notebooks, red traces were seen on its work face when it came out of the ground. The excavators also noted that this tool was 'associated with a small area of red material (ochre?)'. It can be assumed that it processed a red pigment or at least that was one of its uses.

Active miscellanea 1 – set 12 (Amisc1-set12)

Table 4.45. Active miscellanea 1 – set 12 (Amisc1-set12).

Name	Trench:Unit	Prov.	Pres.	Material	Date	L	W	T	Illustr.
S 12	FA:43	C	f	conglom.	Neol.	18.2	8.1	5.1	
S 14	FA:31	C	f	conglom.	Neol.	13.1	8.2	4.5	

Amisc1-set12 comprises two fragmentary tools made of large-grained conglomerate. S 14 includes parts of the curvilinear periphery and two faces of a tool of planoconvex sections. The surface of the flat work face is well cemented, that of the dorsal convex face is crumbly. The work face is smoothed, especially towards its unbroken edge, a possible indication that it was used in an active abrasive manner.

S 12 has two roughly opposite flat work faces broken all around and discontinuously smoothed. It is unclear whether S 12 is a fragment from a larger tool or a piece of conglomerate found and put to use. The current size of this tool makes it adequate for an active abrasive use.

Active miscellanea 1 – set 13 (Amisc1-set13)

Table 4.46. Active miscellanea 1 – set 13 (Amisc1-set13).

Name	Trench:Unit	Prov.	Pres.	Material	Date	L	W	T	Illustr.
FF1:37c	FF1:37	C	f	sandstone	Neol.	13.0	8.1	0.9	
H2A:8/2	H2A:8	C	f	sandstone	Neol.	7.9	5.9	1.4	

Amisc1-set13 consists of two sandstone flakes. FF1:37c preserves what seem to be portions of a flat used area and an unutilized convex surface. This is the only flake found that may originate from a redesigning process. H2A:8/2 has smoothed zones along two of the broken edges—the result of an active or (less likely) passive abrasive use of the flake itself.

Active miscellanea 1 – set 14 (Amisc1-set14)

Table 4.47. Active miscellanea 1 – set 14 (Amisc1-set14).

Name	Trench:Unit	Prov.	Pres.	Material	Date	L	W	T	Illustr.
FS 357	FAS:76	C	f	sandstone	FN	8.6	4.6	5.6	
FS 389	H2A:77	C	f	sandstone	(MN)	4.3	4.0	1.8	
FS 662	Q5S:131	P	f	sandstone	(MN)	9.5	8.7	4.7	
FS 888	L5:62	P	f	sandstone	Neol.	8.4	5.8	2.4	
FF1:37a	FF1:37	C	f	sandstone	Neol.	12.3	6.8	5.0	
H2A:7/1	H2A:7	C	f	sandstone	Neol.	9.6	3.3	3.1	
Q5S:14/4	Q5S:14	P	f	sandstone	Neol.	5.7	3.0	1.9	
S 49	Paralia surf.	P	f	sandstone	Neol.	10.5	9.4	2.5	

Amisc1-set14 comprises eight fragmentary sandstone specimens, about which little can be said. Some carry some abrasive or percussive wear, but the reconstruction of the shape of the original tools is not possible. Others seem to have used areas that are, however, covered by a layer of concretion.

Active miscellanea 1 – set 15 (Amisc1-set15)

Table 4.48. Active miscellanea 1 – set 15 (Amisc1-set15).

Name	Trench:Unit	Prov.	Pres.	Material	Date	L	W	T	Illustr.
FS 199	FA:10	C	f	sandstone	Neol.	14.0	7.9	7.4	
FS 831	HTerrace:9	C	f	sandstone	Neol.	16.8	11.6	5.4	
FS 872	L5:61	P	f	conglom.	FN	10.4	9.2	5.7	
FS 874	L5:61	P	f	conglom.	FN	10.3	7.2	4.9	
S 65	FA:33	C	c	sandstone	Neol.	11.2	10.8	7.9	

Amisc1-set15 consists of five specimens of sandstone and conglomerate. With the exception of S 65, these are fragments carrying no used areas. Such areas may, nevertheless, have belonged to the missing parts. Alternatively, these specimens represent fragments of raw material that was brought to the site to be converted to tools (neither sandstone nor conglomerate occurs naturally at the site).

S 65 is a complete, probably naturally spherical, sandstone cobble ca. 11.0 cm in diameter. It may carry some evidence of active percussive use. If it does not, it can be considered as a piece of raw material brought to the site.

7.2 Active miscellanea 2 (Amisc2)

Active miscellanea 2, or Amisc2, comprises 66 specimens. They are divided into 10 sets. Set 1 is relatively homogeneous, set 2 is totally heterogeneous/artificial, sets 3 through 10 are generally/relatively heterogeneous. They are all presented below.

The drawing of one specimen appears as Figure 32. Photographs of several specimens by set are found in Plates 190–208 on the CD, folder Neolithic/Active/Amisc/Amisc2.

Relatively homogeneous set

Active miscellanea 2 – set 1 (Amisc2-set1)

Table 4.49. Active miscellanea 2 – set 1 (Amisc2-set1).

Name	Trench:Unit	Prov.	Pres.	Material	Date	L	W	T	Illustr.
FS 129	G1:19	C	c	serpentinite	(MN)	4.3	3.4	1.7	Pl. 190
FS 269	A:27	C	c	serpentinite	(FN)	3.2	2.0	1.0	Pl. 191
FS 358	FAS:81	C	c	serpentinite	FN	3.6	2.3	1.2	Pl. 192
FS 579	H2A:144	C	c	limestone	EN	4.7	3.2	2.3	Pl. 194
FS 629	H2APed:172	C	c	quartz	Neol.	3.3	2.5	1.4	Pl. 193
FS 663	H2APed:191	C	c	steatite	Neol.	3.6	2.7	1.8	Pl. 195
FS 768	Q6N:54	P	c	steatite	(EN)	3.3	2.9	1.4	Pl. 196

Amisc2-set1 comprises seven complete, very small, *a posteriori* specimens, mostly of serpentinite and steatite. They come in several shapes. Four have a roughly rectangular, ovate, or triangular plan, and two more or less parallel faces: FS 129 (Pl. 190), FS 269 (Pl. 191), FS 358 (Pl. 192), and FS 629 (Pl. 193). The other three have roughly pyramidal or conical shapes: FS 579 (Pl. 194), FS 663 (Pl. 195), and FS 768 (Pl. 196).

With the exception of FS 579, all were used exclusively in an active abrasive mode. FS 579 (Pl. 194) probably carries additional evidence of an active percussive use. The surfaces of all but one of these specimens are polished as a result of use. The exception is FS 629 (Pl. 193), which is polished only on its periphery, not on its faces. The polished surfaces of some specimens carry scratches caused by the worked material, e.g., FS 269 (Pl. 191), FS 358 (Pl. 192). The scratches on face A of FS 269 are roughly perpendicular to the long axis of the face; the scratches on face B are less consistent in direction, but those visible on the central area tend to be roughly parallel to the face's long axis, those visible on the ends tend to be perpendicular or diagonal to the face's long axis. The periphery of the tool is covered with small scored facets. It must have been easier to use the periphery than the faces given the tool's small thickness.

The scratches visible on the flat parallel faces of FS 358 (Pl. 192) follow different directions, although most of the strongest ones are perpendicular to the faces' long axis. The scratches on the sides, on the other hand, are parallel to each other and diagonal to the sides' long axis. The sides seem more intensely used than the faces—the thinness of the tool may have made inconvenient an equally intensive active abrasive use of the faces.

FS 269 and FS 358, as other specimens in this set, may have served as pot burnishers (personal communication, Vitelli 5/2006; see also Adams and Greenwald 1979:50–51).[56] Their small size may be due to long use, something common for pot burnishers. 'Most of the pots at Franchthi were … burnished', according to Vitelli (1993:8). That so few of the ground stone tools make candidates for pot burnishers suggests perhaps that at this site pot burnishing took place with the help of other materials (perhaps shell, bone, wood, etc.) or in locations not covered by the excavation. Another hypothesis that may fit the less permanent occupation at Franchthi in LN and FN is that, as is often the case with ethnographic examples, the potters were attached to these precious tools and thus took them along when they left the site.

FS 579 (Pl. 194) has a roughly conical shape and several features not seen in the other items of this set: its base is slightly concave, probably the result of an active abrasive use on a convex surface. The tip of the cone, on the other hand, is pitted, perhaps from a light active percussive use in the context of a fine task. The roughly conical shape of this specimen, and the roughly pyramidal shape of FS 663 (Pl. 195) and FS 768 (Pl. 196), may have allowed a more comfortable grip during the abrasive use of these very small tools. Intriguingly, all three specimens have some of their edges chipped, battered, or broken, a wear that can not have been produced in the context of a regular use life as pot burnishers. One specimen of comparable size and shape has been reported from Kitsos and also interpreted as a possible pot burnisher (Perlès 1981:207). Note, however, that Perlès considers it to be the product of manufacture.

Totally heterogeneous/artificial set
Active miscellanea 2 – set 2 (Amisc2-set2)

Table 4.50. Active miscellanea 2 – set 2 (Amisc2-set2).

Name	Trench:Unit	Prov.	Pres.	Material	Date	L	W	T	Illustr.
FS 68	A:40	C	f	soapstone	FN	10.3	7.5	3.5	Pl. 197
FS 230	FA:46	C	c	limestone	FN	8.8	4.1	2.9	Pl. 198
FS 310	HPed:37T	C	c	chert	EN	4.5	2.2	1.3	Pl. 199
FS 891	L5:68	P	f	peridotite	FN	10.7	8.8	5.6	
H1A:84	H1A:84	C	c	ocher?	Neol.	5.0	4.5	2.6	Pl. 200

Amisc2-set2 comprises five complete and fragmentary specimens. Four have unique characteristics in the whole Franchthi stone tool assemblage. One is unique only in the context of the Neolithic material. I discuss each separately.

FS 68 (Pl. 197) is a fragmentary soapstone tool with two generally flat opposite faces that are smoothed and scratched all over from an active abrasive use. The completely preserved face (A) is the most scratched. Some of the scratches are roughly perpendicular to the long axis of this face, others develop diagonally to this axis, while the most intense scratching developed on the face's ends, probably from extra pressure applied there during use. The periphery of the tool carries facets with similar use wear. Such use wear may have been produced from rubbing a wooden surface (see de Beaune 2000:110).

FS 310 (Pl. 199) is a small specimen of chert. It has a rectangular, thin, tabular shape with flat smoothed faces, sides, and ends. Parts of the sides and one of the ends have been chipped, naturally or artificially. It is uncertain if this specimen represents a tool or a non-tool object.

H1A:84 (Pl. 200) is a small red stone—probably ocher. It has a roughly pyramidal shape with a base that has been ground flat. It was probably used for the production of red pigment by grinding. This experimentally and ethnographically documented technique may have been one of those used at Franchthi to produce paint for pottery decoration (Vitelli 1993:101–103) or other purposes. Since this is the only ground pigment found, it may be assumed that this technique was not employed extensively.

FS 891 is a peridotite cobble of elliptical plan and planoconvex sections. Its flat work face was used in active percussion or perhaps combined percussion and abrasion. Whatever the use was, it seems to have interrupted an earlier surface carrying active abrasive wear, a couple of small remnants of which are visible next to the percussively used surface.

FS 230 (Pl. 198) is unique in the Neolithic component only, not the whole Franchthi stone tool assemblage. It is a small, oblong, water-rolled limestone pebble with one end chipped from both faces to form an acute edge.[57] This tool is reminiscent of Upper Mesolithic specimen H1B:108 (Pl. 14). It may have been used as a retoucher or *compresseur* in the manufacture and maintenance of chipped stone tools, as I suggested for Upper Mesolithic H1B:108 and other small Mesolithic limestone pebble tools. FS 230 comes from a FN unit. Given the similarities to pre-Neolithic specimens, I wonder if it originates in the pre-Neolithic occupation, but was picked up by a FN Franchthiote at the surface of the cave or in a pit dug through pre-Neolithic layers.

Generally/relatively heterogeneous sets
Active miscellanea 2 – set 3 (Amisc2-set3)

Table 4.51. Active miscellanea 2 – set 3 (Amisc2-set3).

Name	Trench:Unit	Prov.	Pres.	Material	Date	L	W	T	Illustr.
FS 54	Cave surf.	C	f	serpentinite?	Neol.	4.1	2.4	0.8	
FS 179	G1:8	C	f	serpentinite?	(MN)	3.7	3.6	3.6	
FS 253	G:38	C	c	serpentinite	Neol.	5.3	4.7	3.3	Pl. 201
FS 664	Q5S:144	P	f	serpentinite	MN	6.6	4.6	4.6	
FF1:5	FF1:5	C	f	limestone	Neol.	6.9	3.1	2.7	
S 64	FA:53	C	f	diabase?	Neol.	6.0	5.1	4.2	

Amisc2-set3 comprises six, mostly fragmentary, tools used primarily with their ends. The material of most of them is serpentinite. The single complete specimen, FS 253 (Pl. 201), is 5.3 cm long and none of the fragmentary ones seems to come from an original intact tool longer than 8.0 cm. The complete specimen has a conical shape, the fragmentary ones seem to come from original tools of roughly conical, cylindrical, or simply elongated shapes. The shape of three tools (FS 54, FS 179, and FS 253) is the result of manufacture by pecking and/or grinding; FF1:5 is an *a posteriori* tool; FS 664 and S 64 may or may not be manufactured. Only FS 253 has both ends preserved, the rest have only one. The ends of these tools are generally flat, although the used end (A) of FS 253 has an anomalous (battered) surface. The latter as well as the preserved end of S 64 are ca. 5.0 cm in maximum dimension. The ends of the remaining tools are all much smaller, an indication that they may have been used in the context of fine tasks. All but one of the preserved ends were used exclusively in an active percussive mode. The exception is end A of FS 253, used first in an active abrasive and later in an active percussive mode. In a couple of cases, parts other than the ends may have been additionally used: part of the body of FF1:5 may have been slightly used in an abrasive mode. The body of S 64 may have been used so extensively; alternatively, this was ground in the context of manufacture.

Active miscellanea 2 – set 4 (Amisc2-set4)

Table 4.52. Active miscellanea 2 – set 4 (Amisc2-set4).

Name	Trench:Unit	Prov.	Pres.	Material	Date	L	W	T	Illustr.
FS 171	FF1:39A	C	c	limestone	(MN)	12.2	9.3	7.8	
FS 194	FA:11	C	c	metaquartzite?	Neol.	12.0	7.5	6.5	Pl. 202
FS 456	FAS:120	C	f	limestone	MN	8.1	5.2	3.9	Pl. 203
FS 565	Q5S:4	P	c	limestone	(MN)	11.8	7.9	6.4	
FS 606	L5NE:19	P	c	quartz	FN	8.5	6.6	5.4	
H1:68a	H1:68	C	c	soapstone	Neol.	8.4	6.3	6.2	
Q5S:89/17	Q5S:89	P	f	limestone	Neol.	8.2	6.4	5.4	

Amisc2-set4 comprises seven, mostly complete, *a posteriori* tools. They are mostly of limestone and roughly cylindrical: see FS 194 (Pl. 202); or conical: see FS 171, FS 456 (Pl. 203), H1:68a. These tools were used primarily with the ends as were those of Amisc2-set3. In general, however, they have larger dimensions than the latter, with some being up to ca. 12.0 cm long. Their mostly rounded ends were used in an active percussive mode and perhaps also in an active abrasive mode and in a rotary fashion. Some of these tools, e.g., FS 194 (Pl. 202) and FS 565, may have been used in conjunction with passive tools with cavity made of stone or wood (see Pcav, chapter 3). The base of the conically shaped H1:68a is battered from an active percussive use that apparently followed an active abrasive one—or so is suggested by remnants of an abrasively used surface visible around the battered surface. Parts of the bodies of these tools were used in an active abrasive, and occasionally percussive, mode as well, e.g., FS 194 (Pl. 202), FS 456 (Pl. 203), H1:68a.

Active miscellanea 2 – set 5 (Amisc2-set5)

Table 4.53. Active miscellanea 2 – set 5 (Amisc2-set5).

Name	Trench:Unit	Prov.	Pres.	Material	Date	L	W	T	Illustr.
FS 189	FA:6	C	f	serpentinite	Neol.	6.3	4.4	2.7	
FS 211	H1:20	C	c	serpentinite	Neol.	9.0	6.4	4.0	Pl. 205
FS 215	H1:31	C	c	quartz	Neol.	7.7	5.7	3.4	Pl. 204
FS 255	FAN:74	C	f	quartz	(FN)	6.5	4.1	3.4	
FS 271	A:34	C	c	diabase	Neol.	8.4	4.9	2.5	
FS 290	H1B:94	C	c	serpentinite	Neol.	6.3	6.3	2.7	
FS 452	FAS:117	C	f	serpentinite	(MN)	6.4	5.7	3.8	
FA:24	FA:24	C	f	limestone	Neol.	4.5	2.8	2.5	
FF1:32c	FF1:32	C	c	limestone	(MN)	5.3	3.9	4.1	
FF1:34a*	FF1:34	C	f	limestone	(MN)	6.3	7.8	5.7	
FF1:39Aj*	FF1:39A	C	f	limestone	(MN)	6.0	8.1	5.7	
FF1:40B1b	FF1:40B1	C	c	limestone	MN	6.1	3.1	1.8	
H:24	H:24	C	c	limestone	Neol.	5.7	5.4	3.1	
L5NE:15/10	L5NE:15	P	c	serpentinite	FN	6.7	5.4	2.1	
Q4:72/10	Q4:72	P	c	serpentinite	Neol.	6.3	5.1	1.9	
S 3	Cave surf.	C	c	limestone	Neol.	10.2	9.5	5.8	
S 28	FA:27	C	c	serpentinite	Neol.	7.0	5.6	4.6	
S 35	FA:35	C	f	limestone?	Neol.	7.0	6.5	3.8	
S 60	FA:6	C	f	limestone	Neol.	9.1	6.7	3.9	

Amisc2-set5 comprises 19 complete and fragmentary tools. They are basically water-rolled pebbles and small cobbles modified through use, not manufacture. The most common raw materials in this set are serpentinite and limestone. The complete specimens are between ca. 5.0 and 10.0 cm in maximum dimension, and with a couple of exceptions, none of the fragmentary specimens seems to have exceeded 10.0 cm in maximum dimension in its original intact state. All these specimens were mainly used in an active abrasive mode with one or more areas of their body, e.g., FS 215 (Pl. 204), FS 255, FS 271, FS 452, or with whole faces, e.g., FS 189, FS 290, FF1:39Aj, S 3. With one exception, FS 211 (Pl. 205) (see below), none seems to have been used intensively enough for the shape of the original pebbles and cobbles that served as raw material to change in any significant way. The abrasive use did, nevertheless, produce a strong polish in the affected area of FS 215, whereas the affected areas of some other specimens carry short stries of various directions, e.g., FF1:40B1b, L5NE:15/10, Q4:72/10. Some of these tools also carry percussion marks on the ends, sides, or faces, an indication that they were occasionally used in an active percussive mode, as well (see FS 452, FF1:34a, FF1:39Aj, S 28). FS 290 may have been used in an active or passive percussive mode as indicated by pitting shown in the center of both faces.

Unlike the other specimens in this set, FS 211 (Pl. 205) was used intensively enough in an active abrasive mode for facets to form on its surfaces. This serpentinite tool has a well-smoothed facet that covers a large portion of one face and one side. The location of the facet suggests that the original water-rolled cobble moved over the passive surface at an angle: given the thinness of this tool, that seems to have been the most comfortable way to use this face in an abrasive mode. The second, roughly parallel, face carries a less strong facet that covers about half of its surface, the result of a more limited, but also oblique, active abrasive use. Both facets carry scoring. They may have been produced from smoothing a tool or a non-tool object made of wood.

Active miscellanea 2 – set 6 (Amisc2-set6)

Table 4.54. Active miscellanea 2 – set 6 (Amisc2-set6).

Name	Trench:Unit	Prov.	Pres.	Material	Date	L	W	T	Illustr.
FS 382	FAS:105	C	c	soapstone	LN	7.1	6.3	5.3	Pl. 206
G1:15	G1:15	C	f	soapstone	(MN)	8.5	5.5	3.5	

Amisc2-set6 comprises two tools of soapstone. They are both *a posteriori*—water-rolled cobbles modified by use. Both faces of G1:15 and face A of FS 382 (Pl. 206) were used actively and abrasively in a way that produced a very lustrous surface. This surface carries many fine short stries running in different directions. The pronounced luster may have been produced from smoothing leather.[58] The fine stries could have been caused by tiny particles found on the leather surface. FS 382 carries one facet on face B and one on each of the sides, all used probably in the same way as face A, although not as extensively; that may explain the lack of the characteristic lustrous surface.

Active miscellanea 2 – set 7 (Amisc2-set7)

Table 4.55. Active miscellanea 2 – set 7 (Amisc2-set7).

Name	Trench:Unit	Prov.	Pres.	Material	Date	L	W	T	Illustr.
FS 576	FAS:132	C	f	limestone	EN/MN	6.4	6.3	2.4	
FS 609	L5NE:22	P	c	limestone	FN	12.6	9.6	4.1	
FS 775*	Q5S:216	P	f	limestone	MN	6.6	6.8	6.5	Pl. 207
FS 829	HTerrace:8	C	c	basalt	Neol.	11.6	9.0	5.1	Fig. 32, Pl. 208
H:38	H:38	C	f	limestone	(MN)	6.0	5.1	3.6	
S 31	FA:29	C	f	soapstone	Neol.	8.2	8.0	3.9	
S 42	FA:43	C	c	limestone	Neol.	10.1	9.2	3.9	
S 67	FA:44	C	c	limestone	Neol.	12.5	12.0	4.2	

Amisc2-set7 comprises eight complete and fragmentary specimens mostly of limestone. With one possible exception, FS 775 (Pl. 207), all are *a posteriori* tools—water-rolled cobbles modified by use. They have or had originally an elliptical and more rarely a rectangular plan. The complete among them range from ca. 10.0 to 12.5 cm in maximum dimension and these figures may apply to the original complete tools from which the fragmentary specimens derive. All the specimens in this set have one work face or two opposite ones. The work faces are flattened more or less strongly by an active abrasive use. Active abrasive wear is more rarely visible on the periphery or sides. The reason I put all these specimens in the same set is that the abrasive wear is interrupted in the central area of one or both of the faces by active or passive percussive wear—the result of a secondary use that followed the abrasive use with the entire face. The percussive wear usually takes the form of a pitted surface, see S 42, S 67; or a small depression: see FS 775 (Pl. 207), S 31. The depression seen on one (illustrated) of the faces of FS 775, in particular, is reminiscent of those seen in several Asquare-circ and a few Arect (above, this chapter). Its location in what is now the center of the face may be an indication that it was formed after the fracture of the tool. FS 829 (Fig. 32, Pl. 208) has a much larger battered area on one (illustrated) of its faces. It covers all but the edges of this face and must be the result of a passive percussive use or a combined passive percussive and abrasive use. This area, moreover, carries a yellowish stain, suggesting that the face was involved in the processing of a coloring agent, perhaps ocher. FS 829 is the only tool in the Franchthi ground stone tool assemblage that may have been used with specimens in the Aglobe-stain group (above, this chapter). In a couple of specimens, parts other than the faces were additionally used: the periphery of S 42 seems to have been used in an active percussive mode, whereas the sides of FS 775 (Pl. 207) were so used after being employed in an active abrasive mode.

Active miscellanea 2 – set 8 (Amisc2-set8)

Table 4.56. Active miscellanea 2 – set 8 (Amisc2-set8).

Name	Trench:Unit	Prov.	Pres.	Material	Date	L	W	T	Illustr.
FS 197	FA:11	C	f	serpentinite	Neol.	8.2	6.7	1.4	
FS 507	FAN:148	C	f	limestone	(MN)	3.5	2.3	0.6	
FAN:142	FAN:142	C	f	limestone	(MN)	4.1	3.3	0.7	
FAN:143	FAN:143	C	f	limestone	(MN)	3.1	2.3	0.6	

Amisc2-set8 consists of four flakes. FS 197 comes from a serpentinite cobble and carries scoring next to one of the broken edges, probably from an active abrasive use that took place after the fracture of the original cobble. FS 507 is a limestone flake that may come from a tool or a non-tool object that was pecked. FAN:142 and FAN:143 are small discoidal flakes removed from limestone pebbles. Their surface has pitting and scoring in various directions, use wear that seems to belong to the original pebbles. A number of similar flakes have been retrieved from Upper Mesolithic deposits, whereas negatives of flakes of similar shape and size have been noted on limestone pebbles dated to the same period (see chapter 2). FAN:142 and FAN:143 were excavated in two MN units that also produced some earlier Neolithic material. Given the similarities with the Mesolithic examples, I find it possible that FAN:142 and FAN:143 derive from the Pre-Neolithic component of the site. They may have ended up in later deposits by being picked up by Neolithic inhabitants at the surface of the cave or in pits dug through pre-Neolithic layers.

Active miscellanea 2 – set 9 (Amisc2-set9)

Table 4.57. Active miscellanea 2 – set 9 (Amisc2-set9).

Name	Trench:Unit	Prov.	Pres.	Material	Date	L	W	T	Illustr.
FS 417	FAN:131	C	f	basalt	MN	9.2	4.1	3.2	
FS 422	FAN:133	C	f	serpentinite	MN	5.2	4.6	3.6	
FF1:8c	FF1:8	C	f	serpentinite?	Neol.	5.4	5.4	1.0	
H2APed:187	H2APed:187	C	f	jasper	Neol.	3.2	2.8	1.2	
L5:2/30	L5:2	P	f	serpentinite	FN	5.9	4.0	2.0	
O5:83/12	O5:83	P	f	chlorite schist	EN	4.7	2.0	2.8	
Q5S:52/10	Q5S:52	P	f	serpentinite	Neol.	4.3	3.3	1.4	

Amisc2-set9 comprises seven fragments of pebbles or cobbles of a variety of raw materials, each preserving some evidence of abrasive or percussive use. These fragments are so small or from such a location that reconstruction of the shape of the original tool is not possible.

Active miscellanea 2 – set 10 (Amisc2-set 10)

Table 4.58. Active miscellanea 2 – set 10 (Amisc2-set 10)

Name	Trench:Unit	Prov.	Pres.	Material	Date	L	W	T	Illustr.
FS 646	O5NE:32	P	f	limestone	MN	10.6	5.0	1.9	
FS 780	PQ5:14	P	f	basalt?	MN	6.4	6.2	3.9	

Amisc2-set10 consists of two fragmentary specimens covered with concretion. It is not possible to say whether they were used.

Epilogue

The category of active tools at Franchthi is divided into six more or less homogeneous groups and one heterogeneous one. The first six groups include tools with a more or less specific form, although a specific form is not necessarily combined with a single function. Perhaps the most common characteristic of the active tools is that they served a variety of purposes. With the exception of most Acut and Adisc, most active tools show a variety of kinds of active abrasive and percussive wear, and sometimes, some evidence of passive, mostly percussive, wear as well. The dominant use wear is abrasive, the percussive wear is in general more limited—a pattern seen already among the Neolithic passive tools, as well as in the pre-Neolithic assemblage.

Conspicuous by their absence among the active tools are specimens used consistently for flaking—small, usually ovoid, pebbles with percussive use wear on their ends. The explanation I found likely for a similar absence from the Pre-neolithic deposits—that such implements were too precious to their users to be left behind (chapter 2)—may not be easily entertained for the more or less permanently settled groups of the Neolithic (or at least EN and MN). It may in this case be more likely that flint knapping tools were discarded in specific areas not touched by the excavation. I should, nevertheless, note that lithic debris has been found scattered throughout the site.

NOTES

1. A shorter, and at points different, version of this subchapter has been published in *Hesperia* (Stroulia 2003).
2. I myself used the term 'celts' in an earlier presentation of this material. See previous note.
3. '*Hache*' and '*herminette*' in French respectively.
4. Not 89, as reported in the *Hesperia* article. Since the time of that publication, I decided to transfer FS 737 from this group to the group of Active miscellanea 1 (set 7), (below this chapter).
5. More than 80% of Popen are fragmentary (chapter 3).
6. This number includes one specimen (FS 22) found on the terrace just outside the cave mouth (trench B).
7. For specific assemblages, see Evans and Renfrew 1968:66; Moundréa-Agrafioti and Gnardellis 1994:199; Warren, M. and H. Jarman, Shackleton, and Evans 1968:239, footnote 1.
8. See, for example, Achilleion (Winn and Shimabuku 1989:266), Stavroupoli (Alisøy 2002:562), Makriyalos (Tsoraki 2007:291; Yeroussi 1999:58), Dispilio (Melfos and Stratouli 2002:179; Stratouli 2002:161), and Makri (Melfos, Stratouli, Vavelidis, and Efstratiou 2001:766–767).
9. But at Dispilio nearby outcrops were primarily exploited (Melfos and Stratouli 2002:179; Stratouli 2002:161–162). A similar extraction of blanks from outcrops is reported for Nea Nikomedeia (Rodden 1962:279).
10. For Dispilio see Melfos and Stratouli 2002:177–181; for Makri see Melfos, Stratouli, Vavelidis, and Efstratiou 2001:766–768.
11. According to petrographic analysis, most of the stones used for specimens from Drakaina Cave and Saliagos have sources outside the islands where these two sites are located (Evans and Renfrew 1968:65–66; Oosterom 1968; Stratouli 2005:129; Stratouli and Melfos in press). Stones used for a large number of Sitagroi specimens have been, by similar methods, also shown to be non local (Dixon 2003a; 2003b; Elster 2003a:179). According to macroscopic petrological analysis, the raw material of two specimens from Neolithic Knossos comes from sources about 50 km from the site (Strasser and Fassoulas 2003–2004). The raw materials used for the *haches* from Kitsos and three of the 'axes' found at Tharrounia are also suspected to be of non local origin (Perlès 1981:197; Sugaya 1993:443–444).
12. See, for example, Kozák's account of stone 'ax' manufacture among the Héta Indians of southern Brazil (1972:18).
13. The Acut group is not atypical of Greek Neolithic assemblages of similar tools in this aspect either: flaking has rarely been detected as a manufacturing technique in these assemblages (Perlès 2001:233). More specifically, it has been noticed in specimens from Makriyalos (Yeroussi 1999:61) and Makri (Stroulia 2005b, 2005c). Perlès has also seen examples in materials from western Macedonia (1992:130). Flaking seems to have been more commonly used in the production of cutting edge tools further north. See, for example, the material from Divostin (Prinz 1988) and Selevac (Voytek 1985, 1990).
14. Sawing is defined as splitting a piece of stone by producing opposite narrow grooves through grinding (Wright 1992:57). It involves the use of water with an abrasive material (e.g., sandstone, sand, or emery) and a string or pointed tools of flint, bone, antler, shell, or wood (see Semenov 1964:70-73). The technique of sawing was used to extract raw material from outcrops or produce one or more smaller tools out of a larger one that broke or was no longer useful as such. It has been identified in several Aegean Neolithic assemblages of cutting edge tools: see Nea Nikomedeia (Rodden 1962:279), Sesklo and Dimini (Moundréa-Agrafioti 1981:183-184; Tsountas 1908:315–316), Dispilio (Stratouli 2002:161–162), Olynthos (Mylonas 1929:65), Servia (Mould, Ridley, and Wardle 2000:112, 114), Agios Petros (Efstratiou 1985:45), Megalo Nisi Galanis (Stroulia 2005a), Makriyalos (Tsoraki 2007:291; Yeroussi 1999:35–37).
15. This, nevertheless, is a choice that some modern manufacturers of cutting edge tools are willing to make when dealing with fragile and delicate raw materials. Groups in Irian Jaya, New Guinea, produce 'adze blades' from such materials by a grinding process alone that can last up to two months (Pétrequin and Pétrequin 1993b:363–365).
16. Both this and the following hypothesis have been suggested for many Sesklo specimens that have their proximal parts left unground (Christopoulou 1992:68).
17. But see Ricq-de Bouard and Buret (1987:178–180) who, on the basis of their study of assemblages from Mediterranean France, argue that the presence of 'residual' pecking has probably more to do with the raw material used each time than with hafting.
18. According to Blackwood (1950:16), the differences in the extent of grinding of 'adzes' among the Kukukuku of New Guinea 'appear to be due more to the personal equation rather than to the kind of stone used'.
19. See, however, the Maori who consider grinding 'axes' made of the hard material nephrite 'as a pleasant, even relaxing, activity, and most popular with older men' (Leighton and Dixon 1992:189). I should also note that, according to ethnographic reports, work on the grinding/polishing of the entire tool surface could take place at spare moments over a long period of time and

long after the tools were sufficiently complete to have been put to use (Woodbury 1954:42).

20. E.g., Megalo Nisi Galanis and other sites in the Kozani area (Stroulia 2005a and personal observations 7/2002), Dispilio (personal observations 7/2002), Achilleion (Winn and Shimabuku 1989:266), Makriyalos (Tsoraki 2007:291; Yeroussi 1999:61), and Makri (Stroulia 2005b, 2005c).

21. See, e.g., Edmonds 1995; Lunardi (in press); Voytek 1985.

22. Such features are often mentioned in the ethnographic/ethnoarchaeological literature (see Anderson 1890:74; Dickson 1972:208–209, 1981:42–44; Hampton 1999:69, 93–97). None has so far been identified in Greece (Perlès 2001:233, note 12).

23. For sandstone, see Dickson 1981:156. Clay is a quite good polishing agent according to my own experiments. For an ethnographic example of clay use in this context, see also Kozák 1972:20.

24. Red pigment, though, could have also been used for decorative or symbolic purposes, or in the context of a ritual initiation of the use of the tool (see Hampton 1999:87; Pétrequin and Pétrequin 1993b:367; Toth, Clark, and Ligabue 1992:92).

25. Many more polishing techniques are mentioned in the ethnographic literature. The Maori, for example, are reported to have rubbed their 'adzes' with pieces of a particular kind of wood or with a specific kind of shark oil (Best 1974:46), whereas men in the village of Ormu in Irian Jaya use palm leaves and latex (Pétrequin and Pétrequin 1993a:330).

26. This number refers to the inventoried specimens only. Non-inventoried antler sleeves may exist. Antler sleeves and other antler hafts (some definitely used with cutting edge tools) have been reported from Dimini and Sesklo (Moundréa-Agrafioti 1987; Tsountas 1908:316–318), Dikili Tash (Séfériadès 1992b:105, 109), and Dispilio (Stratouli 2002:171).

27. For what some of these wooden hafts may have looked like, see those preserved in the lacustrine sites of eastern France and Switzerland (Müller-Beck 1965:13–49; Pétrequin and Jeunesse 1995:15–19; Pétrequin and Pétrequin 1988:25, 149–150).

28. For archaeological, experimental, and ethnographic information on techniques of hafting cutting edge tools, see Becker 1945; Blackwood 1950:21–22; Carneiro 1974:110–111, 1979:24–27; Dickson 1981:158–167; Godelier and Garanger 1973:198–200; Hampton 1999:72–88; Heider 1967:56; Hellweg 1984:98; Kozák 1972:21–22; Malinowski 1934:191; Moundréa-Agrafioti 1987; Müller-Beck 1965:13–49; Pétrequin and Jeunesse 1995:15–19; Pétrequin and Pétrequin 1988:25–28, 105–106, 148–153, 1993a:43–59; Pond 1930:93–94; Rostain and Wack 1987:124–130; Schoen 1969:18; Sillitoe 1988:43–50; Steensberg 1980:5–24; Toth, Clark, and Ligabue 1992:92; Tsountas 1908:316–322.

29. But see Ricq-de Bouard and Buret (1987:181), who argue that of the two treatments, only the one involving secondary pecking is related to hafting.

30. Sesklo: concentration of pecked pebbles, roughouts, and broken or blunt tools (Tsountas 1908:316); Dispilio: pieces of serpentinite with evidence of sawing (Melfos and Stratouli 2002:176, 179; Stratouli 2002:161–162); Nea Nikomedeia: 'discarded grooved flakes' or, in other words, byproducts of a sawing process (Rodden 1962:279); Makri: unfinished tools representing different stages of the production sequence (Bekiaris 2007:78–80; Efstratiou and Ntinou 2004; Stroulia 2005b, 2005c); Makriyalos: byproducts of different stages of the manufacturing process (Tsoraki, personal communication 3/07).

31. Such an area is perhaps the one identified by Tsountas at Sesklo (see previous note). See also the controversial evidence for a 'stone-axe workshop' at Makri (Bekiaris 2007:78–80; Efstratiou and Ntinou 2004; Stroulia 2005b, 2005c). A number of prehistoric production sites for cutting edge tools (often called workshops or factories) have been identified in other parts of Europe, e.g., Serbia (Prinz 1988:257–259; Voytek 1985:261–262, 335, 1990:470–473), Bosnia (Benac 1973:82), Turkish Thrace (Erdogu 2000; Ozbek 2000), Great Britain (Edmonds 1993, 1995:49–79), France (Le Roux 1971; Pétrequin and Jeunesse 1995:21–60). I should note that in all the non-Greek cases flaking is part of the manufacturing sequence and that most of these production sites are located away from settlements.

32. There is nothing so complex or extraordinary in the form and size of these tools that would have required a high level of technical expertise. The following observation made by Olausson on the basis of ethnographic and experimental evidence fits the generally small soft Franchthi tools perfectly: 'any individual with strong hands and normal dexterity can easily master the pecking and grinding techniques needed to produce a groundstone axe' (1982–1983:33).

33. See also Taçon, according to whom stone 'axes' were recognized as belonging to men among Australian Aborigines in western Arnhem Land (1991:194–195). An archaeological association of cutting edge tools with males has been noticed in some European contexts (see Farrugia 1992, as cited in Perlès 2001:236; Patton 1991; Pétrequin and Pétrequin 1988:105–106).

34. The first mechanism has been suggested for the material from Saliagos (see Oosterom 1968:100), the second for specimens from Sitagroi, Knossos, and Drakaina Cave (Elster 2003a:179, 185; Strasser and Fassoulas 2003–2004; Stratouli 2005:129; Stratouli and Melfos, in press).

35. The distinction between symmetrical and asymmetrical tools seems more pronounced in the context of some Thessalian assemblages (see Moundréa-Agrafioti 1981; Moundréa-Agrafioti and Gnardellis 1994).

36. See the group of Thessalian sites studied by Moundréa-Agrafioti (1981:186), Dikili Tash (Séfériadès 1992a:88–90, 94), and Stavroupoli (Alisøy 2002:568–569). I have personally seen many such tools in assemblages from the vicinity of Kozani and Kastoria and I suspect that many more exist in other (published and unpublished) Greek assemblages. This edge configuration is also known from Divostin (Prinz 1988).

37. They are common among modern New Guinea groups (see Hampton 1999; Pétrequin and Pétrequin 1993a).

38. Toy tools are documented ethnographically. See, for example, Etheridge (1893:298).

39. For a similar situation see the material from Kitsos (Perlès 1981:199) and Tharrounia (Sugaya 1993:443).

40. To my knowledge, such analysis has been conducted so far on only three Aegean Neolithic assemblages: those from Sesklo A (Christopoulou 1979, 1992), Theopetra Cave (Christopoulou 2000), and Makriyalos (Yeroussi 1999).

41. See also O'Hare for a couple of examples of small flat-edged specimens from Neolithic southern Italy (1990:231).

42. I should note here that flakes that include part of a cutting edge have been reported from Makriyalos. Yeroussi (1999:61–62), citing Voytek, suggests that these flakes were deliberately removed from the tools in the context of a process of edge rejuvenation (see also Tsoraki, personal communication, 8/08). Voytek discovered what she calls 'resharpening flakes' in the material from Selevac (1985:160, 184, 381).

43. I am referring here to FS 525. It is included in the category of ornaments studied for publication by Perlès and Miller (in preparation).

44. O'Hare's (1990:137) hypothesis that the perforation in some southern Italian specimens may have aimed at ritually 'killing' the original complete tools can not be sustained for the Greek specimens; their small size and lack of use wear precludes any original utilitarian function.

45. This is FS 593, mistakenly inventoried as a ground stone artifact. It measures 7.8×5.2×2.0 cm.

46. A couple of flat-edged tools of a size similar to that of FS 210 have been reported from a collection of Euboean material (Sampson and Sugaya 1988–1989:19). Others have been found in prehistoric contexts in Sicily and southern Italy (Leighton and Dixon 1992:192–193).

47. Séfériadès (1992a:93–94) also suspects that some LN specimens from Dikili Tash were used in hide processing. See also Alisøy 2002:571 and Perlès 2001:236. For relevant experiments, see Beugnier 1997.

48. The radiocarbon dates suggest a span of between 400 and 1000 years for EN (see Table 3.1).

49. For ethnographic documentation of such a use see, for example, Strathern 1965:185, 1970:322–323; Rostan and Wack 1987:131–132. Skeletal evidence for the use of such tools for attacking humans comes, for example, from prehistoric cultures of North America (see Strezewski 2006; Willey 1990:114; Willey and Emerson 1993:259).

50. The remaining FN deposits on Paralia consist of graves (Perlès 2004:129; Vitelli 1999:18).

51. A small patch of similar sediment was, however, identified in Paralia trench O5 (Wilkinson and Duhon 1990:44–46, 152).

52. These pits show the highest density of ground stone tools anywhere in the site.

53. Active tools with concave work faces that moved transversally over passive tools with convex work faces are known from the Bronze Age or the Classical era (see Runnels 1981:117–119; Webb 1988, 2000). They are much larger than Arect and typically used for grain grinding.

54. On the efficacy of chert hammers used for pecking, see experiments by Dubreuil (2002:165, 182) and Runnels (1981:249–250).

55. Ethnographic examples of the use of tools of conical shape as meat tenderizers are mentioned by de Beaune (2000:122–123). On the use of ground stone tools for breaking the fibers of meat or hides, see Dubreuil 2002:126; Hamon 2006:99–102.

56. Serpentinite is a common raw material for the Thessalian tools discussed as possible pot burnishers by Moundréa-Agrafioti (1981:257).

57. I should note that the Franchthi assemblage includes two much larger active tools, FS 167 (Pl. 100) and FS 297 (Pl. 98), of peridotite and sandstone respectively, which have an acute edge formed either during a process of manufacture through bifacial chipping/flaking or *a posteriori* as a result of an active percussive use (see Arect, this chapter).

58. An ethnographic example of a water-rolled quartz cobble used in, among other things, the smoothing of leather, is reported by de Beaune (1989a).

CHAPTER FIVE

Summary and Conclusions

The excavations at the site of Franchthi Cave yielded a total of 522 ground stone tools and related manufacturing remains and raw material. Two hundred and fifty-nine, or about half, of the specimens are complete or almost complete; 261 specimens are fragmentary. The remaining two specimens represent roughouts and are, thus, neither complete nor fragmentary. Four hundred and five specimens (78%) were excavated in the cave (including the terrace just outside the cave mouth), 116 (22%) were recovered on Paralia. For one specimen no provenience information whatsoever is available (Appendix A).

Contextual associations with pottery and/or lithics allowed the dating of 265 specimens (about half of the assemblage) to specific pre-Neolithic periods and Neolithic phases. One hundred and forty eight of them are assigned secure dates, 117 are assigned probable dates (the latter include 17 specimens dated to interphases) (Appendix B). The remaining 257 specimens were found in surface or disturbed deposits that yielded Neolithic pottery, along with small quantities of pre-Neolithic lithics and fauna and post-Neolithic pottery.

I divided the whole ground stone tool assemblage into two main components: pre-Neolithic and Neolithic. One surface tool, on the other hand, has characteristics that leave no doubt of its post-Neolithic origin.

The pre-Neolithic component includes 26 specimens that were excavated in stratified deposits dated to various Palaeolithic and Mesolithic periods. All were recovered inside the cave. Another nine specimens found in surface layers or disturbed deposits of the cave show enough similarities to the stratified pre-Neolithic material and differences from the stratified Neolithic material to suggest that they may originate in the pre-Neolithic occupation of the site as well. They are considered as possible pre-Neolithic specimens and they are presented as such in this volume. The pre-Neolithic component is very heterogeneous; thus I was more or less forced to present its members individually. This may be a good thing, after all, since we know nothing about the ground stone tools used in the Aegean before the Neolithic.

The Neolithic component includes 239 specimens that were excavated in stratified deposits of both cave and Paralia and dated to specific Neolithic phases. Another 247 derive from surface or disturbed deposits but show enough similarities to the stratified Neolithic specimens to suggest that they may also originate in the Neolithic occupation of the site. I consider them as Neolithic and they are treated as such in this volume. The Neolithic component thus comprises the vast majority of specimens in the Franchthi ground stone tool assemblage, a total of 486 (93%). I divided this large sample into two broad categories: passive and active. The category of passive tools comprises 112 specimens (23%), that of active tools 374 specimens (77%). Since a number of tools seem to have been used in both a passive and an active mode, these two categories are not mutually exclusive. On the basis of similarities in shape and size, use wear, and, to a larger or smaller degree, raw material—or lack thereof—I created several groups for each category. Three groups have been constructed for the passive tools:

1. Passive open tools (Popen);
2. Passive tools with cavity (Pcav);
3. Passive miscellanea (Pmisc).

Seven groups have been constructed for the far more numerous category of active tools:

1. Active cutting edge tools (Acut);
2. Active discoidal tools (Adisc);
3. Active rectangular tools (Arect);

4. Active square or circular tools (Asquare-circ);
5. Active tools used with ends (Aend);
6. Active globular tools (Aglobe), with two subgroups, Active globular tools with stains (Aglobe-stain) and Active globular tools without stains (Aglobe-nostain);
7. Active miscellanea (Amisc), with two subgroups, Active miscellanea 1 (Amisc1) and Active miscellanea 2 (Amisc2).

In the following sections I summarize the information gleaned from the study of the Franchthi assemblage and articulate its trends along five axes: raw material, manufacture, use and discard, chronological distribution, and spatial distribution.

Raw material

The raw materials used were, in general, collected in the form of water-worn pebbles, cobbles, or small boulders. This is true of both the pre-Neolithic and the Neolithic material. Only for a small number of specimens—all belonging to the Adisc group—is there a suspicion that primary sources (i.e., outcrops) may have been exploited. No specimen in this assemblage has been subjected to thin section petrography but, as I have shown, there are reasons to believe that the water-worn rocks were for the most part picked up in local stream and river beds, or at nearby beaches. Such a raw material procurement strategy required no specialized skills—although one needed to know what kind of rock s/he was looking for—and this is one of the arguments for a general lack of specialization in the production of the Franchthi tools.

A variety of raw materials are represented in the Franchthi assemblage. Some of them were obviously preferred above others. Sandstone (of different types) is by far the most common, and was used for at least 39% of the total number of specimens. Serpentinite and limestone are the next most common raw materials, comprising at least 22% and 10% respectively. Combined, these three materials account for over 70% of the assemblage. Their frequent occurrence is an additional argument for their local origin. Andesite and diabase were used for about 4% of specimens each; peridotite for about 3%, conglomerate, basalt and steatite/soapstone for about 2% each; chert, quartz and a few other materials for less than 2% each.

As I suggested in chapter 2, it is possible that during the Pre-Neolithic periods, some tools of raw material types common in the Franchthi area (e.g., sandstone) came to the site with their mobile users from outside the region. It is also possible that one specimen in the Acut group, whose material seems to be fired steatite, was imported to the site, along with a large number of opaque white beads made in this material. There is one type of stone, however, that is different enough from the local ones to leave little doubt of its exogenous origin: andesite. Two main varieties have been identified at Franchthi, porphyritic and aphanitic, and at least the porphyritic is likely to have come from sources in the Saronic Gulf. Not unlike the local raw materials used, andesite seems to have been collected in the form of water-rolled cobbles and small boulders. Some of the andesite tools are atypical enough to suggest that they probably entered the site ready-made. Others show strong similarities in shape and size to specimens made of local sandstone, an indication that, in this case, it was probably the unworked cobbles/boulders—not the finished tools—that were brought to the site, and Franchthi people the ones who fashioned them into usable implements.

But why was andesite (in either form) brought to Franchthi? Andesite is a good quality material for grinding tools, which is why it was systematically sought after and used in later times (Runnels 1981:142–145, 1985; see also Williams-Thorpe and Thorpe 1993). Yet the small number of andesite specimens found at Franchthi, coupled with their wide chronological distribution—the dated specimens come from all but one of the Neolithic phases[1] as well as the Upper Mesolithic—makes it unlikely that this exogenous raw material entered the site to serve needs that could not be satisfied by local stones (mainly sandstone). There are two other possibilities: 1. Andesitic cobbles and boulders were obtained directly at the sources by Franchthiotes who happened to be there in the context of expeditions with other priorities; 2. The raw material or the finished products were imported to the site through an exchange network that existed not so much to respond to specific technical or economic needs, but rather to enhance contact among groups throughout the Peloponnese and beyond. The first hypothesis may better fit the mobile lifestyle of the Mesolithic foragers, although it is likely that they, like other prehistoric and modern nomadic hunter-gatherers, also participated in exchange systems of a social rather than strictly economic character. If my understanding is correct, the andesite of the single Upper Mesolithic specimen made of this material may have been picked up casually at a source in the area of the Saronic Gulf by people who eventually spent some time at Franchthi. The second scenario may be a better fit with the more sedentary arrangements of Neolithic communities (see Perlès 1992:116–117), although Neolithic examples of direct procurement of raw materials from faraway sources are far from absent (see Perlès 1989; Torrence 1986). If my understanding is correct, most Neolithic andesite specimens (and thus, most of the andesite specimens at Franchthi) or the cobbles/boulders of which they are made were imported to the site through an exchange system that did not aim at satisfying specific technical needs. If so, the role of andesite at Neolithic Franchthi may have been similar to that hypothesized by Perlès for the imported obsidian and honey flint—more social than technical or practical (Perlès 2004:155–158).

I do not know why andesite would have been chosen as one of the goods to circulate in such exchange networks. What I can say, nevertheless, is that there must have been something about this material to justify the consistency with which it entered the site from the Upper Mesolithic through the end of the Neolithic. Whatever this extra-utilitarian value or dimension may have been, it is not expressed in any eloquent way in the andesite tools themselves. The consistency of the import of this material to the site, on the other hand, may imply a continuity, in some sense, between the groups that inhabited it from the Upper Mesolithic through the end of the Neolithic.

Manufacture

A large number of pebbles, cobbles, and boulders collected as raw materials were never subjected to a manufacturing process. They were instead put straight to use; that is why I have called them *a posteriori* tools. About half of the specimens in the pre-Neolithic sample, and probably a similar percentage of the Neolithic sample, are *a posteriori*. Most of the Neolithic *a posteriori* tools belong to the Arect, Asquare-circ, Aglobe, and Amisc groups.

In this assemblage, however, *a posteriori* is not equated with expedient (see Binford 1979). There are, to be sure, *a posteriori* specimens that were used in a very expedient way that left behind very rudimentary use wear and caused little or no change in the shape of the original pebble/cobble. Examples of such tools are found among the Amisc group. That most of them are of sandstone and serpentinite supports the hypothesis that the sandstone and serpentinite used at the site are for the most part local. The Franchthi assemblage, however, also includes *a posteriori* specimens that have been so heavily used in both primary and secondary ways that they acquired very regular, geometric shapes. These are found mostly among the Arect, Asquare-circ and Aglobe groups.

At least half of the Franchthi specimens were manufactured. The manufacturing techniques used for the Franchthi material are chipping/flaking, pecking, and grinding. Of these, pecking is the one that left behind the most traces. Traces of pecking have been identified on two or three pre-Neolithic specimens, and in the Neolithic material, mostly on Popen, Acut, and Aend. The general lack of traces of pecking among Pcav is probably misleading. The technique must have been used for the creation of these tools' cavities, its traces eliminated by a subsequent manufacturing stage of grinding and/or by use. Grinding comes second in frequency of visible traces. Evidence of grinding is found on some pre-Neolithic specimens, and in the Neolithic sample, mostly on Acut and Aend. The traces of flaking/chipping are in general limited. They have been identified on a number of pre-Neolithic specimens. They have also been found on some unutilized surfaces of Popen, Pcav, and Adisc. Nevertheless, the flat or concave work faces of Popen and Adisc suggest that this technique was used extensively at least for a couple of Neolithic groups.

Nothing in the manufacture of the non *a posteriori* specimens points to specialized skills. These tools could have been produced by most, if not all, the adult members of the groups that lived at Franchthi at different times, and perhaps the oldest children as well. If the manufacture of ground stone tools was not a specialized skill or occupation practiced by only a few members of the Franchthi community at any one time, and given the presumed local origin of most of the used raw materials, then one would expect to find pertinent manufacturing debris scattered throughout the site. The pre-Neolithic material does indeed include a few (discoidal) limestone flakes that, I believe, resulted from the on-site production of tools useful in lithic manufacture and maintenance. They are all dated to the Mesolithic period. Yet, very little that could possibly be identified as byproducts of the manufacture of the much more numerous Neolithic material has been located. This can, to some degree, be explained by the fact that two of the three main techniques used in the manufacture of these tools, pecking and grinding, do not leave traces recoverable with conventional excavation techniques. And there are tools (i.e., Acut and Aend) that were fashioned solely by pecking and grinding. Only remains of accidents that occurred during the manufacturing process, along with unutilized raw materials, could be expected in this case, and some evidence of this sort has in fact been identified at the site: three specimens that may have resulted from Acut and/or Aend manufacturing accidents, and an unworked serpentinite cobble that may represent Acut or Aend raw material. What is much more intriguing is the absence of manufacturing debris from the tools for which flaking was part of the manufacturing process. Why were no flakes recovered from the manufacture of Popen, Pcav, and Adisc? Even if the producers tended to carry out the initial flaking at the sources of raw material, some of the flaking must have taken place on-site and produced identifiable flakes. A possible clue as to why no such flakes were recovered may be found in the following two pieces of evidence. The first is the almost complete absence of flakes produced during redesigning processes, processes, that is, that must have taken place on the site. The second is a concentration of a number of sandstone and other cobbles that may represent ground stone tool raw material, in a specific area on the talus, north of Paralia trench L5. On this basis, I am inclined to assume that for some unknown reasons, the flaking involved in the manufacture and redesign of a number of specimens took place in one or more specific areas of the site that were not touched by the excavation or, at most, somewhere in the vicinity. Taboos surrounding specific stages of the ground stone tool manufacturing process are, after all, known ethnographically. Among many groups in Irian Jaya, the grinding of *haches* and *herminettes* is invested with a very strict prohibition along gender lines and must not be carried out within view of women. It thus takes place away from the compounds, usually by a river or stream (Pétrequin and Pétrequin 1988:68, 1993a:371–373, 1993b:368).

Use and discard

There is plenty of evidence to suggest that during the Neolithic the raw materials were not collected randomly. The choice of raw materials was most often dictated by the intended use, as is suggested by a certain division of labor evident in the Neolithic component of the assemblage. Serpentinite is the material of choice for two active tool groups, Acut and Aend (with 74% and 89% respectively made of this material). It is very little used for other tools (basically, only for specimens in the Amisc2 subgroup). Sandstone was used heavily for the category of passive tools as a whole (79%) and for three of the relatively homogeneous active groups (Adisc, Arect, and Asquare-circ with 75–89%). Otherwise, it was used for the vast majority of specimens in the Amisc1 subgroup. Moreover, different types of sandstone were used for different tool groups: a characteristic calcareous variety for the majority of Adisc, a fine-grained variety for most Arect, and a less fine-grained one for most Asquare-circ. Peridotite is the only material used for Aglobe-stain; it was also used for a few Aglobe-nostain. Otherwise, it was occasionally used for Acut and Amisc2. Chert is the raw material of only six tools. Five belong to a single group (Aglobe-nostain), have the same more or less spherical shape, and show active percussive wear all over the surfaces; most likely, all had the same use. Diabase is the raw material of 40% of Aglobe-nostain; it was also used for a few Acut and a couple of Amisc2.

The above distribution of raw materials among the Neolithic tool groups suggests that specific rock types were selected for more or less specific kinds of tools. The relatively specific shape and raw material characterizing most of the Neolithic groups creates the impression that the majority of Neolithic specimens were preconceived as more or less specialized tools. However, the fact that many among them show multiple kinds of use wear—one of which can usually be identified as primary—suggests that during their use life these tools were employed for a number of additional purposes, different from those originally intended. If so, use of relatively specialized tools in additional tasks was something normal in the perceptual system of the users. The emerging picture is thus one of both specialization and flexibility: specialization in the conception of a tool, on the one hand, relative flexibility during its use, on the other. This phrasing reflects my impression that for the most part the people who conceived the tools as more or less specialized in the first place were also the ones who ended up using them in a rather flexible way. I find this scenario more sensible than one that sees these tools as secondarily used by later groups. Although something like that must have taken place during the thousands of years of occupation, and as groups abandoned the site and new groups came to use it, I doubt that it occurred systematically enough to cause the multiple use wear exhibited by a large number of Neolithic tools. Indeed, the fact that multiple use wear is more pronounced in tools exhausted as far as their primary use is concerned (see Asquare-circ and Arect), rather suggests that for the most part the same group of people is responsible for both the primary and the secondary kinds of use wear. Moreover, the fact, that several specimens in a single tool group happen to show similar secondary use wear (see Asquare-circ and Arect) also argues against the hypothesis that these tools represent material left behind by previous Franchthi dwellers and later randomly picked up and used by newcomers.

Although I could identify no relatively homogeneous groups comparable to the Neolithic ones for the pre-Neolithic sample, it is possible to see there, too, cases of combination of a specific raw material, shape, and use wear. I have in mind here the two Mesolithic grooved steatite specimens that may have been used as shaft straighteners, as well as the several small chipped limestone pebbles that may have been used in the context of lithic production and maintenance. These tools seem to have been pretty much specialized. The pestle-like tools, on the other hand, have a specific shape that suggests that they may originally have been conceived as specialized tools; at the same time, they exhibit multiple use wear, indicating that they ended up being used in a variety of tasks and, thus, in a flexible way.

In the small pre-Neolithic sample, abrasion is better represented than percussion; when percussive wear is evident, it almost always accompanies more extensive evidence of abrasion. The tasks in which the pre-Neolithic specimens at Franchthi were or may have been involved include pigment processing or processing of various materials with the help of pigments; lithic manufacture and maintenance; shaft straightening; hide and wood working; and food processing. No specimen discovered in pre-Neolithic deposits, on the other hand, seems to have been a typical flint knapping tool, although lithic debris is found scattered throughout the excavated area. This absence may be explained by a tendency of the flint knappers to take these precious tools along with them.

The picture of the much more numerous Neolithic component is more complex. Again, in general, abrasion is better represented than percussion; when both are evident on the same tools, percussion tends to be secondary to abrasion. The exception to this rule is the relatively spherical tools of the Aglobe-nostain group, and the Aend, which, I believe, were used, for the most part, to peck other tools or non-tool objects to shape (e.g., Acut and Popen) or resharpen blunt tool surfaces. What are missing, again, are typical flint knapping tools. The absence of such tools may not be problematic in LN and FN, when imported obsidian dominates the lithic assemblage: according to Perlès (2004), during these Neolithic phases (as in the two previous ones) obsidian was worked on site (by itinerant flint knapping specialists), but not flaked with stone tools. Local materials, however, were used in substantial quantities in lithic production in EN and MN and byproducts of manufacture have been found throughout the site (Perlès 2004:69–102). One would expect some of the flint knapping tools to have been discarded at the site, especially since their users were less mobile than both their pre-Neolithic and later Neolithic counterparts. One would also expect some of these tools to have been identified and retrieved by the excavators, especially since the water-rolled pebbles of which such tools usually consist do not occur naturally at the area of the site. On this basis, I find it plausible in this case that flint knapping tools were discarded in a specific location that the excavation did not cover—an idea reinforced by the virtual absence of flakes produced during ground stone tool manufacturing and redesigning processes.

Another kind of implement that is largely missing from the Neolithic component is a cutting edge tool large and hard enough for tree felling. As I suggested in chapter 4, there may not have been a substantial need for such tools at Franchthi: the environment may not have been sufficiently forested to make their use compelling. It is also possible that tree-felling techniques not involving this kind of tools were used. There is, on the other hand, a large number of small specimens in the Acut group. These may have been used in light woodworking tasks, for clearing shrubbery and, occasionally, in working hides or clay, although some of them may have been too small and soft even for such tasks. The presence of use wear on their edges confirms that they were used; but exactly how remains unclear. What is perhaps clearer is a certain symbolic value that may have made some of them adequate for ritual killing.

Because of their small sizes, Popen do not seem to have been systematically used for grinding grains. They may have been used for a variety of other grinding tasks, including shaping other tools and non-tool objects of stone, bone, shell, and wood. A few of them have suspicious breakage patterns that led me to hypothesize intentional breakage. Only a very small number of active tools, on the other hand, seem suited for grinding grain. They are all found among Amisc1. The lack of a substantial number of adequate grain grinding tools suggests that Franchthiotes routinely processed grains in ways that did not involve grinding. I should also note here that the few excavated tools with cavity (Pcav as I call them here) do not seem suitable for cereal dehusking. This task must have been accomplished with wooden tools.

Despite the extensive evidence of burnishing in the pottery assemblage, the number of ground stone specimens that could have possibly served as pot burnishers is very small (they are found in Amisc2-set1). This task may have been most often performed with tools of other materials or in locations not covered by the excavation. Moreover, pot burnishers must have been as precious to prehistoric users as they are to modern ones. It is possible, especially in LN and FN, when the Franchthi occupation may not have been year-round, that some of these tools left the site with their users. Perhaps even more puzzling is the small number of pigment processing tools—basically the Aglobe-stain and a few other passive and active tools—despite the extensive evidence of painted decoration on the Franchthi pots and the probable use of pigment in other contexts. The materials ground with Adisc remain largely elusive, whereas Arect and Asquare-circ may have been (at least primarily) used to grind substances such as spices and/or to process hides. Secondary passive or active percussive wear is also seen in the center of the faces of most Asquare-circ, a few Arect, and a couple of specimens in the Amisc group. This may have been produced from a use in nutcracking.

Finally, a few words on the conditions of discard of the Franchthi ground stone tools. Starting with the Neolithic sample, some groups include several exhausted specimens (Adisc, Arect, Asquare-circ, Aglobe). These tools were worn out either from short, but intensive, use or from repeated use over a long period of time. Discard for these tools seems to have been the natural consequence of their exhausted state. I do not consider most of the small Acut exhausted for the simple reason that I do not believe that they were originally much larger. Some of the Neolithic specimens that do not appear exhausted may have been discarded because they were no longer needed—they had served their purpose and their users had no further use for them. Others may have been left behind on abandonment of the site, which happened several times during the long span of the Neolithic. Still others were probably thrown away simply because they happened to break—about half of the Neolithic specimens are fragmentary. Interestingly, however, a few of the broken tools were apparently subjected to a process of redesigning, aimed at producing new small tools adequate for use with one hand. Redesigning processes have mostly targeted the relatively large tools I call Popen. They are attested in all but the last of the Neolithic phases and imply, I believe, a flexible attitude towards tools and raw materials and an attachment of the users to their tools, rather than an environmental constraint.

With one possible exception, there are no specimens that I would consider exhausted in the pre-Neolithic sample. I assume therefore that ground stone tools in the pre-Neolithic periods were discarded when they broke or when their users abandoned the site.

Chronological distribution

The 26 stratified pre-Neolithic specimens are dated to Palaeolithic and Mesolithic periods (Appendix B). Leaving aside the three specimens assigned to the Lower/Upper and Upper/Final Mesolithic interphases, the distribution of the remaining specimens among the four main Pre-Neolithic periods is as follows:

Upper Palaeolithic	7
Lower Mesolithic	8
Upper Mesolithic	6
Final Mesolithic	2

The small size of the pre-Neolithic sample as a whole and the low number of specimens assigned to each of the four periods can be attributed in each case to one or all of the following factors: 1. the very limited or sporadic occupation of the cave; 2. the limited role of the ground stone tool industry in the everyday life of the cave dwellers; 3. a probable tendency for nomadic foragers to take important tools with when abandoning the cave. Yet, even with these generally low frequencies, the near absence of specimens from the Final Mesolithic stands out. This is not surprising: on the contrary, it fits well with the paucity of Final Mesolithic remains in general, which argues for a near-abandonment of the site during the period preceding the Neolithic and, by extension, for a discontinuity between the two periods.

The number of specimens that have been securely or probably dated to specific Neolithic phases (including the Initial Neolithic) or assigned to one of the Neolithic interphases is 239 (Appendix B). Leaving aside the 14 specimens dated to interphases and the single specimen of probable Initial Neolithic date, the distribution of the remaining 224 specimens among the four main Neolithic phases is as follows:

EN	18 (8%)
MN	136 (61%)
LN	11 (5%)
FN	59 (26%)

The distribution is obviously not uniform. Below are some thoughts on the observed differences.

EN is a long phase at Franchthi; it lasted at least 400, and, perhaps, even up to 1000 years (whether the site was occupied continuously or not during this period of time is, however, a matter of debate). There is, moreover, relatively secure evidence for a more or less year-round occupation of the site during this phase as well as evidence for the existence of an open air settlement in front of the cave in what is now Kiladha Bay, of which Paralia was a part (Perlès 2004:69, 135–136; Vitelli 1993:41–48, 210–219). Yet, EN yielded a small number of ground stone tools, especially compared to the following MN. This pattern can be taken as an indication of a limited use of such tools, and, by extension, of a limited need for this kind of material during this phase. There are, however, reasons to believe that more ground stone tools were used in the course of EN than this number suggests. According to Vitelli (1993:44), later Neolithic as well as post-Neolithic activities probably destroyed some EN deposits inside the cave. If so, some EN specimens may occur among those found in disturbed or surface cave deposits and considered here as generally Neolithic. Moreover, the massive quantities of shell bead manufacturing debris, as well as lithics related to shell bead manufacture that were found in EN deposits of Paralia (see Miller 1996; Perlès 2001:223–226, 2004:151–154), suggest a substantial use of ground stone tools—active percussive tools were necessary in the manufacture of lithic tools, passive abrasive tools were necessary in the manufacture of shell beads. That such tools were not found in significant numbers in EN strata means perhaps that they were discarded in unexcavated locations of the site, including the submerged area in front of Paralia.

The EN sample includes four specimens of each of the two kinds of tools traditionally associated with the Neolithic culture: cutting edge tools (Acut) and open passive abrasive tools (Popen). Yet these specimens in general do not appear well suited for the uses traditionally attributed to such tools—tree-felling and grain grinding respectively. Acut have no equivalent in any pre-Neolithic period. The Upper Mesolithic, on the other hand, yielded a fragment of what seems to be a passive abrasive tool of substantial size, but this seems to have had a rim around its work face, a configuration not encountered among the Neolithic tools I call Popen. Two other new tools, a Pcav and an Arect, are also included in the EN sample. All these specimens rather argue for a discontinuity between the Mesolithic and the Neolithic at Franchthi, a hypothesis that is supported by geostratigraphical and other evidence (see, e.g., Farrand 2000:96–97; Hansen 1991:174–183).

The following phase, MN, is characterized by a much larger number of ground stone tools when compared to EN. MN is in fact the phase with the largest concentration of ground stone tools in the Neolithic, suggesting that in this phase the ground stone tool industry was an important one. The large number of specimens is accompanied by an increase in diversity. Aend and Aglobe appear now for the first time. These two groups, as well as Arect, Acut, and Popen seem to have been used mostly in MN.

LN shows the lowest frequency of ground stone tools of all Neolithic phases. The low quantities of LN ceramic material, along with its limited distribution, exclusively inside the cave, led Vitelli to hypothesize an occupation consisting of intermittent visits by otherwise mobile groups. Indeed, the particular characteristics of the LN pottery point, according to her, to gatherings of a ceremonial character (Vitelli 1999:10–11, 96–104). Perlès accepts the hypothesis of brief visits to the cave only for the earlier part of LN on the basis of the very low relative densities of the lithic, ceramic, and botanical remains. However, she finds the densities of the same kinds of remains for the later part of LN too similar to those for MN to support this hypothesis for later LN. Using this and other evidence, she suggests that in this part of LN the cave was used for longer stretches of time—although not necessarily throughout the year—by people who practiced cereal agriculture nearby and perhaps also had an open-air settlement that was complementary to the cave and is now submerged somewhere in Kiladha Bay. Ceremonies, according to this scenario, could very well have been carried out inside the cave (Perlès 2004:104–106, 115–116). None of the few ground stone tools originating in LN deposits has any extraordinary characteristics that could point to a ceremonial use; they seem to have been used in ordinary domestic activities. The possibility, however, that they were used to produce substances or fashion artifacts that could participate in one way or another in ceremonial contexts cannot be ruled out.

According to Perlès, the densities of FN ceramic, lithic, and botanical materials are all comparable to those observed in MN, arguing against Vitelli's hypothesis for an FN occupation consisting of a series of relatively brief visits separated by periods of limited, if any, occupation. On the basis of this and other evidence, Perlès proposed that in FN too the site was used for longer stretches of time during the year (Perlès 2004:129–130; see also Vitelli 1999:89–93). This hypothesis seems to be reinforced by the FN ground stone tool sample. FN shows the second highest frequency of ground stone tools after MN. In fact, considering that the FN occupation at Franchthi was neither as permanent nor as long as the MN occupation, I would argue that FN displays the highest density of ground stone tools in the whole Neolithic sequence. This implies a very intensive use of these tools and it may be fair to suggest that the ground stone tool industry was more important in FN than in MN.

The FN ground stone tool sample seems, moreover, to support Perlès' portrayal of FN Franchthi as the locus of some specialized activities of primarily domestic character (Perlès 2004:128–131). This sample includes the most specialized of all Neolithic groups: Adisc. Not only is this the most homogeneous of the Neolithic groups in terms of raw material, shape, and size, but it is also the only group made up of tools that for the most part show a single kind of use wear. This suggests that at least one specialized activity involving ground stone tools took place at the site during FN. No Adisc has been identified from any of the other Neolithic phases, an indication perhaps that, whatever the activity in which these tools were involved was, it did not take place at any time before FN. Alternatively, such an activity was carried out with the help of tools of other materials.

In short, it is likely that the groups which inhabited the site in EN used more ground stone tools than the number of the recovered EN specimens indicates. The very large number of specimens dated to MN suggests that the need for ground stone tools was very pronounced during this phase. Little use of ground stone tools is, on the other hand, suggested for LN. FN, finally, did not last long but seems to have witnessed the most intensive use of ground stone tools.

Spatial distribution

All the pre-Neolithic material was found inside the cave and this is where it was probably used and/or kept between use episodes. The Neolithic material, on the other hand, comes from both the cave and Paralia: 369 specimens (76%) were found in the cave (including the terrace just outside the cave mouth), 116 specimens (24%) were found on Paralia; for one specimen no provenience information is available (see Appendices A–B). The percentages of Neolithic tools found in the cave and on Paralia perfectly match the volumes of Neolithic sediment removed from the two sectors of the site during the excavations, 76% from the cave, 24% from Paralia respectively (Jacobsen and Farrand 2000:28–29; Farrand, e-mail communication 1/1998). If, however, the specimens with a specific date from the two areas are broken down by Neolithic phase (both secure and probable dates are taken into consideration), a more complex picture emerges, as shown in this table:

	EN	MN	LN	FN
Cave	5 (28%)	110 (81%)	11 (100%)	31 (53%)
Paralia	13 (72%)	26 (19%)	0 (0%)	28 (47%)

I offer here some thoughts on the differences observed. The distributions of the EN and LN material between the cave and Paralia are rather as expected. More specifically, the EN sample is very small and, thus, problematic for statistical use. Yet it is probably not accidental that most EN specimens were found on Paralia: this is after all the sector of the site where other kinds of EN material, such as pottery and lithics, tend to concentrate (see Perlès 2004:82–83; Vitelli 1993:41–48). This may have to do with a more intensive use of Paralia in EN (after all, walls and terraces were constructed there during this phase); it may also, or alternatively, have to do with disturbances of EN deposits inside the cave that caused the 'loss' of some EN material (see above). As for the concentration of the LN ground stone tools exclusively inside the cave, it is not at all surprising: no archaeological material dated to LN was found on Paralia.

The distribution of MN and FN specimens between the two sectors of the site are, on the other hand, unexpected. Starting with the MN specimens, the vast majority were found inside the cave, while other kinds of MN material, such as lithics and pottery (see Perlès 2004:100; Vitelli 1993:50), are distributed much more evenly between the cave and Paralia. The very large difference between the numbers of specimens found inside the cave and on Paralia must reflect a tendency in MN to use and discard ground stone tools inside the cave. We are, in other words, witnessing a choice by MN Franchthiotes to carry out the majority of tasks involving ground stone tools inside the cave, at the same time that they carried out other tasks in a more indiscriminate way both inside the cave and on Paralia. This should perhaps be taken as evidence of a certain organization and specialization of space, and perhaps also of a division of labor, regarding ground stone tools. I do not know what attracted the users of ground stone tools to the inside of the cave in MN. My only suspicion is that this preference has perhaps something to do with the existence of hearths in this part of the cave, since it is true that a number of MN specimens (Arect, Aend, Aglobe, Popen, and Acut) were found roughly speaking in hearth contexts.

The distribution of FN specimens between the cave and Paralia is, by contrast, roughly balanced. This is odd in light of the fact that most of the FN lithics and pottery were found inside the cave (Perlès 2004:117–119; Vitelli 1999:88–89). The symmetrical distribution of the ground stone tools between the two sectors of the site may be an indication of a special use of Paralia in relation to this material during this phase.

Table 5.1 compares the percentages of Neolithic sediments removed from different cave trenches[2] with the percentages of ground stone tools excavated in these sediments. Trenches with heavily disturbed deposits (e.g., FA) have not been taken into consideration. This comparison reveals a very high density of ground stone tools in FAN/FAS, and a very low density of this kind of material in trench A and in the G–G1 cluster of trenches. Are these strong density differences perhaps an indication that some parts of the cave were more preferred than others for ground stone tool-related activities and/or for the discard of this kind of material?

Table 5.2 compares the percentages of Neolithic sediments removed from Paralia trenches[3] with the percentages of ground stone tools excavated in those sediments. This comparison shows a very high density of specimens in the L5 cluster of trenches. Twenty-eight of the thirty-six specimens recovered there are dated to FN. These, along with 20 spindle whorls, about 35 kg of pottery,

Table 5.1. Correlations of percentages of volume of sediment removed and percentages of ground stone tools excavated from different trenches or trench clusters inside the cave.

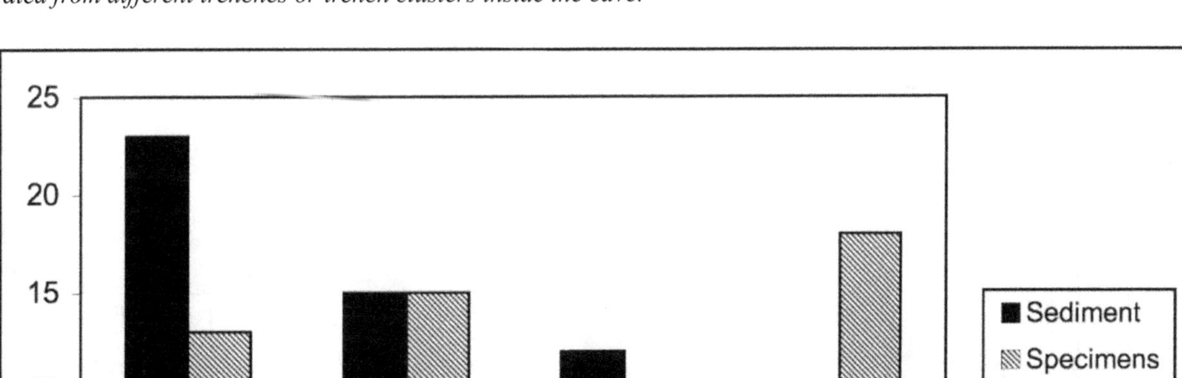

and a substantial amount of lithic material were excavated in an arrangement of pits that is likely to have been originally used for lime production (Vitelli 1999:90–91; Perlès 2004:117–118). Vitelli suggested that this material may initially have been utilized elsewhere on Paralia and was finally placed, perhaps in a ritualized way, inside the pit formation by an FN group that chose to eliminate any visible traces of its activity on Paralia. This hypothesis is reinforced not only by the discovery of a similar pit formation at FN Lerna, but also by the intact state of a number of lithic tools found within the Paralia pit formation (see Perlès 2004:117–118; Vitelli 1999:90–91).[4] More than half of the ground stone tools found there are complete. The latter include some perfectly usable items, but also a few that could be considered exhausted.

Having reached the end of this study, I have to admit that I did not answer all the questions I had when I started this journey. I can, in fact, assure the reader that I now have more questions about this material than I had originally. Some will never find an answer. Others may be answered in time as the field of Aegean ground stone studies develops. If this volume serves to inspire others to examine other assemblages more closely and publish them systematically, then it will have served its purpose.

NOTES

1. None of the dated andesite tools comes from EN, yet crushed andesite is included in the temper of what is probably locally produced EN pottery (the so-called andesite ware) (Vitelli 1993:208–209). This suggests that andesite was imported to the site during this phase as well. However, since andesite had been used at the site before EN, it is also possible that abandoned tools or the raw material itself were found on the surface or in pits dug through pre-Neolithic layers.

2. As provided in Jacobsen and Farrand 2000:28–29.

3. As provided by Farrand, e-mail communication 1/1998.

4. Perlès (2004:118) entertained the alternative hypothesis of a secondary use of the pit formation as a dump, but even she finds that Vitelli's hypothesis can better accommodate the intact chipped stone tools, especially arrowheads, found there.

Table 5.2. Correlations of percentages of volume of sediment removed and percentages of ground stone tools excavated from different trenches in Paralia.

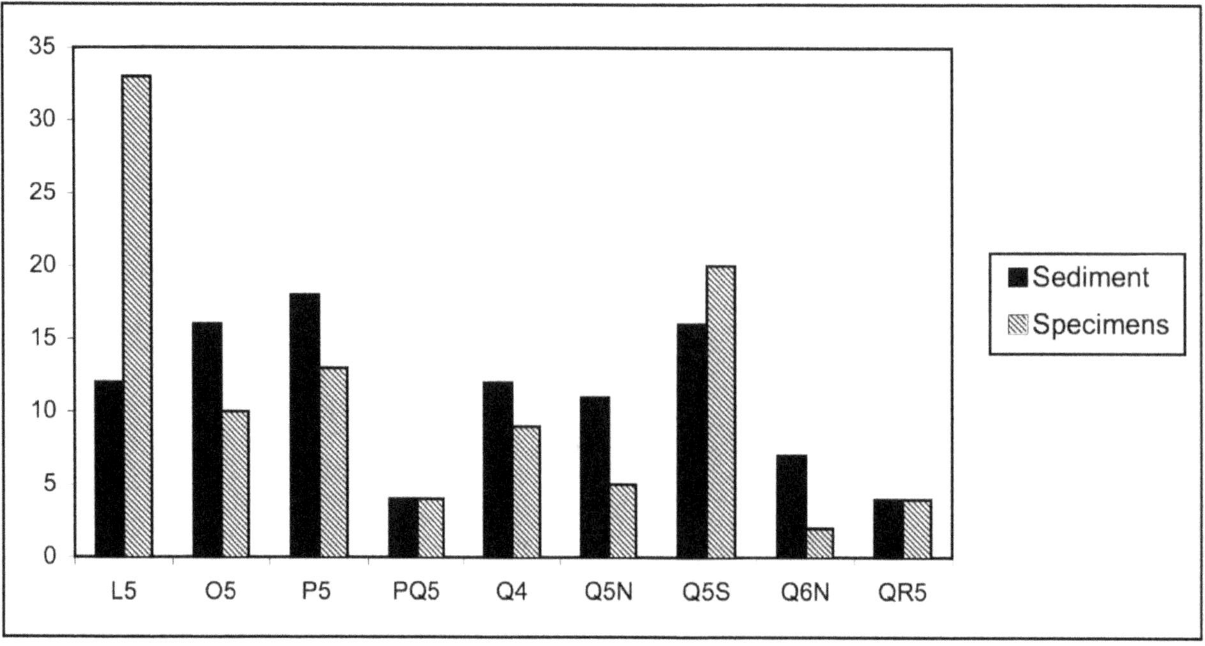

REFERENCES

Adams, Jenny
1988. 'Use-Wear Analyses on Manos and Hide-Processing Stones.' *Journal of Field Archaeology* 15:307–315.
1989a. 'Methods for Improving Ground Stone Artifacts Analysis: Experiments in Mano Wear Patterns.' In Daniel S. Amick and Raymond P. Mauldin, eds., *Experiments in Lithic Technology*, pp. 259–276. BAR International Series 528, Oxford.
1989b. 'Experimental Replication of the Use of Ground Stone Tools.' *KIVA* 54:261–271.
1994. *The Development of Prehistoric Grinding Technology in the Point of Pines.* Ph.D. Dissertation, University of Arizona.
1995. 'The Development of Prehistoric Grinding Technology in the Point of Pines Area, East-Central Arizona.' *Museum Anthropology* 19:17–29.
1997. *Manual for a Technological Approach to Ground Stone Analysis.* Center for Desert Archaeology, Tuscon.
2002. *Ground Stone Analysis: A Technological Approach.* The University of Utah Press, Salt Lake City.
2008. 'Beyond the Broken.' In Yorke Rowan and Jennie Ebeling, eds., *New Approaches to Old Stones: Recent Studies of Ground Stone Artifacts*, pp. 213–229. Equinox, London.

Adams, Jenny, and David Greenwald
1979. *Stone Artifacts from Walpi, Part II. Walpi Archaeological Project, Phase II.* Vol. 4. Museum of Northern Arizona, Flagstaff.

Agatzioti, Sophia
2000. *Τριπτά λίθινα εργαλεία από τον οικισμό της Τούμπας Θεσσαλονίκης.* M.A. Thesis, Aristotle University of Thessaloniki.

Alisøy, Hege Agathe
2002. 'Consumption of Ground Stone Tools at Stavroupoli.' In Dimitris Grammenos and Stavros Kotsos, eds., *Σωστικές Ανασκαφές στο νεολιθικό οικισμό Σταυρούπολης Θεσσαλονίκης*, pp. 561–608. Publications of the Archaeological Institute of Northern Greece, Thessaloniki.

Anderson, William
1890. 'Description of Some Stone Weapons and Implements Used by the Aborigines of New South Wales.' *Records of the Geological Survey of New South Wales* 2:73–81.

Atalay, Sonya, and Christine A. Hastorf
2006. 'Food, Meals, and Daily Activities: Food *Habitus* at Neolithic Çatalhöyük.' *American Antiquity* 71(2):283–319.

Avitsur, Shmuel
1975. 'The Way to Bread: The Example of the Land of Israel.' *Tools and Tillage* 2(4):228–241.

Banks, Kimbal M.
1982. 'Late Paleolithic and Neolithic Grinding Implements in Egypt.' *Lithic Technology* 11(1):12–20.

Baudais, Dominique, and Karen Lundström-Baudais
2002. 'Enquête ethnoarchéologique dans un village du nord-ouest du Népal: Les instruments de mouture et de broyage.' In Hara Procopiou and René Treuil, eds., *Moudre et broyer I: Méthodes*, pp. 155–180. CTHS, Paris.

Baysal, Adnan, and Katherine Wright
2005a. 'Cooking, Crafts and Curation: Ground-Stone Artifacts from Çatalhöyük.' In Ian Hodder, ed., *Changing Materialities at Çatalhöyük: Reports from the 1995-99 Seasons*, pp. 307–324. McDonald Institute for Archaeological Research and British Institute at Ankara, Cambridge and London.
2005b. 'Ground-Stone Artifacts: Discussion of Contexts.' In Ian Hodder, ed., *Changing Materialities at Çatalhöyük: Reports from the 1995-99 Seasons*, pp. 559–588. McDonald Institute for Archaeological Research and British Institute at Ankara, Cambridge and London.

Becker, C. J.
1945. 'New Finds of Hafted Neolithic Celts.' *Acta Archaeologica* 16:155–175.

Bekiaris, Tasos
2007. *Τριπτά εργαλεία από το Νεολιθικό οικισμό της Μάκρης Έβρου.* M.A. Thesis, Aristotle University of Thessaloniki.

Benac, Alojz
1973. 'Obre II, a Neolithic Settlement of the Butmir Group at Gornje Polje.' *Wissenschaftliche Mitteilungen des Bosnisch-Herzegowinischen Landesmuseums* 3:5–191.

Best, Elsdon
1974. *Stone Implements of the Maori.* A.R. Shearer, Government Printer, Wellington, New Zealand.

Bétirac, B.
1956. 'Sur la fragmentation volontaire des meules et polissoires néolithiques.' *Bulletin de la Société Préhistorique Française* 53:42.

Beugnier, Valérie.
1997. *L'usage du silex dans l'acquisition et le traitement des matières animales dans le Néolithique de Chalain et Clairvaux. La Motte-aux-Magnins et Chalain 3 (Jura, France), 3700–2980 av. J.C.* Ph.D. Dissertation, Paris X - Nanterre.

Binford, Lewis R.
1979. 'Organization and Formation Processes: Looking at Curated Technologies.' *Journal of Anthropological Research* 35:255–273.

Blackwood, Beatrice
1950. *The Technology of a Modern Stone Age People in New Guinea.* Oxford University Press, Oxford.

Boshier, Adrian K.
1965. 'Effects of Pounding by Africans of North-West Transvaal on Hard and Soft Stones.' *Makapansgat: The South African Archaeological Bulletin* 20(79):131–136.

Bottema, Sytze
1990. 'Holocene Environment of the Southern Argolid: A Pollen Core from Kiladha Bay.' In Tony J. Wilkinson and Susan T. Duhon, *Franchthi Paralia: The Sediments, Stratigraphy, and Offshore Investigations*, pp. 117–138. Indiana University Press, Bloomington and Indianapolis.

Bradley, Richard
2005. *Ritual and Domestic Life in Prehistoric Europe.* Routledge, London and New York.

Bradley, Richard, and Mark Edmonds
1993. *Interpreting the Axe Trade: Production and Exchange in Neolithic Britain.* Cambridge University Press, Cambridge.

Braidwood, Robert, J., et al.
1953. 'Did Man Once Live by Beer Alone?' *American Anthropologist* 55:515–526.

Brass, L. J.
1941. 'Stone Age Agriculture in New Guinea.' *Geographical Review* 31:555–569.

Britt, Claude, Jr.
1973. 'Historical Evidence for a Use of Cupstones.' *Ohio Archaeologist* 23:26–27.

Bulmer, Ralph, and Susan Bulmer
1962. 'Figurines and Other Stones of Power Among the Kyaka of Central New Guinea.' *The Journal of the Polynesian Society* 71:192–208.

Campana, Douglas V.
1987. 'The Manufacture of Bone Tools in the Zagros and the Levant.' *MASCA Journal* 4(3):110–121.
1989. *Natufian and Protoneolithic Bone Tools: The Manufacture and Use of Bone Implements in the Zagros and the Levant.* BAR International Series 494, Oxford.

Carneiro, Robert L.
1974. 'On the Use of the Stone Axe by the Amahuaca Indians of Eastern Peru.' *Ethnologische Zeitschrift Zürich* 1:107–122.
1979. 'Tree Felling with the Stone Ax: An Experiment Carried Out Among the Yanomamö Indians of Southern Venezuela.' In Carol Kramer, ed., *Ethnoarchaeology: Implications of Ethnography for Archaeology*, pp. 21–58. Columbia University Press, New York.

Carter, George F.
1977. 'The Metate: An Early Grain-Grinding Implement in the New World.' In Charles Reed, ed., *Origins of Agriculture*, pp. 693–712. Mouton Publishers, Paris.

Chapman, John
2000. *Fragmentation in Archaeology: People, Places, and Broken Objects in the Prehistory of South-Eastern Europe.* Routledge, London and New York.

Christensen, Marianne, and François Valla
1999. 'Pour relancer un débat: Que sont les pierres à rainure du Natoufien Proche-Oriental?' *Bulletin de la Société Préhistorique Française* 96(2):247–252.

Christopoulou, Alexandra
1979. *Microwear Analysis of the Chipped and Ground Stone Tools from Sesklo A.* Ph.D. Dissertation, Institute of Archaeology, London.
1992. ''Ιχνη χρήσης στα λειασμένα λίθινα εργαλεία του Σέσκλου Α.' In *Διεθνές Συνέδριο για την Αρχαία Θεσσαλία στη μνήμη του Δημήτρη Θεοχάρη*, pp. 64–70. Greek Ministry of Culture, Athens.
2000. 'Τα λειασμένα λίθινα εργαλεία του σπηλαίου Θεόπετρας.' In Nina Kyparissi-Apostolika, ed., *Theopetra Cave: Twelve Years of Excavation and Research 1987–1998,* pp. 293–305. Institute for Aegean Prehistory, Athens.

Cohen, Ronald, and Curtis N. Runnels
1981. 'The Source of the Kitsos Millstones.' In Nicole Lambert, ed., *La grotte préhistorique de Kitsos (Attique): Missions 1968–1978*, pp. 233–239. A.D.P.F. École Française d'Athènes, Athens.

Cook, Della
2000. 'Skeletal Evidence for Nutrition in Mesolithic and Neolithic Greece: A View from Franchthi Cave.' In Sarah J. Vaughan and William D.E. Coulson, eds., *Palaeodiet in the Aegean,* pp. 99–104. Oxbow Books, Oxford.

Cosner, Aaron J.
1951. 'Arrowshaft-Straightening with a Grooved Stone.' *American Antiquity* 17(2):147–148.

Cullen, Tracey
1995. 'Mesolithic Mortuary Ritual at Franchthi Cave, Greece.' *Antiquity* 69:270–289.
1999. 'Scattered Human Bones at Franchthi Cave: Remnants of Ritual or Refuse?' In Philip P. Betancourt, Vassos Karageorghis, Robert Laffineur, and Wolf-Dietrich Niemeier, eds., *Meletemata: Studies in Aegean Archaeology Presented to Malcolm H. Wiener as He Enters His 65th Year*, pp. 165–170. Université de Liège and University of Texas at Austin, Liège and Austin.

Cullen, Tracey, and Anastasia Papathanasiou
(In preparation). *Human Remains from Franchthi Cave.* Indiana University Press, Bloomington and Indianapolis.

D'Andrea, A.C.
2003. 'Social and Technological Aspects of Non-Mechanised Emmer Processing.' In Patricia C. Anderson, Linda S. Cummings, Thomas K. Schippers, and Bernard Simonel, eds., *Le Traitement des récoltes: un regard sur la diversité du Néolithique au présent*, pp. 47–60. APDCA, Antibes.

Danforth, Loring M.
1982. *The Death Rituals of Rural Greece.* Princeton University Press, Princeton.

David, Nicholas
1998. 'The Ethnoarchaeology and Field Archaeology of Grinding at Sukur, Adamawa State, Nigeria.' *African Archaeological Review* 15(1):13–63.

Davidson, Daniel S., and Frederick D. McCarthy
1957. 'The Distribution and Chronology of Some Important Types of Stone Implements in Western Australia.' *Anthropos* 52:390–458.

Davis, Michael K.
1982. 'The Çayönü Ground Stone.' In Linda S. Braidwood and Robert J. Braidwood, eds., *Prehistoric Village Archaeology in South-Eastern Turkey: The Eighth Millennium B.C. Site at Çayönü: Its Chipped and Ground Stone Industries and Faunal Remains*, pp. 73–151. BAR International Series 138, Oxford.

de Beaune, Sophie A.
1989a. 'Exemple ethnographique de l'usage pluri-fonctionnel d'un galet de quartz.' *Bulletin de la Société Préhistorique Française* 86(2):61–64.
1989b. 'Essai d'une classification typologique des galets et plaquettes utilisés au Paléolithique.' *Gallia Préhistoire* 31:27–64.
1993. 'Nonflint Stone Tools of the Early Upper Paleolithic.' In Heidi Knecht, Anne Pike-Tay, and Randall White, eds., *Before Lascaux: The Complex Record of the Early Upper Paleolithic*, pp. 163–191. CRC Press, Boca Raton, Florida.
1997. *Les galets utilisés au Paléolithique Supérieur: Approche archéologique et expérimentale.* CNRS, Paris.
2000. *Pour une archéologie du geste.* CNRS, Paris.

Deith, M.R., and N.J. Shackleton
1988. 'Oxygen Isotope Analysis of Marine Molluscs from Franchthi Cave.' In Judith C. Shackleton, *Marine Molluscan Remains from Franchthi Cave*, pp. 133–156. Indiana University Press, Bloomington and Indianapolis.

Dengate, James A.
1999. 'Post-Neolithic Franchthi.' In Karen Vitelli, *Franchthi Neolithic Pottery.* Vol. 2. *The Later Neolithic Phases 3–5*, pp. 111–117. Indiana University Press, Bloomington and Indianapolis.

Dickson, Frank P.
1972. 'Ground Edge Axes.' *Mankind* 8:206–211.
1981. *Australian Stone Hatchets: A Study in Design and Dynamics.* Academic Press, Sydney.

Dixon, John
2003a. 'Lithic Petrology.' In Ernestine S. Elster and Colin Renfrew, eds., *Prehistoric Sitagroi: Excavations in Northeast Greece, 1968–1970.* Vol. 2. *The Final Report*, pp. 133–146. Monumenta Archaeologica 20. Cotsen Institute of Archaeology at UCLA, Los Angeles.
2003b. 'Appendix 4.1. Petrological Analysis.' In Ernestine S. Elster and Colin Renfrew, eds., *Prehistoric Sitagroi: Excavations in Northeast Greece, 1968–1970.* Vol. 2. *The Final Report*, pp. 147–174. Monumenta Archaeologica 20. Cotsen Institute of Archaeology at UCLA, Los Angeles.

Dubreuil, Laure
2002. *Étude fonctionnelle des outils de broyage natoufiens: nouvelles perspectives sur*

l'émergence de l'agriculture au Proche-Orient. Ph.D. Dissertation, Université Bordeaux I.

Ebeling, Jennie R., and Yorke M. Rowan
2004. 'The Archaeology of the Daily Grind: Ground Stone Tools and Food Production in the Southern Levant.' *Near Eastern Archaeology* 67(2):108–117.

Edmonds, Mark
1993. 'Towards a Context for Production and Exchange: The Polished Axe in Earlier Neolithic Britain.' In Chris Scarre and Frances Healy, eds., *Trade and Exchange in Prehistoric Europe. Proceedings of a Conference Held at the University of Bristol, April 1992*, pp. 69–86. Oxbow Books, London.
1995. *Stone Tools and Society: Working Stone in Neolithic and Bronze Age Britain.* B.T. Batsford Ltd, London.

Efstratiou, Nikos
1985. *Agios Petros: A Neolithic Site in the Northern Sporades.* BAR International Series 241, Oxford.

Efstratiou, Nikos, and Maria Ntinou
2004. ''Ένα εργαστήριο κατασκευής λίθινων αξινών στη Νεολιθική Μάκρη.' In Polyxeni Adam-Veleni, et al., eds., *Αρχαιολογικό Έργο στη Μακεδονία και Θράκη* 16:1–7. Ministry of Culture and Ministry of Macedonia and Thrace, Thessaloniki.

Elster, Ernestine S.
2003a. 'Grindstones, Polished Edge-Tools, and Other Stone Artifacts.' In Ernestine S. Elster and Colin Renfrew, eds., *Prehistoric Sitagroi: Excavations in Northeast Greece, 1968–1970.* Vol. 2. *The Final Report*, pp. 175–195. Monumenta Archaeologica 20. Cotsen Institute of Archaeology at UCLA, Los Angeles.
2003b. 'Catalog of Grindstones, Polished Edge-Tools, and Other Stone Artifacts.' In Ernestine S. Elster and Colin Renfrew, eds., *Prehistoric Sitagroi: Excavations in Northeast Greece, 1968–1970, vol. 2: The Final Report*, pp. 204–227. Monumenta Archaeologica 20. Cotsen Institute of Archaeology at UCLA, Los Angeles.

Erdogu, Burçin
2000. 'The Problems of Dating Prehistoric Axe Factories and Neolithisation in Turkish Thrace.' *Documenta Praehistorica* 27:155–166.

Ertug-Yaras, Füsun
2002. 'Pounders and Grinders in a Modern Central Anatolian Village.' In Hara Procopiou and René Treuil, eds., *Moudre et broyer II: Archéologie et histoire,* pp. 211–225. CTHS, Paris.

Etheridge, R. Jr
1893. 'Notes on Australian Aboriginal Stone Weapons and Implements.' *Proceedings of the Linnean Society of New South Wales* 8:295–299.

Euler, Robert C., and Henry F. Dobyns
1983. 'The Ethnoarchaeology of Pai Milling Stones.' In Nancy L. Fox, ed., *Collected Papers in Honor of Charlie R. Steen, Jr.,* pp. 253–267. Albuquerque Archaeological Society Press, Albuquerque.

Evans, John D.
1964. 'Excavations in the Neolithic Settlement of Knossos, 1957–60. Part I.' *The Annual of the British School at Athens* 59:141–240.

Evans, John D., and Colin Renfrew
1968. *Excavations at Saliagos near Antiparos.* The British School of Archaeology at Athens, Thames and Hudson.

Farrand, William R.
2000. *Depositional History of Franchthi Cave: Sediments, Stratigraphy, and Chronology.* Indiana University Press, Bloomington and Indianapolis.
2003. 'Depositional Environments and Site Formation during the Mesolithic Occupations of Franchthi Cave, Peloponnesos, Greece.' In Nena Galanidou and Catherine Perlès, eds., *The Greek Mesolithic: Problems and Perspectives*, pp. 69–78. British School at Athens, London.

Formenti, Françoise, and Hara Procopiou
1998. 'Analyse chromatographique de traces d'acides gras sur l'outillage de mouture. Contribution à son interprétation fonctionnelle.' *Cahiers de l'Euphrate* 8:151–177.

Foxhall, Lin, and Hamish A. Forbes
1982. 'Σιτομετρεία: The Role of Grain as a Staple Food in Classical Antiquity.' *Chiron* 12:73–81.

Fratt, Lee
1992. 'Ground Stone in Arizona.' In Mark C. Slaughter et al., *Making and Using Stone Artifacts: A Context for Evaluating Lithic Sites in Arizona*, pp. 16–25. Arizona State Parks, State Historic Preservation Office, Phoenix.

Fujimoto, Tsuyoshi
1993. 'Studies of Wear on Grinding Stones.' In Lech Krzyżaniak, Michał Kobusiewicz, and John Alexander, eds., *Environmental Change and Human Culture in the Nile Basin and Northern Africa until the Second Millennium B.C.*, pp. 485–490. Poznań Archaeological Museum, Poznań.

Galdikas, Birutė
1988. 'Milling Stones.' In Alan McPherron and Dragoslav Srejović, eds., *Divostin and the Neolithic of Central Serbia*, pp. 338–341. Department of Anthropology, University of Pittsburgh, Pittsburgh.

Godelier, Maurice, and José Garanger
1973. 'Outils de pierre, outils d'acier chez les Baruya de Nouvelle-Guinée.' *L'Homme* 13:185–220.

González, Jesús Emilio, and Juan José Ibáñez
2002. 'The Use of Pebbles in Eastern Vizcaya between 12000 and 10000 B.P.' In Hara Procopiou and René Treuil, eds., *Moudre et broyer I: Méthodes*, pp. 69–80. CTHS, Paris.

Goodarzi-Tabrizi, Shoki
1999. *The Worked Bone Remains of Hallan Çemi Tepesi, An Early Neolithic Site in Southeastern Turkey*. Ph.D. Dissertation, University of California, Berkeley.

Goren-Inbar, Naama, Gonen Sharon, Yoel Melamed, and Mordechai Kislev
2002. 'Nuts, Nut Cracking, and Pitted Stones at Gesher Benot Ya'aqov, Israel.' *Proceedings of the National Academy of Sciences* 99(4):2455–2460.

Graham, Martha
1994. *Mobile Farmers: An Ethnoarchaeological Approach to Settlement Organization among the Rarámuri of Northwestern Mexico*. International Monographs in Prehistory, Ann Arbor.

Grégoire, J.-P.
1992. 'Les grandes unités de transformation des céreals: L'exemple des minoteries de la Mésopotamie du sud à la fin du IIIe millénaire avant notre ère.' In Patricia Anderson, ed., *Préhistoire de l'agriculture: nouvelles approches expérimentales et ethnographiques*, pp. 321–339. CNRS, Paris.

Haaland, Randi
1987. *Socio-Economic Differentiation in the Neolithic Sudan.* BAR International Series 350, Oxford.
1995. 'Sedentism, Cultivation, and Plant Domestication in the Holocene Middle Nile Region.' *Journal of Field Archaeology* 22:157–174.

Hamon, Caroline
2006. *Broyage et abrasion au Néolithique ancien: Caractérisation technique et fonctionnelle des outillages en grès du Bassin parisien.* BAR International Series 1551, Oxford.

Hampton, O.W. 'Bud'
1999. *Culture of Stone: Sacred and Profane Uses of Stone among the Dani*. Texas A&M University Press, College Station, Texas.

Hansen, Julie M.
1991. *The Palaeoethnobotany of Franchthi Cave.* Indiana University Press, Bloomington and Indianapolis.
2000. 'Palaeoethnobotany and Palaeodiet in the Aegean Region: Notes on Legume Toxicity and Related Pathologies.' In Sarah J. Vaughan and William D.E. Coulson, eds., *Palaeodiet in the Aegean*, pp. 13–27. Oxbow Books, Oxford.

Harlan, Jack R.
1967. 'A Wild Wheat Harvest in Turkey.' *Archaeology* 20:197–201.

Hayden, Brian
1987a. 'Traditional Metate Manufacturing in Guatemala Using Chipped Stone Tools.' In Brian Hayden, ed., *Lithic Studies Among the Contemporary Highland Maya*, pp. 9–119. The University of Arizona Press, Tucson.
1987b. 'Past to Present Uses of Stone Tools in the Maya Highlands.' In Brian Hayden, ed., *Lithic Studies Among the Contemporary Highland Maya*, pp. 160–234. The University of Arizona Press, Tucson.

Heider, Karl G.
1967. 'Archaeological Assumptions and Ethnographical Facts: A Cautionary Tale from New Guinea.' *Southwestern Journal of Anthropology* 23:52–64.

Hellweg, Paul.
1984. *Flintknapping: The Art of Making Stone Tools.* Canyon Publishing Company, Canoga Park, California.

Hersh, Theresa Lillian
1981. *Grinding Stones and Food Processing Techniques of the Neolithic Societies of Turkey and Greece: Statistical, Experimental and Ethnographic Approaches to Archaeological Problem-Solving.* Ph.D. Dissertation, Columbia University.

Herz, Norman
1992. 'Provenance Determination of Neolithic Mediterranean Marbles by Stable Isotopes.' *Archaeometry* 34(2):185–194.

Hillman, Gordon
1981a. 'Reconstructing Crop Husbandry Practices from Charred Remains of Crops.' In Roger Mercer, ed., *Farming Practice in British Prehistory*, pp. 123–162. Edinburgh University Press, Edinburgh.
1981b. 'Possible Evidence of Grain-Roasting at Iron Age Pembrey.' *The Carmarthenshire Antiquary* 16:25-32.

1983. 'Interpretation of Archaeological Plant Remains: The Application of Ethnographic Models from Turkey.' In W. Van Zeist and W.A. Casparie, eds., *Plants and Ancient Man: Studies in Palaeoethnobotany*, pp. 1–41. A.A. Balkema, Rotterdam and Boston.

1984. 'Traditional Husbandry and Processing of Archaic Cereals in Recent Times: The Operations, Products and Equipment Which Might Feature in Sumerian Texts. Part I: The Glume Wheats.' *Bulletin of Sumerian Agriculture* 1:114–152.

Hodder, Ian, and Paul Lane

1982. 'A Contextual Examination of Neolithic Axe Distribution in Britain.' In Jonathan E. Erickson and Timothy K. Earle, eds., *Contexts for Prehistoric Exchange*, pp. 213–235. Academic Press, New York.

Hole, Frank, Kent V. Flannery, and James A. Neely

1969. *Prehistory and Human Ecology of the Deh Luran Plain: An Early Village Sequence from Khuzistan, Iran.* University of Michigan, Ann Arbor.

Holmes, William H.

1919. *Handbook of Aboriginal American Antiquities. Part I: Introductory: The Lithic Industries.* Bureau of American Ethnology, Washington, D.C.

Ibáñez Estévez, Juan José, and Jesús Emilio González Urquijo

1996. *From Tool Use to Site Function: Use-Wear Analysis in Some Final Upper Palaeolithic Sites in the Basque Country.* Tempvs Reparatvm, Oxford.

Iversen, Johannes

1956. 'Forest Clearance in the Stone Age.' *Scientific American* 194:36–41.

Jacobsen, Thomas W., and William R. Farrand

1987. *Franchthi Cave and Paralia: Maps, Plans, and Sections.* Indiana University Press, Bloomington and Indianapolis.

2000. 'Excavation History and Methodology.' In William R. Farrand, *Depositional History of Franchthi Cave: Sediments, Stratigraphy, and Chronology*, pp. 11–29. Indiana University Press, Bloomington and Indianapolis.

Jameson, Michael H., Curtis Runnels, and Tjeerd H. van Andel

1994. *A Greek Countryside: The Southern Argolid from Prehistory to Present Day.* Stanford University Press, Stanford.

Julien, Michèle

1985. 'L'outillage lithique non façonné.' In Danièle Lavallée, Michèle Julien, Jane Wheeler, and Claudine Karlin, eds., *Telarmachay. Chasseurs et pasteurs préhistoriques des Andes I.* Recherche sur les Civilisations, Paris.

Kardulias, P. Nick, and Curtis Runnels

1995. 'The Lithic Artifacts: Flaked Stone and Other Nonflaked Lithics.' In Curtis Runnels, Daniel J. Pullen, and Susan Langdon, eds., *Artifact and Assemblage. The Finds from a Regional Survey of the Southern Argolid, Greece.* Vol. 1. *The Prehistoric and Early Iron Age Pottery and the Lithic Artifacts,* pp. 74–139. Stanford University Press, Stanford.

Katz, Solomon H., and Mary M. Voigt

1986. 'Bread and Beer: The Early Use of Cereals in the Human Diet.' *Expedition* 28(2):23–34.

Kingery, W. David, Pamela B. Vandiver, and Martha Prickett

1988. 'The Beginnings of Pyrotechnology, Part II: Production and Use of Lime and Gypsum Plaster in the Pre-Pottery Neolithic Near East.' *Journal of Field Archaeology* 15:219–244.

Kozák, Vladimir

1972. 'Stone Age Revisited.' *Natural History* 81:14–24.

Kraybill, Nancy

1977. 'Pre-Agricultural Tools for the Preparation of Foods in the Old World.' In Charles Reed, ed., *Origins of Agriculture*, pp. 485–521. Mouton Publishers, Paris.

Leighton, Robert, and John E. Dixon

1992. 'Jade and Greenstone in the Prehistory of Sicily and Southern Italy.' *Oxford Journal of Archaeology* 11:179–200.

Leroi-Gourhan, André

1971. *Évolution et techniques: L'homme et la matière.* Albin Michel, Paris.

Le Roux, C.-T.

1971. 'A Stone Axe-Factory in Brittany.' *Antiquity* 45:283–288.

Lidström Holmberg, Cecilia

2004. 'Saddle Querns and Gendered Dynamics of the Early Neolithic in Mid Central Sweden.' In Helena Knuttson, ed., *Arrival: Coast to Coast 10*, pp. 199–231. Uppsala.

Lunardi, Anna

In press. 'Quinzano and Rivoli—Two Middle Neolithic Sites in the Adige Valley (Verona, North-Eastern Italy): Lithic Choices and Functional Aspects of the Non-Flint Stone Implements.' In *Non-flint Raw Material Use in Prehistory: Old Prejudices and New Directions. Proceedings of the XV Congress of the U.I.S.P.P.* ArchaeoPress, Oxford.

Malinowski, Bronislaw

1934. 'Stone Implements in Eastern New Guinea.' In E.E. Evans-Pritchard, Raymond Firth, Bronislaw Malinowski, and Isaac Schapera, eds., *Essays Presented to C.G. Seligman*, pp. 189–196. Kegan Paul, Trench Trubner and Co., London.

McCarthy, Frederick D.

1941. 'Aboriginal Grindstones and Mortars.' *The Australian Museum Magazine* 7:329–333.

Megaloudi, Fragkiska

2006. *Plants and Diet in Greece from Neolithic to Classic Periods: The Archaeobotanical Remains.* BAR International Series 1516, Oxford.

Melfos, Vassilis, and Georgia Stratouli

2002. 'Η προέλευση των πρώτων υλών για τα τέχνεργα του οικισμού.' In Georgios Hourmouziadis, ed., *Δισπηλιό 7500 χρόνια μετά*, pp. 175–183. University Studio Press, Thessaloniki.

Melfos, Vassilis, Georgia Stratouli, Michael Vavelidis, and Nikos Efstratiou

2001. 'Provenance and Flow of Raw Materials Used for the Polished Stone Tools Manufacture from the Neolithic Settlement of Makri, Aegean Thrace.' In Yannis Bassiakos, Eleni Aloupi, and Yorgos Facorellis, eds., *Archaeometry Issues in Greek Prehistory and Antiquity*, pp. 763–778. Hellenic Society of Archaeometry and Society of Messenian Archaeological Studies, Athens.

Menasanch, Montserrat, Roberto Risch, and José Antonio Soldevilla

2002. 'Las tecnologías del procesado de cereal en el sudeste de la peninsula ibèrica durante el III y el II milenio A.N.E.' In Hara Procopiou and René Treuil, eds., *Moudre et broyer I: Méthodes*, pp. 81–110. CTHS, Paris.

Meurers-Balke, Jutta, and Jens Lüning

1992. 'Some Aspects and Experiments Concerning the Processing of Glume Wheats.' In Patricia Anderson, ed., *Préhistoire de l'agriculture: nouvelles approches expérimentales et ethnographiques*, pp. 341–362. CNRS, Paris.

M'Guire, Joseph D.

1892. 'Materials, Apparatus and Processes of the Aboriginal Lapidary.' *The American Anthropologist* 5:165–176.

Miller, Michele A.

1996. 'The Manufacture of Cockle Shell Beads at Early Neolithic Franchthi Cave, Greece: A Case of Craft Specialization?' *Journal of Mediterranean Archaeology* 9(1):7–37.

1997. *Jewels of Shell and Stone, Clay and Bone: The Production, Function, and Distribution of Aegean Stone Age Ornaments.* Ph.D. Dissertation, Boston University.

1998. 'The Distribution of Opaque White Beads.' Paper presented at the 63rd Annual Meeting of the Society for American Archaeology, Seattle, Washington State.

2002. 'Grindstones in Greek Neolithic Ornament Production.' In Hara Procopiou and René Treuil, eds., *Moudre et broyer II: Archéologie et histoire,* pp. 45–55. CTHS, Paris.

Moore, A.M.T.

2000. 'Stone and Other Artifacts.' In A.M.T. Moore, G.C. Hillman, and A.J. Legge, eds., *Village on the Euphrates: From Foraging to Farming at Abu Hureyra*, pp. 165–186. Oxford University Press, Oxford.

Moritz, Ludwig A.

1958. *Grain-mills and Flour in Classical Antiquity.* Oxford University Press, Oxford.

Mould, Catharine A., Cressida Ridley, and Kenneth A. Wardle

2000. 'The Stone Small Finds.' In Cressida Ridley, Kenneth A. Wardle, and Catharine A. Mould, eds., *Servia I: Anglo-Hellenic Rescue Excavations*, pp. 112–161. British School at Athens, London.

Moundréa-Agrafioti, Antiklia

1981. *La Thessalie du Sud-Est au Néolithique: Outillage lithique et osseux.* Ph.D. Dissertation, Université de Paris X.

1987. 'Problèmes d'emmanchement dans le Néolithique Grec: Les gaines et manches en bois de cervidé.' In Danielle Stordeur, ed., *La main et l'outil. Manches et emmanchements préhistoriques*, pp. 247–256. G.S. Maison de l'Orient, Paris.

1992. 'Εργαλεία από λειασμένο λίθο.' In Lila Marangou, ed., *Μινωϊκός και Ελληνικός πολιτισμός από την συλλογή Μητσοτάκη*, pp. 174–180. Nicholas P. Goulandris Foundation, Athens.

1996. 'Tools.' In George Papathanassopoulos, ed., *Neolithic Culture in Greece,* pp. 103–106. Nicholas P. Goulandris Foundation, Athens.

2002. 'Moudre et broyer dans l'espace construit d'une ville du début du Bronze recent égéen (Akrotiri, Théra).' In Hara Procopiou and René Treuil, eds., *Moudre et broyer II: Archéologie et histoire,* pp. 93–106. CTHS, Paris.

Moundréa-Agrafioti, Antiklia, and Charalambos Gnardellis

1994. 'Classification des outils tranchants thessaliens en pierre polie par les méthodes multidimensionnelles.' In *La Thessalie: Quinze années de recherches archéologiques, 1975-1990. Bilans et perspectives,* vol. 1, pp. 189–200. Greek Ministry of Culture, Editions Kapon, Athens.

Müller-Beck, Hansjürgen
1965. *Seeberg Burgäschisee-Süd V: Holzgeräte und Holzbearbeitung.* Verlag Stämpfli & Cie, Bern.

Mylonas, George E.
1929. *Excavations at Olynthus.* Vol. 1. *The Neolithic Settlement.* Johns Hopkins University Press, Baltimore.

Nami, Hugo G.
1984. 'Experimental Approach to the Manufacture of Chipped and Ground Stone Artifacts from the Túnel Site, Tierra Del Fuego, Argentina.' *Lithic Technology* 13:102–107.

Nelson, Margaret
1987. 'Contemporary Specialization and Marketing of Manos and Metates in the Maya Highlands.' In Brian Hayden, ed., *Lithic Studies Among the Contemporary Highland Maya*, pp. 148–159. The University of Arizona Press, Tuscon.

Nesbitt Mark, and Delwen Samuel
1996. 'From Staple Crop to Extinction? The Archaeology and History of the Hulled Wheats.' In S. Padulosi, K. Hammer, and J. Heller, eds., *Hulled Wheats*, pp. 41–101. International Plant Genetic Resources Institute, Rome.

Nierlé, M.C.
1983. 'Mureybet et Cheikh Hassan (Syrie): Outillage de mouture et de broyage (9ème et 8ème millénaires).' *Cahiers de l'Euphrate* 3:177–216.

Ninou, Ismini
2006. *Analysis of Grinding Stones from Neolithic Sites of Northern Greece: Dispilio and Apsalos.* M.A. Thesis, University of Southampton.

O'Brien, Patrick K.
1994. *An Experimental Study of Ground Stone Use-Wear.* M.A. Thesis, University of Arizona.

O'Hare, Graham B.
1990. 'A Preliminary Study of Polished Stone Artifacts in Prehistoric Southern Italy.' *Proceedings of the Prehistoric Society* 56:123–152.

Olausson, Deborah
1982–1983. 'Flint and Groundstone Axes in the Scanian Neolithic: An Evaluation of Raw Materials Based on Experiment.' *Scripta Minora* 1982–1983 (2).

Oosterom, M.G.
1968. 'Appendix II: Mineralogical Investigations of Archaeological Specimens from Saliagos.' In John D. Evans and Colin Renfrew, *Excavations at Saliagos near Antiparos*, pp. 99–100. The British School of Archaeology at Athens, Thames and Hudson.

Ozbek, Onur
2000. 'A Prehistoric Stone Axe Production Site in Turkish Thrace: Hamaylitarla.' *Documenta Praehistorica* 27:167–171.

Panourgia, Neni
1995. *Fragments of Death, Fables of Identity: An Athenian Anthropography.* The University of Wisconsin Press, Madison.

Patton, Mark, A.
1991. 'Axes, Men, and Women: Symbolic Dimensions of Neolithic Exchange in Armorica (North-West France).' In Paul Garwood, David Jennings, Robin Skeates, and Judith Toms, eds., *Sacred and Profane: Proceedings of a Conference on Archaeology, Ritual and Religion, Oxford, 1989*, pp. 65–79. Oxford University Committee for Archaeology, Oxford.

Perlès, Catherine
1981. 'Industries lithiques.' In Nicole Lambert, ed., *La grotte préhistorique de Kitsos (Attique). Missions 1968–1978,* pp. 123–222. A.D.P.F. École Française d'Athènes, Athens.
1987. *Les Industries lithiques taillées de Franchthi (Argolide, Grèce).* Vol. 1. *Présentation générale et industries paléolithiques.* Indiana University Press, Bloomington and Indianapolis.
1989. *From Stone Procurement to Neolithic Society in Greece.* David Skomp Distinguished Lecture in Anthropology, Indiana University, Bloomington.
1990. *Les Industries lithiques taillées de Franchthi (Argolide, Grèce).* Vol. 2. *Les industries du Mésolithique et du Néolithique initial.* Indiana University Press, Bloomington and Indianapolis.
1992. 'Systems of Exchange and Organization of Production in Neolithic Greece,' *Journal of Mediterranean Archaeology* 5:115–164.
1999. 'Long-Term Perspectives on the Occupation of the Franchthi Cave: Continuity and Discontinuity.' In G.N. Bailey, E. Adam, E. Panagopoulou, C. Perlès, and K. Zachos, eds., *The Palaeolithic Archaeology of Greece and Adjacent Areas*, pp. 311–318. British School at Athens, London.
2001. *The Early Neolithic in Greece.* Cambridge University Press, Cambridge.

2003. 'The Mesolithic at Franchthi: An Overview of the Data and Problems.' In Nena Galanidou and Catherine Perlès, eds., *The Greek Mesolithic: Problems and Perspectives*, pp. 79–87. British School at Athens, London.

2004. *Les Industries lithiques taillées de Franchthi (Argolide, Grèce)*. Vol. 3. *Du Néolithique ancient au Néolithique final*. Indiana University Press, Bloomington and Indianapolis.

Perlès, Catherine, and Michelle Miller

In preparation. *The Ornaments from Franchthi Cave*. Indiana University Press, Bloomington and Indianapolis.

Pétrequin, Pierre, and Christian Jeunesse

1995. *La hache de pierre: Carriéres vosgiennes et échanges de lames polies pendant le Néolithique (5400–2100 av. J.-C.)*. Errance, Paris.

Pétrequin, Pierre, and Anne-Marie Pétrequin

1988. *Le Néolithique des lacs: Préhistoire des lacs de Chalain et de Clairvaux (4000–2000 av. J.C.)*. Errance, Paris.

1993a. *Écologie d'un outil: la hache de pierre en Irian Jaya (Indonésie)*. CNRS, Paris.

1993b. 'From Stone Tool to Sacred Axe: The Axes of the Danis of Irian Jaya, Indonesia.' In Arlette Berthelet and Jean Chavaillon, eds., *The Use of Tools by Human and Non-Human Primates*, pp. 359–377. Clarendon Press, Oxford.

Philibert, Sylvie

1993. 'Quelle interprétation fonctionnelle pour les grattoirs ocrés de la Balma Margineda (Andorre)?' In Patricia C. Anderson, Sylvie Beyries, Marcel Otte, and Hugues Plisson, eds., *Traces et fonction: les gestes retrouvés*, Vol. 1, pp. 131–137. ERAUL, Liège.

Poissonnier, Bertrand

2002. 'Pilons, broyeurs, bouchardes, marteaux et autres percuteurs: les interprétations fonctionnelles au risque de l'expérimentation.' In Hara Procopiou and René Treuil, eds., *Moudre et broyer I: Méthodes*, pp. 141–152. CTHS, Paris.

Pond, Alonzo W.

1930. *Primitive Methods of Working Stone Based on Experiments of Halvor L. Skavlem*. Logan Museum, Beloit College, Beloit.

Prinz, Beth

1988. 'The Ground Stone Industry from Divostin.' In Alan McPherron and Dragoslav Srejović, eds., *Divostin and the Neolithic of Central Serbia*, pp. 255–299. University of Pittsbutgh, Pittsburgh.

Procopiou, Hara

1998. *L'outillage de mouture et de broyage en Crète minoenne*. Ph.D. Dissertation, Université de Paris I – Sorbonne.

2003. 'Les techniques de décorticage dans le monde égéen. Étude ethnoarchéologique dans les Cyclades.' In Patricia C. Anderson, Linda S. Cummings, Thomas K. Schippers, and Bernard Simonel, eds., *Le Traitement des récoltes: un regard sur la diversité du Néolithique au présent*, pp. 115–136. APDCA, Antibes.

Procopiou, Hara, Patricia Anderson, Françoise Formenti, and Juan Tresseras Jordi

2002. 'Étude des matières transformées sur les outils de mouture: Identification des résidus et des traces d'usure par analyse chimique et par observations en microscopie optique et électronique.' In Hara Procopiou and René Treuil, eds., *Moudre et broyer I: Méthodes*, pp. 111–127. CTHS, Paris.

Renfrew, Jane M.

1973. 'Agriculture.' In Demetrios Theocharis, ed., *Neolithic Greece*, pp. 147–164. National Bank of Greece, Athens.

Ricou, Christian, and Thimus Esnard

1996. 'Utilisation des galets ouvragés du site de Ponthezières à Saint-Georges d'Oléron (Charente-Maritime).' *Bulletin de la Société Française* 94(4):546–548.

Ricq-de Bouard, Monique

1983. *Les outils lithiques polis du sud de la France*. CNRS, Paris.

Ricq-de Bouard, Monique, and Catherine Buret

1987. 'Traces superficielles et emmanchement.' In Danielle Stordeur, ed., *La main et l'outil. Manches et emmanchements préhistoriques*, pp. 177–184. G.S. Maison de l'Orient, Paris.

Risch, Roberto

2002. *Recursos naturales, medios de producción y explotación social. Un análisis económico de la industria lítica de Fuente Álamo (Almería), 2250–1400 antes de nuestra era*. Verlag Philipp von Zabern, Mainz.

Ritchie, William A.

1929. *Hammerstones, Anvils and Certain Pitted Stones*. The New York State Archaeological Association, Lewis H. Morgan Chapter, Rochester, New York.

Rodden, Robert J.

1962. 'Excavations at the Early Neolithic Site at Nea Nikomedeia, Greek Macedonia (1961 Season).' *Proceedings of the Prehistoric Society* 28:267–288.

Rodden, R.J., and J.M. Rodden

1964. 'A European Link with Chatal Huyuk: The 7th Millennium Settlement of Nea Nikomedeia in Macedonia. Part II: Burials and the Shrine.' *The Illustrated London News* (April):604–607.

Roodenberg, Jacob J.
1986. *Le mobilier en pierre de Bouqras: Utilisation de la pierre dans un site néolithique sur le Moyen Euphrate (Syrie).* Nederlands Historisch-Archaeologisch Instituut Te Istanbul, Istanbul.

Rosenberg, Michael, Mark Nesbitt, Richard W. Redding, and Thomas F. Strasser
1995. 'Hallan Çemi Tepesi: Some Preliminary Observations Concerning Early Neolithic Subsistence Behaviors in Eastern Anatolia.' *Anatolica* 21:1–12.

Rostain, Stéphen, and Yves Wack
1987. 'Haches et herminettes en pierre de Guyane Française.' *Journal de la Société des Américanistes* 73:107–138.

Roubet, Colette
1989. 'Methods of Analysis of Grinding Implements.' In Angela E. Close, ed., *The Prehistory of Wadi Kubbaniya,* vol. 3, pp. 470–489. Southern Methodist University Press, Dallas.

Roux, Valentine
1985. *Le matériel de broyage. Étude ethnoarchéologique à Tichitt, Mauritanie.* Recherche sur les Civilisations, Paris.

Rowan, Yorke, and Jennie Ebeling
2008. 'Introduction: Keeping Our Nose to the Grinding Stone.' In Yorke Rowan and Jennie Ebeling, eds., *New Approaches to Old Stones: Recent Studies of Ground Stone Artifacts*, pp. 1–15. Equinox, London.

Rowe, Roger
1995. 'Towards Cupstone Classification: An Experimental Approach.' *Ohio Archaeologist* 45(3):11–17.

Runnels, Curtis N.
1981. *A Diachronic Study and Economic Analysis of Millstones from the Argolid, Greece.* Ph.D. Dissertation, Indiana University.
1985. 'Trade and the Demand for Millstones in Southern Greece in the Neolithic and the Early Bronze Age.' In Bernard A. Knapp and Tamara Stech, eds., *Prehistoric Production and Exchange: The Aegean and Eastern Mediterranean*, pp. 30–43. University of California, Los Angeles.
1988. 'Early Bronze-Age Stone Mortars from the Southern Argolid.' *Hesperia* 57:257–272.
1996. 'The Stone Artifacts from the Neolithic Period.' In Berit Wells, ed., *The Berbati-Limnes Archaeological Survey 1988-1990*, pp. 40–43. Astroms, Jonsered.

Runnels, Curtis N., and Priscilla M. Murray
1983. 'Milling in Ancient Greece.' *Archaeology* 36(6):62–63, 75.

Sampson, Adamantios
1988. *Η Νεολιθική κατοίκηση στο Γυαλί της Νισύρου.* Euboean Antiquarian Society, Athens.

Sampson, Adamantios, and Chicako Sugaya
1988–1989. 'The Ground Stone Axes from Euboea.' *Annals of Anthropology and Archaeology* 3:11–45.

Samuel, Delwen
1993. 'Ancient Egyptian Cereal Processing: Beyond the Artistic Record.' *Cambridge Archaeological Journal* 3(2):276–283.
1999. 'Bread Making and Social Interactions at the Amarna Workmen's Village, Egypt.' In Kenneth David Thomas, ed., *Food Technology and Its Social Context: Production, Processing and Storage. World Archaeology* 31(1):121–144.

Sarpaki, Anaya
2001. 'Processed Cereals and Pulses from the Late Bronze Age Site of Akrotiri, Thera; Preparations Prior to Consumption: A Preliminary Approach to Their Study.' *Annual of the British School at Athens* 96:27–40.

Schelberg, John D.
1997. 'The Metates of Chaco Canyon, New Mexico.' In Frances Joan Mathien, ed., *Ceramics, Lithics and Ornaments of Chaco Canyon: Analyses of Artifacts from the Chaco Project 1971–1978*, vol. 3, pp. 1013–1117. National Park Service, Santa Fe.

Schlanger, Sarah H.
1991. 'On Manos, Metates, and the History of Site Occupations.' *American Antiquity* 56(3):460–474.

Schmandt-Besserat, Denise
1980. 'Ocher in Prehistory: 300,000 Years of the Use of Iron Ores as Pigments.' In Theodore A. Wertime and James D. Muhly, eds., *The Coming of the Age of Iron*, pp. 127–150. Yale University Press, New Haven and London.

Schneider, Joan S.
1996. 'Quarrying and Production of Milling Implements at Antelope Hill, Arizona.' *Journal of Field Archaeology* 23:299–311.
2002. 'Milling Tool Design, Stone Textures, and Function.' In Hara Procopiou and René Treuil, eds., *Moudre et broyer I: Méthodes*, pp. 31–53. CTHS, Paris.

Schoen, I.L.
1969. 'Contact with the Stone Age.' *Natural History* 78:10–18, 66–67.

Schön, Werner, and Uta Holter
1990. 'Grinding Implements from the Neolithic and Recent Times in Desert Areas in Egypt and Sudan.' *Beitrage zur allgemeinen und vergleichenden Archäologie* 9–10:359–379.
Schroth, Adella B.
1996. 'An Ethnographic Review of Grinding, Pounding, Pulverizing, and Smoothing with Stones.' *Pacific Coast Archaeological Society Quarterly* 32(4):55–75.
Séfériadès, Michel
1992a. 'La pierre polie.' In René Treuil, ed., *Dikili Tash: Village Préhistorique de Macédoine orientale, Fouilles de Jean Deshayes (1961-1975),* vol. 1, pp. 84–99. *Bulletin de Correspondence Hellénique* Supplement 16, École Française d'Athènes, Athens.
1992b. 'L'os et le bois de cervidé.' In René Treuil, ed., *Dikili Tash: Village Préhistorique de Macédoine orientale, Fouilles de Jean Deshayes (1961–1975),* vol. 1, pp. 99–112. *Bulletin de Correspondence Hellénique* Supplement 16, École Française d'Athènes, Athens.
Semenov, Sergei Aristarkhovich
1964. *Prehistoric Technology*. Barnes and Noble, London.
Shackleton, Judith C.
1988. *Marine Molluscan Remains from Franchthi Cave.* Indiana University Press, Bloomington and Indianapolis.
Shott, Michael J.
1989. 'On Tool-Class Use Lives and the Formation of Archaeological Assemblages.' *American Antiquity* 54:9–30.
Sillitoe, Paul
1988. *Made in Niugini: Technology in the Highlands of Papua New Guinea*. British Museum Publications, London.
Skeates, Robin
1995. 'Animate Objects: A Biography of Prehistoric 'Axe-Amulets' in the Central Mediterranean Region.' *Proceedings of the Prehistoric Society* 61:279–301.
Smoor, Bert
1976. 'Polished Stone Tools.' In Marija Gimbutas, ed., *Neolithic Macedonia: As Reflected by Excavation at Anza, Southeast Yugoslavia*, pp. 177–188. Institute of Archaeology, University of California, Los Angeles.
Solecki, Rose L.
1969. 'Milling Tools and the Epi-paleolithic in the Near East.' In Mireille Ters, ed., *Études sur le Quaternaire dans le monde,* vol. 2, pp. 989–994. CNRS, Paris.
Solecki, Rose L., and Ralph S. Solecki
1970. 'Grooved Stones from Zawi Chemi Shanidar, A Protoneolithic Site in Northern Iraq.' *American Anthropologist* 72:831–841.
Sonnenfeld, J.
1962. 'Interpreting the Function of Primitive Implements.' *American Antiquity* 28(1):56–65.
Spears, Carol S.
1975. 'Hammers, Nuts and Jolts, Cobbles, Cobbles, Cobbles: Experiments in Cobble Technologies in Search of Correlates.' In Charles M. Baker, ed., *Arkansas Eastman Archaeological Project*, pp. 83–116. Research Report No. 6, Arkansas Archaeological Survey, Fayetteville, Arkansas.
Spenneman, D.H.R.
1987. 'On the Use-Wear of Stone Adzes and Axes and Its Implication for the Assessment of Humans Handedness.' *Lithic Technology* 16:22–27.
Stahl, Ann
1989. 'Plant-Food Processing: Implications for Dietary Quality.' In David R. Harris and Gordon C. Hillman, eds., *Foraging and Farming: The Evolution of Plant Exploitation*, pp. 171–194. Unwin Hyman, London.
Starnini, Elisabetta, and Barbara Voytek
1997. 'New Lights on Old Stones: The Ground Stone Assemblage from the Bernabò Brea Excavation at Arene Candide.' *Memorie dell'Istituto Italiano di Paleontologia Umana* 5:427–511.
Steensberg, Axel
1980. *New Guinea Gardens: A Study of Husbandry with Parallels in Prehistoric Europe*. Academic Press, London.
Stout, Dietrich
2002. 'Skill and Cognition in Stone Tool Production.' *Current Anthropology* 43:693–722.
Strasser, Thomas F., and Charalambos G. Fassoulas
2003–2004. 'Granodiorite Axes from Knossos and their Implications for Neolithic Trade on Crete.' *Aegean Archaeology* 7:9–12.
Strathern, Marilyn
1965. 'Axe Types and Quarries: A Note on the Classification of Stone Axe Blades from the Hagen Area, New Guinea.' *The Journal of the Polynesian Society* 74:182–191.
1970. 'Stone Axes and Flake Tools: Evaluations from Two New Guinea Highlands Societies.' *Proceedings of the Prehistoric Society* 35:311–329.
Stratouli, Georgia
2002. 'Τα εργαλεία από λειασμένο λίθο, οστό και κέρατο.' In Georgios Hourmouziadis,

ed., *Δισπηλιό 7500 χρόνια μετά*, pp. 155–174. University Studio Press, Thessaloniki.
2005. 'Symbolic Behaviour at Places of Social Activity Beyond the Domestic Area in the Ionian Neolithic.' *Documenta Praehistorica* 32:123–132.

Stratouli, Georgia, and Vassilis Melfos
In press. 'Exchange Networks in the Neolithic of Greece: Gabbro and Talc Objects from Drakaina Cave, Kephalonia Island, Western Greece.' In *Proceedings of the 4th Symposium of Archaeometry of the Hellenic Society of Archaeometry, 28–31 May 2003*. Athens.

Strezewski, Michael
2006. 'Patterns of Interpersonal Violence at the Fisher Site.' *Midcontinental Journal of Archaeology* 31(2):249–279.

Stroulia, Anna
2003. 'Ground Stone Celts from Franchthi Cave: A Close Look.' *Hesperia* 72:1–30.
2005a. 'Λίθινα τριπτά απο την Κίτρινη Λίμνη Κοζάνης: Πρώτη προσέγγιση, πρώτα ερωτήματα.' In Polyxeni Adam-Veleni, et al., eds., *Αρχαιολογικό Έργο στη Μακεδονία και Θράκη* 17(2003):571–580. Ministry of Culture and Ministry of Macedonia and Thrace, Thessaloniki.
2005b. 'Redefining the So-Called Stone Celt Workshop at Makri, Thrace, Greece.' Paper delivered at the 82nd Central States Anthropological Society Annual Meeting, Miami University, Oxford, Ohio.
2005c. 'Making Celts, Un-making Celt Workshops at Neolithic Makri, Greece.' Paper delivered at the 70th Annual Meeting of the Society for American Archaeology, Salt Lake City, Utah.
In preparation. 'Ground Stone Tools from Kitrini Limni, Kozani.'

Sugaya, Chicako
1992. 'The Function of the Neolithic Stone Axe.' In *Διεθνές Συνέδριο για την Αρχαία Θεσσαλία στη μνήμη του Δημήτρη Θεοχάρη*, pp. 71–77. Greek Ministry of Culture, Athens.
1993. 'The Stone Axes of Tharrounia.' In Adamantios Sampson, ed., *Σκοτεινή Θαρρουνίων. Το σπήλαιο, ο οικισμός και το νεκροταφείο*, pp. 442–447. Privately published, Athens.

Taçon, Paul S.C.
1991. 'The Power of Stone: Symbolic Aspects of Stone Use and Tool Development in Western Arnhem Land, Australia.' *Antiquity* 65:192–207.

Talalay, Lauren E.
1987. 'Rethinking the Function of Clay Figurine Legs from Neolithic Greece: An Argument by Analogy.' *American Journal of Archaeology* 91:161–169.
1993. *Deities, Dolls, and Devices: Neolithic Figurines from Franchthi Cave, Greece.* Indiana University Press, Bloomington and Indianapolis.

Torrence, Robin
1986. *Production and Exchange of Stone Tools: Prehistoric Obsidian in the Aegean.* Cambridge University Press, Cambridge.

Toth, Nicholas, Desmond Clark, and Giancarlo Ligabue
1992. 'The Last Stone Ax Makers.' *Scientific American* 267:88–93.

Touloumis, Kosmas
2002. 'Η οικονομία ενός Νεολιθικού λιμναίου οικισμού.' In Georgios Hourmouziadis, ed., *Δισπηλιό 7500 χρόνια μετά*, pp. 89–113. University Studio Press, Thessaloniki.

Townsend, William H.
1969. 'Stone and Steel Tool Use in a New Guinea Society.' *Ethnology* 8:199–205.

Tsoraki, Christina
2007. 'Unravelling Ground Stone Life Histories: The Spatial Organization of Stone Tools and Human Activities at LN Makriyalos, Greece.' *Documenta Praehistorica* 34:289–297.

Tsountas, Christos
1901. 'Λίθινα εργαλεία εκ Πελοποννήσου.' *Αρχαιολογική Εφημερίς* 1901:85–90.
1908. *Αι προϊστορικαί Ακροπόλεις Σέσκλου και Διμηνίου.* Sakellariou, Athens.

Valamoti, Soultana-Maria
1994. 'Η επεξεργασία και η αποθήκευση του σιταριού μέσα από αρχαιοβοτανικά δεδομένα: Μία εισαγωγή.' In *"Ο Άρτος ημών": Από το σιτάρι στο ψωμί*, pp. 46–54. Cultural Technological Foundation ETBA, Athens.
2007. 'Traditional Foods and Culinary Novelties in Neolithic and Bronze Age Northern Greece: An Overview of the Archaeobotanical Evidence.' In Christopher Mee and Josette Renard, eds., *Cooking up the Past: Food and Culinary Practices in the Neolithic and Bronze Age Aegean*, pp. 89–108. Oxbow Books, Oxford.

van Andel, Tjeerd H., and Charles J. Vitaliano
1987. 'Water and Other Resources.' In Tjeerd H. van Andel and Susan Buck Sutton, *Landscape and People of the Franchthi Region*, pp. 17–20. Indiana University Press, Bloomington and Indianapolis.

VanPool, Todd L., and Robert D. Leonard
2002. 'Specialized Ground Stone Production in the Casas Grandes Region of Northern Chihuahua, Mexico.' *American Antiquity* 67(4):710–730.

Vaughan, Patrick C.
1990. 'Use-Wear Analysis of Mesolithic Chipped-Stone Artifacts from Franchthi Cave.' In Catherine Perlès, *Les Industries lithiques taillées de Franchthi (Argolide, Grèce),* vol. 2*: Les industries du Mésolithique et du Néolithique initial*, pp. 239–253. Indiana University Press, Bloomington and Indianapolis.

Vial, L.G.
1940–1941. 'Stone Axes of Mount Hagen, New Guinea.' *Oceania* 11:157–163.

Vialou, D.
1981. 'La parure.' In Nicole Lambert, ed., *La grotte préhistorique de Kitsos (Attique). Missions 1968-1978,* pp. 391–419. A.D.P.F. École Française d'Athènes, Athens.

Vitaliano, Charles J.
1987. 'Geological History.' In Tjeerd H. van Andel and Susan Buck Sutton, *Landscape and People of the Franchthi Region*, pp. 12–17. Indiana University Press, Bloomington and Indianapolis.
N.d. 'Geology of the Koilada-Fournoi-Kranidhi Region, Peloponnesos, Greece.' Unpublished manuscript.

Vitelli, Karen D.
1993. *Franchthi Neolithic Pottery.* Vol. 1. *Classification and Ceramic Phases 1 and 2.* Indiana University Press, Bloomington and Indianapolis.
1999. *Franchthi Neolithic Pottery.* Vol. 2. *The Later Neolithic Phases 3–5.* Indiana University Press, Bloomington and Indianapolis.

Voytek, Barbara
1985. *The Exploitation of Lithic Resources in Neolithic Southeast Europe.* Ph.D. Dissertation, University of California, Berkeley.
1990. 'The Use of Stone Resources.' In Ruth Tringham and Dušan Krstić, eds., *Selevac: A Neolithic Village in Yugoslavia*, pp. 437–484. Institute of Archaeology, University of California, Los Angeles.

Wace, A.J.B., and M.S. Thompson
1912. *Prehistoric Thessaly.* Cambridge University Press, Cambridge.

Warren, Peter M., M.R. Jarman, H.N. Jarman, N.J. Shackleton, and John D. Evans
1968. 'Knossos Neolithic, Part II.' *The Annual of the British School at Athens* 63:239–276.

Webb, Jennifer M.
1998. 'Lithic Technology and Discard at Marki, Cyprus: Consumer Behavior and Site Formation in the Prehistoric Bronze Age.' *Antiquity* 72:796–805.
2000. 'Curation, Expediency and Discard: The Ground Stone Industry at Marki-*Alonia.*' In G.K. Ioannides and S. Hadjistellis, eds.*, Acts of the Third International Congress of Cypriot Studies (Nicosia, 16–20 April, 1996)*, pp. 261–279. Society of Cypriot Studies, Nicosia.

White, Peter J., and N. Modjeska
1978. 'Acquirers, Users, Finders, Losers: The Use Axe Blades Make of the Duna.' *Mankind* 11:276–287.

Wijnen, Marie-Hélène
1982. *The Early Neolithic I at Sesklo: An Early Farming Community in Thessaly, Greece.* Universitaire Pers Leiden, Leiden.

Wilke, Philip J., and Leslie A. Quintero
1996. 'Near Eastern Neolithic Millstone Production: Insights from Research in the Arid Southwestern United States.' In Stefan Karol Kozlowski and Hans Georg Gebel, eds., *Neolithic Chipped Stone Industries of the Fertile Crescent, and Their Contemporaries in Adjacent Regions*, pp. 243–260. Ex oriente, Berlin.

Wilkinson, Tony J., and Susan T. Duhon
1990. *Franchthi Paralia: The Sediments, Stratigraphy, and Offshore Investigations.* Indiana University Press, Bloomington and Indianapolis.

Willcox, George
2002. 'Charred Plant Remains from a 10th Millennium B.P. Kitchen at Jerf el Ahmar (Syria).' *Vegetation History and Archaeobotany* 11(1–2):55–60.

Willey, P.
1990. *Prehistoric Warfare on the Great Plains: Skeletal Analysis of the Crow Creek Massacre Victims.* Garland, New York and London.

Willey, P., and Thomas E. Emerson
1993. 'The Osteology and Archaeology of the Crow Creek Massacre.' *Plains Anthropologist* 38:227–269.

Williams-Thorpe, Olwen, and Richard S. Thorpe
1993. 'Geochemistry and Trade of Eastern Mediterranean Millstones from the Neolithic to Roman Periods.' *Journal of Archaeological Science* 20:263–320.

Winn, Shan, and Daniel Shimabuku
1989. 'Bone and Ground Stone Tools.' In Marija Gimbutas, Shan Winn, and Daniel Shimabuku, eds., *Achilleion: A Neolithic Settlement in Thessaly, Greece, 6400–5600*

BC, pp. 259–272. Monumenta Archaeologica 14. Institute of Archaeology, University of California, Los Angeles.

Woodbury, Richard B.

1954. *Prehistoric Stone Implements of Northeastern Arizona.* Harvard University, Cambridge, Massachusetts.

Wright, Katherine I.

1991. 'The Origins and Development of Ground Stone Assemblages in Late Pleistocene Southwest Asia.' *Paléorient* 17(1):19–45.

1992. 'A Classification System for Ground Stone Tools from the Prehistoric Levant.' *Paléorient* 18(2):53–81.

1993. 'Early Holocene Ground Stone Assemblages in the Levant.' *Levant* 25:93–111.

1994. 'Ground-Stone Tools and Hunter-Gatherer Subsistence in Southwest Asia: Implications for the Transition to Farming.' *American Antiquity* 59(2):238–263.

Yalouri, Eleana

1994. 'Μεταποίηση των σιτηρών κατά τη Νεολιθική περίοδο και την Εποχή του Χαλκού: Πειραματικές προσεγγίσεις.' In In *"Ο Άρτος ημών": Από το σιτάρι στο ψωμί*, pp. 55–71. Cultural Technological Foundation ETBA, Athens.

Yeroussi, Soultana

1999. *Τριπτά και λειασμένα εργαλεία από το Μακρύγιαλο Πιερίας.* M.A. Thesis, Aristotle University of Thessaloniki.

Yohe, Robert M., Margaret E. Newman, and Joan S. Schneider

1991. 'Immunological Identification of Small-Mammal Proteins on Aboriginal Milling Equipment.' *American Antiquity* 56(4):659–666.

Zurro, Débora, Roberto Risch, and Ignacio Clemente Conte

2005. 'Analysis of an Archaeological Grinding Tool: What to Do With Archaeological Artefacts?' In Xavier Terradas, ed, *Lithic Toolkits in Ethnoarchaeological Contexts*, pp. 57–64. BAR International Series 1370, Oxford.

APPENDIX A

List of all Franchthi ground stone tools and related specimens by trench and unit

KEY: Prov.=Provenience, Pres.=Preservation, C=Cave, P=Paralia, c=complete, f=fragmentary, Palaeol.=Palaeolithic, Mesol.=Mesolithic, (Upper/Final Mesol.)=probably Upper/Final Mesolithic interphase, (Final Mesol.)=probable Final Mesolithic, Pre-Neol.=Pre-Neolithic, Neol.=Neolithic, (Initial Neol.)=probable Initial Neolithic, EN=Early Neolithic, MN=Middle Neolithic, LN=Late Neolithic, FN=Final Neolithic, (EN)=probable Early Neolithic, (MN)=probable Middle Neolithic, (LN)=probable Late Neolithic, (FN)=probable Final Neolithic, EN/MN=Early/Middle Neolithic interphase, MN/LN=Middle/Late Neolithic interphase, surf.=surface, n/ap=non applicable, conglom.=conglomerate, sandstone/conglom.=sandstone combined with conglomerate

Note: G:lot 28 refers to units G:19-24.

Trench:unit	Prov.	Name	Pres.	Material	Date	Group
A:5	C	FS 6	f	serpentinite	Neol.	Acut
A:5	C	FS 273	c	diabase	Neol.	Aglobe-nostain
A:18	C	FS 7	c	serpentinite	Neol.	Aend
A:19	C	FS 52	c	serpentinite	Neol.	Acut
A:24	C	FS 14	c	sandstone	FN	Adisc
A:25	C	FS 13	c	sandstone	FN	Pcav
A:27	C	FS 21	c	serpentinite	(FN)	Acut
A:27	C	FS 269	c	serpentinite	(FN)	Amisc2-set1
A:27	C	FS 270	c	sandstone	(FN)	Amisc1-set10
A:30	C	FS 12	c	serpentinite	Neol.	Acut
A:34	C	FS 271	c	diabase	Neol.	Amisc2-set5
A:37	C	FS 37	c	argillite	Neol.	Acut
A:40	C	FS 34	c	serpentinite	FN	Acut
A:40	C	FS 59	c	sandstone	FN	Pcav
A:40	C	FS 68	f	soapstone	FN	Amisc2-set2
A:45	C	FS 32	c	diabase	Neol.	Acut
A:46	C	FS 36	n/ap	andesite	Neol.	Acut
A:55	C	FS 64	f	sandstone	Neol.	Amisc1-set1
A:55	C	FS 73	f	sandstone	Neol.	Popen
A:65	C	FS 74	c	sandstone	(Initial Neol.)	Amisc1-set4
B:3	C	FS 22	c	serpentinite	Neol.	Acut
BE:4	C	FS 303	c	sandstone	Neol.	Amisc1-set11
C:4	C	FS 272	c	diabase	Neol.	Aglobe-nostain
F:3	C	S 54	f	sandstone	Pre-Neol.?	possible Pre-Neol.
F:4	C	S 33	f	sandstone?	Neol.	Amisc1-set11
F:6	C	S 52	f	andesite	Neol.	Popen
F:15	C	S 55	f	andesite	Neol.	Popen
F:16	C	S 56	f	diorite?	Neol.	Aglobe-nostain
F:20	C	S 57	f	serpentinite	Neol.	Acut
FA	C	S 61	f	andesite	Neol.	Popen
FA	C	S 68	c	limestone	Pre-Neol.?	possible Pre-Neol.
FA	C	S 2	c	conglom.?	Neol.	Amisc1-set6
FA scarp	C	FS 226	c	serpentinite	Neol.	Acut

Trench:unit	Prov.	Name	Pres.	Material	Date	Group
FA surf.	C	FS 795	c	andesite	Neol.	Popen
FA surf.	C	S 27	c	basalt	Neol.	Asquare-circ
FA surf.	C	S 58	c	sandstone	Neol.	Amisc1-set11
FA:4	C	FS 186	c	sandstone	Neol.	Amisc1-set9
FA:6	C	FS 188	c	sandstone	Neol.	Adisc
FA:6	C	FS 189	f	serpentinite	Neol.	Amisc2-set5
FA:6	C	S 59	f	andesite	Neol.	Popen
FA:6	C	S 60	f	limestone	Neol.	Amisc2-set5
FA:7	C	S 24	f	andesite	Neol.	Popen
FA:8	C	FS 187	c	sandstone	Neol.	Adisc
FA:10	C	FS 192	c	serpentinite	Neol.	Aend
FA:10	C	FS 199	f	sandstone	Neol.	Amisc1-set15
FA:10	C	S 11	f	sandstone	Neol.	Popen
FA:10	C	S 25	f	sandstone	Neol.	Popen
FA:10	C	S 38a	f	sandstone	Neol.	Popen
FA:11	C	FS 194	c	metaquartzite?	Neol.	Amisc2-set4
FA:11	C	FS 196	c	sandstone	Neol.	Amisc1-set11
FA:11	C	FS 197	f	serpentinite	Neol.	Amisc2-set8
FA:15	C	S 34	f	sandstone	Neol.	Popen
FA:19	C	S 46	f	sandstone	Neol.	Amisc1-set11
FA:21	C	S 16	f	conglom.?	Neol.	Amisc1-set11
FA:24	C	FS 204	f	serpentinite	Neol.	Acut fragment?
FA:24	C	FS 207	c	serpentinite	Neol.	Acut
FA:24	C	FA:24	f	limestone	Neol.	Amisc2-set5
FA:27	C	S 28	c	serpentinite	Neol.	Amisc2-set5
FA:28	C	FA:28	f	serpentinite	Neol.	Acut
FA:28	C	FA:28a	f	serpentinite	Neol.	Acut fragment?
FA:29	C	FS 223	c	metaandesite?	Neol.	Asquare-circ
FA:29	C	S 31	f	soapstone	Neol.	Amisc2-set7
FA:29	C	S 32	f	sandstone	Neol.	Popen
FA:29	C	S 39	f	sandstone	Neol.	Popen
FA:30	C	S 45	f	sandstone	Neol.	Asquare-circ
FA:31	C	S 14	f	conglom.	Neol.	Amisc1-set12
FA:33	C	S 62	c	sandstone	Neol.	Asquare-circ
FA:33	C	S 65	c	sandstone	Neol.	Amisc1-set15
FA:33A	C	FS 210	c	serpentinite	Neol.	Acut
FA:33A	C	FS 212	c	serpentinite	Neol.	Acut
FA:33A	C	S 22	c	sandstone	Neol.	Adisc
FA:33A	C	S 40	f	sandstone	Neol.	Amisc1-set11
FA:33B	C	S 30	c	sandstone	Neol.	Popen
FA:33B	C	S 38	f	sandstone	Neol.	Popen
FA:34	C	S 29	f	sandstone	Neol.	Popen
FA:34	C	S 41	f	sandstone	Neol.	Popen
FA:34	C	S 48	c	sandstone	Neol.	Arect
FA:34	C	S 51	f	conglom.?	Neol.	Amisc1-set11
FA:35	C	FS 214	f	sandstone	Neol.	Pcav
FA:35	C	FS 220	c	sandstone	Neol.	Asquare-circ
FA:35	C	S 35	f	limestone?	Neol.	Amisc2-set5
FA:35	C	S 36	f	andesite	Neol.	Amisc1-set5
FA:35	C	S 37	f	sandstone	Neol.	Popen
FA:37	C	FS 219	c	serpentinite	Neol.	Acut
FA:37	C	S 19	c	sandstone	Neol.	Adisc
FA:37	C	S 50	f	sandstone	Neol.	Asquare-circ
FA:39	C	FS 221	c	felsite porphyry	FN	Acut

Trench:unit	Prov.	Name	Pres.	Material	Date	Group
FA:41	C	S 17	f	sandstone	Neol.	Pcav
FA:41	C	S 18	c	sandstone/conglom.	Neol.	Adisc
FA:41	C	S 26	f	sandstone	Neol.	Popen
FA:41	C	S 53	f	conglom.	Neol.	Popen
FA:42	C	FS 225	c	serpentinite	Neol.	Aend
FA:42	C	FA:42a	c	limestone	Pre-Neol.?	possible Pre-Neol.
FA:42	C	FA:42b	c	limestone	Pre-Neol.?	possible Pre-Neol.
FA:42	C	S 21	f	sandstone	Neol.	Popen
FA:42	C	S 44	f	sandstone	Neol.	Popen
FA:43	C	FS 227	c	peridotite	Neol.	Acut
FA:43	C	S 12	f	conglom.	Neol.	Amisc1-set12
FA:43	C	S 42	c	limestone	Neol.	Amisc2-set7
FA:43	C	S 66	f	andesite	Neol.	Popen
FA:44	C	S 43	f	volcanic rock	Neol.	Popen
FA:44	C	S 67	c	limestone	Neol.	Amisc2-set7
FA:45	C	FS 231	c	sandstone	FN	Asquare-circ
FA:46	C	FS 230	c	limestone	FN	Amisc2-set2
FA:49	C	FS 260	f	sandstone	Neol.	Adisc
FA:53	C	S 64	f	diabase?	Neol.	Amisc2-set3
FA:54	C	FS 239	c	serpentinite	Neol.	Acut
FA:54	C	FS 240	f	serpentinite	Neol.	Acut manuf. remain?
FA:54	C	S 69	f	sandstone	Neol.	Amisc1-set11
FAN:59	C	FS 258	c	sandstone	FN	Adisc
FAN:59	C	FS 261	c	sandstone	FN	Amisc1-set11
FAN:61	C	FAN:61	c	conglom.	FN	Adisc
FAN:61	C	FAN:61/1	c	sandstone/conglom.	FN	Adisc
FAN:63	C	FAN:63	c	sandstone?	FN	Pmisc
FAN:74	C	FS 255	f	quartz	(FN)	Amisc2-set5
FAN:86	C	FAN:86	f	sandstone	(LN)	Popen
FAN:89	C	FAN:89	c	sandstone	LN	Amisc1-set11
FAN:91	C	FS 299	f	sandstone	(FN)	Adisc
FAN:91	C	FS 300	c	sandstone/conglom.	(FN)	Adisc
FAN:117	C	FS 285	c	sandstone	LN	Popen
FAN:117	C	FS 287	c	sandstone?	LN	Amisc1-set1
FAN:117	C	FS 288	f	serpentinite	LN	Acut fragment?
FAN:119	C	FS 297	c	sandstone	(LN)	Arect
FAN:121	C	FS 396	f	sandstone	MN/LN	Popen
FAN:129	C	FAN:129	f	serpentinite	MN	Acut
FAN:131	C	FS 417	f	basalt	MN	Amisc2-set9
FAN:132	C	FS 418	f	sandstone	MN	Popen
FAN:132	C	FS 419	f	siltstone	MN	Popen
FAN:132	C	FS 420	c	serpentinite	MN	Aend
FAN:133	C	FS 422	f	serpentinite	MN	Amisc2-set9
FAN:134	C	FS 423	f	sandstone	MN	Popen
FAN:134	C	FS 424	f	andesite	MN	Popen
FAN:134	C	FS 425	f	serpentinite	MN	Acut
FAN:134	C	FS 426	f	serpentinite	MN	Acut fragment?
FAN:136	C	FS 432	f	serpentinite	MN	Aend
FAN:136	C	FS 433	f	sandstone	MN	Popen
FAN:136	C	FS 434	f	sandstone	MN	Popen
FAN:137	C	FS 435	f	sandstone	MN	Amisc1-set11
FAN:142	C	FS 505	c	serpentinite	(MN)	Acut
FAN:142	C	FAN:142	f	limestone	(MN)	Amisc2-set8
FAN:143	C	FAN:143	f	limestone	(MN)	Amisc2-set8
FAN:148	C	FS 507	f	limestone	(MN)	Amisc2-set8

Trench:unit	Prov.	Name	Pres.	Material	Date	Group
FAN:174	C	FS 549	f	quartzite	Final Mesol.	Pre-Neol.
FAN:177	C	FS 551	f	andesite	Upper Mesol.	Pre-Neol.
FAS:61	C	FS 304	c	sandstone	FN	Adisc
FAS:69	C	FS 317	c	sandstone	FN	Adisc
FAS:70	C	FS 318	c	sandstone	FN	Asquare-circ
FAS:71	C	FS 320	f	sandstone	FN	Popen
FAS:71	C	FS 315	c	diabase	FN	Aglobe-nostain
FAS:71	C	FS 324	f	andesite	FN	Popen
FAS:72	C	FS 311	n/ap	peridotite	FN	Acut
FAS:72	C	FS 322	c	conglom.	FN	Amisc1-set11
FAS:73	C	FS 350	f	andesite	FN	Amisc1-set5
FAS:76	C	FS 357	f	sandstone	FN	Amisc1-set14
FAS:81	C	FS 358	c	serpentinite	FN	Amisc2-set1
FAS:83	C	FS 360	f	sandstone	(FN)	Asquare-circ
FAS:93	C	FS 368	f	sandstone	LN	Popen
FAS:102	C	FS 379	f	sandstone	(LN)	Amisc1-set10
FAS:102	C	FS 380	f	andesite	LN	Popen
FAS:105	C	FS 382	c	soapstone	LN	Amisc2-set6
FAS:107	C	FS 385	f	serpentinite	LN	Acut
FAS:116	C	FS 442	f	sandstone	MN/LN	Popen
FAS:117	C	FS 445	f	sandstone?	(MN)	Amisc1-set7
FAS:117	C	FS 452	f	serpentinite	(MN)	Amisc2-set5
FAS:117	C	FAS:117	f	?	(MN)	Amisc1-set1
FAS:120	C	FS 455	f	sandstone	MN	Amisc1-set9
FAS:120	C	FS 456	f	limestone	MN	Amisc2-set4
FAS:121	C	FS 464	f	sandstone	MN	Popen
FAS:123	C	FS 465	f	sandstone	MN	Popen
FAS:123	C	FS 466	f	sandstone	MN	Popen
FAS:124	C	FS 467	f	sandstone	(MN)	Popen
FAS:125	C	FS 468	f	sandstone	MN	Popen
FAS:132	C	FS 576	f	limestone	EN/MN	Amisc2-set7
FAS:159	C	FAS:159	f	limestone	Upper Mesol.	Pre-Neol.
FAS:166	C	FS 701	c	limestone	Upper Mesol.	Pre-Neol.
FAS:184	C	FS 706	f	sandstone	Lower Mesol.	Pre-Neol.
FAS:191	C	FS 725	c	limestone	Lower Mesol.	Pre-Neol.
FAS:204	C	FS 750	c	sandstone	Upper Palaeol.	Pre-Neol.
FF1:5	C	FF1:5	f	limestone	Neol.	Amisc2-set3
FF1:5	C	FF1:5a	f	sandstone	Neol.	Amisc1-set7
FF1:6	C	FS 95	c	sandstone	Neol.	Arect
FF1:6	C	FS 121	c	sandstone	Neol.	Adisc
FF1:6	C	FF1:6	c	diabase	Neol.	Aglobe-nostain
FF1:6	C	FF1:6a	f	andesite?	Neol.	Popen
FF1:6	C	FF1:6B	c	sandstone	Neol.	Asquare-circ
FF1:6	C	FF1:6c	f	sandstone	Neol.	Popen
FF1:6	C	FF1:6E	c	olivine gabbro	Neol.	Asquare-circ
FF1:7	C	FS 93	c	serpentinite	Neol.	Acut
FF1:8	C	FS 114	f	andesite	Neol.	Popen
FF1:8	C	FF1:8a	c	limestone	Pre-Neol.?	possible Pre-Neol.
FF1:8	C	FF1:8b	c	sandstone	Neol.	Amisc1-set9
FF1:8	C	FF1:8c	f	serpentinite?	Neol.	Amisc2-set9
FF1:9	C	FS 94	c	serpentinite	Neol.	Acut
FF1:9	C	FF1:9	f	peridotite	Neol.	Aglobe-nostain
FF1:10	C	FS 124	f	andesite	Neol.	Popen
FF1:11	C	FF1:11	c	diabase	Neol.	Aglobe-nostain
FF1:11	C	FF1:11a	c	sandstone	Neol.	Amisc1-set9

Trench:unit	Prov.	Name	Pres.	Material	Date	Group
FF1:11	C	FF1:11b	c	sandstone	Neol.	Amisc1-set9
FF1:13	C	FF1:13	c	diabase	Neol.	Aglobe-nostain
FF1:14	C	FF1:14a	f	sandstone	Neol.	Popen
FF1:14	C	FF1:14b	f	sandstone	Neol.	Popen
FF1:20	C	FF1:20	f	sandstone	Neol.	Popen
FF1:24	C	FS 112	f	serpentinite	Neol.	Acut
FF1:26	C	FS 117	c	serpentinite	Neol.	Acut
FF1:26	C	FS 118	c	serpentinite	Neol.	Acut
FF1:26	C	FS 120	c	serpentinite	Neol.	Aend
FF1:29	C	FF1:29	f	serpentinite	Neol.	Acut
FF1:29	C	FF1:29C	c	diabase	Neol.	Aglobe-nostain
FF1:30	C	FS 181	f	serpentinite	(MN)	Acut fragment?
FF1:32	C	FS 132	c	metaquartzite	(MN)	Arect
FF1:32	C	FS 133	c	sandstone	(MN)	Arect
FF1:32	C	FF1:32A	f	sandstone	(MN)	Amisc1-set11
FF1:32	C	FF1:32b	f	sandstone	(MN)	Popen
FF1:32	C	FF1:32c	c	limestone	(MN)	Amisc2-set5
FF1:34	C	FS 134	c	sandstone	(MN)	Arect
FF1:34	C	FF1:34a	f	limestone	(MN)	Amisc2-set5
FF1:34	C	FF1:34f	f	sandstone	(MN)	Popen
FF1:34	C	FF1:34g	f	sandstone	(MN)	Popen
FF1:35	C	FF1:35B	c	diabase	(MN)	Aglobe-nostain
FF1:36	C	FF1:36	f	sandstone	(MN)	Popen
FF1:37	C	FS 136	c	serpentinite	Neol.	Aend
FF1:37	C	FF1:37a	f	sandstone	Neol.	Amisc1-set14
FF1:37	C	FF1:37c	f	sandstone	Neol.	Amisc1-set13
FF1:39A	C	FS 170	f	sandstone	(MN)	Popen
FF1:39A	C	FS 171	c	limestone	(MN)	Amisc2-set4
FF1:39A	C	FF1:39Aj	f	limestone	(MN)	Amisc2-set5
FF1:39B2	C	FS 149	c	serpentinite	MN	Acut
FF1:40B1	C	FS 180	f	serpentinite	MN	Acut
FF1:40B1	C	FF1:40B1a	c	peridotite	MN	Aglobe-stain
FF1:40B1	C	FF1:40B1b	c	limestone	MN	Amisc2-set5
G:2	C	FS 11	c	serpentinite	Neol.	Acut
G:2	C	FS 47	f	steatite	Pre-Neol.?	possible Pre-Neol.
G:3	C	FS 23	c	serpentinite	Neol.	Acut
G:6	C	FS 48	c	andesite	Neol.	Amisc1-set6
G:12	C	FS 44	c	serpentinite	Neol.	Acut
G:17	C	FS 24	c	diabase	Neol.	Acut
G:17	C	FS 25	c	serpentinite	Neol.	Aend
G:19	C	FS 53	c	sandstone	(MN)	Arect
G:20	C	FS 38	f	serpentinite	(MN)	Acut
G:20	C	FS 50	c	serpentinite	(MN)	Aend
G:20	C	FS 51	f	silstone	(MN)	Pmisc
G:21	C	FS 33	c	serpentinite	(MN)	Acut
G:24	C	FS 35	f	serpentinite	(MN)	Acut fragment?
G:32	C	FS 252	c	limestone	Pre-Neol.?	possible Pre-Neol.
G:38	C	FS 253	c	serpentinite	Neol.	Amisc2-set3
G:lot28	C	FS 81	c	sandstone	(MN)	Popen
G:lot28	C	FS 82	c	sandstone	(MN)	Popen
G:lot28	C	FS 83	f	sandstone	(MN)	Popen
G:lot28	C	FS 84	c	sandstone	(MN)	Arect
G:lot28	C	FS 85	c	sandstone	(MN)	Aglobe-nostain
G1:1	C	FS 113	c	sandstone	Neol.	Adisc
G1:4	C	FS 90	c	serpentinite	Neol.	Acut

Trench:unit	Prov.	Name	Pres.	Material	Date	Group
G1:5	C	FS 115	c	sandstone	Neol.	Asquare-circ
G1:8	C	FS 98	f	serpentinite	(MN)	Acut
G1:8	C	FS 179	f	serpentinite?	(MN)	Amisc2-set3
G1:9	C	FS 123	c	sandstone	(MN)	Arect
G1:10	C	FS 174	c	sandstone	(MN)	Popen
G1:10	C	FS 175	c	sandstone	(MN)	Popen
G1:11	C	FS 126	c	sandstone	(MN)	Popen
G1:11	C	FS 178	f	serpentinite	(MN)	Acut
G1:11	C	FS 108	c	serpentinite	(MN)	Aend
G1:11	C	FS 125	c	sandstone	(MN)	Arect
G1:11	C	FS 107	c	sandstone?	(MN)	Amisc1-set10
G1:13	C	FS 122	c	diorite	(MN)	Aglobe-nostain
G1:15	C	G1:15	f	soapstone	(MN)	Amisc2-set6
G1:15	C	FS 106	c	limestone	(MN)	Aglobe-nostain
G1:15	C	FS 116	c	serpentinite	(MN)	Acut
G1:16	C	FS 111	c	peridotite	(MN)	Aglobe-stain
G1:17	C	FS 109	c	serpentinite	(MN)	Aend
G1:17	C	FS 119	c	serpentinite	(MN)	Acut raw material?
G1:18	C	G1:18/1	c	sandstone	(MN)	Popen
G1:18	C	G1:18/2	f	sandstone	(MN)	Popen
G1:19	C	FS 110	c	sandstone	(MN)	Arect
G1:19	C	FS 128	c	conglom.	(MN)	Aglobe-nostain
G1:19	C	FS 129	c	serpentinite	(MN)	Amisc2-set1
G1:19	C	FS 173	c	sandstone	(MN)	Popen
G1:20	C	FS 168	f	sandstone	MN	Popen
G1:32	C	G1:32	c	limestone	(Upper/Final Mesol.)	Pre-Neol.
G1:34	C	FS 156	c	steatite	Upper Mesol.	Pre-Neol.
G1:50	C	FS 183	f	diabase	Lower Mesol.	Pre-Neol.
G1:54	C	FS 184	f	limestone	Lower Mesol.	Pre-Neol.
H	C	S 72	c	sandstone	Neol.	Asquare-circ
H:2	C	FS 142	c	basalt	Neol.	Acut
H:2	C	H:2	f	sandstone	Neol.	Amisc1-set9
H:13	C	FS 153	c	serpentinite	Neol.	Acut
H:13	C	FS 154	c	andesite	Neol.	Amisc1-set4
H:17	C	H:17	f	serpentinite	Neol.	Acut
H:21	C	FS 155	c	sandstone	Neol.	Amisc1-set4
H:23	C	FS 159	c	serpentinite	(MN)	Acut
H:23	C	FS 165	c	sandstone	(MN)	Popen
H:24	C	FS 167	c	peridotite	Neol.	Arect
H:24	C	H:24	c	limestone	Neol.	Amisc2-set5
H:34	C	FS 160	f	serpentinite	(MN)	Acut
H:35	C	FS 157	c	serpentinite	(MN)	Acut
H:38	C	H:38	f	limestone	(MN)	Amisc2-set7
H:39	C	H:39	f	serpentinite	MN	Acut fragment?
H:40	C	H:40	f	slate	Neol.	Amisc1-set7
H:57A2	C	FS 169	f	basalt	Pre-Neol.?	possible Pre-Neol.
H:67B2	C	H:67B2	f	limestone	Pre-Neol.?	possible Pre-Neol.
HPed:37N	C	FS 323	c	sandstone	(MN)	Amisc1-set8
HPed:37T	C	FS 310	c	chert	EN	Amisc2-set2
HPed:37Y	C	FS 321	f	sandstone	EN	Popen
HTerrace:8	C	FS 829	c	basalt	Neol.	Amisc2-set7
HTerrace:9	C	FS 828	c	sandstone	Neol.	Amisc1-set8
HTerrace:9	C	FS 831	f	sandstone	Neol.	Amisc1-set15
HTerrace:9	C	FS 833	c	sandstone	Neol.	Amisc1-set11

Trench:unit	Prov.	Name	Pres.	Material	Date	Group
HTerrace:16	C	FS 848	f	sandstone	Neol.	Arect
HTerrace:16	C	FS 841	c	diabase	Neol.	Aglobe-nostain
HTerrace:16	C	FS 850	c	sandstone	Neol.	Amisc1-set11
HTerrace:20	C	FS 849	f	sandstone	Neol.	Arect
HTerrace:21	C	FS 840	c	diabase	Neol.	Aglobe-nostain
H1:5	C	FS 826	c	serpentinite	Neol.	Acut
H1:8	C	FS 832	f	andesite	Neol.	Popen
H1:9	C	FS 830	f	sandstone	Neol.	Popen
H1:12	C	FS 201	c	serpentinite	Neol.	Acut
H1:13	C	FS 852	c	sandstone	Neol.	Popen
H1:14	C	FS 877	f	serpentinite	Neol.	Acut fragment?
H1:16	C	FS 837	c	serpentinite	Neol.	Acut
H1:16	C	FS 838	f	serpentinite	Neol.	Acut
H1:20	C	FS 211	c	serpentinite	Neol.	Amisc2-set5
H1:25	C	H1:25	f	sandstone	Neol.	Popen
H1:31	C	FS 215	c	quartz	Neol.	Amisc2-set5
H1:41	C	FS 222	c	serpentinite	Neol.	Acut
H1:41	C	H1:41	c	sandstone	Neol.	Amisc1-set3
H1:47	C	H1:47	f	sandstone	Neol.	Popen
H1:52	C	H1:52	c	sandstone	Neol.	Popen
H1:56	C	FS 229	c	serpentinite	Neol.	Acut
H1:58	C	H1:58	f	sandstone	Neol.	Popen
H1:59	C	FS 228	c	serpentinite	Neol.	Aend
H1:64	C	H1:64	c	serpentinite	Neol.	Aend
H1:68	C	H1:68	f	sandstone	Neol.	Popen
H1:68	C	H1:68a	c	soapstone	Neol.	Amisc2-set4
H1A:72	C	FS 247	f	sandstone	Neol.	Popen
H1A:72	C	H1:72	f	sandstone	Neol.	Amisc1-set3
H1A:84	C	H1A:84	c	ocher?	Neol.	Amisc2-set2
H1A:91	C	H1A:91	c	diabase	EN/MN	Aglobe-nostain
H1A:93	C	H1A:93	c	sandstone	(EN)	Amisc1-set8
H1A:94	C	FS 257	f	sandstone	(EN)	Amisc1-set11
H1A:100	C	FS 256	c	sandstone	Neol.	Arect
H1A:120	C	FS 296	f	sandstone	Lower/Upper Mesol.	Pre-Neol.
H1A:124	C	FS 274	f	metaquartzite	Lower Mesol.	Pre-Neol.
H1A:127	C	FS 275	f	sandstone	Lower Mesol.	Pre-Neol.
H1A:179	C	FS 377	c	sandstone	Upper Palaeol.	Pre-Neol.
H1A:179	C	FS 378	f	limestone	Upper Palaeol.	Pre-Neol.
H1A:181	C	FS 386	f	limestone	Upper Palaeol.	Pre-Neol.
H1A:198	C	H1A:198/20	f	limestone	Upper Palaeol.	Pre-Neol.
H1A:207	C	H1A:207/21	f	limestone	Upper Palaeol.	Pre-Neol.
H1A:215	C	FS 454	f	sandstone	Upper Palaeol.	Pre-Neol.
H1B:78	C	FS 284	c	sandstone	Neol.	Amisc1-set8
H1B:82	C	FS 278	c	serpentinite	Neol.	Acut
H1B:83	C	FS 277	f	serpentinite	Neol.	Aend
H1B:88	C	FS 302	f	conglom.	Neol.	Amisc1-set11
H1B:92	C	FS 301	f	sandstone	Neol.	Popen
H1B:94	C	FS 289	c	serpentinite	Neol.	Acut
H1B:94	C	FS 290	c	serpentinite	Neol.	Amisc2-set5
H1B:95	C	FS 295	f	sandstone	Neol.	Amisc1-set7
H1B:95	C	FS 298	c	peridotite	Neol.	Aglobe-stain
H1B:108	C	H1B:108	c	limestone	Upper Mesol.	Pre-Neol.
H1B:114	C	H1B:114/25	f	limestone	Upper Mesol.	Pre-Neol.
H1B:121	C	FS 530	f	steatite	Lower Mesol.	Pre-Neol.

Trench:unit	Prov.	Name	Pres.	Material	Date	Group
H1B:144	C	FS 594	c	limestone	Lower Mesol.	Pre-Neol.
H1B scarp	C	FS 276	c	sandstone	Neol.	Amisc1-set9
H1B surf.	C	S 71	f	andesite	Neol.	Popen
H2A:7	C	H2A:7/1	f	sandstone	Neol.	Amisc1-set14
H2A:8	C	H2A:8/2	f	sandstone	Neol.	Amisc1-set13
H2A:9	C	H2A:9a	f	serpentinite	Neol.	Acut manuf. remain?
H2A:9	C	H2A:9b	f	sandstone	Neol.	Amisc1-set9
H2A:23	C	H2A:23/4	c	sandstone	Neol.	Amisc1-set9
H2A:40	C	FS 344	f	slate	MN	Acut fragment?
H2A:41	C	H2A:41/7	f	sandstone	Neol.	Popen
H2A:58	C	FS 359	f	serpentinite	(MN)	Acut fragment?
H2A:66	C	FS 362	c	serpentinite	(MN)	Aend
H2A:75	C	FS 374	c	serpentinite	MN	Acut
H2A:75	C	FS 371	c	peridotite	MN	Aglobe-stain
H2A:75	C	FS 372	c	peridotite	MN	Aglobe-stain
H2A:75	C	FS 373	c	sandstone	MN	Amisc1-set9
H2A:75	C	FS 375	c	limestone	MN	Aglobe-nostain
H2A:75	C	H2A:75/21	f	peridotite	MN	Aglobe-nostain
H2A:77	C	FS 389	f	sandstone	(MN)	Amisc1-set14
H2A:77	C	FS 390	c	andesite	(MN)	Popen
H2A:84	C	FS 388	c	sandstone	MN	Popen
H2A:95	C	FS 471	c	sandstone	(MN)	Amisc1-set8
H2A:122	C	FS 531	c	sandstone	MN	Amisc1-set1
H2A:129	C	FS 550	f	serpentinite	Neol.	Acut fragment?
H2A:144	C	FS 579	c	limestone	EN	Amisc2-set1
H2A:163	C	H2A:163	f	limestone	(Upper/Final Mesol.)	Pre-Neol.
H2APed:172	C	FS 629	c	quartz	Neol.	Amisc2-set1
H2APed:186	C	FS 645	f	sandstone	Neol.	Popen
H2APed:187	C	H2APed:187	f	jasper	Neol.	Amisc2-set9
H2APed:191	C	FS 663	c	steatite	Neol.	Amisc2-set1
H2APed:195	C	FS 666	f	limestone	Neol.	Acut
H2APed:203	C	FS 691	f	limestone	(Final Mesol.)	Pre-Neol.
H2B:13	C	FS 395	f	sandstone	(MN)	Popen
H2B:16	C	H2B:16	f	sandstone	(MN)	Popen
H2B:17	C	FS 398	c	serpentinite	(MN)	Acut
H2B:25	C	FS 472	c	conglom.	(MN)	Pcav
H2B:33	C	FS 414	f	sandstone	(MN)	Amisc1-set7
H2B:34	C	H2B:34	f	sandstone	(MN)	Popen
H2B:50	C	FS 428	c	basalt	(MN)	Acut
Cave surf.	C	FS 1	c	diabase	Neol.	Acut
Cave surf.	C	FS 185	c	diabase	Neol.	Acut
Cave surf.	C	S 9	f	sandstone	Neol.	Popen
Cave surf.	C	FS 54	f	serpentinite?	Neol.	Amisc2-set3
Cave surf.	C	S 3	c	limestone	Neol.	Amisc2-set5
Cave surf.	C	S 1	f	conglom.	Post-Neol.	Post-Neol.
L5:1	P	FS 737	f	sandstone	FN	Amisc1-set7
L5:2	P	FS 575	f	sandstone	FN	Adisc
L5:2	P	L5:2/30	f	serpentinite	FN	Amisc2-set9
L5:26	P	FS 740	c	sandstone	(MN)	Amisc1-set4
L5:34	P	FS 760	c	diorite	EN/MN	Aglobe-nostain
L5:37	P	FS 758	f	sandstone	EN	Amisc1-set11
L5:60	P	FS 885	c	basalt	FN	Acut
L5:60	P	FS 871	c	diorite	FN	Aglobe-nostain
L5:61	P	FS 870	c	sandstone	FN	Asquare-circ
L5:61	P	FS 872	f	conglom.	FN	Amisc1-set15

Trench:unit	Prov.	Name	Pres.	Material	Date	Group
L5:61	P	FS 873	f	conglom.	FN	Popen
L5:61	P	FS 874	f	conglom.	FN	Amisc1-set15
L5:62	P	FS 888	f	sandstone	Neol.	Amisc1-set14
L5:68	P	FS 891	f	peridotite	FN	Amisc2-set2
L5:79	P	L5:79/47	f	sandstone	Neol.	Popen
L5:91	P	FS 910	c	sandstone	EN/MN	Pcav
L5:99	P	L5:99/51	c	peridotite	MN	Aglobe-nostain
L5NE:7	P	FS 589	c	steatite	FN	Acut
L5NE:7	P	FS 595	f	sandstone	FN	Adisc
L5NE:7	P	L5NE:7	f	chert	FN	Aglobe-nostain
L5NE:15	P	FS 596	c	sandstone	FN	Adisc
L5NE:15	P	FS 597	f	sandstone	FN	Amisc1-set3
L5NE:15	P	FS 598	c	sandstone/conglom.	FN	Adisc
L5NE:15	P	L5NE:15/10	c	serpentinite	FN	Amisc2-set5
L5NE:18	P	FS 602	c	diabase	FN	Aend
L5NE:18	P	FS 603	f	sandstone	FN	Popen
L5NE:18	P	FS 604	f	sandstone	FN	Adisc
L5NE:18	P	FS 605	c	sandstone/conglom.	FN	Amisc1-set2
L5NE:18	P	FS 612	c	sandstone/conglom.	FN	Amisc1-set2
L5NE:19	P	FS 600	c	serpentinite	FN	Acut
L5NE:19	P	FS 606	c	quartz	FN	Amisc2-set4
L5NE:19	P	FS 607	c	sandstone	FN	Amisc1-set11
L5NE:19	P	FS 608	c	sandstone	FN	Adisc
L5NE:19	P	L5NE:19/25	c	sandstone/conglom.	FN	Adisc
L5NE:22	P	FS 609	c	limestone	FN	Amisc2-set7
L5NE:33	P	FS 621	c	sandstone	Neol.	Adisc
O5:4	P	FS 695	c	diabase	Neol.	Aglobe-nostain
O5:34	P	FS 726	c	serpentinite	(MN)	Acut
O5:43	P	FS 734	f	serpentinite	Neol.	Acut manuf. remain?
O5:59	P	FS 751	f	basalt	EN/MN	Acut
O5:81	P	FS 759	f	sandstone	EN	Popen
O5:83	P	O5:83/12	f	chlorite schist	EN	Amisc2-set9
O5:84	P	O5:84	f	serpentinite	(EN)	Acut
O5:116	P	O5:116/13	c	peridotite	Neol.	Aglobe-stain
O5N:14	P	FS 680	c	serpentinite	Neol.	Acut
O5NE:25	P	FS 644	f	limestone	Neol.	Acut fragment?
O5NE:32	P	FS 646	f	limestone	MN	Amisc2-set10
P5:77	P	FS 757	f	sandstone	MN	Amisc1-set3
P5:89	P	FS 765	f	conglom.?	(MN)	Popen
P5:91	P	FS 767	f	serpentinite	Neol.	Acut
P5:92	P	FS 766	f	basalt	MN	Aend
P5:152	P	FS 788	c	sandstone	Neol.	Amisc1-set11
P5:153	P	FS 789	f	serpentinite	Neol.	Acut
P5:162	P	FS 790	f	serpentinite	(MN)	Acut fragment?
P5:174	P	FS 883	c	serpentinite	MN	Acut
P5:178	P	P5:178/13	c	peridotite	MN	Aglobe-stain
P5:179	P	P5:179	c	chert	MN	Aglobe-nostain
P5:183	P	FS 876	c	chert	MN	Aglobe-nostain
P5:186	P	FS 889	c	limestone	MN	Aglobe-nostain
P5:190	P	FS 899	c	serpentinite	MN	Acut
P5:191	P	FS 902	c	steatite	MN	Acut
PQ5:9	P	FS 772	f	serpentinite	Neol.	Acut
PQ5:9	P	FS 771	f	sandstone	Neol.	Arect
PQ5:14	P	FS 780	f	basalt?	MN	Amisc2-set10
PQ5:28	P	FS 779	c	serpentinite	MN	Acut

Trench:unit	Prov.	Name	Pres.	Material	Date	Group
Q4 backfill	P	FS 827	c	chert	Neol.	Aglobe-nostain
Q4:1	P	FS 693	c	diorite	Neol.	Acut
Q4:3	P	Q4:3/2	c	goethite	Neol.	Aglobe-nostain
Q4:58	P	FS 715	f	serpentinite	Neol.	Acut
Q4:59	P	FS 714	f	serpentinite	Neol.	Acut
Q4:72	P	Q4:72/10	c	serpentinite	Neol.	Amisc2-set5
Q4:86	P	Q4:86/11	f	sandstone	EN	Popen
Q4:87	P	Q4:87/14	f	sandstone	EN	Popen
Q4:87	P	Q4:87/12	c	sandstone	EN	Amisc1-set7
Q4:100	P	FS 749	f	sandstone	EN	Pcav
Q4:109	P	Q4:109/19	f	andesite	EN/MN	Popen
Q4:128	P	FS 755	c	diabase	EN	Acut
Q5N:2	P	Q5N:2/1	f	magnetite?	Neol.	Aglobe-nostain
Q5N:3	P	FS 363	c	serpentinite	Neol.	Acut
Q5N:23	P	FS 430	f	peridotite	EN	Acut
Q5N:24	P	FS 436	f	serpentinite	(EN)	Acut
Q5N:42	P	FS 509	f	sandstone	Neol.	Popen
Q5N:43	P	FS 508	f	serpentinite	EN/MN	Acut fragment?
Q5N:103	P	Q5N:103/13	f	sandstone	MN	Popen
Q5S:2	P	Q5S:2/1	f	serpentinite	Neol.	Aglobe-nostain
Q5S:4	P	FS 562	f	serpentinite	(MN)	Acut fragment?
Q5S:4	P	FS 565	c	limestone	(MN)	Amisc2-set4
Q5S:14	P	FS 577	f	serpentinite	Neol.	Acut
Q5S:14	P	Q5S:14/4	f	sandstone	Neol.	Amisc1-set14
Q5S:50	P	FS 617	f	peridotite	Neol.	Acut
Q5S:52	P	Q5S:52/10	f	serpentinite	Neol.	Amisc2-set9
Q5S:76	P	FS 634	f	sandstone	MN	Pcav
Q5S:89	P	Q5S:89/17	f	limestone	Neol.	Amisc2-set4
Q5S:90	P	Q5S:90/18	c	serpentinite	Neol.	Aend
Q5S:91	P	Q5S:91/19	c	magnetite	Neol.	Acut
Q5S:92	P	FS 624	c	sandstone	Neol.	Popen
Q5S:131	P	FS 661	f	sandstone	(MN)	Popen
Q5S:131	P	FS 662	f	sandstone	(MN)	Amisc1-set14
Q5S:144	P	FS 664	f	serpentinite	MN	Amisc2-set3
Q5S:154	P	FS 667	f	andesite	Neol.	Amisc1-set3
Q5S:154	P	FS 668	f	sandstone	Neol.	Popen
Q5S:177	P	FS 723	f	sandstone	Neol.	Popen
Q5S:186	P	Q5S:186/44	c	sandstone	EN/MN	Amisc1-set7
Q5S:216	P	FS 774	c	sandstone	MN	Arect
Q5S:216	P	FS 775	f	limestone	MN	Amisc2-set7
Q5S:223	P	FS 786	c	sandstone	EN	Arect
Q6N:38	P	FS 752	f	sandstone	EN/MN	Amisc1-set1
Q6N:54	P	FS 768	c	steatite	(EN)	Amisc2-set1
QR5:6	P	QR5:6/2	c	chert	Neol.	Aglobe-nostain
QR5:12	P	FS 884	c	basalt	EN/MN	Acut
QR5:29	P	FS 892	f	sandstone	EN/MN	Popen
QR5:29	P	FS 893	c	serpentinite	EN/MN	Acut
Paralia surf.	P	S 8	c	peridotite	Neol.	Aglobe-stain
Paralia surf.	P	S 4	f	sandstone	Neol.	Popen
Paralia surf.	P	S 6	c	sandstone	Neol.	Arect
Paralia surf.	P	S 49	f	sandstone	Neol.	Amisc1-set14
n/a	n/a	S 73	f	sandstone	Neol.	Amisc1-set3

APPENDIX B

List of all Franchthi ground stone tools dated to specific pre-Neolithic periods and interphases, or specific Neolithic phases and interphases

KEY: Prov.=Provenience, Pres.=Preservation, C=Cave, P=Paralia, c=complete, f=fragmentary, Palaeol.=Palaeolithic, Mesol.=Mesolithic, (Upper/Final Mesol.)=probably Upper/Final Mesolithic interphase, (Final Mesol.)=probable Final Mesolithic, pre-Neol.=pre-Neolithic, Neol.=Neolithic, (Initial Neol.)=probable Initial Neolithic, EN=Early Neolithic, MN=Middle Neolithic, LN=Late Neolithic, FN=Final Neolithic, (EN)=probable Early Neolithic, (MN)=probable Middle Neolithic, (LN)=probable Late Neolithic, (FN)=probable Final Neolithic, EN/MN=Early/Middle Neolithic interphase, MN/LN=Middle/Late Neolithic interphase, n/ap=non applicable, conglom.=conglomerate sandstone/conglom.=sandstone combined with conglomerate

Note: G:lot 28 refers to units G:19-24.

Date	Trench:unit	Prov.	Name	Pres.	Material	Group
Upper Palaeol.	FAS:204	C	FS 750	c	sandstone	Pre-Neol.
Upper Palaeol.	H1A:179	C	FS 377	c	sandstone	Pre-Neol.
Upper Palaeol.	H1A:179	C	FS 378	f	limestone	Pre-Neol.
Upper Palaeol.	H1A:181	C	FS 386	f	limestone	Pre-Neol.
Upper Palaeol.	H1A:198	C	H1A:198/20	f	limestone	Pre-Neol.
Upper Palaeol.	H1A:207	C	H1A:207/21	f	limestone	Pre-Neol.
Upper Palaeol.	H1A:215	C	FS 454	f	sandstone	Pre-Neol.
Lower Mesol.	FAS:184	C	FS 706	f	sandstone	Pre-Neol.
Lower Mesol.	FAS:191	C	FS 725	c	limestone	Pre-Neol.
Lower Mesol.	G1:50	C	FS 183	f	diabase	Pre-Neol.
Lower Mesol.	G1:54	C	FS 184	f	limestone	Pre-Neol.
Lower Mesol.	H1A:124	C	FS 274	f	metaquartzite	Pre-Neol.
Lower Mesol.	H1A:127	C	FS 275	f	sandstone	Pre-Neol.
Lower Mesol.	H1B:121	C	FS 530	f	steatite	Pre-Neol.
Lower Mesol.	H1B:144	C	FS 594	c	limestone	Pre-Neol.
Lower/Upper Mesol.	H1A:120	C	FS 296	f	sandstone	Pre-Neol.
Upper Mesol.	FAN:177	C	FS 551	f	andesite	Pre-Neol.
Upper Mesol.	FAS:159	C	FAS:159	f	limestone	Pre-Neol.
Upper Mesol.	FAS:166	C	FS 701	c	limestone	Pre-Neol.
Upper Mesol.	G1:34	C	FS 156	c	steatite	Pre-Neol.
Upper Mesol.	H1B:108	C	H1B:108	c	limestone	Pre-Neol.
Upper Mesol.	H1B:114	C	H1B:114/25	f	limestone	Pre-Neol.
(Upper/Final Mesol.)	G1:32	C	G1:32	c	limestone	Pre-Neol.
(Upper/Final Mesol.)	H2A:163	C	H2A:163	f	limestone	Pre-Neol.
Final Mesol.	FAN:174	C	FS 549	f	quartzite	Pre-Neol.
(Final Mesol.)	H2APed:203	C	FS 691	f	limestone	Pre-Neol.
(Initial Neol.)	A:65	C	FS 74	c	sandstone	Amisc1-set4
EN	HPed:37Y	C	FS 321	f	sandstone	Popen
EN	HPed:37T	C	FS 310	c	chert	Amisc2-set2
EN	H2A:144	C	FS 579	c	limestone	Amisc2-set1
EN	L5:37	P	FS 758	f	sandstone	Amisc1-set11
EN	O5:81	P	FS 759	f	sandstone	Popen
EN	O5:83	P	O5:83/12	f	chlorite schist	Amisc2-set9

Date	Trench:unit	Prov.	Name	Pres.	Material	Group
EN	Q4:86	P	Q4:86/11	f	sandstone	Popen
EN	Q4:87	P	Q4:87/12	c	sandstone	Amisc1-set7
EN	Q4:87	P	Q4:87/14	f	sandstone	Popen
EN	Q4:100	P	FS 749	f	sandstone	Pcav
EN	Q4:128	P	FS 755	c	diabase	Acut
EN	Q5N:23	P	FS 430	f	peridotite	Acut
EN	Q5S:223	P	FS 786	c	sandstone	Arect
(EN)	H1A:93	C	H1A:93	c	sandstone	Amisc1-set8
(EN)	H1A:94	C	FS 257	f	sandstone	Amisc1-set11
(EN)	O5:84	P	O5:84	f	serpentinite	Acut
(EN)	Q5N:24	P	FS 436	f	serpentinite	Acut
(EN)	Q6N:54	P	FS 768	c	steatite	Amisc2-set1
EN/MN	FAS:132	C	FS 576	f	limestone	Amisc2-set7
EN/MN	H1A:91	C	H1A:91	c	diabase	Aglobe-nostain
EN/MN	L5:34	P	FS 760	c	diorite	Aglobe-nostain
EN/MN	L5:91	P	FS 910	c	sandstone	Pcav
EN/MN	O5:59	P	FS 751	f	basalt	Acut
EN/MN	Q4:109	P	Q4:109/19	f	andesite	Popen
EN/MN	Q5N:43	P	FS 508	f	serpentinite	Acut fragment?
EN/MN	Q5S:186	P	Q5S:186/44	c	sandstone	Amisc1-set7
EN/MN	Q6N:38	P	FS 752	f	sandstone	Amisc1-set1
EN/MN	QR5:12	P	FS 884	c	basalt	Acut
EN/MN	QR5:29	P	FS 893	c	serpentinite	Acut
EN/MN	QR5:29	P	FS 892	f	sandstone	Popen
MN	FAN:129	C	FAN:129	f	serpentinite	Acut
MN	FAN:131	C	FS 417	f	basalt	Amisc2-set9
MN	FAN:132	C	FS 418	f	sandstone	Popen
MN	FAN:132	C	FS 419	f	siltstone	Popen
MN	FAN:132	C	FS 420	c	serpentinite	Aend
MN	FAN:133	C	FS 422	f	serpentinite	Amisc2-set9
MN	FAN:134	C	FS 423	f	sandstone	Popen
MN	FAN:134	C	FS 424	f	andesite	Popen
MN	FAN:134	C	FS 425	f	serpentinite	Acut
MN	FAN:134	C	FS 426	f	serpentinite	Acut fragment?
MN	FAN:136	C	FS 432	f	serpentinite	Aend
MN	FAN:136	C	FS 433	f	sandstone	Popen
MN	FAN:136	C	FS 434	f	sandstone	Popen
MN	FAN:137	C	FS 435	f	sandstone	Amisc1-set11
MN	FAS:120	C	FS 455	f	sandstone	Amisc1-set9
MN	FAS:120	C	FS 456	f	limestone	Amisc2-set4
MN	FAS:121	C	FS 464	f	sandstone	Popen
MN	FAS:123	C	FS 465	f	sandstone	Popen
MN	FAS:123	C	FS 466	f	sandstone	Popen
MN	FAS:125	C	FS 468	f	sandstone	Popen
MN	FF1:39B2	C	FS 149	c	serpentinite	Acut
MN	FF1:40B1	C	FS 180	f	serpentinite	Acut
MN	FF1:40B1	C	FF1:40B1a	c	peridotite	Aglobe-stain
MN	FF1:40B1	C	FF1:40B1b	c	limestone	Amisc2-set5
MN	G1:20	C	FS 168	f	sandstone	Popen
MN	H:39	C	H:39	f	serpentinite	Acut fragment?
MN	H2A:40	C	FS 344	f	slate	Acut fragment?
MN	H2A:75	C	FS 371	c	peridotite	Aglobe-stain
MN	H2A:75	C	FS 372	c	peridotite	Aglobe-stain
MN	H2A:75	C	FS 373	c	sandstone	Amisc1-set9

Date	Trench:unit	Prov.	Name	Pres.	Material	Group
MN	H2A:75	C	FS 374	c	serpentinite	Acut
MN	H2A:75	C	FS 375	c	limestone	Aglobe-nostain
MN	H2A:75	C	H2A:75/21	f	peridotite	Aglobe-nostain
MN	H2A:84	C	FS 388	c	sandstone	Popen
MN	H2A:122	C	FS 531	c	sandstone	Amisc1-set1
MN	L5:99	P	L5:99/51	c	peridotite	Aglobe-nostain
MN	O5NE:32	P	FS 646	f	limestone	Amisc2-set10
MN	P5:77	P	FS 757	f	sandstone	Amisc1-set3
MN	P5:92	P	FS 766	f	basalt	Aend
MN	P5:174	P	FS 883	c	serpentinite	Acut
MN	P5:178	P	P5:178/13	c	peridotite	Aglobe-stain
MN	P5:179	P	P5:179	c	chert	Aglobe-nostain
MN	P5:183	P	FS 876	c	chert	Aglobe-nostain
MN	P5:186	P	FS 889	c	limestone	Aglobe-nostain
MN	P5:190	P	FS 899	c	serpentinite	Acut
MN	P5:191	P	FS 902	c	steatite	Acut
MN	PQ5:14	P	FS 780	f	basalt?	Amisc2-set10
MN	PQ5:28	P	FS 779	c	serpentinite	Acut
MN	Q5N:103	P	Q5N:103/13	f	sandstone	Popen
MN	Q5S:76	P	FS 634	f	sandstone	Pcav
MN	Q5S:144	P	FS 664	f	serpentinite	Amisc2-set3
MN	Q5S:216	P	FS 774	c	sandstone	Arect
MN	Q5S:216	P	FS 775	f	limestone	Amisc2-set7
(MN)	FAN:142	C	FS 505	c	serpentinite	Acut
(MN)	FAN:142	C	FAN:142	f	limestone	Amisc2-set8
(MN)	FAN:143	C	FAN:143	f	limestone	Amisc2-set8
(MN)	FAN:148	C	FS 507	f	limestone	Amisc2-set8
(MN)	FAS:117	C	FS 445	f	sandstone?	Amisc1-set7
(MN)	FAS:117	C	FS 452	f	serpentinite	Amisc2-set5
(MN)	FAS:117	C	FAS:117	f	?	Amisc1-set1
(MN)	FAS:124	C	FS 467	f	sandstone	Popen
(MN)	FF1:30	C	FS 181	f	serpentinite	Acut fragment?
(MN)	FF1:32	C	FS 132	c	metaquartzite	Arect
(MN)	FF1:32	C	FS 133	c	sandstone	Arect
(MN)	FF1:32	C	FF1:32A	f	sandstone	Amisc1-set11
(MN)	FF1:32	C	FF1:32b	f	sandstone	Popen
(MN)	FF1:32	C	FF1:32c	c	limestone	Amisc2-set5
(MN)	FF1:34	C	FS 134	c	sandstone	Arect
(MN)	FF1:34	C	FF1:34a	f	limestone	Amisc2-set5
(MN)	FF1:34	C	FF1:34f	f	sandstone	Popen
(MN)	FF1:34	C	FF1:34g	f	sandstone	Popen
(MN)	FF1:35	C	FF1:35B	c	diabase	Aglobe-nostain
(MN)	FF1:36	C	FF1:36	f	sandstone	Popen
(MN)	FF1:39A	C	FS 170	f	sandstone	Popen
(MN)	FF1:39A	C	FS 171	c	limestone	Amisc2-set4
(MN)	FF1:39A	C	FF1:39Aj	f	limestone	Amisc2-set5
(MN)	G:19	C	FS 53	c	sandstone	Arect
(MN)	G:20	C	FS 38	f	serpentinite	Acut
(MN)	G:20	C	FS 50	c	serpentinite	Aend
(MN)	G:20	C	FS 51	f	silstone	Pmisc
(MN)	G:21	C	FS 33	c	serpentinite	Acut
(MN)	G:24	C	FS 35	f	serpentinite	Acut fragment?
(MN)	G:lot28	C	FS 81	c	sandstone	Popen
(MN)	G:lot28	C	FS 82	c	sandstone	Popen

Date	Trench:unit	Prov.	Name	Pres.	Material	Group
(MN)	G:lot28	C	FS 83	f	sandstone	Popen
(MN)	G:lot28	C	FS 84	c	sandstone	Arect
(MN)	G:lot28	C	FS 85	c	sandstone	Aglobe-nostain
(MN)	G1:8	C	FS 98	f	serpentinite	Acut
(MN)	G1:8	C	FS 179	f	serpentinite?	Amisc2-set3
(MN)	G1:9	C	FS 123	c	sandstone	Arect
(MN)	G1:10	C	FS 174	c	sandstone	Popen
(MN)	G1:10	C	FS 175	c	sandstone	Popen
(MN)	G1:11	C	FS 107	c	sandstone?	Amisc1-set10
(MN)	G1:11	C	FS 108	c	serpentinite	Aend
(MN)	G1:11	C	FS 125	c	sandstone	Arect
(MN)	G1:11	C	FS 126	c	sandstone	Popen
(MN)	G1:11	C	FS 178	f	serpentinite	Acut
(MN)	G1:13	C	FS 122	c	diorite	Aglobe-nostain
(MN)	G1:15	C	FS 106	c	limestone	Aglobe-nostain
(MN)	G1:15	C	FS 116	c	serpentinite	Acut
(MN)	G1:15	C	G1:15	f	soapstone	Amisc2-set6
(MN)	G1:16	C	FS 111	c	peridotite	Aglobe-stain
(MN)	G1:17	C	FS 109	c	serpentinite	Aend
(MN)	G1:17	C	FS 119	c	serpentinite	Acut raw material?
(MN)	G1:18	C	G1:18/1	c	sandstone	Popen
(MN)	G1:18	C	G1:18/2	f	sandstone	Popen
(MN)	G1:19	C	FS 110	c	sandstone	Arect
(MN)	G1:19	C	FS 128	c	conglom.	Aglobe-nostain
(MN)	G1:19	C	FS 129	c	serpentinite	Amisc2-set1
(MN)	G1:19	C	FS 173	c	sandstone	Popen
(MN)	H:23	C	FS 159	c	serpentinite	Acut
(MN)	H:23	C	FS 165	c	sandstone	Popen
(MN)	H:34	C	FS 160	f	serpentinite	Acut
(MN)	H:35	C	FS 157	c	serpentinite	Acut
(MN)	H:Ped37N	C	FS 323	c	sandstone	Amisc1-set8
(MN)	H:38	C	H:38	f	limestone	Amisc2-set7
(MN)	H2A:58	C	FS 359	f	serpentinite	Acut fragment?
(MN)	H2A:66	C	FS 362	c	serpentinite	Aend
(MN)	H2A:77	C	FS 389	f	sandstone	Amisc1-set14
(MN)	H2A:77	C	FS 390	c	andesite	Popen
(MN)	H2A:95	C	FS 471	c	sandstone	Amisc1-set8
(MN)	H2B:13	C	FS 395	f	sandstone	Popen
(MN)	H2B:16	C	H2B:16	f	sandstone	Popen
(MN)	H2B:17	C	FS 398	c	serpentinite	Acut
(MN)	H2B:25	C	FS 472	c	conglom.	Pcav
(MN)	H2B:33	C	FS 414	f	sandstone	Amisc1-set7
(MN)	H2B:34	C	H2B:34	f	sandstone	Popen
(MN)	H2B:50	C	FS 428	c	basalt	Acut
(MN)	L5:26	P	FS 740	c	sandstone	Amisc1-set4
(MN)	O5:34	P	FS 726	c	serpentinite	Acut
(MN)	P5:89	P	FS 765	f	conglom.	Popen
(MN)	P5:162	P	FS 790	f	serpentinite	Acut fragment?
(MN)	Q5S:4	P	FS 562	f	serpentinite	Acut fragment?
(MN)	Q5S:4	P	FS 565	c	limestone	Amisc2-set4
(MN)	Q5S:131	P	FS 661	f	sandstone	Popen
(MN)	Q5S:131	P	FS 662	f	sandstone	Amisc1-set14
MN/LN	FAN:121	C	FS 396	f	sandstone	Popen
MN/LN	FAS:116	C	FS 442	f	sandstone	Popen

Date	Trench:unit	Prov.	Name	Pres.	Material	Group
LN	FAN:89	C	FAN:89	c	sandstone	Amisc1-set11
LN	FAN:117	C	FS 285	c	sandstone	Popen
LN	FAN:117	C	FS 287	c	sandstone?	Amisc1-set1
LN	FAN:117	C	FS 288	f	serpentinite	Acut fragment?
LN	FAS:102	C	FS 380	f	andesite	Popen
LN	FAS:105	C	FS 382	c	soapstone	Amisc2-set6
LN	FAS:107	C	FS 385	f	serpentinite	Acut
LN	FAS:93	C	FS 368	f	sandstone	Popen
(LN)	FAN:86	C	FAN:86	f	sandstone	Popen
(LN)	FAN:119	C	FS 297	c	sandstone	Arect
(LN)	FAS:102	C	FS 379	f	sandstone	Amisc1-set10
FN	A:24	C	FS 14	c	sandstone	Adisc
FN	A:25	C	FS 13	c	sandstone	Pcav
FN	A:40	C	FS 34	c	serpentinite	Acut
FN	A:40	C	FS 59	c	sandstone	Pcav
FN	A:40	C	FS 68	f	soapstone	Amisc2-set2
FN	FA:39	C	FS 221	c	felsite porphyry	Acut
FN	FA:45	C	FS 231	c	sandstone	Asquare-circ
FN	FA:46	C	FS 230	c	limestone	Amisc2-set2
FN	FAN:59	C	FS 258	c	sandstone	Adisc
FN	FAN:59	C	FS 261	c	sandstone	Amisc1-set11
FN	FAN:61	C	FAN:61	c	conglom.	Adisc
FN	FAN:61	C	FAN:61/1	c	sandstone/conglom.	Adisc
FN	FAN:63	C	FAN:63	c	sandstone?	Pmisc
FN	FAS:61	C	FS 304	c	sandstone	Adisc
FN	FAS:69	C	FS 317	c	sandstone	Adisc
FN	FAS:70	C	FS 318	c	sandstone	Asquare-circ
FN	FAS:71	C	FS 315	c	diabase	Aglobe-nostain
FN	FAS:71	C	FS 320	f	sandstone	Popen
FN	FAS:71	C	FS 324	f	andesite	Popen
FN	FAS:72	C	FS 311	n/ap	peridotite	Acut
FN	FAS:72	C	FS 322	c	conglom.	Amisc1-set11
FN	FAS:73	C	FS 350	f	andesite	Amisc1-set5
FN	FAS:76	C	FS 357	f	sandstone	Amisc1-set14
FN	FAS:81	C	FS 358	c	serpentinite	Amisc2-set1
FN	L5:1	P	FS 737	f	sandstone	Amisc1-set7
FN	L5:2	P	FS 575	f	sandstone	Adisc
FN	L5:2	P	L5:2/30	f	serpentinite	Amisc2-set9
FN	L5:60	P	FS 871	c	diorite	Aglobe-nostain
FN	L5:60	P	FS 885	c	basalt	Acut
FN	L5:61	P	FS 870	c	sandstone	Asquare-circ
FN	L5:61	P	FS 872	f	conglom.	Amisc1-set15
FN	L5:61	P	FS 873	f	conglom.	Popen
FN	L5:61	P	FS 874	f	conglom.	Amisc1-set15
FN	L5:68	P	FS 891	f	peridotite	Amisc2-set2
FN	L5NE:7	P	FS 589	c	steatite	Acut
FN	L5NE:7	P	FS 595	f	sandstone	Adisc
FN	L5NE:7	P	L5NE:7	f	chert	Aglobe-nostain
FN	L5NE:15	P	FS 596	c	sandstone	Adisc
FN	L5NE:15	P	FS 597	f	sandstone	Amisc1-set3
FN	L5NE:15	P	FS 598	c	sandstone/conglom.	Adisc
FN	L5NE:15	P	L5NE:15/10	c	serpentinite	Amisc2-set5
FN	L5NE:18	P	FS 602	c	diabase	Aend
FN	L5NE:18	P	FS 603	f	sandstone	Popen

Date	Trench:unit	Prov.	Name	Pres.	Material	Group
FN	L5NE:18	P	FS 604	f	sandstone	Adisc
FN	L5NE:18	P	FS 605	c	sandstone/conglom.	Amisc1-set2
FN	L5NE:18	P	FS 612	c	sandstone/conglom.	Amisc1-set2
FN	L5NE:19	P	FS 600	c	serpentinite	Acut
FN	L5NE:19	P	FS 606	c	quartz	Amisc2-set4
FN	L5NE:19	P	FS 607	c	sandstone	Amisc1-set11
FN	L5NE:19	P	FS 608	c	sandstone	Adisc
FN	L5NE:19	P	L5NE:19/25	c	sandstone/conglom.	Adisc
FN	L5NE:22	P	FS 609	c	limestone	Amisc2-set7
(FN)	A:27	C	FS 21	c	serpentinite	Acut
(FN)	A:27	C	FS 269	c	serpentinite	Amisc2-set1
(FN)	A:27	C	FS 270	c	sandstone	Amisc1-set10
(FN)	FAN:74	C	FS 255	f	quartz	Amisc2-set5
(FN)	FAN:91	C	FS 299	f	sandstone	Adisc
(FN)	FAN:91	C	FS 300	c	sandstone/conglom.	Adisc
(FN)	FAS:83	C	FS 360	f	sandstone	Asquare-circ

APPENDIX C

Master List

KEY: Prov.=Provenience, Pres.=Preservation, C=Cave, P=Paralia, c=complete, f=fragmentary, Palaeol.=Palaeolithic, Mesol.=Mesolithic, (Upper/Final Mesol.)=probably Upper/Final Mesolithic interphase, (Final Mesol.)=probable Final Mesolithic, pre-Neol.=pre-Neolithic, Neol.=Neolithic, (Initial Neol.)=probable Initial Neolithic, EN=Early Neolithic, MN=Middle Neolithic, LN=Late Neolithic, FN=Final Neolithic, (EN)=probable Early Neolithic, (MN)=probable Middle Neolithic, (LN)=probable Late Neolithic, (FN)=probable Final Neolithic, EN/MN=Early/Middle Neolithic interphase, MN/LN=Middle/Late Neolithic interphase, n/ap=non applicable, surf.=surface, conglom.=conglomerate, sandstone/conglom.=sandstone combined with conglomerate

Note: G:lot 28 refers to units G:19-24.

Name	Trench:unit	Prov.	Pres.	Material	Date	Group
FS 1	Cave surf.	C	c	diabase	Neol.	Acut
FS 6	A:5	C	f	serpentinite	Neol.	Acut
FS 7	A:18	C	c	serpentinite	Neol.	Aend
FS 11	G:2	C	c	serpentinite	Neol.	Acut
FS 12	A:30	C	c	serpentinite	Neol.	Acut
FS 13	A:25	C	c	sandstone	FN	Pcav
FS 14	A:24	C	c	sandstone	FN	Adisc
FS 21	A:27	C	c	serpentinite	(FN)	Acut
FS 22	B:3	C	c	serpentinite	Neol.	Acut
FS 23	G:3	C	c	serpentinite	Neol.	Acut
FS 24	G:17	C	c	diabase	Neol.	Acut
FS 25	G:17	C	c	serpentinite	Neol.	Aend
FS 32	A:45	C	c	diabase	Neol.	Acut
FS 33	G:21	C	c	serpentinite	(MN)	Acut
FS 34	A:40	C	c	serpentinite	FN	Acut
FS 35	G:24	C	f	serpentinite	(MN)	Acut fragment?
FS 36	A:46	C	n/ap	andesite	Neol.	Acut
FS 37	A:37	C	c	argillite	Neol.	Acut
FS 38	G:20	C	f	serpentinite	(MN)	Acut
FS 44	G:12	C	c	serpentinite	Neol.	Acut
FS 47	G:2	C	f	steatite	Pre-Neol.?	possible Pre-Neol.
FS 48	G:6	C	c	andesite	Neol.	Amisc1-set6
FS 50	G:20	C	c	serpentinite	(MN)	Aend
FS 51	G:20	C	f	silstone	(MN)	Pmisc
FS 52	A:19	C	c	serpentinite	Neol.	Acut
FS 53	G:19	C	c	sandstone	(MN)	Arect
FS 54	Cave surf.	C	f	serpentinite?	Neol.	Amisc2-set3
FS 59	A:40	C	c	sandstone	FN	Pcav
FS 64	A:55	C	f	sandstone	Neol.	Amisc1-set1
FS 68	A:40	C	f	soapstone	FN	Amisc2-set2
FS 73	A:55	C	f	sandstone	Neol.	Popen
FS 74	A:65	C	c	sandstone	(Initial Neol.)	Amisc1-set4
FS 81	G:lot28	C	c	sandstone	(MN)	Popen
FS 82	G:lot28	C	c	sandstone	(MN)	Popen
FS 83	G:lot28	C	f	sandstone	(MN)	Popen

Name	Trench:unit	Prov.	Pres.	Material	Date	Group
FS 84	G:lot28	C	c	sandstone	(MN)	Arect
FS 85	G:lot28	C	c	sandstone	(MN)	Aglobe-nostain
FS 90	G1:4	C	c	serpentinite	Neol.	Acut
FS 93	FF1:7	C	c	serpentinite	Neol.	Acut
FS 94	FF1:9	C	c	serpentinite	Neol.	Acut
FS 95	FF1:6	C	c	sandstone	Neol.	Arect
FS 98	G1:8	C	f	serpentinite	(MN)	Acut
FS 106	G1:15	C	c	limestone	(MN)	Aglobe-nostain
FS 107	G1:11	C	c	sandstone?	(MN)	Amisc1-set10
FS 108	G1:11	C	c	serpentinite	(MN)	Aend
FS 109	G1:17	C	c	serpentinite	(MN)	Aend
FS 110	G1:19	C	c	sandstone	(MN)	Arect
FS 111	G1:16	C	c	peridotite	(MN)	Aglobe-stain
FS 112	FF1:24	C	f	serpentinite	Neol.	Acut
FS 113	G1:1	C	c	sandstone	Neol.	Adisc
FS 114	FF1:8	C	f	andesite	Neol.	Popen
FS 115	G1:5	C	c	sandstone	Neol.	Asquare-circ
FS 116	G1:15	C	c	serpentinite	(MN)	Acut
FS 117	FF1:26	C	c	serpentinite	Neol.	Acut
FS 118	FF1:26	C	c	serpentinite	Neol.	Acut
FS 119	G1:17	C	c	serpentinite	(MN)	Acut raw material?
FS 120	FF1:26	C	c	serpentinite	Neol.	Aend
FS 121	FF1:6	C	c	sandstone	Neol.	Adisc
FS 122	G1:13	C	c	diorite	(MN)	Aglobe-nostain
FS 123	G1:9	C	c	sandstone	(MN)	Arect
FS 124	FF1:10	C	f	andesite	Neol.	Popen
FS 125	G1:11	C	c	sandstone	(MN)	Arect
FS 126	G1:11	C	c	sandstone	(MN)	Popen
FS 128	G1:19	C	c	conglom.	(MN)	Aglobe-nostain
FS 129	G1:19	C	c	serpentinite	(MN)	Amisc2-set1
FS 132	FF1:32	C	c	metaquartzite	(MN)	Arect
FS 133	FF1:32	C	c	sandstone	(MN)	Arect
FS 134	FF1:34	C	c	sandstone	(MN)	Arect
FS 136	FF1:37	C	c	serpentinite	Neol.	Aend
FS 142	H:2	C	c	basalt	Neol.	Acut
FS 149	FF1:39B2	C	c	serpentinite	MN	Acut
FS 153	H:13	C	c	serpentinite	Neol.	Acut
FS 154	H:13	C	c	andesite	Neol.	Amisc1-set4
FS 155	H:21	C	c	sandstone	Neol.	Amisc1-set4
FS 156	G1:34	C	c	steatite	Upper Mesol.	Pre-Neol.
FS 157	H:35	C	c	serpentinite	(MN)	Acut
FS 159	H:23	C	c	serpentinite	(MN)	Acut
FS 160	H:34	C	f	serpentinite	(MN)	Acut
FS 165	H:23	C	c	sandstone	(MN)	Popen
FS 167	H:24	C	c	peridotite	Neol.	Arect
FS 168	G1:20	C	f	sandstone	MN	Popen
FS 169	H:57A2	C	f	basalt	Pre-Neol.?	possible Pre-Neol.
FS 170	FF1:39A	C	f	sandstone	(MN)	Popen
FS 171	FF1:39A	C	c	limestone	(MN)	Amisc2-set4
FS 173	G1:19	C	c	sandstone	(MN)	Popen
FS 174	G1:10	C	c	sandstone	(MN)	Popen
FS 175	G1:10	C	c	sandstone	(MN)	Popen
FS 178	G1:11	C	f	serpentinite	(MN)	Acut
FS 179	G1:8	C	f	serpentinite?	(MN)	Amisc2-set3
FS 180	FF1:40B1	C	f	serpentinite	MN	Acut

Name	Trench:unit	Prov.	Pres.	Material	Date	Group
FS 181	FF1:30	C	f	serpentinite	(MN)	Acut fragment?
FS 183	G1:50	C	f	diabase	Lower Mesol.	Pre-Neol.
FS 184	G1:54	C	f	limestone	Lower Mesol.	Pre-Neol.
FS 185	Cave surf.	C	c	diabase	Neol.	Acut
FS 186	FA:4	C	c	sandstone	Neol.	Amisc1-set9
FS 187	FA:8	C	c	sandstone	Neol.	Adisc
FS 188	FA:6	C	c	sandstone	Neol.	Adisc
FS 189	FA:6	C	f	serpentinite	Neol.	Amisc2-set5
FS 192	FA:10	C	c	serpentinite	Neol.	Aend
FS 194	FA:11	C	c	metaquartzite?	Neol.	Amisc2-set4
FS 196	FA:11	C	c	sandstone	Neol.	Amisc1-set11
FS 197	FA:11	C	f	serpentinite	Neol.	Amisc2-set8
FS 199	FA:10	C	f	sandstone	Neol.	Amisc1-set15
FS 201	H1:12	C	c	serpentinite	Neol.	Acut
FS 204	FA:24	C	f	serpentinite	Neol.	Acut fragment?
FS 207	FA:24	C	c	serpentinite	Neol.	Acut
FS 210	FA:33A	C	c	serpentinite	Neol.	Acut
FS 211	H1:20	C	c	serpentinite	Neol.	Amisc2-set5
FS 212	FA:33A	C	c	serpentinite	Neol.	Acut
FS 214	FA:35	C	f	sandstone	Neol.	Pcav
FS 215	H1:31	C	c	quartz	Neol.	Amisc2-set5
FS 219	FA:37	C	c	serpentinite	Neol.	Acut
FS 220	FA:35	C	c	sandstone	Neol.	Asquare-circ
FS 221	FA:39	C	c	felsite porphyry	FN	Acut
FS 222	H1:41	C	c	serpentinite	Neol.	Acut
FS 223	FA:29	C	c	metaandesite?	Neol.	Asquare-circ
FS 225	FA:42	C	c	serpentinite	Neol.	Aend
FS 226	FA scarp	C	c	serpentinite	Neol.	Acut
FS 227	FA:43	C	c	peridotite	Neol.	Acut
FS 228	H1:59	C	c	serpentinite	Neol.	Aend
FS 229	H1:56	C	c	serpentinite	Neol.	Acut
FS 230	FA:46	C	c	limestone	FN	Amisc2-set2
FS 231	FA:45	C	c	sandstone	FN	Asquare-circ
FS 239	FA:54	C	c	serpentinite	Neol.	Acut
FS 240	FA:54	C	f	serpentinite	Neol.	Acut manuf. remain?
FS 247	H1A:72	C	f	sandstone	Neol.	Popen
FS 252	G:32	C	c	limestone	Pre-Neol.?	possible Pre-Neol.
FS 253	G:38	C	c	serpentinite	Neol.	Amisc2-set3
FS 255	FAN:74	C	f	quartz	(FN)	Amisc2-set5
FS 256	H1A:100	C	c	sandstone	Neol.	Arect
FS 257	H1A:94	C	f	sandstone	(EN)	Amisc1-set11
FS 258	FAN:59	C	c	sandstone	FN	Adisc
FS 260	FA:49	C	f	sandstone	Neol.	Adisc
FS 261	FAN:59	C	c	sandstone	FN	Amisc1-set11
FS 269	A:27	C	c	serpentinite	(FN)	Amisc2-set1
FS 270	A:27	C	c	sandstone	(FN)	Amisc1-set10
FS 271	A:34	C	c	diabase	Neol.	Amisc2-set5
FS 272	C:4	C	c	diabase	Neol.	Aglobe-nostain
FS 273	A:5	C	c	diabase	Neol.	Aglobe-nostain
FS 274	H1A:124	C	f	metaquartzite	Lower Mesol.	Pre-Neol.
FS 275	H1A:127	C	f	sandstone	Lower Mesol.	Pre-Neol.
FS 276	H1B scarp	C	c	sandstone	Neol.	Amisc1-set9
FS 277	H1B:83	C	f	serpentinite	Neol.	Aend
FS 278	H1B:82	C	c	serpentinite	Neol.	Acut
FS 284	H1B:78	C	c	sandstone	Neol.	Amisc1-set8

Name	Trench:unit	Prov.	Pres.	Material	Date	Group
FS 285	FAN:117	C	c	sandstone	LN	Popen
FS 287	FAN:117	C	c	sandstone?	LN	Amisc1-set1
FS 288	FAN:117	C	f	serpentinite	LN	Acut fragment?
FS 289	H1B:94	C	c	serpentinite	Neol.	Acut
FS 290	H1B:94	C	c	serpentinite	Neol.	Amisc2-set5
FS 295	H1B:95	C	f	sandstone	Neol.	Amisc1-set7
FS 296	H1A:120	C	f	sandstone	Lower/Upper Mesol.	Pre-Neol.
FS 297	FAN:119	C	c	sandstone	(LN)	Arect
FS 298	H1B:95	C	c	peridotite	Neol.	Aglobe-stain
FS 299	FAN:91	C	f	sandstone	(FN)	Adisc
FS 300	FAN:91	C	c	sandstone/conglom.	(FN)	Adisc
FS 301	H1B:92	C	f	sandstone	Neol.	Popen
FS 302	H1B:88	C	f	conglom.	Neol.	Amisc1-set11
FS 303	BE:4	C	c	sandstone	Neol.	Amisc1-set11
FS 304	FAS:61	C	c	sandstone	FN	Adisc
FS 310	HPed:37T	C	c	chert	EN	Amisc2-set2
FS 311	FAS:72	C	n/ap	peridotite	FN	Acut
FS 315	FAS:71	C	c	diabase	FN	Aglobe-nostain
FS 317	FAS:69	C	c	sandstone	FN	Adisc
FS 318	FAS:70	C	c	sandstone	FN	Asquare-circ
FS 320	FAS:71	C	f	sandstone	FN	Popen
FS 321	HPed:37Y	C	f	sandstone	EN	Popen
FS 322	FAS:72	C	c	conglom.	FN	Amisc1-set11
FS 323	HPed:37N	C	c	sandstone	(MN)	Amisc1-set8
FS 324	FAS:71	C	f	andesite	FN	Popen
FS 344	H2A:40	C	f	slate	MN	Acut fragment?
FS 350	FAS:73	C	f	andesite	FN	Amisc1-set5
FS 357	FAS:76	C	f	sandstone	FN	Amisc1-set14
FS 358	FAS:81	C	c	serpentinite	FN	Amisc2
FS 359	H2A:58	C	f	serpentinite	(MN)	Acut fragment?
FS 360	FAS:83	C	f	sandstone	(FN)	Asquare-circ
FS 362	H2A:66	C	c	serpentinite	(MN)	Aend
FS 363	Q5N:3	P	c	serpentinite	Neol.	Acut
FS 368	FAS:93	C	f	sandstone	LN	Popen
FS 371	H2A:75	C	c	peridotite	MN	Aglobe-stain
FS 372	H2A:75	C	c	peridotite	MN	Aglobe-stain
FS 373	H2A:75	C	c	sandstone	MN	Amisc1-set9
FS 374	H2A:75	C	c	serpentinite	MN	Acut
FS 375	H2A:75	C	c	limestone	MN	Aglobe-nostain
FS 377	H1A:179	C	c	sandstone	Upper Palaeol.	Pre-Neol.
FS 378	H1A:179	C	f	limestone	Upper Palaeol.	Pre-Neol.
FS 379	FAS:102	C	f	sandstone	(LN)	Amisc1-set10
FS 380	FAS:102	C	f	andesite	LN	Popen
FS 382	FAS:105	C	c	soapstone	LN	Amisc2-set6
FS 385	FAS:107	C	f	serpentinite	LN	Acut
FS 386	H1A:181	C	f	limestone	Upper Palaeol.	Pre-Neol.
FS 388	H2A:84	C	c	sandstone	MN	Popen
FS 389	H2A:77	C	f	sandstone	(MN)	Amisc1-set14
FS 390	H2A:77	C	c	andesite	(MN)	Popen
FS 395	H2B:13	C	f	sandstone	(MN)	Popen
FS 396	FAN:121	C	f	sandstone	MN/LN	Popen
FS 398	H2B:17	C	c	serpentinite	(MN)	Acut
FS 414	H2B:33	C	f	sandstone	(MN)	Amisc1-set7
FS 417	FAN:131	C	f	basalt	MN	Amisc2-set9
FS 418	FAN:132	C	f	sandstone	MN	Popen

Name	Trench:unit	Prov.	Pres.	Material	Date	Group
FS 419	FAN:132	C	f	siltstone	MN	Popen
FS 420	FAN:132	C	c	serpentinite	MN	Aend
FS 422	FAN:133	C	f	serpentinite	MN	Amisc2-set9
FS 423	FAN:134	C	f	sandstone	MN	Popen
FS 424	FAN:134	C	f	andesite	MN	Popen
FS 425	FAN:134	C	f	serpentinite	MN	Acut
FS 426	FAN:134	C	f	serpentinite	MN	Acut fragment?
FS 428	H2B:50	C	c	basalt	(MN)	Acut
FS 430	Q5N:23	P	f	peridotite	EN	Acut
FS 432	FAN:136	C	f	serpentinite	MN	Aend
FS 433	FAN:136	C	f	sandstone	MN	Popen
FS 434	FAN:136	C	f	sandstone	MN	Popen
FS 435	FAN:137	C	f	sandstone	MN	Amisc1-set11
FS 436	Q5N:24	P	f	serpentinite	(EN)	Acut
FS 442	FAS:116	C	f	sandstone	MN/LN	Popen
FS 445	FAS:117	C	f	sandstone?	(MN)	Amisc1-set7
FS 452	FAS:117	C	f	serpentinite	(MN)	Amisc2-set5
FS 454	H1A:215	C	f	sandstone	Upper Palaeol.	Pre-Neol.
FS 455	FAS:120	C	f	sandstone	MN	Amisc1-set9
FS 456	FAS:120	C	f	limestone	MN	Amisc2-set4
FS 464	FAS:121	C	f	sandstone	MN	Popen
FS 465	FAS:123	C	f	sandstone	MN	Popen
FS 466	FAS:123	C	f	sandstone	MN	Popen
FS 467	FAS:124	C	f	sandstone	(MN)	Popen
FS 468	FAS:125	C	f	sandstone	MN	Popen
FS 471	H2A:95	C	c	sandstone	(MN)	Amisc1-set8
FS 472	H2B:25	C	c	conglom.	(MN)	Pcav
FS 505	FAN:142	C	c	serpentinite	(MN)	Acut
FS 507	FAN:148	C	f	limestone	(MN)	Amisc2-set8
FS 508	Q5N:43	P	f	serpentinite	EN/MN	Acut fragment?
FS 509	Q5N:42	P	f	sandstone	Neol.	Popen
FS 530	H1B:121	C	f	steatite	Lower Mesol.	Pre-Neol.
FS 531	H2A:122	C	c	sandstone	MN	Amisc1-set1
FS 549	FAN:174	C	f	quartzite	Final Mesol.	Pre-Neol.
FS 550	H2A:129	C	f	serpentinite	Neol.	Acut fragment?
FS 551	FAN:177	C	f	andesite	Upper Mesol.	Pre-Neol.
FS 562	Q5S:4	P	f	serpentinite	(MN)	Acut fragment?
FS 565	Q5S:4	P	c	limestone	(MN)	Amisc2-set4
FS 575	L5:2	P	f	sandstone	FN	Adisc
FS 576	FAS:132	C	f	limestone	EN/MN	Amisc2-set7
FS 577	Q5S:14	P	f	serpentinite	Neol.	Acut
FS 579	H2A:144	C	c	limestone	EN	Amisc2-set1
FS 589	L5NE:7	P	c	steatite	FN	Acut
FS 594	H1B:144	C	c	limestone	Lower Mesol.	Pre-Neol.
FS 595	L5NE:7	P	f	sandstone	FN	Adisc
FS 596	L5NE:15	P	c	sandstone	FN	Adisc
FS 597	L5NE:15	P	f	sandstone	FN	Amisc1-set3
FS 598	L5NE:15	P	c	sandstone/conglom.	FN	Adisc
FS 600	L5NE:19	P	c	serpentinite	FN	Acut
FS 602	L5NE:18	P	c	diabase	FN	Aend
FS 603	L5NE:18	P	f	sandstone	FN	Popen
FS 604	L5NE:18	P	f	sandstone	FN	Adisc
FS 605	L5NE:18	P	c	sandstone/conglom.	FN	Amisc1-set2
FS 606	L5NE:19	P	c	quartz	FN	Amisc2-set4
FS 607	L5NE:19	P	c	sandstone	FN	Amisc1-set11

Name	Trench:unit	Prov.	Pres.	Material	Date	Group
FS 608	L5NE:19	P	c	sandstone	FN	Adisc
FS 609	L5NE:22	P	c	limestone	FN	Amisc2-set7
FS 612	L5NE:18	P	c	sandstone/conglom.	FN	Amisc1-set2
FS 617	Q5S:50	P	f	peridotite	Neol.	Acut
FS 621	L5NE:33	P	c	sandstone	Neol.	Adisc
FS 624	Q5S:92	P	c	sandstone	Neol.	Popen
FS 629	H2APed:172	C	c	quartz	Neol.	Amisc2-set1
FS 634	Q5S:76	P	f	sandstone	MN	Pcav
FS 644	O5NE:25	P	f	limestone	Neol.	Acut fragment?
FS 645	H2APed:186	C	f	sandstone	Neol.	Popen
FS 646	O5NE:32	P	f	limestone	MN	Amisc2-set10
FS 661	Q5S:131	P	f	sandstone	(MN)	Popen
FS 662	Q5S:131	P	f	sandstone	(MN)	Amisc1-set14
FS 663	H2APed:191	C	c	steatite	Neol.	Amisc2-set1
FS 664	Q5S:144	P	f	serpentinite	MN	Amisc2-set3
FS 666	H2APed:195	C	f	limestone	Neol.	Acut
FS 667	Q5S:154	P	f	andesite	Neol.	Amisc1-set3
FS 668	Q5S:154	P	f	sandstone	Neol.	Popen
FS 680	O5N:14	P	c	serpentinite	Neol.	Acut
FS 691	H2APed:203	C	f	limestone	(Final Mesol.)	Pre-Neol.
FS 693	Q4:1	P	c	diorite	Neol.	Acut
FS 695	O5:4	P	c	diabase	Neol.	Aglobe-nostain
FS 701	FAS:166	C	c	limestone	Upper Mesol.	Pre-Neol.
FS 706	FAS:184	C	f	sandstone	Lower Mesol.	Pre-Neol.
FS 714	Q4:59	P	f	serpentinite	Neol.	Acut
FS 715	Q4:58	P	f	serpentinite	Neol.	Acut
FS 723	Q5S:177	P	f	sandstone	Neol.	Popen
FS 725	FAS:191	C	c	limestone	Lower Mesol.	Pre-Neol.
FS 726	O5:34	P	c	serpentinite	(MN)	Acut
FS 734	O5:43	P	f	serpentinite	Neol.	Acut manuf. remain?
FS 737	L5:1	P	f	sandstone	FN	Amisc1-set7
FS 740	L5:26	P	c	sandstone	(MN)	Amisc1-set4
FS 749	Q4:100	P	f	sandstone	EN	Pcav
FS 750	FAS:204	C	c	sandstone	Upper Palaeol.	Pre-Neol.
FS 751	O5:59	P	f	basalt	EN/MN	Acut
FS 752	Q6N:38	P	f	sandstone	EN/MN	Amisc1-set1
FS 755	Q4:128	P	c	diabase	EN	Acut
FS 757	P5:77	P	f	sandstone	MN	Amisc1-set3
FS 758	L5:37	P	f	sandstone	EN	Amisc1-set11
FS 759	O5:81	P	f	sandstone	EN	Popen
FS 760	L5:34	P	c	diorite	EN/MN	Aglobe-nostain
FS 765	P5:89	P	f	conglom.?	(MN)	Popen
FS 766	P5:92	P	f	basalt	MN	Aend
FS 767	P5:91	P	f	serpentinite	Neol.	Acut
FS 768	Q6N:54	P	c	steatite	(EN)	Amisc2-set1
FS 771	PQ5:9	P	f	sandstone	Neol.	Arect
FS 772	PQ5:9	P	f	serpentinite	Neol.	Acut
FS 774	Q5S:216	P	c	sandstone	MN	Arect
FS 775	Q5S:216	P	f	limestone	MN	Amisc2-set7
FS 779	PQ5:28	P	c	serpentinite	MN	Acut
FS 780	PQ5:14	P	f	basalt?	MN	Amisc2-set10
FS 786	Q5S:223	P	c	sandstone	EN	Arect
FS 788	P5:152	P	c	sandstone	Neol.	Amisc1-set11
FS 789	P5:153	P	f	serpentinite	Neol.	Acut
FS 790	P5:162	P	f	serpentinite	(MN)	Acut fragment?

Name	Trench:unit	Prov.	Pres.	Material	Date	Group
FS 795	FA surf.	C	c	andesite	Neol.	Popen
FS 826	H1:5	C	c	serpentinite	Neol.	Acut
FS 827	Q4 backfill	P	c	chert	Neol.	Aglobe-nostain
FS 828	HTerrace:9	C	c	sandstone	Neol.	Amisc1-set8
FS 829	HTerrace:8	C	c	basalt	Neol.	Amisc2-set7
FS 830	H1:9	C	f	sandstone	Neol.	Popen
FS 831	HTerrace:9	C	f	sandstone	Neol.	Amisc1-set15
FS 832	H1:8	C	f	andesite	Neol.	Popen
FS 833	HTerrace:9	C	c	sandstone	Neol.	Amisc1-set11
FS 837	H1:16	C	c	serpentinite	Neol.	Acut
FS 838	H1:16	C	f	serpentinite	Neol.	Acut
FS 840	HTerrace:21	C	c	diabase	Neol.	Aglobe-nostain
FS 841	HTerrace:16	C	c	diabase	Neol.	Aglobe-nostain
FS 848	HTerrace:16	C	f	sandstone	Neol.	Arect
FS 849	HTerrace:20	C	f	sandstone	Neol.	Arect
FS 850	HTerrace:16	C	c	sandstone	Neol.	Amisc1-set11
FS 852	H1:13	C	c	sandstone	Neol.	Popen
FS 870	L5:61	P	c	sandstone	FN	Asquare-circ
FS 871	L5:60	P	c	diorite	FN	Aglobe-nostain
FS 872	L5:61	P	f	conglom.	FN	Amisc1-set15
FS 873	L5:61	P	f	conglom.	FN	Popen
FS 874	L5:61	P	f	conglom.	FN	Amisc1-set15
FS 876	P5:183	P	c	chert	MN	Aglobe-nostain
FS 877	H1:14	C	f	serpentinite	Neol.	Acut fragment?
FS 883	P5:174	P	c	serpentinite	MN	Acut
FS 884	QR5:12	P	c	basalt	EN/MN	Acut
FS 885	L5:60	P	c	basalt	FN	Acut
FS 888	L5:62	P	f	sandstone	Neol.	Amisc1-set14
FS 889	P5:186	P	c	limestone	MN	Aglobe-nostain
FS 891	L5:68	P	f	peridotite	FN	Amisc2-set2
FS 892	QR5:29	P	f	sandstone	EN/MN	Popen
FS 893	QR5:29	P	c	serpentinite	EN/MN	Acut
FS 899	P5:190	P	c	serpentinite	MN	Acut
FS 902	P5:191	P	c	steatite	MN	Acut
FS 910	L5:91	P	c	sandstone	EN/MN	Pcav
FA:24	FA:24	C	f	limestone	Neol.	Amisc2-set5
FA:28	FA:28	C	f	serpentinite	Neol.	Acut
FA:28a	FA:28	C	f	serpentinite	Neol.	Acut fragment?
FA:42a	FA:42	C	c	limestone	Pre-Neol.?	possible Pre-Neol.
FA:42b	FA:42	C	c	limestone	Pre-Neol.?	possible Pre-Neol.
FAN:61	FAN:61	C	c	conglom.	FN	Adisc
FAN:61/1	FAN:61	C	c	sandstone/conglom.	FN	Adisc
FAN:63	FAN:63	C	c	sandstone?	FN	Pmisc
FAN:86	FAN:86	C	f	sandstone	(LN)	Popen
FAN:89	FAN:89	C	c	sandstone	LN	Amisc1-set11
FAN:129	FAN:129	C	f	serpentinite	MN	Acut
FAN:142	FAN:142	C	f	limestone	(MN)	Amisc2-set8
FAN:143	FAN:143	C	f	limestone	(MN)	Amisc2-set8
FAS:117	FAS:117	C	f	?	(MN)	Amisc1-set1
FAS:159	FAS:159	C	f	limestone	Upper Mesol.	Pre-Neol.
FF1:5	FF1:5	C	f	limestone	Neol.	Amisc2-set3
FF1:5a	FF1:5	C	f	sandstone	Neol.	Amisc1-set7
FF1:6	FF1:6	C	c	diabase	Neol.	Aglobe-nostain
FF1:6a	FF1:6	C	f	andesite?	Neol.	Popen
FF1:6B	FF1:6	C	c	sandstone	Neol.	Asquare-circ

Name	Trench:unit	Prov.	Pres.	Material	Date	Group
FF1:6c	FF1:6	C	f	sandstone	Neol.	Popen
FF1:6E	FF1:6	C	c	olivine gabbro	Neol.	Asquare-circ
FF1:8a	FF1:8	C	c	limestone	Pre-Neol.?	possible Pre-Neol.
FF1:8b	FF1:8	C	c	sandstone	Neol.	Amisc1-set9
FF1:8c	FF1:8	C	f	serpentinite?	Neol.	Amisc2-set9
FF1:9	FF1:9	C	f	peridotite	Neol.	Aglobe-nostain
FF1:11	FF1:11	C	c	diabase	Neol.	Aglobe-nostain
FF1:11a	FF1:11	C	c	sandstone	Neol.	Amisc1-set9
FF1:11b	FF1:11	C	c	sandstone	Neol.	Amisc1-set9
FF1:13	FF1:13	C	c	diabase	Neol.	Aglobe-nostain
FF1:14a	FF1:14	C	f	sandstone	Neol.	Popen
FF1:14b	FF1:14	C	f	sandstone	Neol.	Popen
FF1:20	FF1:20	C	f	sandstone	Neol.	Popen
FF1:29	FF1:29	C	f	serpentinite	Neol.	Acut
FF1:29C	FF1:29	C	c	diabase	Neol.	Aglobe-nostain
FF1:32A	FF1:32	C	f	sandstone	(MN)	Amisc1-set11
FF1:32b	FF1:32	C	f	sandstone	(MN)	Popen
FF1:32c	FF1:32	C	c	limestone	(MN)	Amisc2-set5
FF1:34a	FF1:34	C	f	limestone	(MN)	Amisc2-set5
FF1:34f	FF1:34	C	f	sandstone	(MN)	Popen
FF1:34g	FF1:34	C	f	sandstone	(MN)	Popen
FF1:35B	FF1:35	C	c	diabase	(MN)	Aglobe-nostain
FF1:36	FF1:36	C	f	sandstone	(MN)	Popen
FF1:37a	FF1:37	C	f	sandstone	Neol.	Amisc1-set14
FF1:37c	FF1:37	C	f	sandstone	Neol.	Amisc1-set13
FF1:39Aj	FF1:39A	C	f	limestone	(MN)	Amisc2-set5
FF1:40B1a	FF1:40B1	C	c	peridotite	MN	Aglobe-stain
FF1:40B1b	FF1:40B1	C	c	limestone	MN	Amisc2-set5
G1:15	G1:15	C	f	soapstone	(MN)	Amisc2-set6
G1:18/1	G1:18	C	c	sandstone	(MN)	Popen
G1:18/2	G1:18	C	f	sandstone	(MN)	Popen
G1:32	G1:32	C	c	limestone	(Upper/Final Mesol.)	Pre-Neol.
H:2	H:2	C	f	sandstone	Neol.	Amisc1-set9
H:17	H:17	C	f	serpentinite	Neol.	Acut
H:24	H:24	C	c	limestone	Neol.	Amisc2-set5
H:38	H:38	C	f	limestone	(MN)	Amisc2-set7
H:39	H:39	C	f	serpentinite	MN	Acut fragment?
H:40	H:40	C	f	slate	Neol.	Amisc1-set7
H:67B2	H:67B2	C	f	limestone	Pre-Neol.?	possible Pre-Neol.
H1:25	H1:25	C	f	sandstone	Neol.	Popen
H1:41	H1:41	C	c	sandstone	Neol.	Amisc1-set3
H1:47	H1:47	C	f	sandstone	Neol.	Popen
H1:52	H1:52	C	c	sandstone	Neol.	Popen
H1:58	H1:58	C	f	sandstone	Neol.	Popen
H1:64	H1:64	C	c	serpentinite	Neol.	Aend
H1:68	H1:68	C	f	sandstone	Neol.	Popen
H1:68a	H1:68	C	c	soapstone	Neol.	Amisc2-set4
H1:72	H1A:72	C	f	sandstone	Neol.	Amisc1-set3
H1A:84	H1A:84	C	c	ocher?	Neol.	Amisc2-set2
H1A:91	H1A:91	C	c	diabase	EN/MN	Aglobe-nostain
H1A:93	H1A:93	C	c	sandstone	(EN)	Amisc1-set8
H1A:198/20	H1A:198	C	f	limestone	Upper Palaeol.	Pre-Neol.
H1A:207/21	H1A:207	C	f	limestone	Upper Palaeol.	Pre-Neol.
H1B:108	H1B:108	C	c	limestone	Upper Mesol.	Pre-Neol.
H1B:114/25	H1B:114	C	f	limestone	Upper Mesol.	Pre-Neol.

Name	Trench:unit	Prov.	Pres.	Material	Date	Group
H2A:7/1	H2A:7	C	f	sandstone	Neol.	Amisc1-set14
H2A:8/2	H2A:8	C	f	sandstone	Neol.	Amisc1-set13
H2A:9a	H2A:9	C	f	serpentinite	Neol.	Acut manuf. remain?
H2A:9b	H2A:9	C	f	sandstone	Neol.	Amisc1-set9
H2A:23/4	H2A:23	C	c	sandstone	Neol.	Amisc1-set9
H2A:41/7	H2A:41	C	f	sandstone	Neol.	Popen
H2A:75/21	H2A:75	C	f	peridotite	MN	Aglobe-nostain
H2A:163	H2A:163	C	f	limestone	(Upper/Final Mesol.)	Pre-Neol.
H2APed:187	H2APed:187	C	f	jasper	Neol.	Amisc2-set9
H2B:16	H2B:16	C	f	sandstone	(MN)	Popen
H2B:34	H2B:34	C	f	sandstone	(MN)	Popen
L5:2/30	L5:2	P	f	serpentinite	FN	Amisc2-set9
L5:79/47	L5:79	P	f	sandstone	Neol.	Popen
L5:99/51	L5:99	P	c	peridotite	MN	Aglobe-nostain
L5NE:7	L5NE:7	P	f	chert	FN	Aglobe-nostain
L5NE:15/10	L5NE:15	P	c	serpentinite	FN	Amisc2-set5
L5NE:19/25	L5NE:19	P	c	sandstone/conglom.	FN	Adisc
O5:83/12	O5:83	P	f	chlorite schist	EN	Amisc2-set9
O5:84	O5:84	P	f	serpentinite	(EN)	Acut
O5:116/13	O5:116	P	c	peridotite	Neol.	Aglobe-stain
P5:178/13	P5:178	P	c	peridotite	MN	Aglobe-stain
P5:179	P5:179	P	c	chert	MN	Aglobe-nostain
Q4:3/2	Q4:3	P	c	goethite	Neol.	Aglobe-nostain
Q4:72/10	Q4:72	P	c	serpentinite	Neol.	Amisc2-set5
Q4:86/11	Q4:86	P	f	sandstone	EN	Popen
Q4:87/12	Q4:87	P	c	sandstone	EN	Amisc1-set7
Q4:87/14	Q4:87	P	f	sandstone	EN	Popen
Q4:109/19	Q4:109	P	f	andesite	EN/MN	Popen
Q5N:2/1	Q5N:2	P	f	magnetite?	Neol.	Aglobe-nostain
Q5N:103/13	Q5N:103	P	f	sandstone	MN	Popen
Q5S:2/1	Q5S:2	P	f	serpentinite	Neol.	Aglobe-nostain
Q5S:14/4	Q5S:14	P	f	sandstone	Neol.	Amisc1-set14
Q5S:52/10	Q5S:52	P	f	serpentinite	Neol.	Amisc2-set9
Q5S:89/17	Q5S:89	P	f	limestone	Neol.	Amisc2-set4
Q5S:90/18	Q5S:90	P	c	serpentinite	Neol.	Aend
Q5S:91/19	Q5S:91	P	c	magnetite	Neol.	Acut
Q5S:186/44	Q5S:186	P	c	sandstone	EN/MN	Amisc1-set7
QR5:6/2	QR5:6	P	c	chert	Neol.	Aglobe-nostain
S 1	Cave surf.	C	f	conglom.	Post-Neol.	Post-Neol.
S 2	FA	C	c	conglom.?	Neol.	Amisc1-set6
S 3	Cave surf.	C	c	limestone	Neol.	Amisc2-set5
S 4	Paralia surf.	P	f	sandstone	Neol.	Popen
S 6	Paralia surf.	P	c	sandstone	Neol.	Arect
S 8	Paralia surf.	P	c	peridotite	Neol.	Aglobe-stain
S 9	Cave surf.	C	f	sandstone	Neol.	Popen
S 11	FA:10	C	f	sandstone	Neol.	Popen
S 12	FA:43	C	f	conglom.	Neol.	Amisc1-set12
S 14	FA:31	C	f	conglom.	Neol.	Amisc1-set12
S 16	FA:21	C	f	conglom.?	Neol.	Amisc1-set11
S 17	FA:41	C	f	sandstone	Neol.	Pcav
S 18	FA:41	C	c	sandstone/conglom.	Neol.	Adisc
S 19	FA:37	C	c	sandstone	Neol.	Adisc
S 21	FA:42	C	f	sandstone	Neol.	Popen
S 22	FA:33A	C	c	sandstone	Neol.	Adisc
S 24	FA:7	C	f	andesite	Neol.	Popen

Name	Trench:unit	Prov.	Pres.	Material	Date	Group
S 25	FA:10	C	f	sandstone	Neol.	Popen
S 26	FA:41	C	f	sandstone	Neol.	Popen
S 27	FA surf.	C	c	basalt	Neol.	Asquare-circ
S 28	FA:27	C	c	serpentinite	Neol.	Amisc2-set5
S 29	FA:34	C	f	sandstone	Neol.	Popen
S 30	FA:33B	C	c	sandstone	Neol.	Popen
S 31	FA:29	C	f	soapstone	Neol.	Amisc2-set7
S 32	FA:29	C	f	sandstone	Neol.	Popen
S 33	F:4	C	f	sandstone?	Neol.	Amisc1-set11
S 34	FA:15	C	f	sandstone	Neol.	Popen
S 35	FA:35	C	f	limestone?	Neol.	Amisc2-set5
S 36	FA:35	C	f	andesite	Neol.	Amisc1-set5
S 37	FA:35	C	f	sandstone	Neol.	Popen
S 38	FA:33B	C	f	sandstone	Neol.	Popen
S 38a	FA:10	C	f	sandstone	Neol.	Popen
S 39	FA:29	C	f	sandstone	Neol.	Popen
S 40	FA:33A	C	f	sandstone	Neol.	Amisc1-set11
S 41	FA:34	C	f	sandstone	Neol.	Popen
S 42	FA:43	C	c	limestone	Neol.	Amisc2-set7
S 43	FA:44	C	f	volcanic rock	Neol.	Popen
S 44	FA:42	C	f	sandstone	Neol.	Popen
S 45	FA:30	C	f	sandstone	Neol.	Asquare-circ
S 46	FA:19	C	f	sandstone	Neol.	Amisc1-set11
S 48	FA:34	C	c	sandstone	Neol.	Arect
S 49	Paralia surf.	P	f	sandstone	Neol.	Amisc1-set14
S 50	FA:37	C	f	sandstone	Neol.	Asquare-circ
S 51	FA:34	C	f	conglom.?	Neol.	Amisc1-set11
S 52	F:6	C	f	andesite	Neol.	Popen
S 53	FA:41	C	f	conglom.	Neol.	Popen
S 54	F:3	C	f	sandstone	Pre-Neol.?	possible Pre-Neol.
S 55	F:15	C	f	andesite	Neol.	Popen
S 56	F:16	C	f	diorite?	Neol.	Aglobe-nostain
S 57	F:20	C	f	serpentinite	Neol.	Acut
S 58	FA surf.	C	c	sandstone	Neol.	Amisc1-set11
S 59	FA:6	C	f	andesite	Neol.	Popen
S 60	FA:6	C	f	limestone	Neol.	Amisc2-set5
S 61	FA	C	f	andesite	Neol.	Popen
S 62	FA:33	C	c	sandstone	Neol.	Asquare-circ
S 64	FA:53	C	f	diabase?	Neol.	Amisc2-set3
S 65	FA:33	C	c	sandstone	Neol.	Amisc1-set15
S 66	FA:43	C	f	andesite	Neol.	Popen
S 67	FA:44	C	c	limestone	Neol.	Amisc2-set7
S 68	FA	C	c	limestone	Pre-Neol.?	possible Pre-Neol.
S 69	FA:54	C	f	sandstone	Neol.	Amisc1-set11
S 71	H1B surf.	C	f	andesite	Neol.	Popen
S 72	H	C	c	sandstone	Neol.	Asquare-circ
S 73	n/a	n/a	f	sandstone	Neol.	Amisc1-set3

FIGURES

Figure 1. Franchthi Cave in the southern Argolid (reproduced from Jacobsen and Farrand 1987, Figure 1).

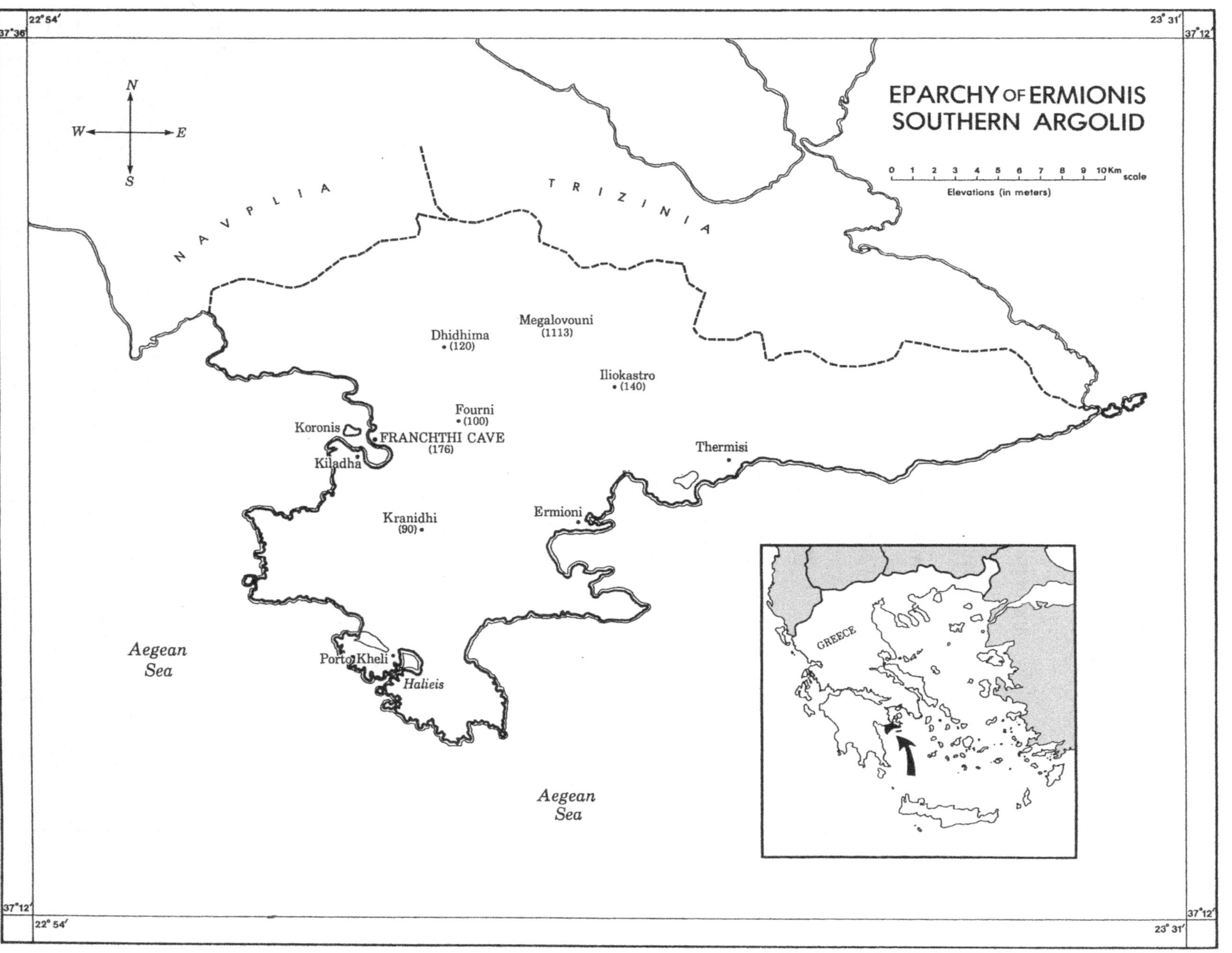
EPARCHY OF ERMIONIS
SOUTHERN ARGOLID
0 1 2 3 4 5 6 7 8 9 10 Km scale
Elevations (in meters)
N
W
E
S
NAVPLIA
TRIZINIA
Dhidhima (120)
Megalovouni (1113)
Iliokastro (140)
Fourni (100)
Koronis
FRANCHTHI CAVE (176)
Kiladha
Thermisi
Kranidhi (90)
Ermioni
Porto Kheli
Halieis
Aegean Sea
Aegean Sea
GREECE
22° 54′
23° 31′
37°36′
37°12′

Figure 2. Franchthi Cave and Paralia, showing excavated areas (modified from Figure 2 in Shackleton 1988).

Note: Some of the trench names indicate the location of more than one trench. More specifically:

'E' indicates area of trenches E and BE.

'F' indicates area of trench F and portion of F1.

'FF1' indicates area of trench FF1 and portion of F1.

'A' indicates area of trench A and portion of FA.

'FAS' indicates area of trench FAS and portion of FA.

'FAN' indicates area of trench FAN and portion of FA.

'H' indicates area of trenches H, HA, HB, and H Pedestal.

'L5' indicates area of trenches L5 and L5NE.

'O5' indicates area of trenches O5, O5N, and O5NE.

'P5' indicates area of trenches P5 and PQ5.

'Q5' indicates area of trenches Q5S and Q5N.

'Q6' indicates area of trenches Q6N and Q6NE.

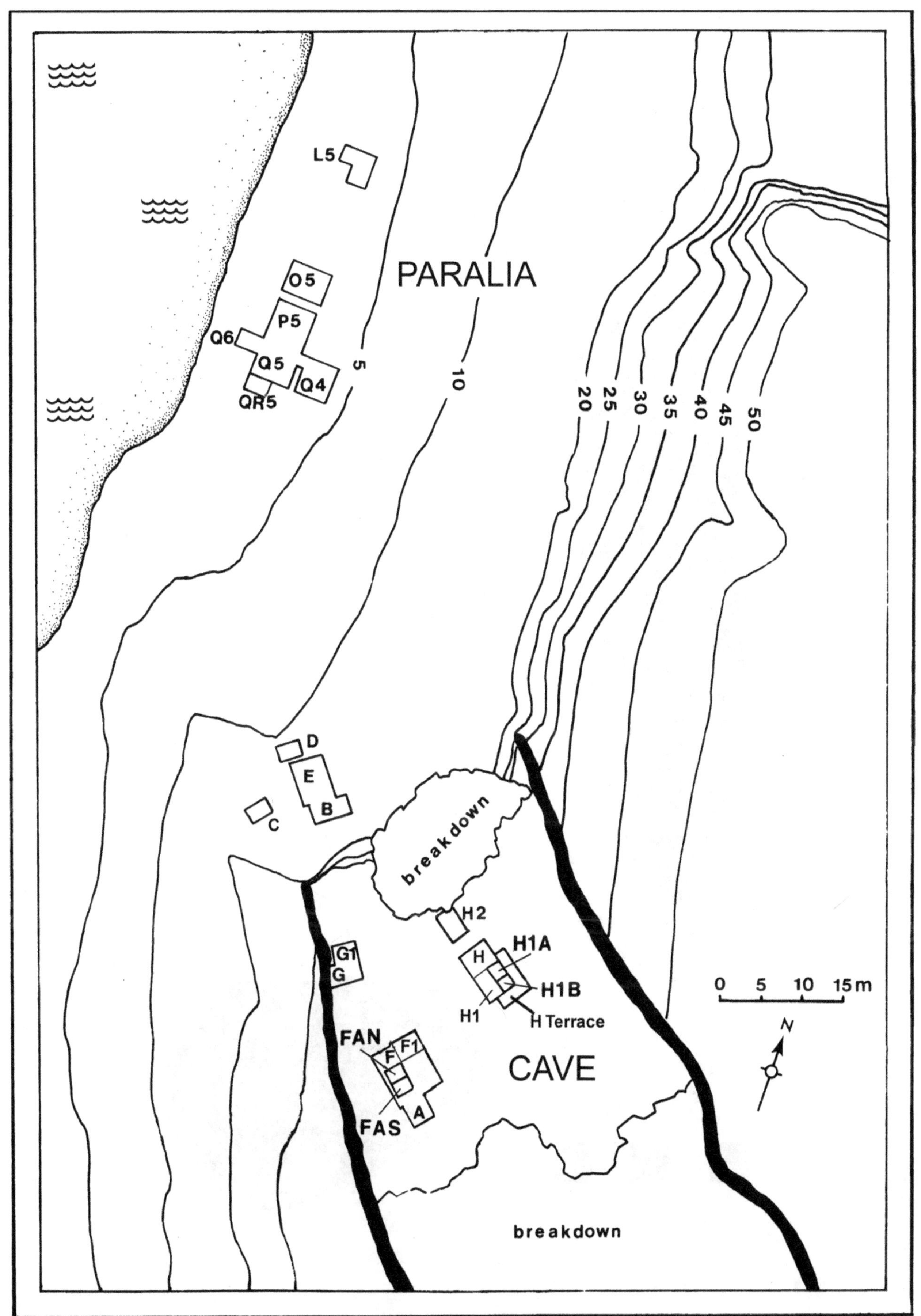
PARALIA
L5
O5
P5
Q6
Q5
Q4
QR5
5
10
20
25
30
35
40
45
50
D
E
B
C
breakdown
H2
H1A
H
H1B
H1
H Terrace
G1
G
FAN
F1
F
FAS
A
CAVE
breakdown
0 5 10 15m
N

Figure 3. FS 750: Plan view, longitudinal and transverse sections. Scale 3:4.

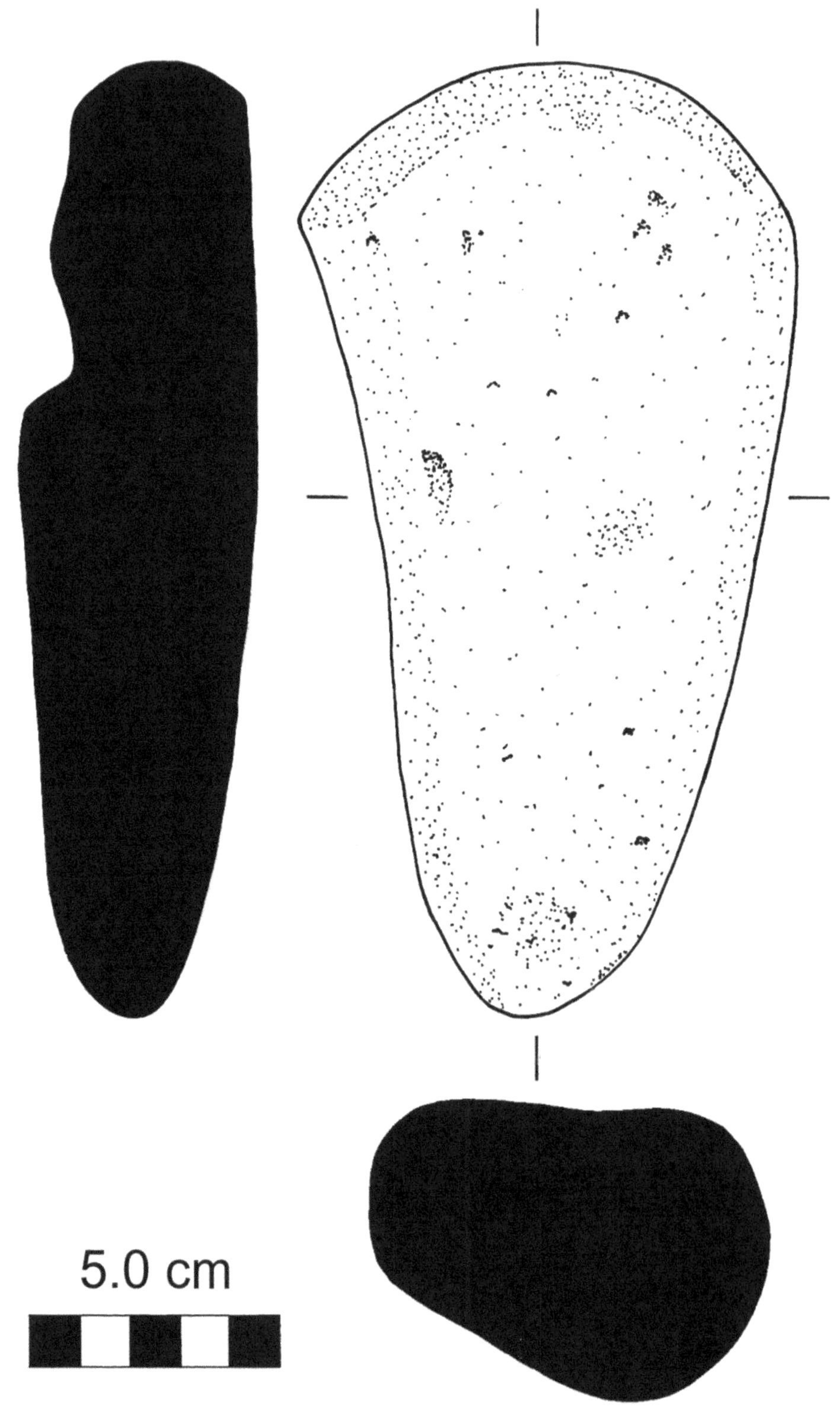

Figure 4. FS 390: Work face, longitudinal and transverse sections. Scale 1:2.

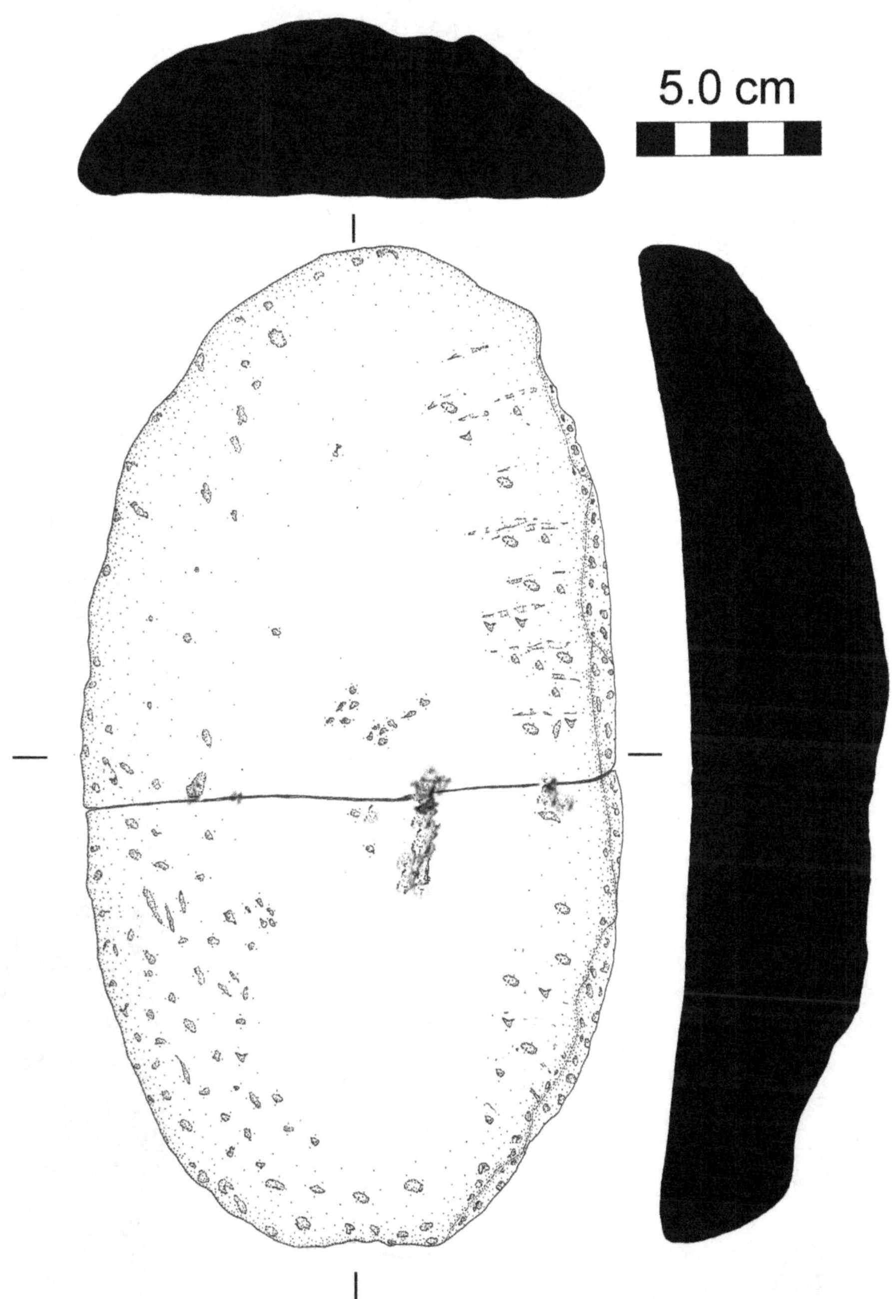

Figure 5. G1:18/1: Work face, longitudinal and transverse sections. Scale 3:4.

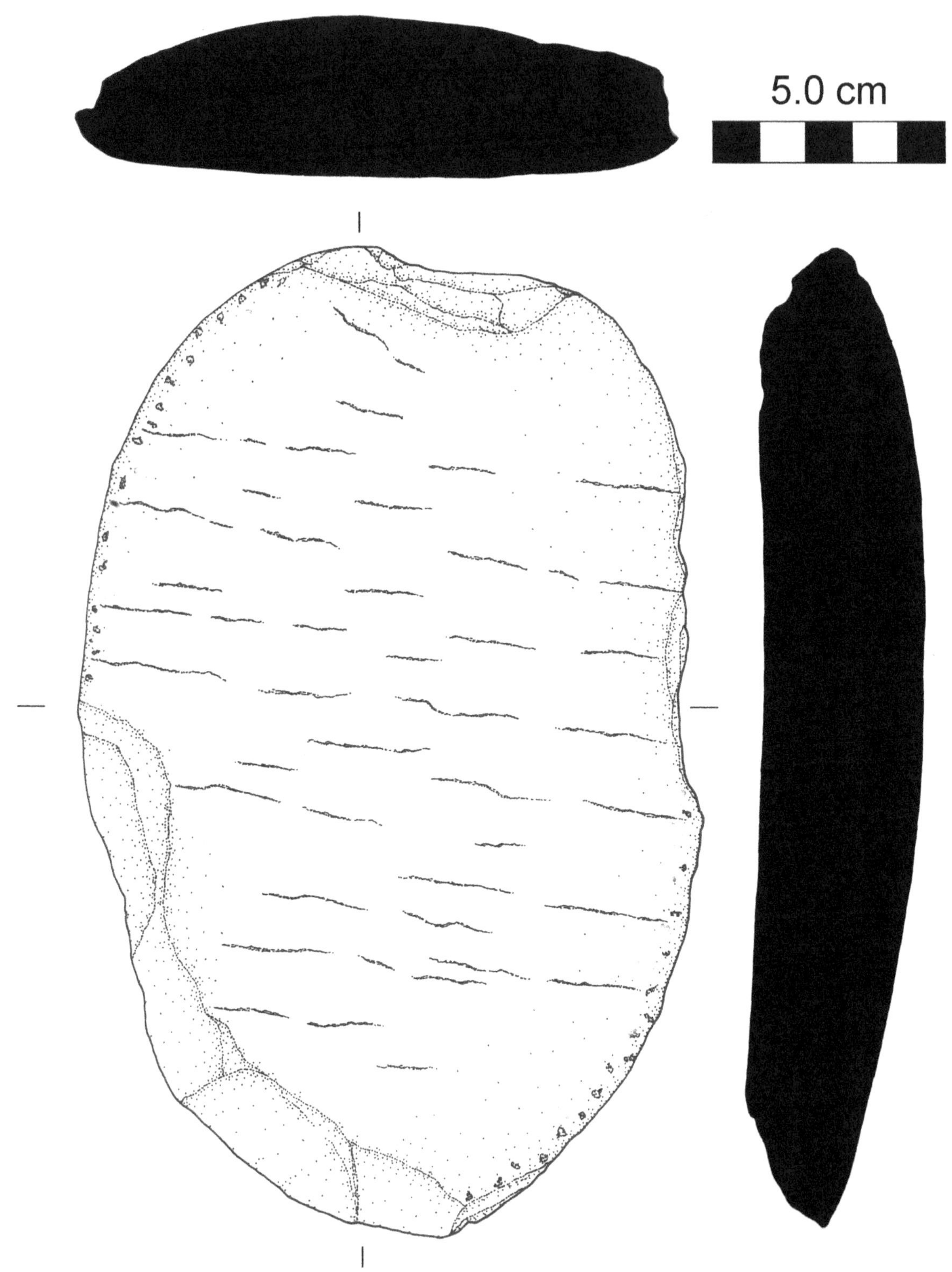

Figure 6. FS 723: One of two work faces, longitudinal and transverse sections. Scale 3:4.

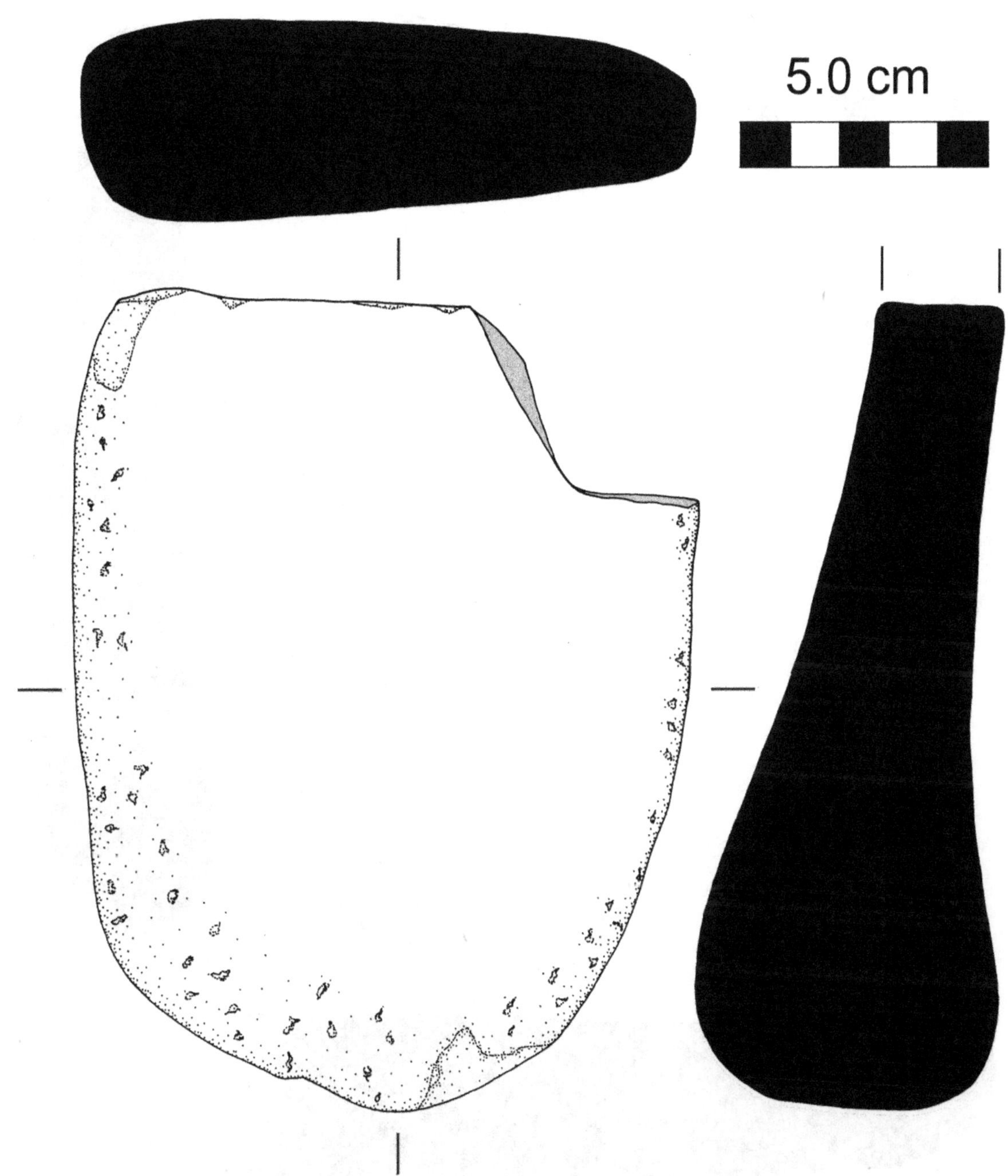

Figure 7. FS 892: Work face, longitudinal and transverse sections. Scale 3:4.

(The line crossing the groove represents a natural crack.)

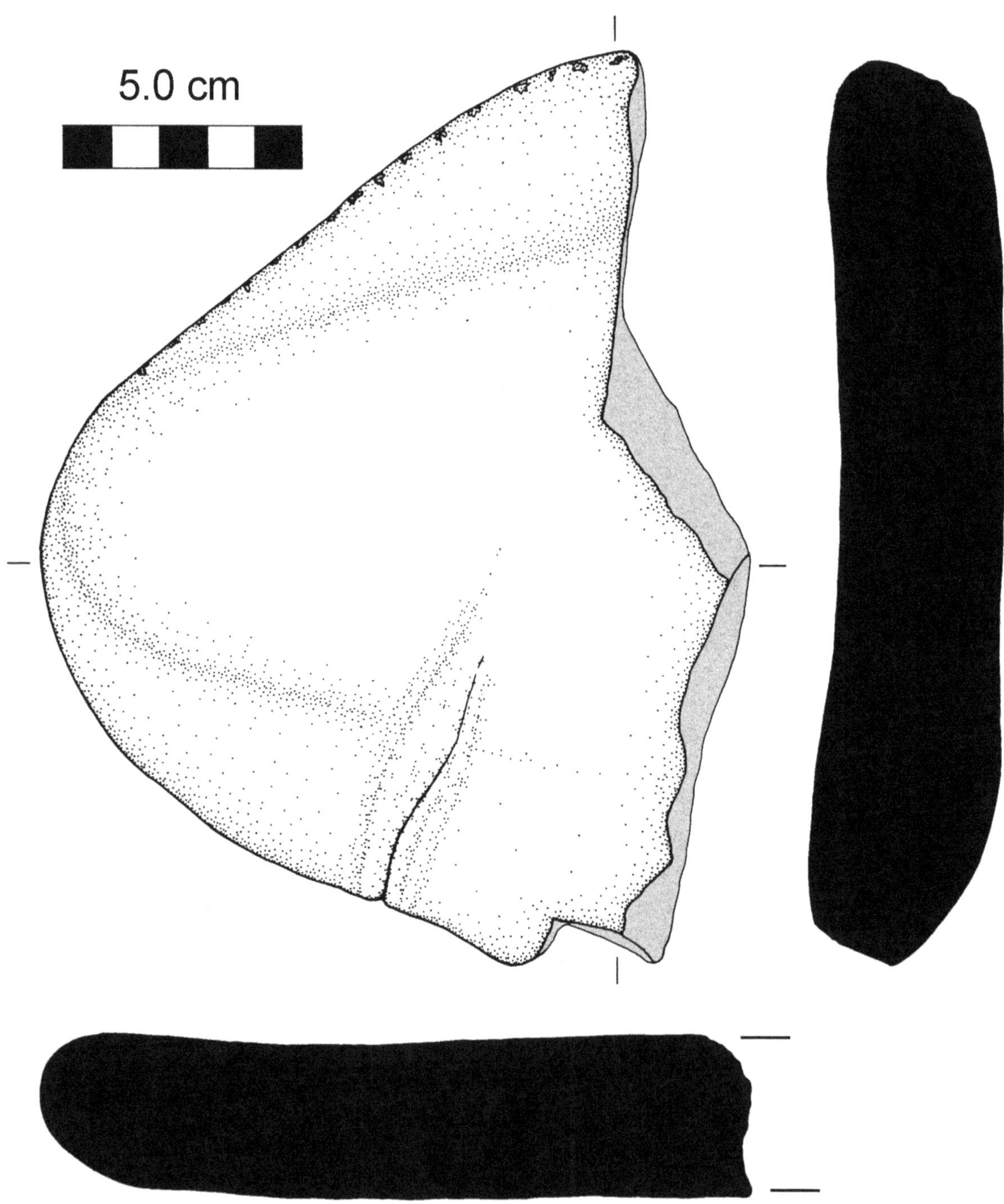

Figure 8. H1:68: Work face, two longitudinal sections (aa+bb), transverse section. Scale 1:2.

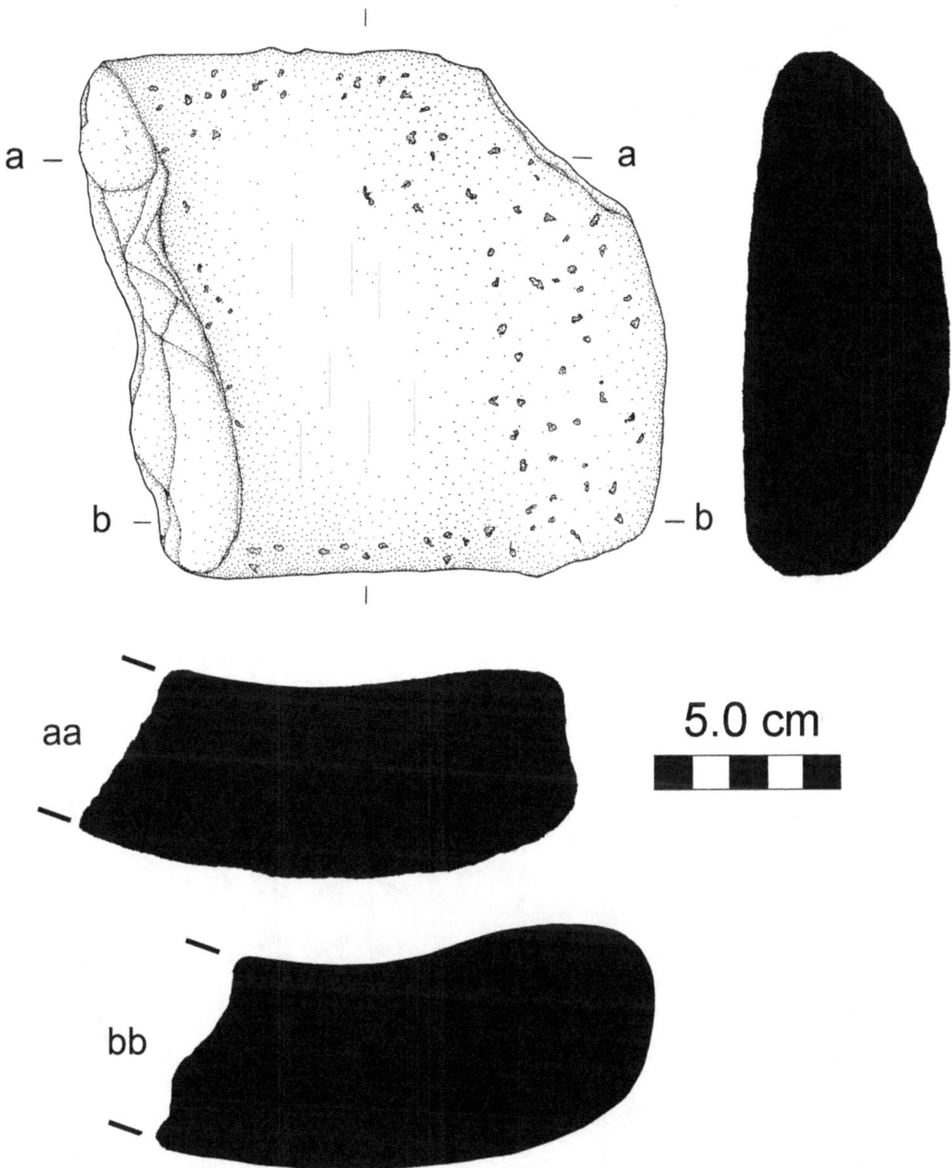

Figure 9. FS 126: Work face, side with facet, and transverse section. Scale 1:2.

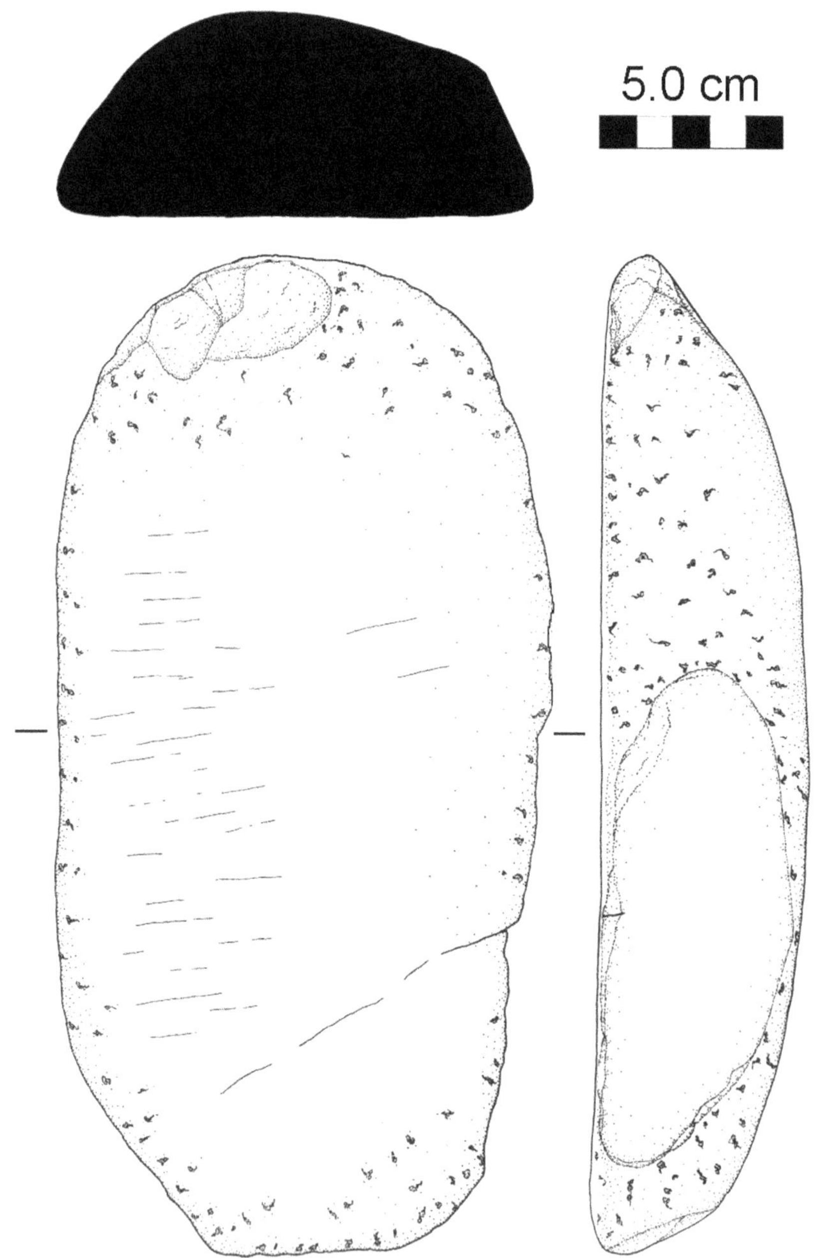

Figure 10. FS 165: Work faces (A+B), longitudinal and transverse sections. Scale 1:2.

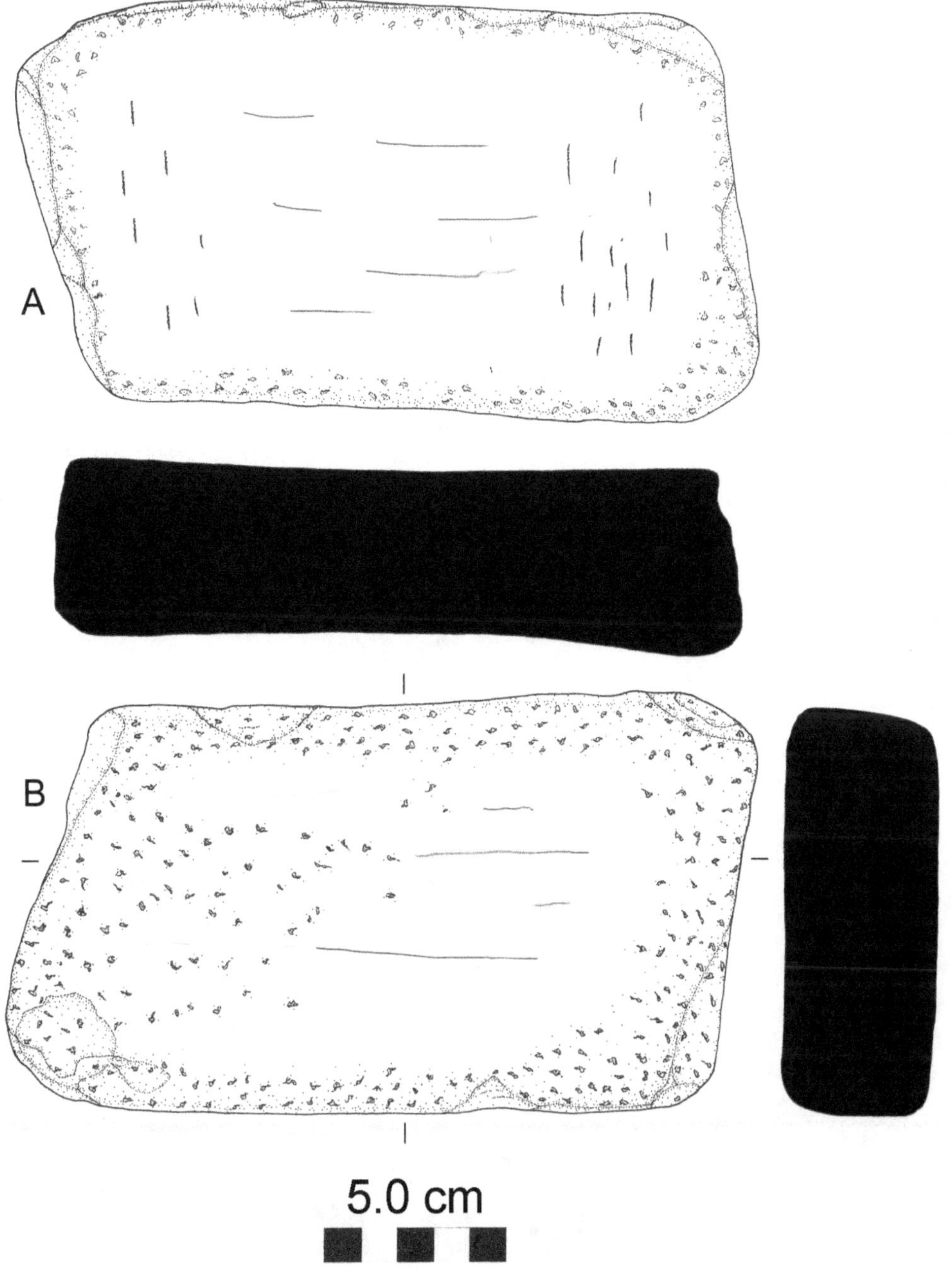

Figure 11. FS 174: Work face and one of the sides. Scale 3:4.

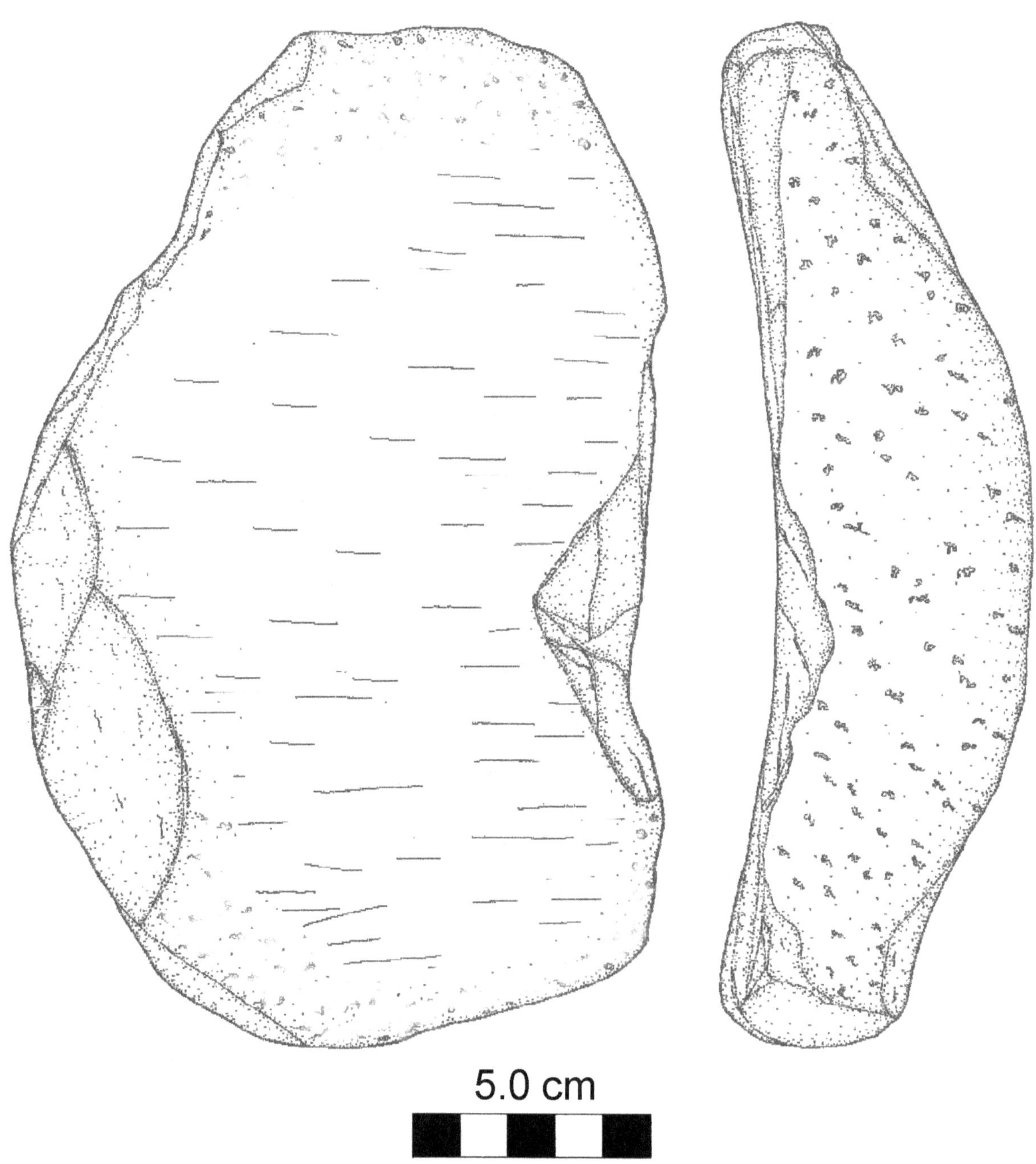

Figure 12. FS 83: Work face, longitudinal and transverse sections. Scale 1:1.

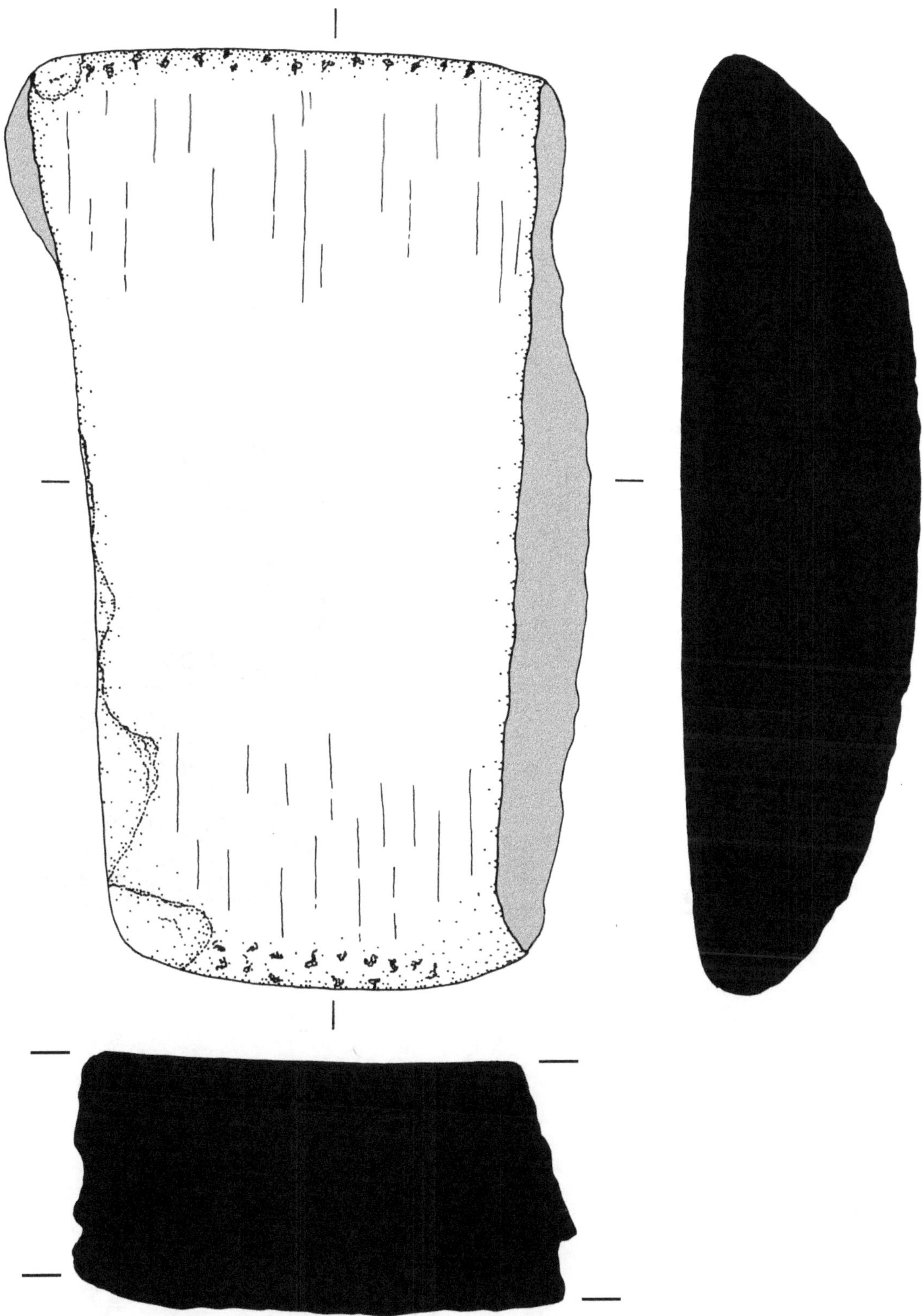

Figure 13. FS 321: Work face A and transverse section. Scale 1:1.

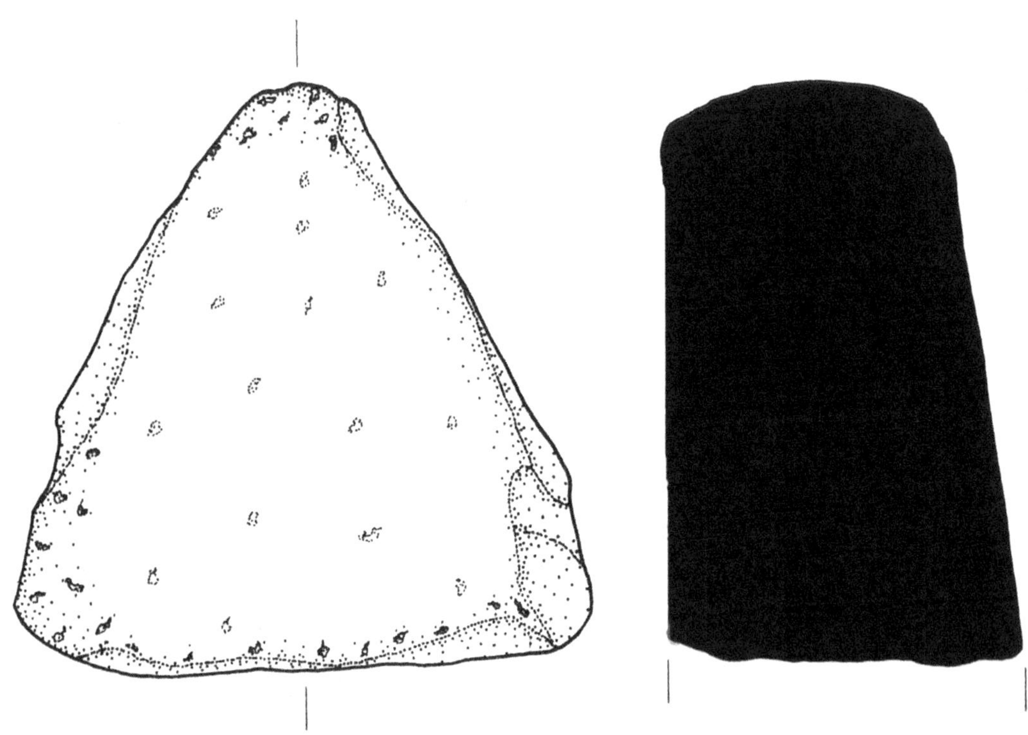

Figure 14. FS 13: Work face, transverse section. Scale 1:2.

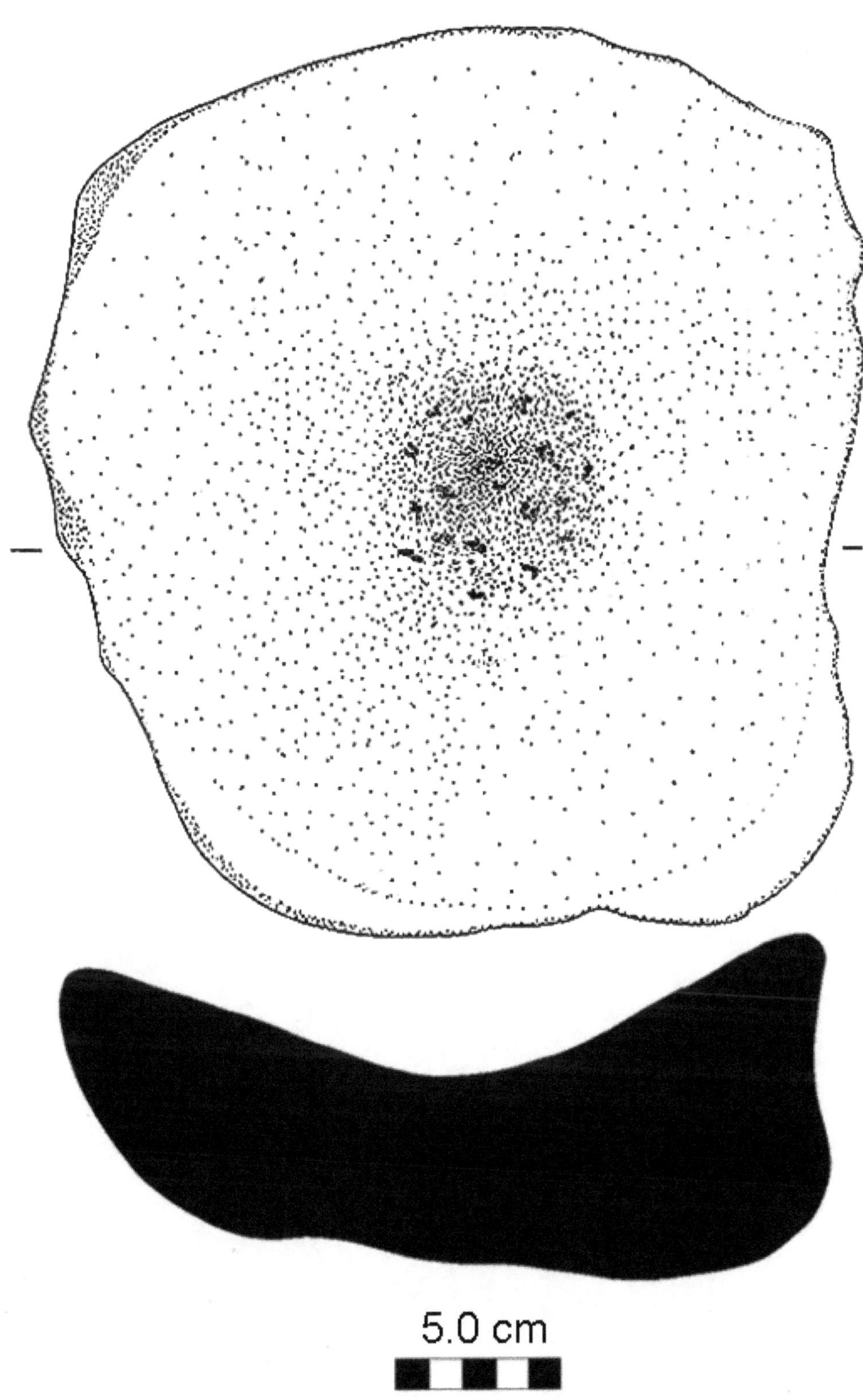

Figure 15. Scale 1:1.

FS 44: One face, longitudinal and transverse sections.

FS 363: Faces, longitudinal section, working edge in front view.

FS 680: One face, one side, working edge in front view.

FS 201: One face, one side, transverse section.

FS 883: One face, one side, transverse section.

FS 884: One face, one side, transverse section.

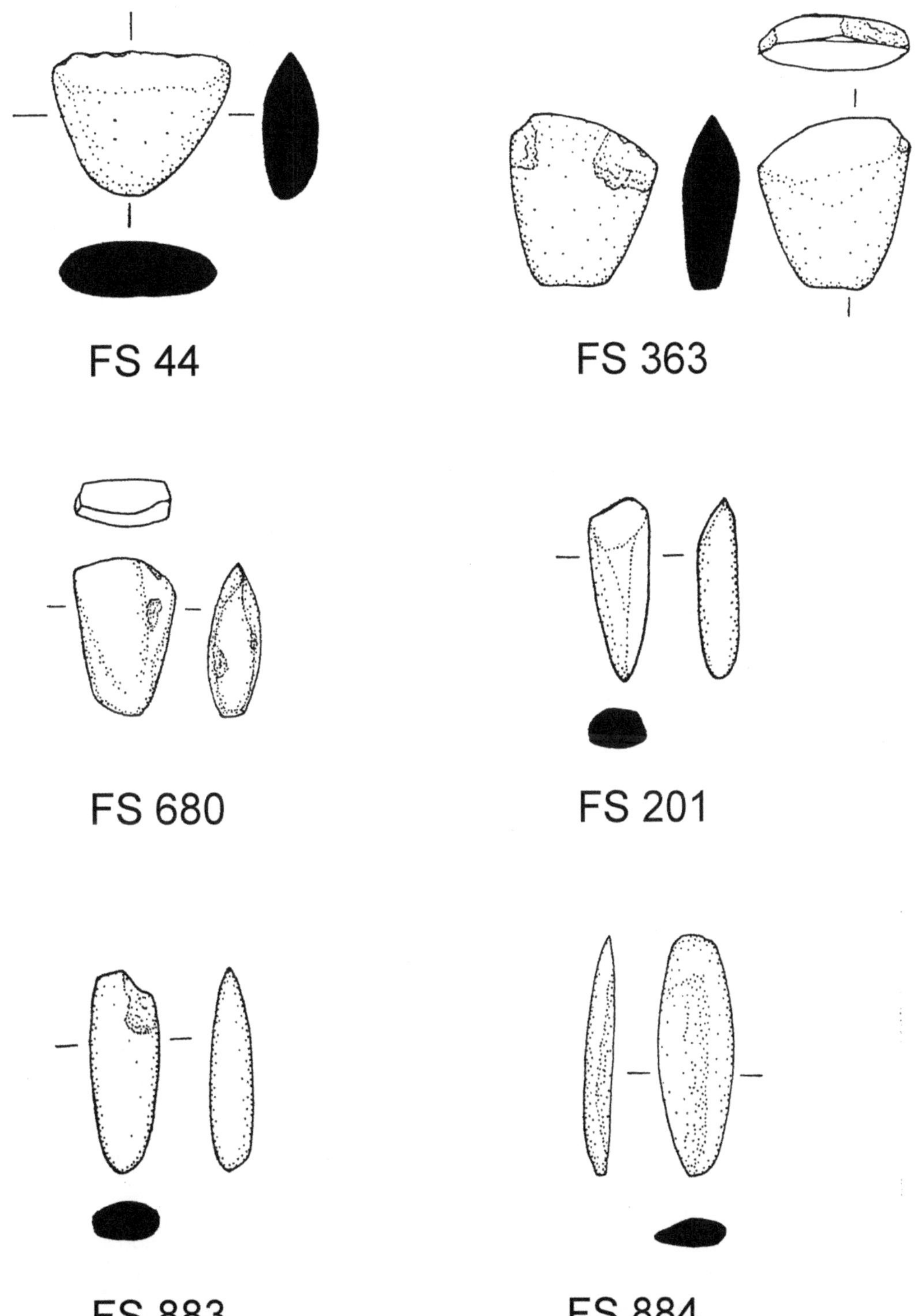
FS 44
FS 363
FS 680
FS 201
FS 883
FS 884

Figure 16. Scale 1:1.

FS 52: One face, longitudinal and transverse sections.

FS 589: One face, longitudinal and transverse sections.

FS 37: One face, one side, and proximal end in front view.

FS 893: One face, one side, and transverse section.

FS 222: One face, one side, and transverse section.

FS 779: One face, longitudinal and transverse sections.

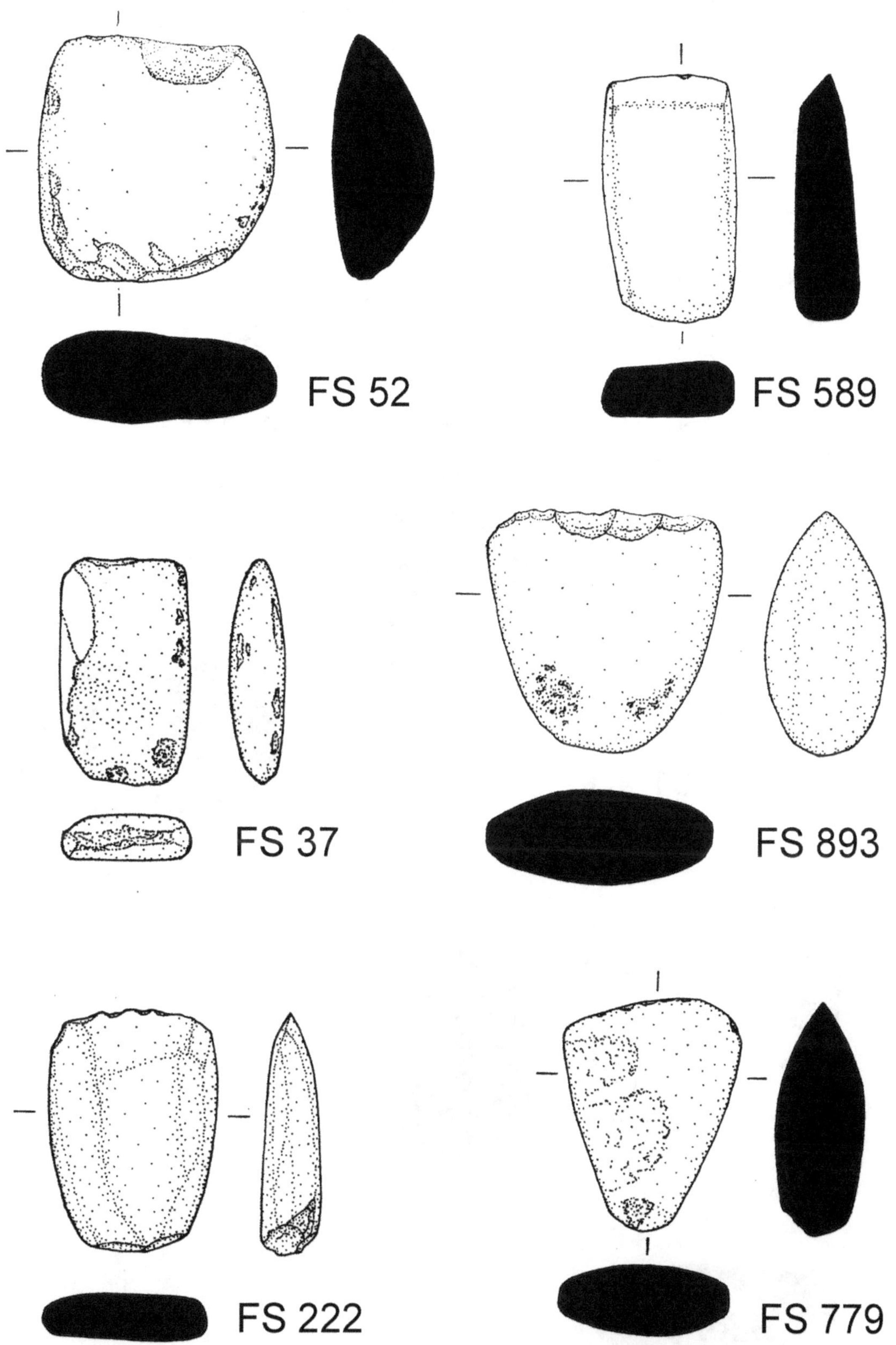
FS 52
FS 589
FS 37
FS 893
FS 222
FS 779

Figure 17. Scale 1:1.

FS 751: One face, working edge in front view, and longitudinal section.

FS 112: One face, transverse section.

FS 21: One face, longitudinal and transverse sections.

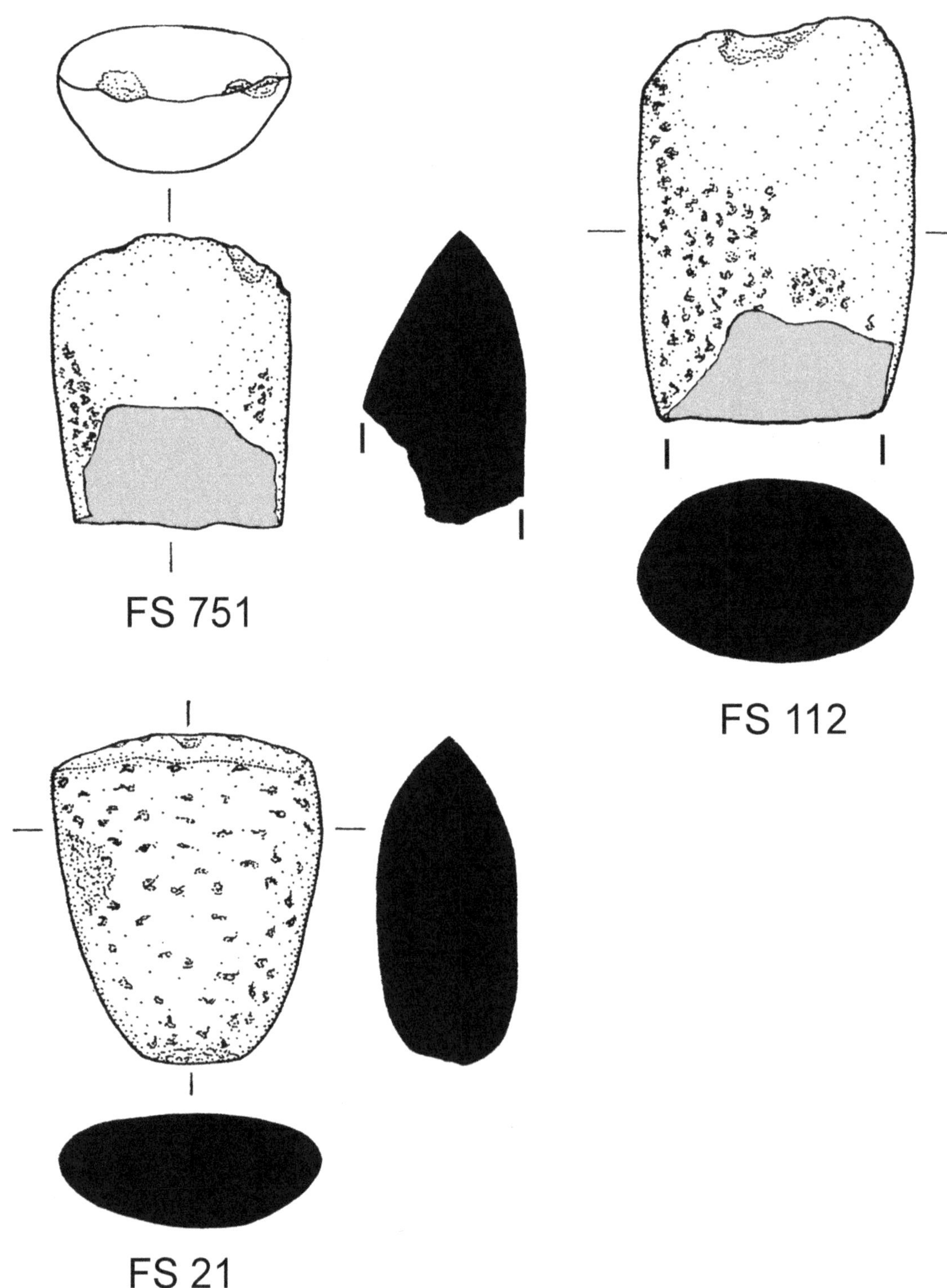

Figure 18. Scale 1:1.

FS 33: One face, longitudinal and transverse sections.

FS 430: One face, longitudinal and transverse sections.

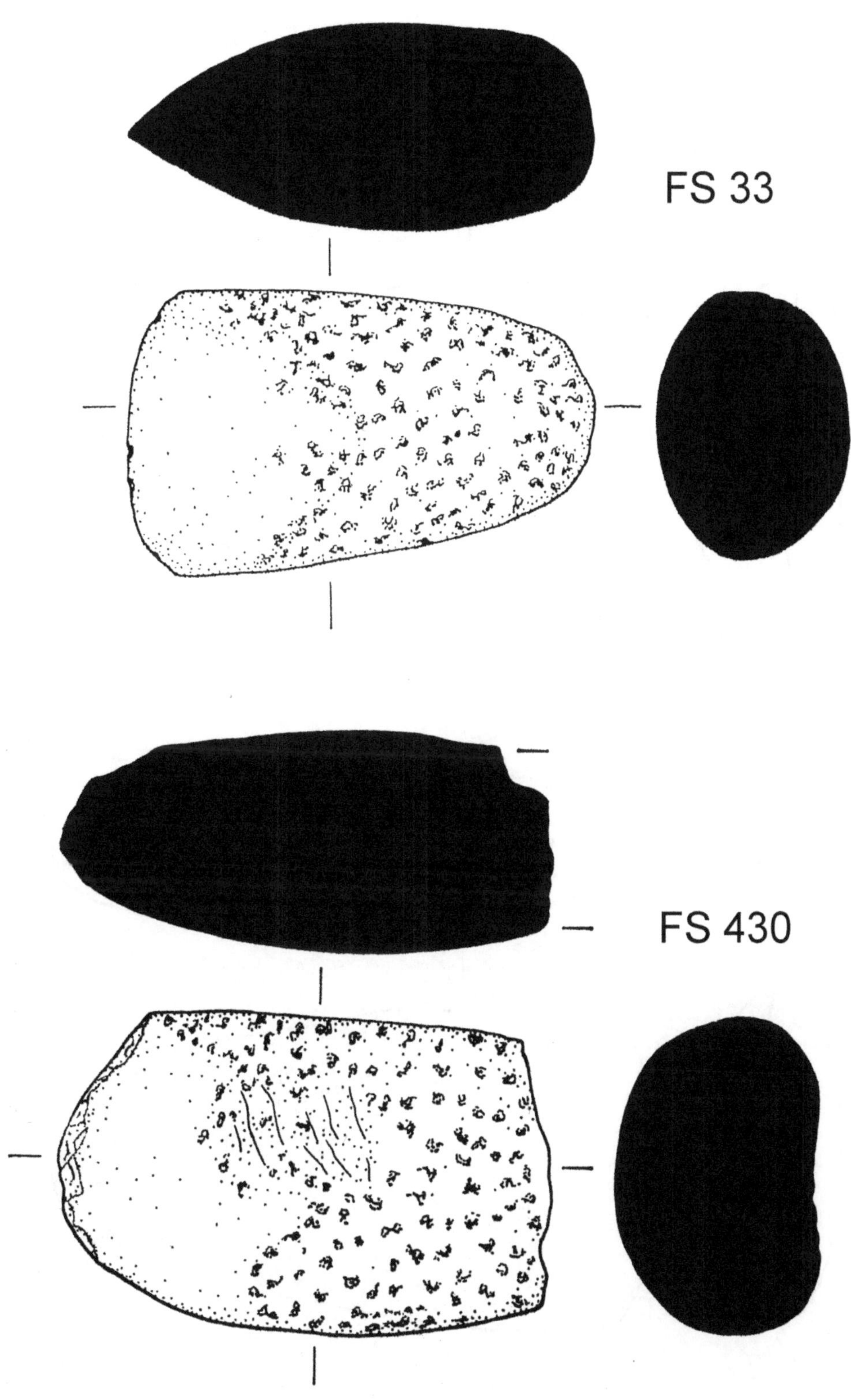

Figure 19. Scale 1:1.

FS 117: One face, one side, working edge in front view.

FS 837: One face, one side, working edge in front view.

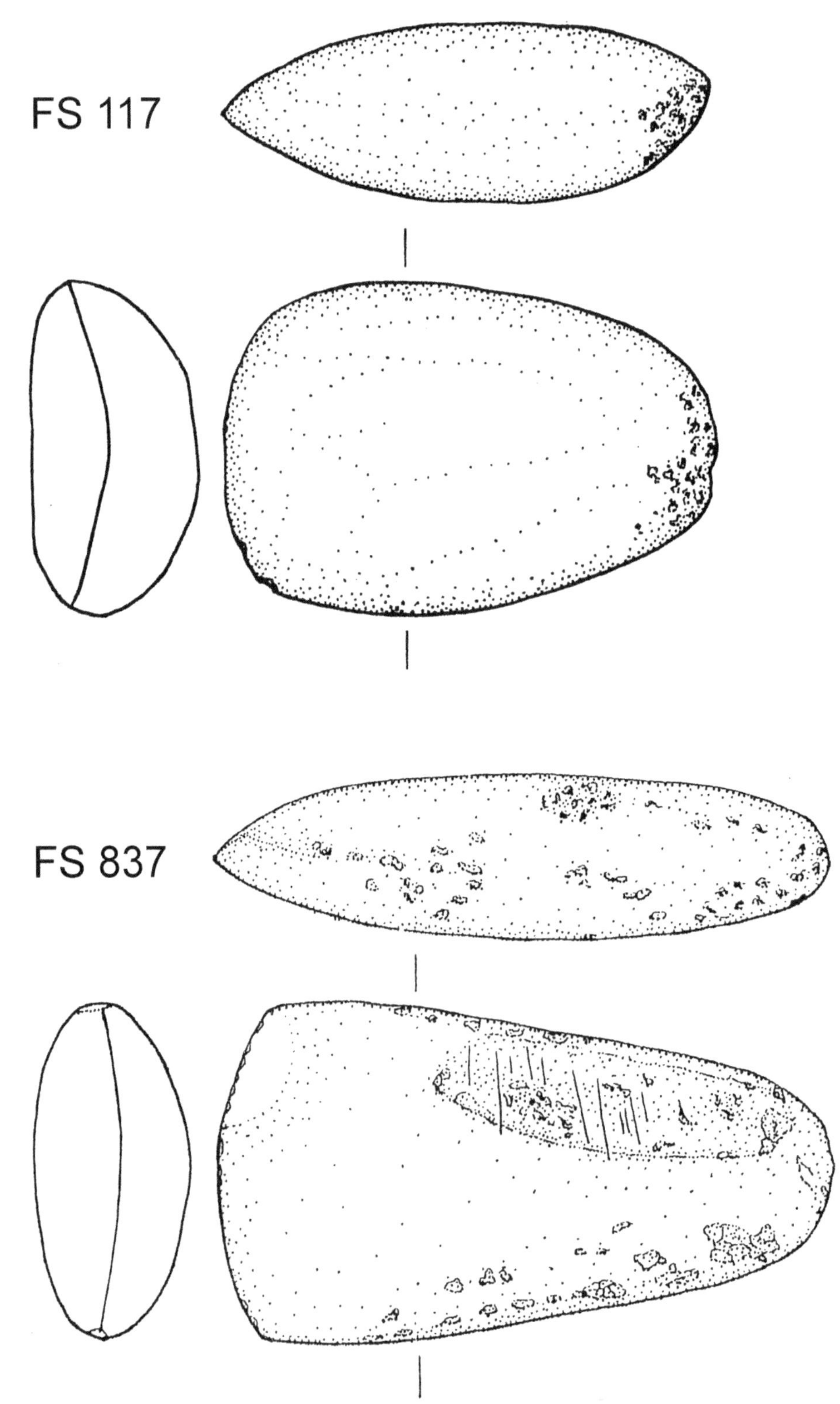

Figure 20. FAN:61/1: Work face, longitudinal and transverse sections. Scale 1:1.

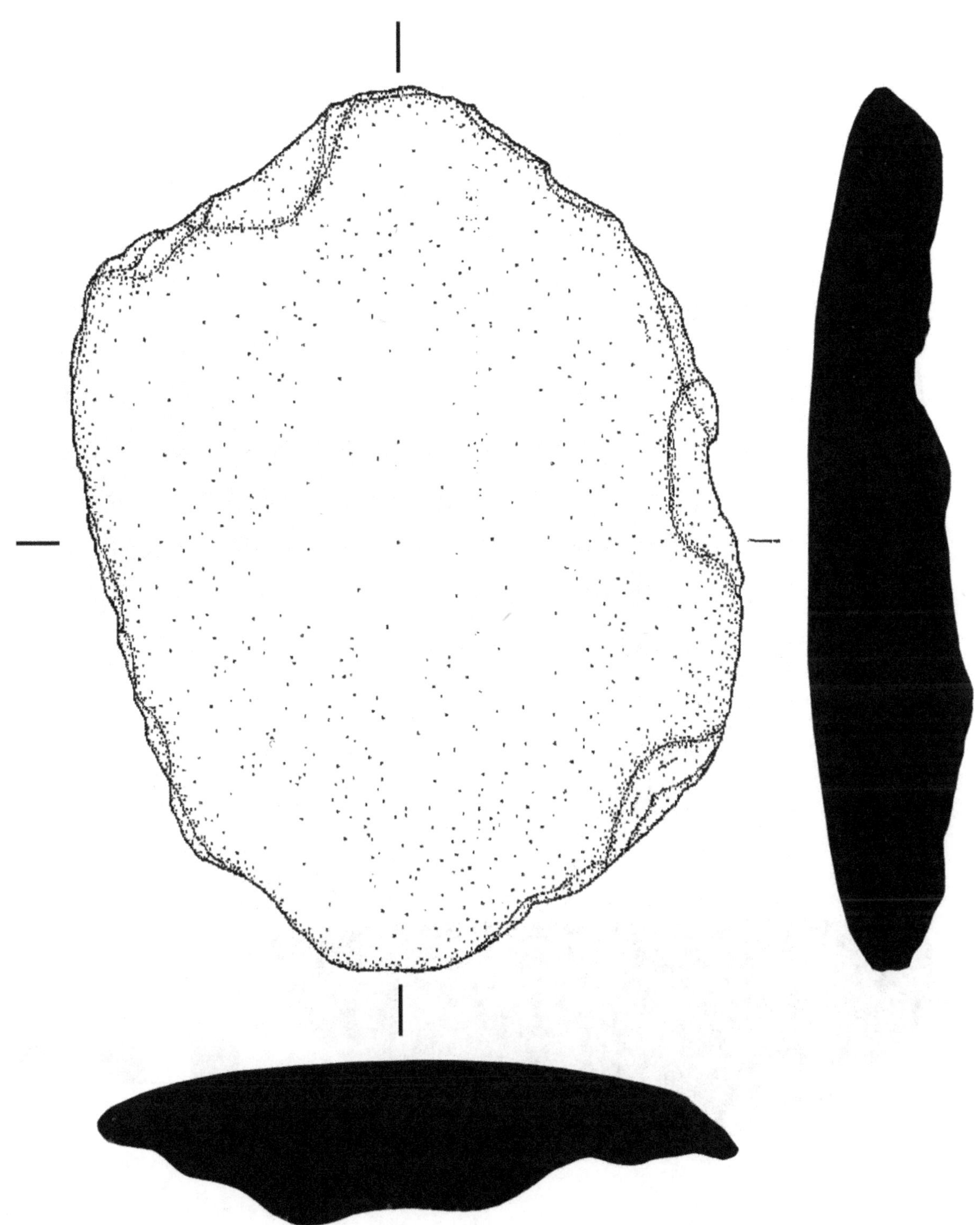

Figure 21. FS 14: Work face, part of periphery, transverse section. Scale 3:4.

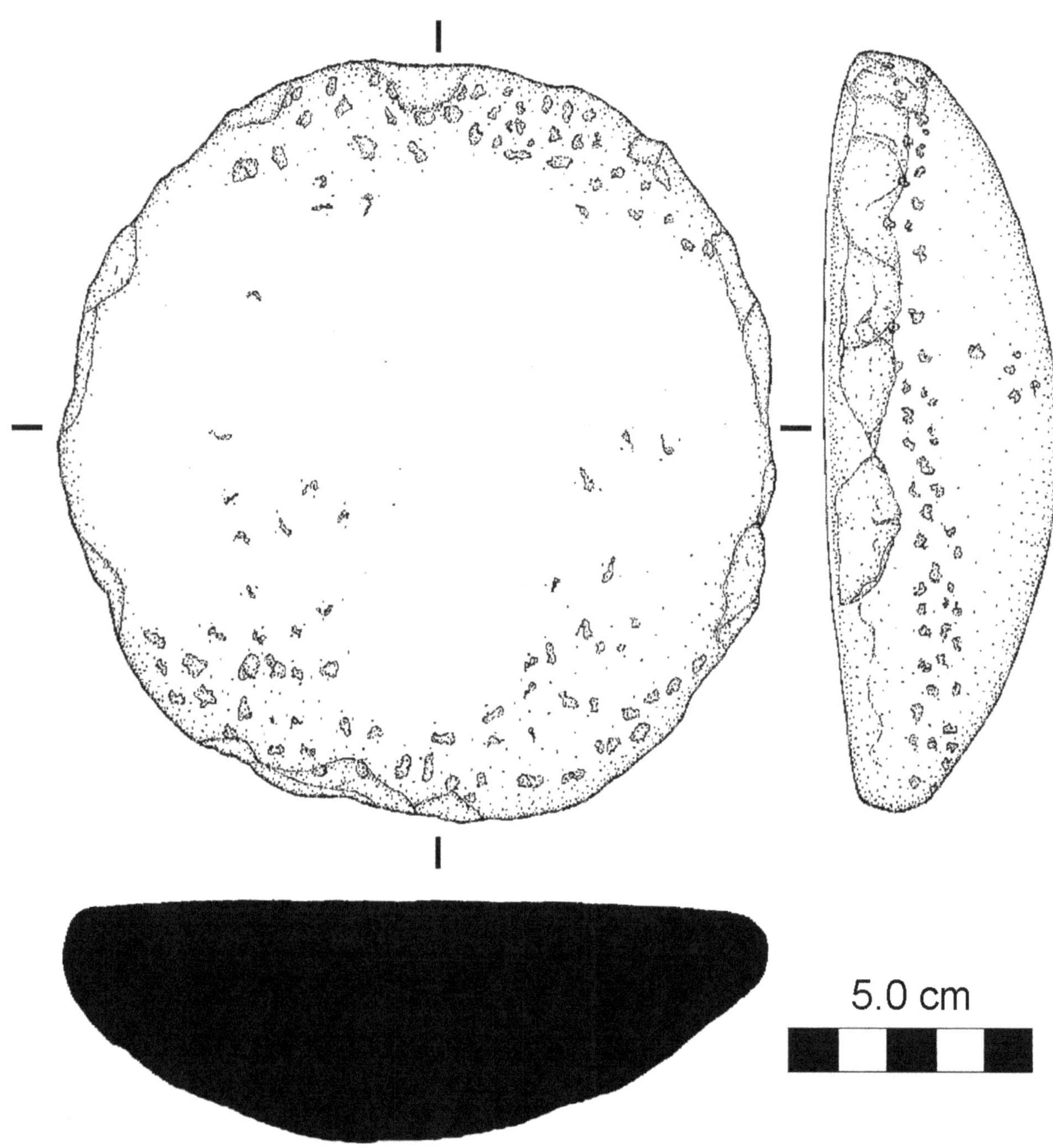

Figure 22. FS 317: Work face, part of periphery, transverse section. Scale 1:1.

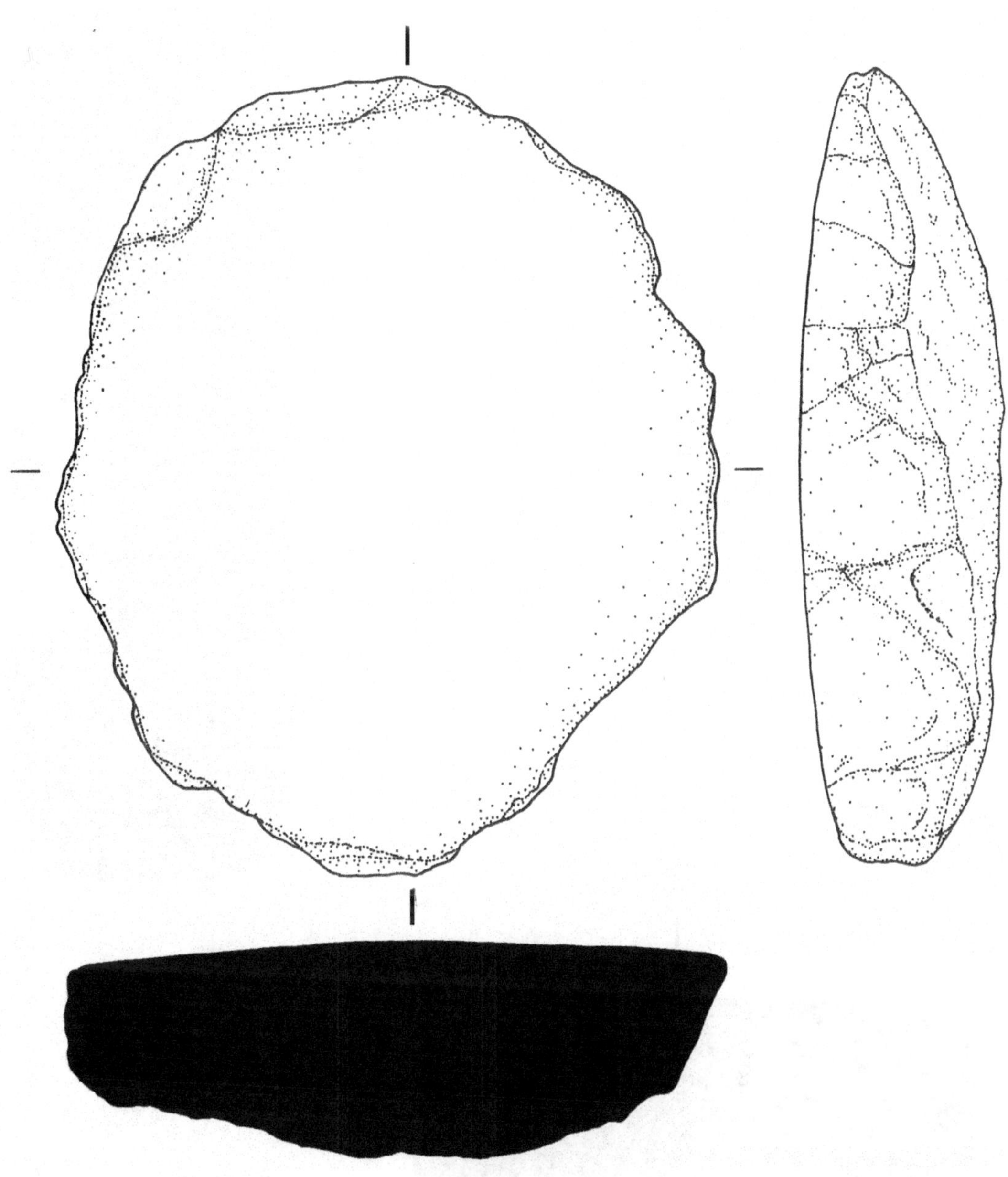

Figure 23. FS 256: One of the faces, longitudinal and transverse sections. Scale 1:1.

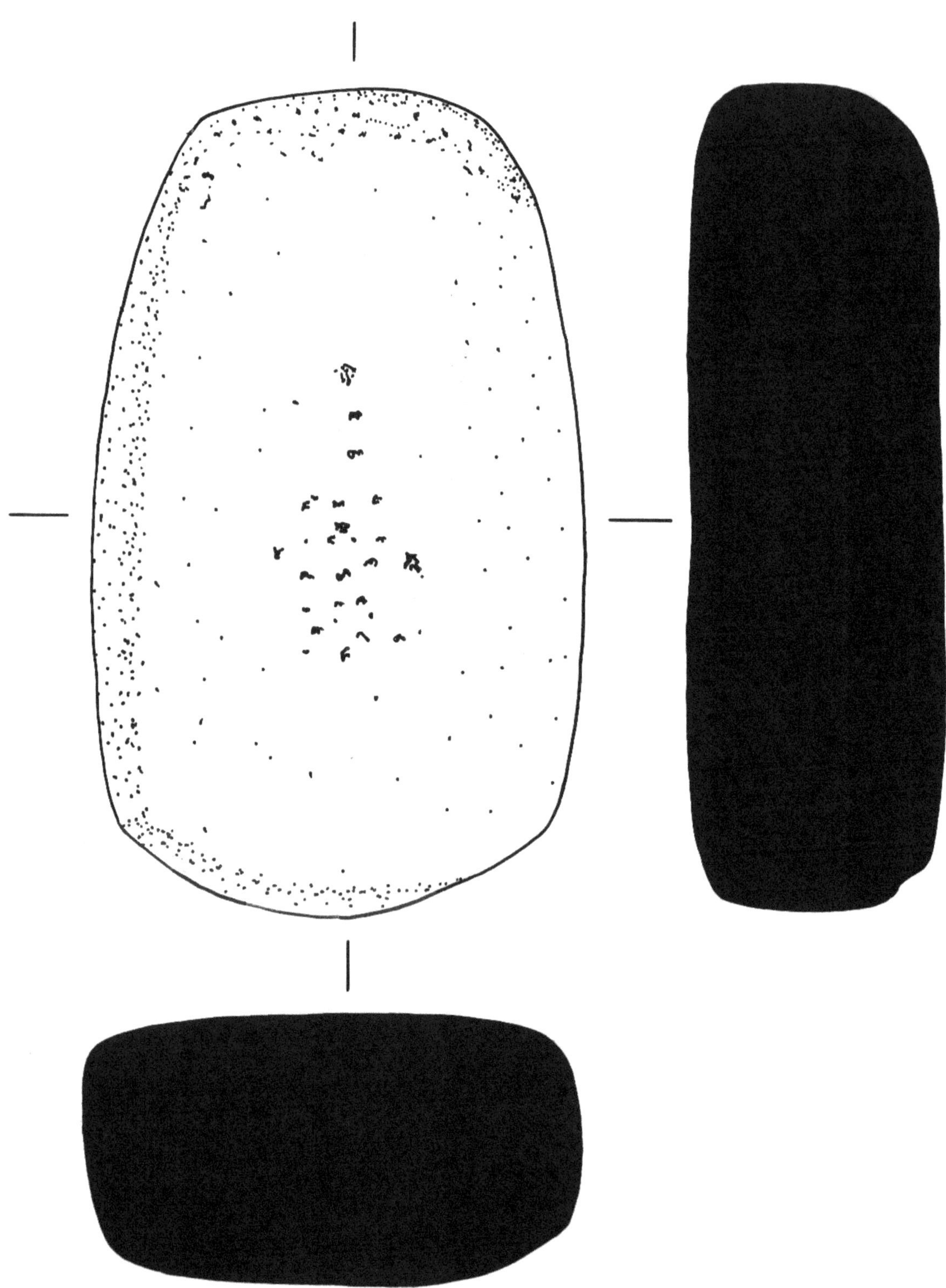

Figure 24. FS 53: One of the faces, one of the sides, transverse section. Scale 1:1.

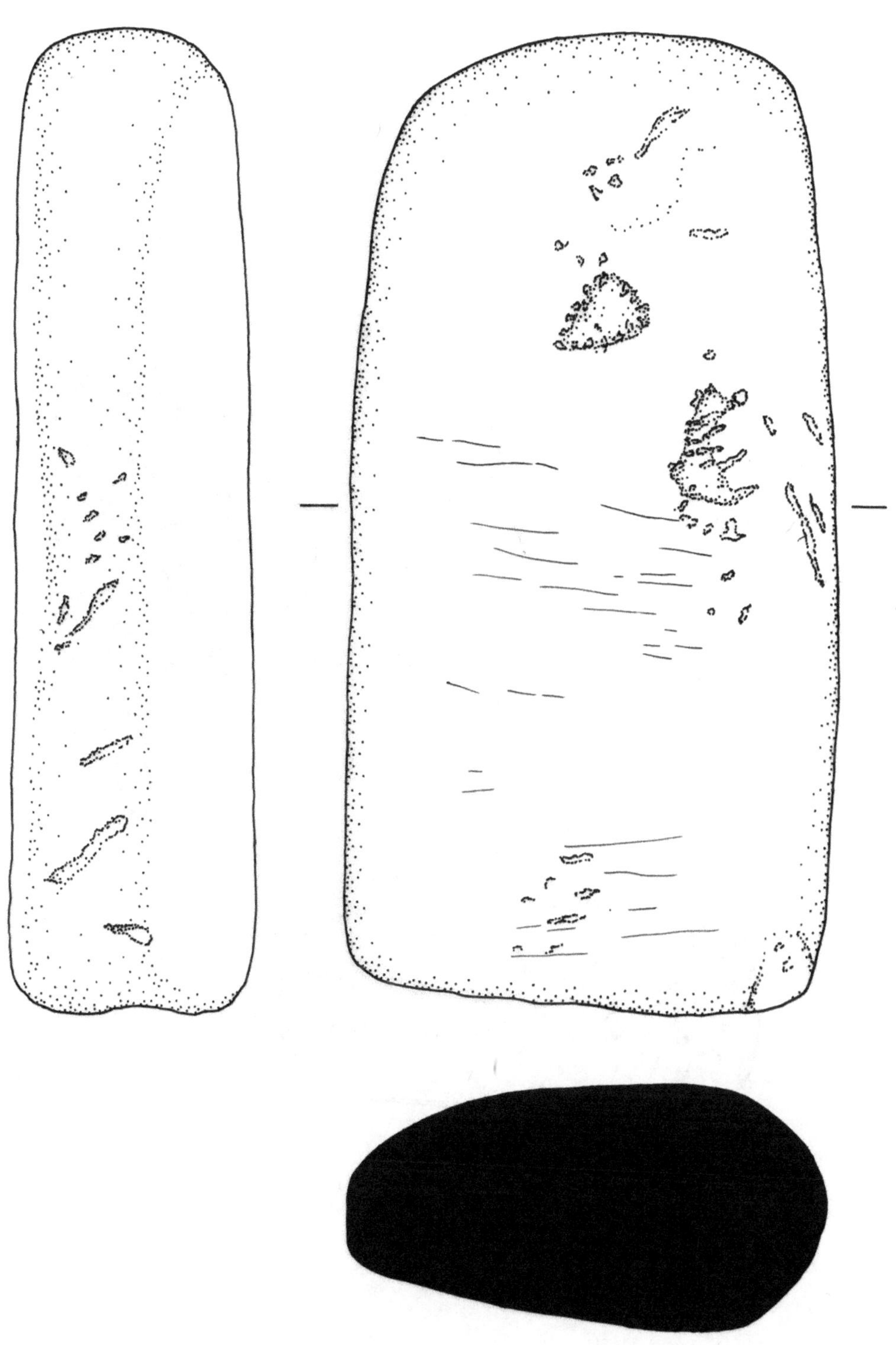

Figure 25. FS 223: One of the faces, part of periphery, one section. Scale 1:1.

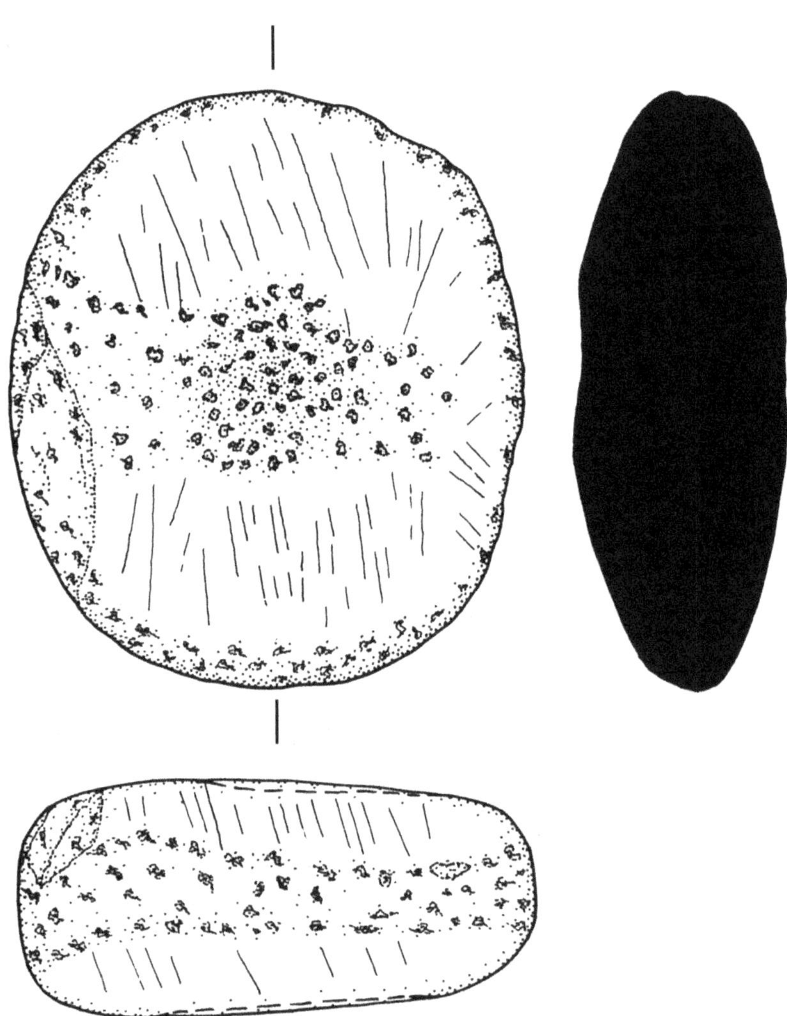

Figure 26. FS 870: One of the faces, both sections. Scale 1:1.

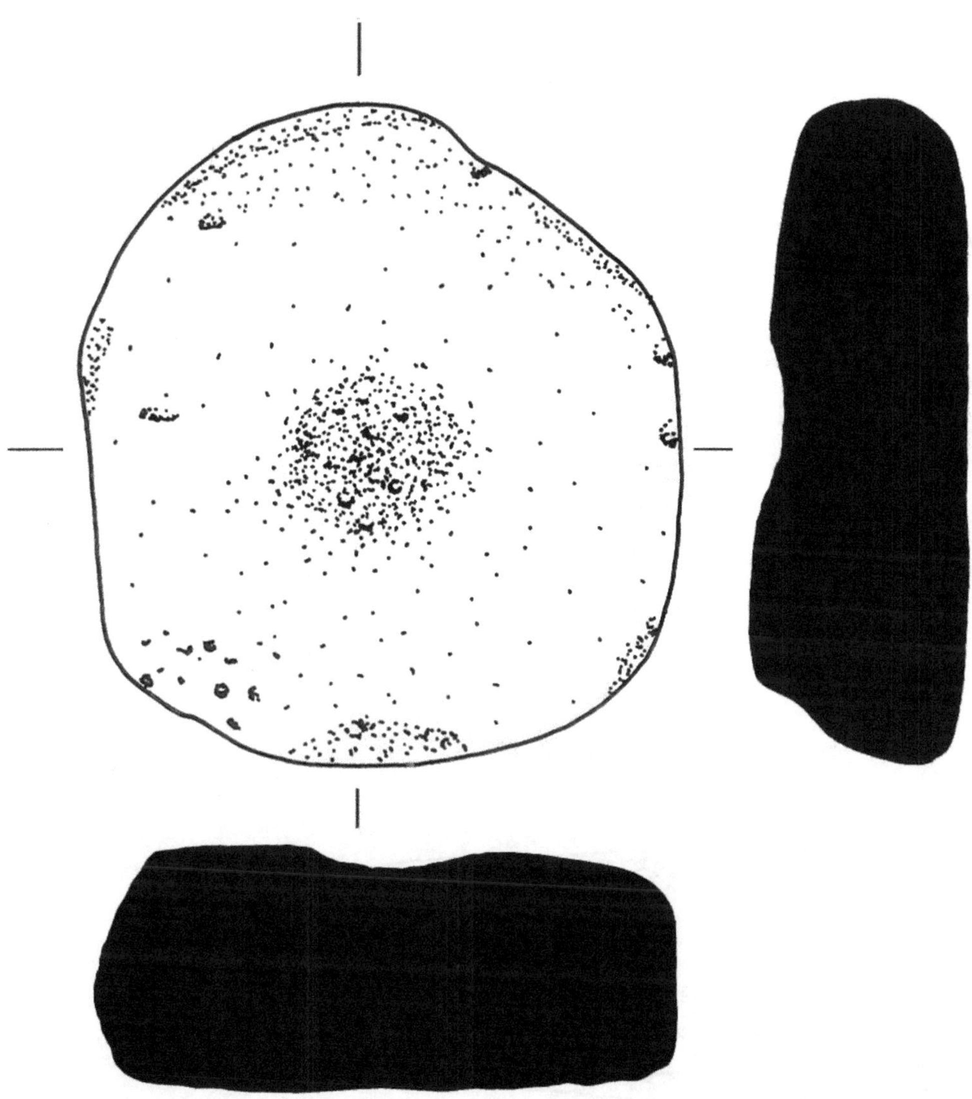

Figure 27. S 62: One of the faces, two parts of the periphery. Scale 1:1.

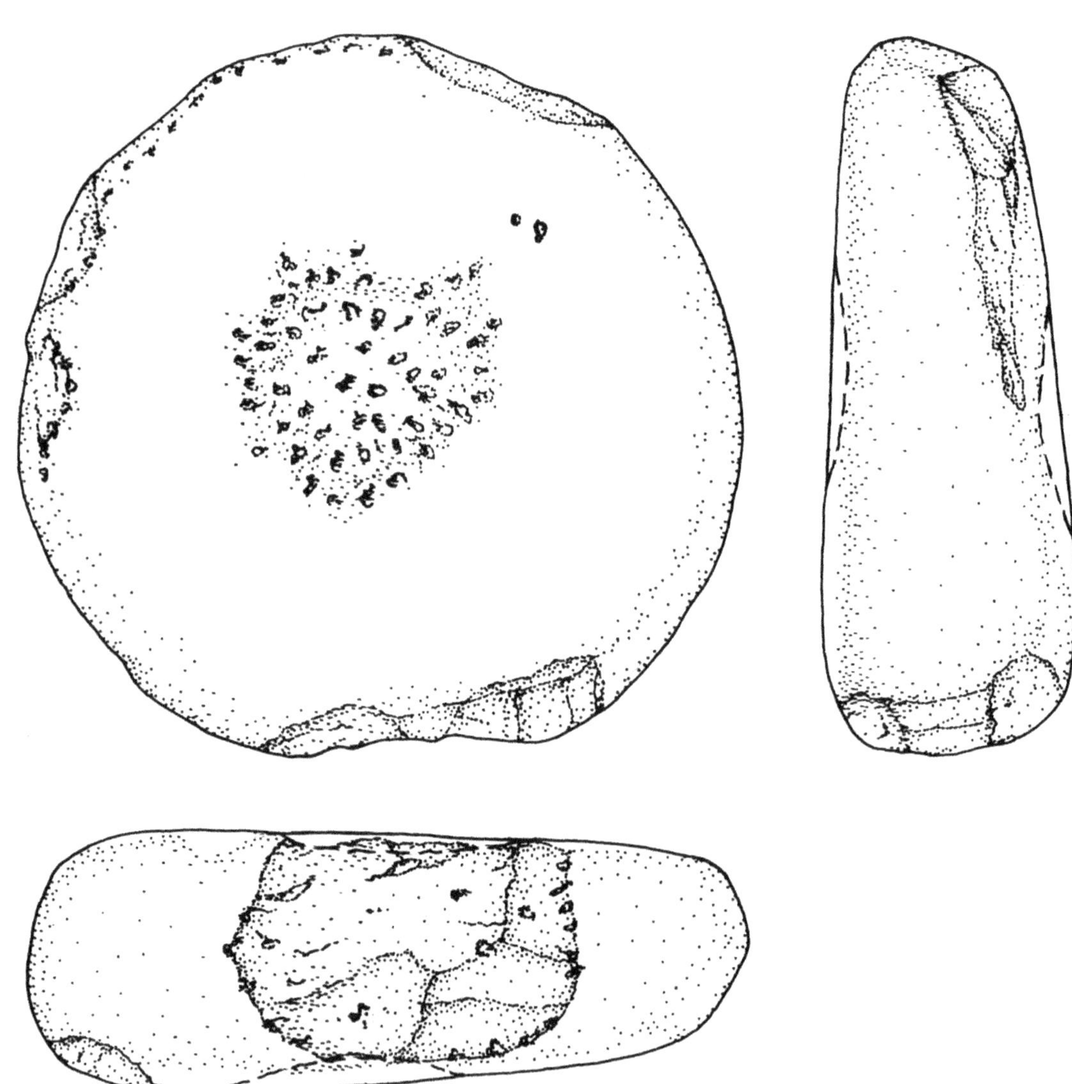

Figure 28. FS 115: Face A, two sides. Scale 1:1.

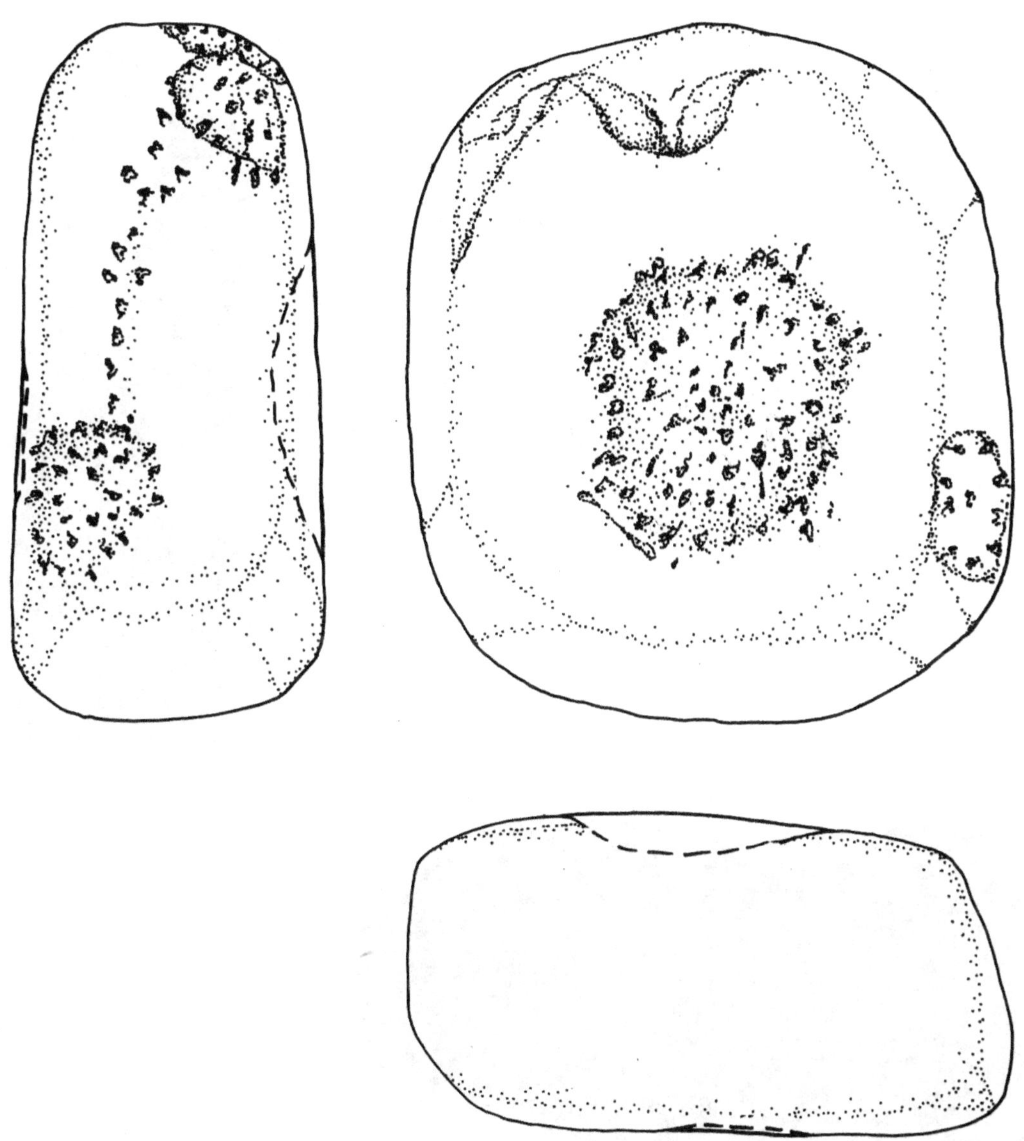

Figure 29. FS 318: One of the faces, both sections. Scale 1:1.

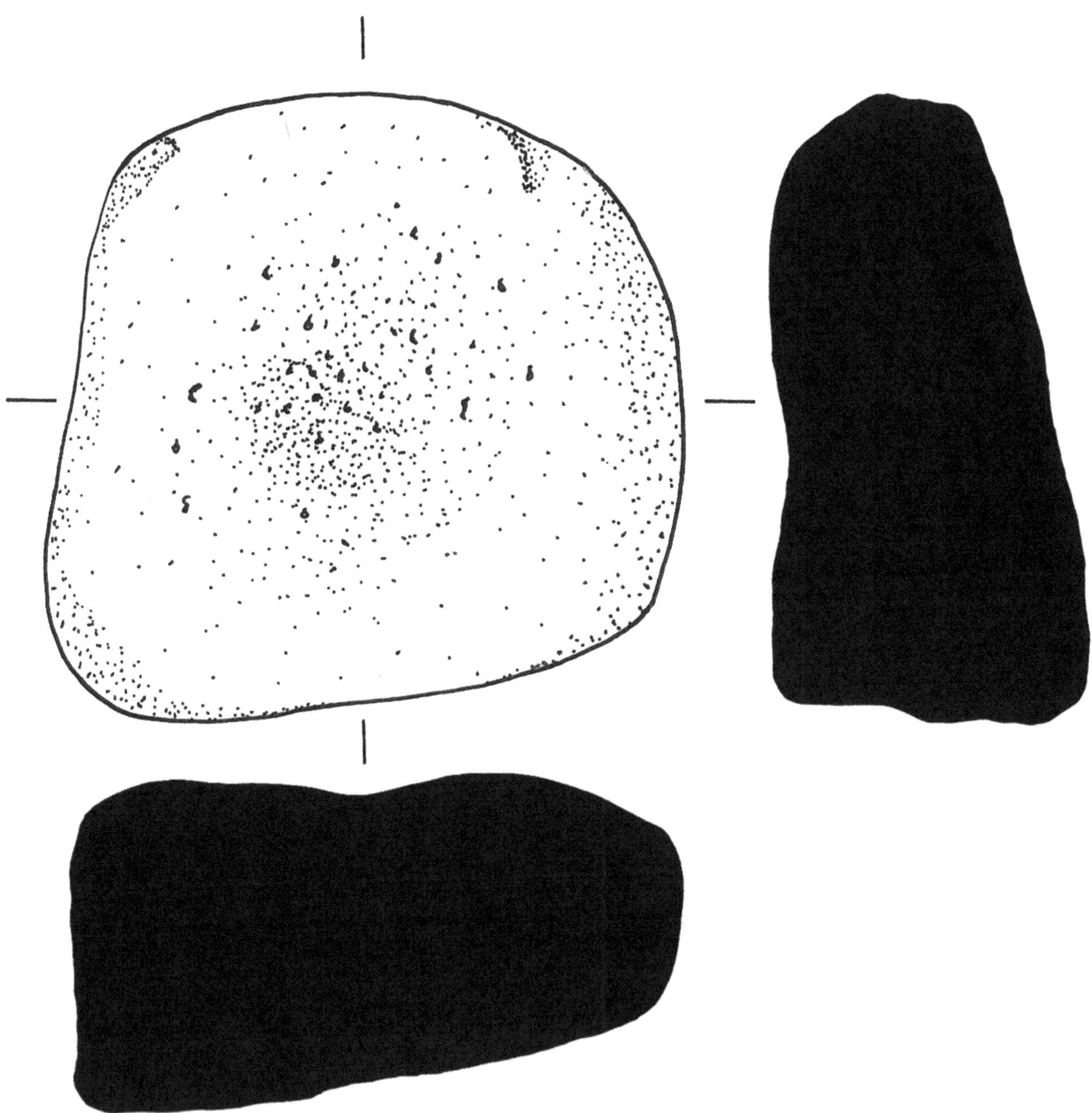

Figure 30. FF1:6B: Face A, two parts of the periphery. Scale 1:1.

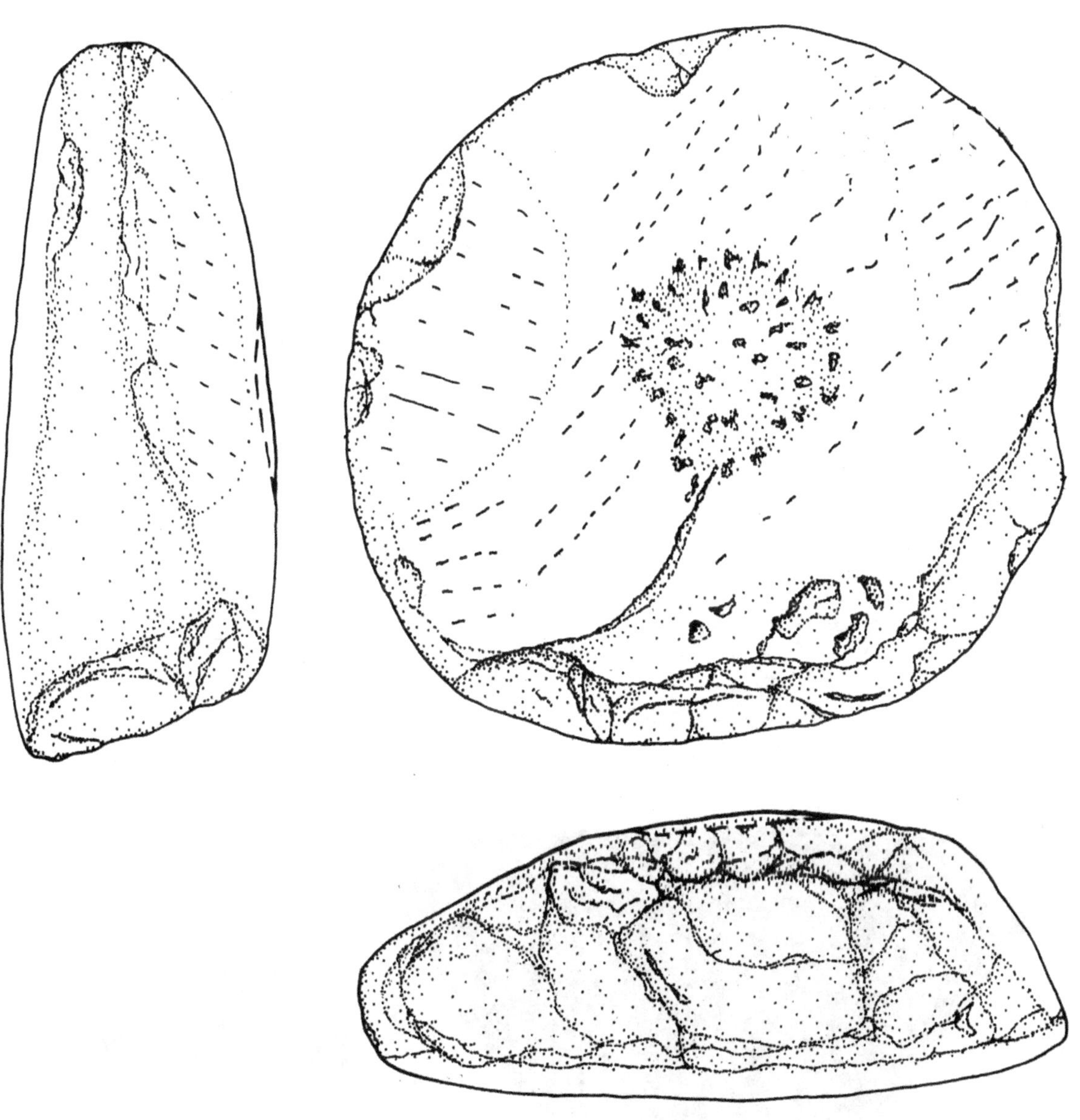

Figure 31. FS 261: Work face, one side, transverse section. Scale 3:4.

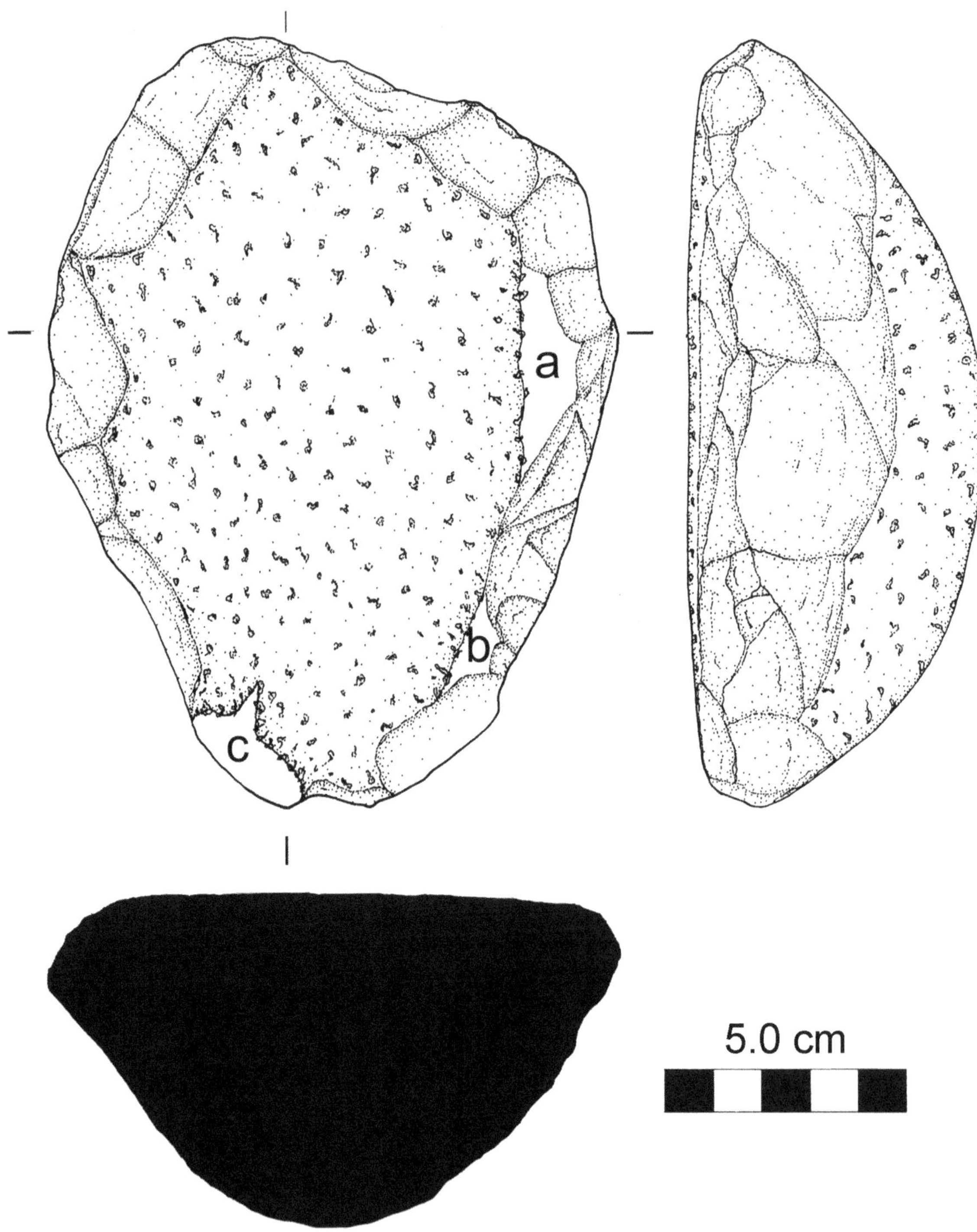

Figure 32. FS 829: Face with battered area, transverse section. Scale 1:1.

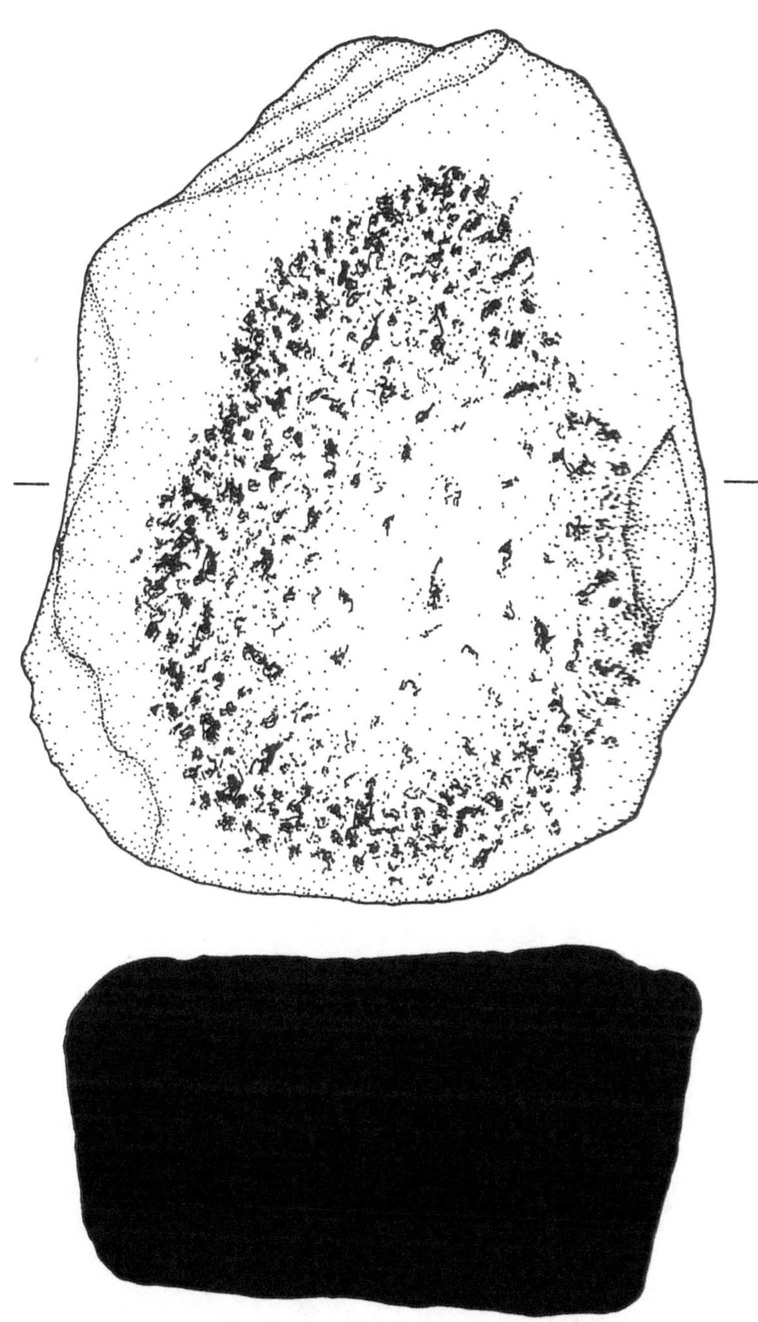

INDEX

Following Vitelli (1993), I prepared this index to be a reference to discussions that are not apparent from the Table of Contents and the illustrations. The pre-Neolithic material from the site, for example, has its own separate section in the text, but some references to it are made in other sections. Only the latter references are indexed. The index also includes references to the definitions of terms in the text.

www.ingramcontent.com/pod-product-compliance
Lightning Source LLC
LaVergne TN
LVHW082004060826
844660LV00031B/1271

* 9 7 8 0 2 5 3 2 2 1 7 8 0 *